MW01631404

Warfare and Logistics along the US-Canadian Border during the War of 1812

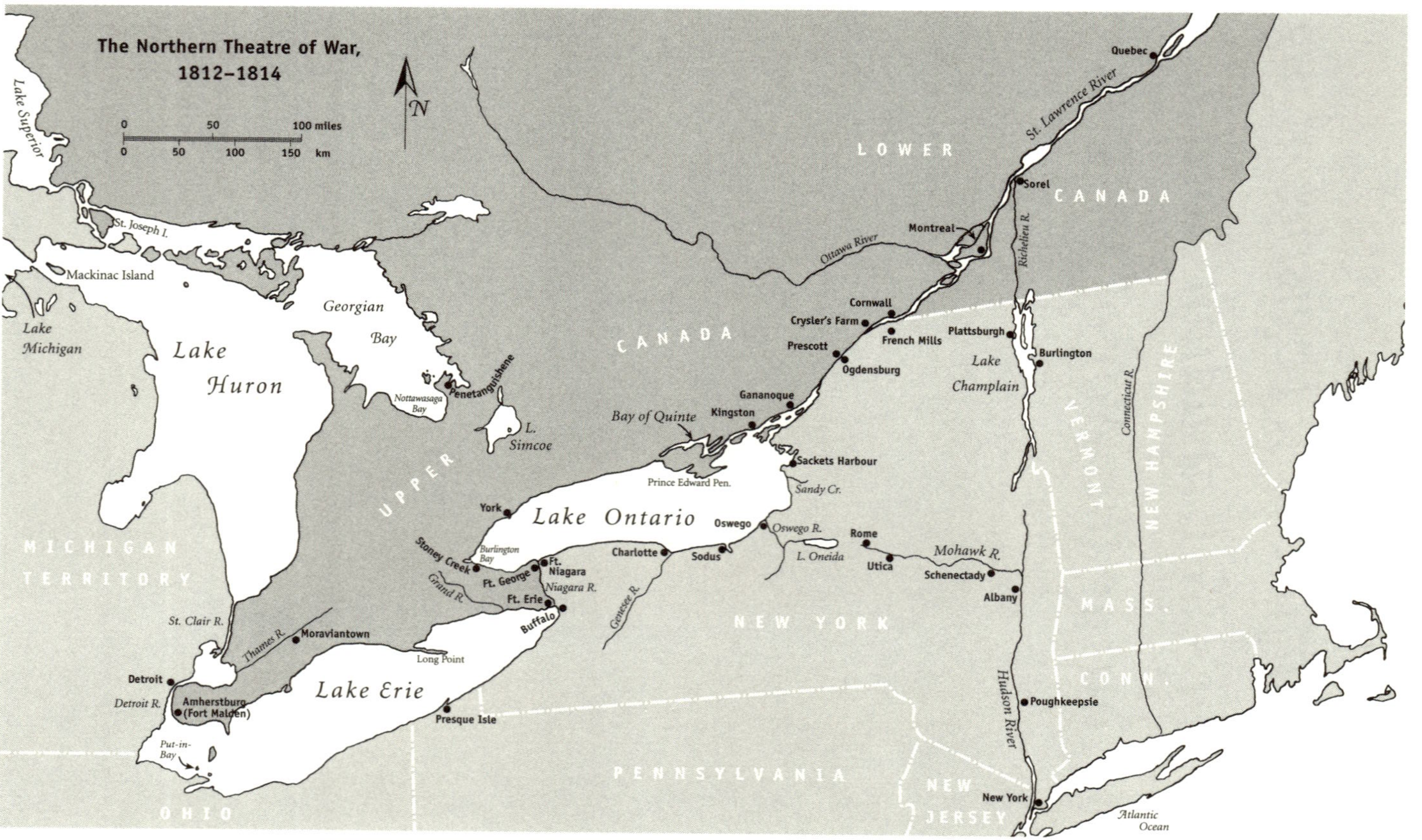

The Northern Theatre of War,
1812–1814
0
50
100 miles
0
50
100
150
km
N
Lake Superior
St. Joseph I.
Mackinac Island
Lake
Michigan
Lake
Huron
Georgian
Bay
Nottawasaga
Bay
Penetanguishene
L.
Simcoe
LOWER
CANADA
UPPER
CANADA
Quebec
St. Lawrence River
Sorel
Richelieu R.
Montreal
Ottawa River
Cornwall
Crysler's Farm
French Mills
Prescott
Ogdensburg
Plattsburgh
Burlington
Lake
Champlain
Gananoque
Kingston
Bay of Quinte
Sackets Harbour
Prince Edward Pen.
Sandy Cr.
York
Lake Ontario
Oswego
Oswego R.
Burlington
Bay
Stoney Creek
Grand R.
Ft. George
Ft.
Niagara
Niagara R.
Ft. Erie
Buffalo
Charlotte
Sodus
Genesee R.
Rome
Utica
Mohawk R.
L. Oneida
Schenectady
Albany
MICHIGAN
TERRITORY
St. Clair R.
Thames R.
Moraviantown
Long Point
Lake Erie
Detroit
Detroit R.
Amherstburg
(Fort Malden)
Presque Isle
Put-in-
Bay
OHIO
PENNSYLVANIA
NEW YORK
NEW
JERSEY
New York
Atlantic
Ocean
Hudson River
Poughkeepsie
VERMONT
NEW HAMPSHIRE
Connecticut R.
MASS.
CONN.

Warfare and Logistics along the US-Canadian Border during the War of 1812

Christopher D. Dishman

University Press of Kansas

Published by the University Press of Kansas (Lawrence, Kansas 66045), which was organized by the Kansas Board of Regents and is operated and funded by Emporia State University, Fort Hays State University, Kansas State University, Pittsburg State University, the University of Kansas, and Wichita State University

Library of Congress Cataloging-in-Publication Data

Names: Dishman, Chris D., 1972– author.
Title: Warfare and logistics along the US-Canadian border during the War of 1812 / Christopher D. Dishman.
Description: Lawrence : University Press of Kansas, 2021. | Includes bibliographical references and index.
Identifiers: LCCN 2021012564 (print) | LCCN 2021012565 (ebook)
ISBN 9780700632701 (cloth)
ISBN 9780700632718 (ebook)
Subjects: LCSH: United States—History—War of 1812—Campaigns. | Canada—History, Military—19th century.
Classification: LCC E355 .D57 2021 (print) | LCC E355 (ebook) | DDC 973.5/23—dc23
LC record available at https://lccn.loc.gov/2021012564.
LC ebook record available at https://lccn.loc.gov/2021012565.

British Library Cataloguing-in-Publication Data is available.

Printed in the United States of America
10 9 8 7 6 5 4 3 2 1

The paper used in this publication is acid free and meets the minimum requirements of the American National Standard for Permanence of Paper for Printed Library Materials Z39.48-1992.

Dedicated to the memory of Tim Denison, whose wit, humor, and passion for history inspired me to complete this book

CONTENTS

MAPS AND ILLUSTRATIONS

MAPS

ILLUSTRATIONS

PREFACE

This book provides a comprehensive study of the combat that took place along the US-Canadian border during the War of 1812. The bulk of the war's fighting occurred in this frontier wilderness, which in 1811 included the Great Lakes, the Old Northwest of the United States, and Upper and Lower Canada. The region's size, varied topography, and undeveloped infrastructure made this a challenging environment to move troops and supplies to the battlefield. Few large settlements or all-season roads intersected the border frontier, so reinforcements, food, and ammunition could be weeks or months away from their destination depending on the time of year. In this theater, the safe and timely arrival of soldiers, shipwrights, cannon, and other provisions often dictated a battle's outcome before a shot was fired.

The US northern frontier remained the focus of the country's military efforts throughout the war. President James Madison and the US Congress declared war on Britain to force its leaders to rescind measures that, among other American objections, infringed on America's maritime trade. Madison believed that war was necessary to convince Britain to submit to American demands since diplomacy had failed to alter British policies. The burden, then, fell to America to launch military operations to force Britain to negotiate, and America's only viable offensive military option was to invade Canada, a country that retained a long and poorly developed border that would require a substantial number of troops to defend. In 1812, Britain, which was engaged in a war against Napoleon, could not supply enough soldiers to North America to guard the entire Canadian border. British leaders in Canada would need to focus their finite resources around garrisons, settlements, and other strategic points, and be prepared to move troops to other locations as needed. Once the danger from Napoleon subsided in 1814, England allocated additional soldiers to the theater, which enabled its commanders to conduct robust cross-border operations.

In this book, I examine the battles that occurred on the US-

Canadian frontier between 1812 and 1814 and assess the successes and failures of military operations in the region and evaluate the performance of the military officers there. I also highlight the interdependencies between the many land and naval operations conducted on the border frontier during the war. British or American victories often depended on the success of other operations, such as naval control of the Great Lakes or a successful attack on a supply depot. I also look at Britain's and America's frontier objectives and how those objectives changed based on political or military factors. The war's battles are brought to life with personal and professional stories from soldiers and civilians who participated in or observed these events, including a few humorous anecdotes that help humanize the soldiers. Backgrounds on some military officers who played key roles along the border frontier help illuminate their expertise and decision-making.

Not found herein is an examination of the actions outside of the US-Canadian border, including Britain's invasions of Maryland, the District of Columbia, and New Orleans, or of the popular blue water ship engagements that occurred in the Atlantic. The assaults on Baltimore, Fort McHenry, and the District of Columbia were designed, in part, to draw American troops away from the northern frontier so Britain could conduct a major offensive thrust into New York State, and that campaign is the focus of the last chapter.

In these pages, I also detail the importance of logistics in the frontier war. Victory for either side often depended on enough men and supplies arriving promptly at a remote outpost or dockyard. This dependence on external supplies meant that military operations in one theater could produce cascading effects hundreds of miles from the battle. Garrisons relied on the arrival of food rations and other supplies transported from distant supply depots. Britain faced a monumental challenge in this regard. Reinforcements and military provisions traveled from Britain to Halifax, Nova Scotia, after which shippers loaded them into boats to travel to Montreal for further shipment west on the St. Lawrence and Great Lakes. Britain's western flank hung at the far end of this extended supply line, 1,300 miles from Halifax.

Supplies imported into Canada from Britain or the West Indies included cannon, ammunition, and guns, and also ship components, such as anchors, rope, and sails. Canada could not produce any of these items within the country, so the United States retained a distinct advantage with its indigenous metal works and iron industries. These components proved critical in a war that depended on the rushed construction of vessels that could outgun their enemy. For both sides, if a ship's mechanisms failed to arrive on time, naval officers might be forced to deploy incomplete and defective ships for combat and would be in danger of losing a critical naval engagement.

Cattle, pork, and flour provided the primary food source for soldiers garrisoning distant outposts in Upper Canada and in the Old Northwest. Armies depended on an external source for food because the surrounding countryside rarely possessed enough crops or livestock to support an army. Canada relied on food imports from Britain and the West Indies, and the United States hired private contractors to purchase and consolidate food rations from farmers within the country.

Britain also relied on supplies to cement their alliance with local tribes in Upper Canada. Native Americans helped augment British forces, and British Indian agents rewarded their loyalty with food, muskets, knives, liquor, and other gifts. In August 1814, when Upper Canada suffered supply shortages, the commissary general of British North America was alarmed to learn that half of the 14,000 rations issued daily to the soldiers went to Native Americans and their families, which reduced his estimations for how long the supplies would last.[1]

Much of the border frontier contained forest and woodlands, with few villages, good roads, or settlements. Heavy rains turned trails into muddy pits, and weak bridges could not handle heavy loads. As a result, Britain relied on boats to move provisions through the St. Lawrence River and Great Lakes. The waterway offered the most efficient method to transport troops and supplies from east to west, but heavy gales, storms, sandbars, and other hazards threatened to sink vessels that made the trip. Transporters captained forty-foot-long batteaux that carried up to nine tons combined of passengers and freight and drew only twenty inches of water. They also piloted a larger and more durable sixty-foot-long Durham boat, which carried heavier cargoes of iron, grain, and timber.

Britain recognized the importance of the St. Lawrence and the Great Lakes early in the mid-eighteenth century. Its soldiers erected or reinforced garrisons that protected vital choke points through its passage, and they also built or refurbished vessels for combat on the lakes. One English journalist wrote toward the end of the war: "Everything in Canada depends on the Lakes; and . . . those who are masters of them, are in fact, the masters of the Canadas."

America's efforts to control the waterways lacked urgency until after a few disastrous battlefield losses. The governor of the Michigan Territory, General William Hull, had warned the US War Department in 1809 about the importance of the lakes: "I would suggest for consideration the expediency of building some armed vessels on Lake Erie for the purpose of preserving the communication." Two years later, when asked to take command of an army in the region, Hull told US secretary of war William Eustis that "if there is a prospect of war with England, what measures are most expedient? In my mind there can be no doubt. Prepare a naval force on Lake Erie superiour to the British, and sufficient to preserve your communication."[2]

Hull's concern about Lake Erie was grounded in his understanding of the isolated countryside that surrounded Detroit. No roads existed from Urbana, Ohio—a consolidation point for supplies and soldiers—to Detroit, and the route traversed 200 miles of wilderness, including the "Black Swamp." In the eastern United States, rivers, roads, and canals in New York and Pennsylvania offered more efficient pathways for moving supplies. These routes enabled American industry and navy yards to support the country's shipbuilding efforts on Lakes Erie, Ontario, and Champlain.

America and Britain planned many of their US-Canadian border objectives around the disruption or preservation of logistics lines. Unlike the American West, which stretched from Detroit to New Orleans, Britain's string of settlements lacked north–south depth as they curled along the northern or eastern shores of the St. Lawrence River and Great Lakes. This horizontal supply route placed Britain's entire line of communication laterally across Canada's frontier. An American assault against any point on the route would starve outposts west of the invasion point of supplies and reinforcements. America's roads, in contrast, ran north to south—at a right angle—to the Canadian border, so Britain could not interdict US shipments unless they conducted a major invasion of the country. The Madison administration eventually recognized Britain's logistical vulnerability and aimed to sever this logistics line to weaken British forces in Upper Canada. Ultimately, the Great Lakes proved the central battleground in the contest over logistics in the border region, and each side performed shipbuilding miracles to produce vessels quickly that were customized for combat on the lakes.

I am indebted to the many scholars who provided important insights and feedback on the manuscript. I am grateful to Edward Coss, who read early versions of this text, and I am especially appreciative to Tanya J. Grodzinski, who reviewed multiple versions of the book and provided invaluable insights, feedback, and corrections. I also appreciate the support from Walter Borneman, who—albeit many years ago—provided important words of encouragement that helped me maintain momentum for this effort throughout the years.

I am also thankful to the many people who assisted in providing me primary research materials. For some, this assistance occurred a while ago, but their efforts still contributed to the creation of this book. I greatly appreciate the staff at Britain's National Archives and Canada's Library and Archives (LAC), who helped me locate important War of 1812 holdings at their respective facilities. I am particularly indebted to Suzanne Lemaire at LAC, who saved me many hours by identifying pertinent War of 1812 holdings related to my research topic. I also appreciate the help of Annabelle Schattmann, who assisted in providing some of the images used in this book despite the closure of the LAC because of SARS-COVID-19 protocols. Other researchers also identified important research materials and went out of their way to support the project. Mary Doehla from the Special Collections branch at Historic Cherry Hill; Jennifer Duplaga at the Kentucky Historical Society; Christine Beauregard from Manuscripts and Special Collections at the New York State Library; Michael Burgess from Special Collections at the Feinberg Library at SUNY Plattsburgh; and James Holberg at the Filson Historical Society, among many others.

This work relies heavily on the quality scholarship already produced on the war, including by Donald Graves, J. Mackay Hitsman, Robert Malcolmson, and Donald Hickey, among many others. Together they built a solid scholarly foundation that greatly aided me in developing this book.

I would also like to thank the University Press of Kansas, and especially Joyce Harrison for her steadfast support and her faith in the story being told within these pages.

Finally, any errors are strictly my own.

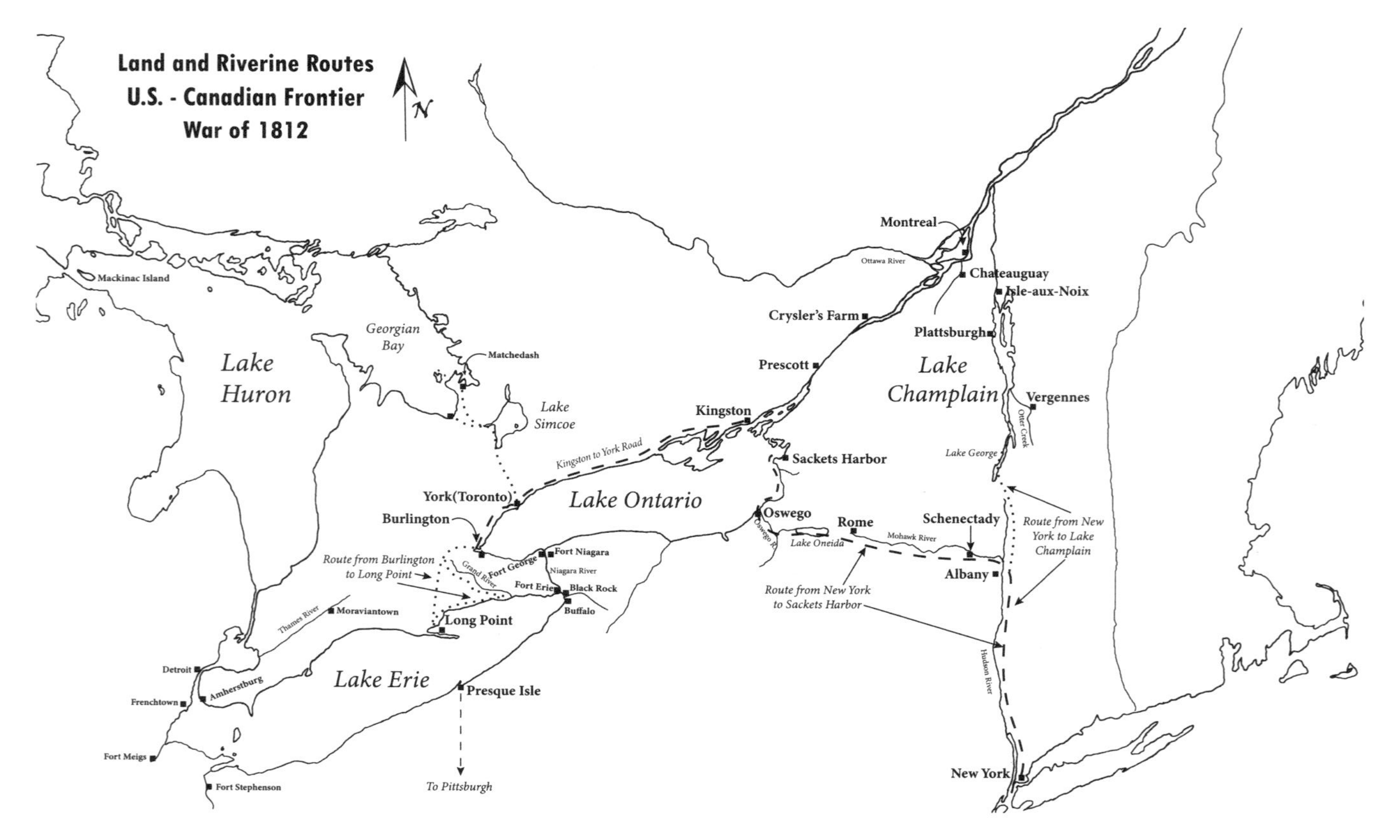

Land and Riverine Routes
U.S. - Canadian Frontier
War of 1812
N
Mackinac Island
Lake Huron
Georgian Bay
Matchedash
Lake Simcoe
York(Toronto)
Burlington
Kingston to York Road
Kingston
Lake Ontario
Route from Burlington to Long Point
Grand River
Fort George
Fort Niagara
Niagara River
Fort Erie
Black Rock
Buffalo
Long Point
Moraviantown
Thames River
Detroit
Amherstburg
Frenchtown
Fort Meigs
Fort Stephenson
Lake Erie
Presque Isle
To Pittsburgh
Montreal
Ottawa River
Chateauguay
Isle-aux-Noix
Crysler's Farm
Plattsburgh
Prescott
Lake Champlain
Vergennes
Otter Creek
Lake George
Sackets Harbor
Oswego
Oswego R.
Lake Oneida
Rome
Mohawk River
Schenectady
Albany
Route from New York to Lake Champlain
Route from New York to Sackets Harbor
Hudson River
New York

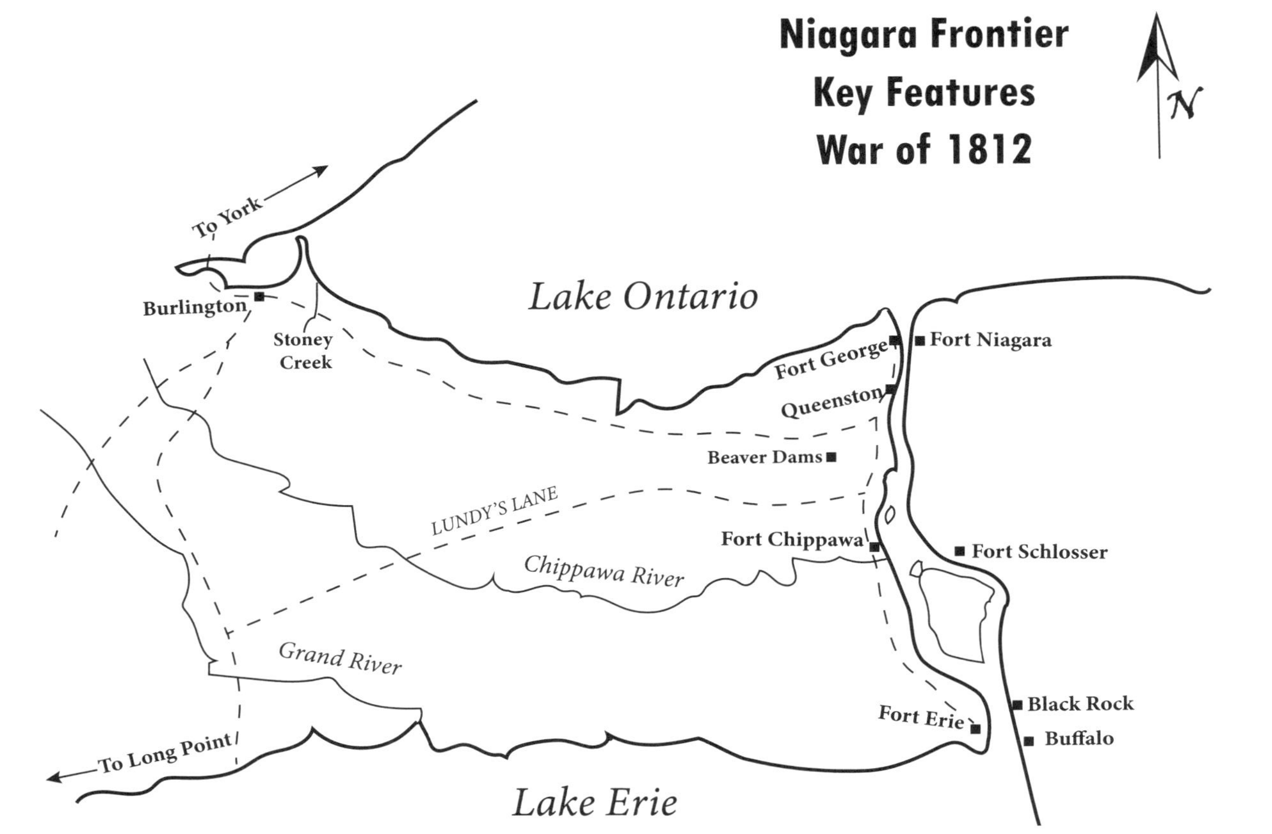
Niagara Frontier
Key Features
War of 1812
N
To York
Lake Ontario
Burlington
Stoney Creek
Fort George
Fort Niagara
Queenston
Beaver Dams
LUNDY'S LANE
Fort Chippawa
Fort Schlosser
Chippawa River
Grand River
Fort Erie
Black Rock
Buffalo
To Long Point
Lake Erie

1

Origins of War and the Border Frontier

The roads were so execrably bad that no words can give you an idea of them.
—A traveler commenting on the roads in Upper Canada, quoted in Edwin Guillet, *Pioneer Travel in Upper Canada*

On June 1, 1812, President James Madison dispatched a message to Congress requesting a declaration of war on Britain. The memo detailed examples of British infringement on US territorial and economic rights. The president cited Britain's impressment of American seamen, Britain's incitement of Native Americans, and the Royal Navy's seizure of neutral shipping. He closed: "We behold, in fine, on the side of Great Britain, a state of war against the United States, and on the side of the United States a state of peace toward Great Britain." Madison's war message wisely encompassed a range of issues that appealed to the broadest possible constituency. The Democratic-Republican "war hawks," a group of pro-war congressmen, had been lobbying for Madison to make such an address, but moderate Democratic-Republicans believed that America should avoid war and pursue other measures to achieve resolution to the issues. Madison's message sought to convince moderates to join him in declaring war against Britain, because with complete Republican support, the declaration would pass.[1]

Two weeks earlier in London, a disgruntled merchant assassinated Britain's hardline prime minister, Spencer Perceval, who had ignored American complaints about Britain's policies and was unwavering in his support of British maritime measures. Following his death, King George III selected Robert Banks Jenkinson, the second Earl of Liverpool and the secretary of state for war and the colonies, as Perceval's successor. Liverpool's fragile coalition government, which lacked parliamentary support, sought to avoid conflict with the United States and focus on the war against Napoleon. On June 16, Foreign Minister Viscount Castlereagh, Liverpool's leader in the House of Commons, announced in Parliament that Britain would allay one of America's grievances and suspend the Orders in Council, with the hope of avoiding war and restarting its profitable trade with the country.[2]

In 1807, Parliament had issued the Orders in Council to prevent America from trading with Britain's enemies and profiting from the Napoleonic War. The Orders in Council permitted British captains to seize neutral American merchant vessels that traded with France and other European countries. The directives also ordered all neutral vessels seeking to trade with Europe to first enter a British port, where their goods would be subject to customs duties. France issued a similar decree, and the implementation of the two directives crippled American trade to Europe.

Before 1807, Britain had largely ignored America's growing share of maritime shipping and the profit that American traders generated during the Napoleonic War. During the conflict, the United States, which retained the second largest merchant marine fleet in the world, engaged in "carryover" trade where American merchant vessels circumvented Britain's navigation laws by reexporting foreign cargo from their own ports. Foreign-produced goods, such as rum from the West Indies, arrived in New England to be transferred to American ships, after which the cargo obtained neutral status. The goods could then be shipped to France or Britain without interference from the Royal Navy. In 1806, America exported 2 million pounds of cotton and 146 million pounds of sugar to Europe that had been imported into American ports. The country's carryover trade increased 200 percent before 1812 and helped sustain America's maritime-based economy. In 1807, American exports peaked at $108 million, but less than half of that trade included goods or raw materials produced in America.[3]

News of the repeal of the Orders in Council took weeks to arrive in America. On June 17, 1812, one day after the British government rescinded the Orders in Council, the US Senate, unaware of the decision, approved a declaration of war on Britain by a vote of 19 to 13. The vote was cast largely along partisan lines, with Democratic-Republicans, including moderates, supporting Madison's war declaration. If notice of the revocation of the orders had arrived earlier, Madison would have likely still pressed for war. Britain would not relinquish its right to impress British deserters, especially during its war with France, and this issue was paramount in Madison's mind.[4]

America's vibrant seafaring trade required experienced sailors to man its merchant fleet, which put its traders in competition with Britain for experienced seamen. During the Napoleonic Wars, Britain could not fully man its extensive naval squadron while also maintaining its legal commitment that Britons occupied three-fourths of the crews on British merchant ships (later lowered to one-fourth). The implementation of a continental blockade against Europe drained the service of men and ships, and the navy still maintained responsibility of protecting shipping lanes and opening new markets. By 1809, the Royal Navy required 125,000 men to operate its warships, compared to only 40,000 sailors needed during peacetime. Desertion, death, and disability decreased the number of available seamen, and combat led to further reductions. Since 1793, Britain had engaged in six major naval battles and had suffered 5,749 casualties in those affairs. The Royal Navy required around 10,000 new men each year to man its vessels and replace those lost to disease, desertion, and combat.[5]

Poor medical care, long times at sea, and terrible food prompted some British sailors to desert the service to seek a better life elsewhere. Some joined the American merchant marine, which offered higher wages without the risk of combat. British deserters on American ships often obtained fraudulent citizenship certificates or became naturalized US citizens. British captains, desperate for men, searched American and European merchant vessels for deserters and sometimes seized legitimate Americans. In such cases, the Admiralty rarely punished the offenders.[6]

In the view of English leaders, British subjects could not renounce their loyalty to the king and service in the navy, otherwise known as "indefeasible allegiance." A subject included anyone who previously served in the Royal Navy, married or settled in England, or expatriates who became naturalized citizens of another country. Impressment of British subjects enabled Britain to rely primarily on Britons to man its ships, rather than accept foreigners into the service, as was customary in other navies. The Royal Navy and press gangs seized anyone fitting these broad criteria from American ships, even if the sailor possessed a US citizenship certificate. More than 10,000 Americans may have been impressed by the Royal Navy between 1803 and 1812.[7]

British apprehension about American shippers recruiting its sailors grew in the years before the war. The US government rarely sought out British deserters to return them to England, and American authorities did not prosecute individuals who sold fraudulent citizenship certificates. The government also lacked a centralized system for tracking and regulating citizenship, which hindered efforts to identify and remove deserters. Even with the necessary laws and enforcement mechanisms, most American merchants would still have ignored the rules. The country's seafaring trade depended on experienced sailors serving in its fleet, so America's shippers would not willingly prevent non-American sailors from joining their crews.[8]

The powder keg erupted in 1807 off the coast of Virginia when the British frigate *Leopard* demanded to board the US frigate *Chesapeake* to search for deserters. The frigate's captain refused to allow the *Leopard*'s crew to board the ship. In response, the *Leopard* fired on the smaller vessel, which quickly succumbed to the barrage. The *Leopard*'s sailors boarded the crippled American vessel and detained four seamen. One of the crewmen was a British deserter and three others were Americans. The Admiralty hung the Briton for treason and released two Americans, and one died in jail. Despite British amends for the attack, anger toward Britain flared throughout the United States. In Norfolk and New York, crowds destroyed British water casks and damaged a British ship. American leaders viewed the impressment of the *Chesapeake*'s seamen as a slight to the country's honor because they regarded a single impressed seaman as a violation of American rights.[9]

Many Britons were incensed that America would declare war on the country while Britain was engaged in a war with Napoleon. In the view of many British leaders, England was Western civilization's last defense against this steamrolling tyrant; the Royal Navy was the "last hope of Europe." Americans, they believed, should be grateful for Britain's protection from France, but instead America engaged in treasonous behavior by stealing sailors from the Royal Navy. Many British leaders, furious that Madison declared war while they battled France, wanted to squash the destabilizing upstart.[10] The *Staffordshire Advertiser* wrote:

> America, like a child that has been introduced too soon into life, has conducted herself with an offensive pertness and a ridiculous dignity. She would require that England bend to her in mock-tragedy, like the giant paying his court to Tom Thumb. If America chose to balance peace and war on the childish resentment and antipathy which she has displayed towards our ambassador, let her blow the trumpet; and when she has learned to distinguish it as a challenge to arms, from a play thing, we shall find in her more prudence.[11]

Madison hoped only a short war would be necessary to force England to meet America's demands: "The sword was scarcely out of the scabbard before the enemy was apprised of the reasonable terms on which it would be resheathed." He exploited Britain's situation by declaring war at a time when he believed that the ministry could not divert resources away from the European continent. The president also naïvely believed that British leaders would be more receptive to addressing America's grievances because they would seek to avoid combatting France and America simultaneously. In truth, Madison possessed as many reasons to declare war with France as he did with Britain. France continued to capture American merchant ships, especially those supplying food to the British Army in Spain and Portugal. Federalists, the minority party in 1812, believed that Napoleon—not Britain—was the real threat to America, and they wanted Madison to declare war on France. Madison, aware of these political dynamics, briefly considered war with both powers, a "triangular war," as he referred to it, but he dismissed the idea since it proposed a "thousand difficulties."[12]

Thus on June 18, 1812, Madison signed Congress's declaration of war and the course was set for America to conduct military operations against Britain. Madison and his administration believed that America should strike first to achieve a quick military victory. A military thrust into Canada was the only viable option to achieve this goal. If America seized a portion of Canada, they reasoned, Prime Minister Liverpool should be willing to discuss America's grievances in exchange for the land's return to Britain.

American leaders were optimistic about the potential success of such an assault. In 1812, Thomas Jefferson wrote that America's invasion of Canada would involve a "mere matter of marching" for the country's army. Many Americans shared Jefferson's zealous assessment. British North America (the empire's colonial territories in North America) contained few habitants, crumbling garrisons, an indefensibly long border, and an infrastructure incapable of handling large numbers of troops and supplies. The United States, in contrast, could raise a substantial army from its population of 7.7 million, and British North America, with around 500,000 inhabitants, did not possess enough citizens to field a large force. The militia in British North America would also draw from some populations with lukewarm allegiance to the Crown, including recent American immigrants and a French-speaking population inherited from New France. Britain also faced the daunting task of reinforcing Canada's isolated interior through an overextended line of communication that stretched from England to Halifax and westward to Canada's interior. A successful journey to bring troops or heavy stores from England to Upper Canada could be derailed by Native Americans, storms, rapids, or numerous other obstacles. America, it seemed, retained a distinct military advantage along the border frontier.

The US invasion of Canada was not the first foray into the country. In December 1775, America attempted to assault Quebec City during the Revolutionary War, but British defenders routed the American force during a blizzard. After that war, 50,000 British loyalists departed the United States for Canada and the British Isles. Many of these immigrants, perhaps around 30,000, settled in present-day Ontario along the St. Lawrence and Detroit Rivers. Pioneers also joined the movement, attracted by cheap land, and together the two groups grew the population of Canada's isolated western frontier. In 1791, the government split the province of Quebec at the Ottawa River into Upper Canada (western Quebec) and Lower Canada to govern the new arrivals. By 1811, Upper Canada's population reached 77,000 people.[13]

Despite the creation of the new province, the lack of all-season roads hindered movement into the region. The government of Upper Canada possessed insufficient funds to construct new roads, so farmers waited until winter to travel on oxen-pulled sleds known as jumpers. Travelers could cross hundreds of miles on jumpers to visit friends or trade supplies. Farmers also used wagons or carts to bring produce to market during the summer. Britain attempted to requisition these carts throughout the war, but the inhabitants in Upper Canada lacked sufficient oxen and carts to support military operations. The British Commissariat, which was responsible for transporting military provisions, had difficulty securing enough wagons to carry the required supplies.[14]

Roads in Canada and the United States exhibited similar characteristics. Road construction consisted of men expanding wetland walking trails by laying cut trees side by side to allow travelers to drag wagons across them. Known as "corduroy roads," the logs prevented wagons from sinking into the mud, but horses and oxen often slipped on the logs. Road construction circumvented large trees, which could be a major obstacle for carts and wagons. Ravines posed another problem since few durable bridges existed over the gaps. As noted by one writer, "Bridges were rare, and those that existed were often viewed as objects of dread." Heavy rains washed away smaller bridges, and stronger, planked bridges could still be dangerous to cross.[15]

Roads in Canada and the United States often cut through land managed by absentee landowners who ignored repairs needed on their stretch of road. In many cases, farmers became occupied with their own crops, and they could not dedicate time to repairing damaged roads. The repeated use of heavy wagons dug deep divots into roads, making them unusable, and large bodies of troops required hundreds of wagons. In August 1813, for example, the British Commissariat allotted eleven carts per 100 men, so a force of 1,000 soldiers would be accompanied by 110 wagons. These wagons could quickly ruin a road, or, more likely, a broken path would damage the cart's wheels. In 1837, one traveler in Upper Canada noted that "the roads were so execrably bad that no words can give you an idea of them. We often sank in mudholes above the axel tree . . . a wheel here and there, or a broken shaft lying by the roadside, told of former wrecks and disasters."[16]

In the United States, some roads in New York State underwent significant improvements before the war. The turnpike, or toll road, transformed the quality of roads around Albany. A company built a turnpike from private capital, and they refunded themselves and performed maintenance by collecting tolls from travelers. The company placed gates every ten miles where travelers paid a fee to continue down the path. These hard-surfaced roads were graded and contained gullies to ensure proper drainage. Before the war, a series of connected turnpikes stretched from Albany to Utica, near Rome, and construction was under way for the road to continue westward. By 1807, 234 miles of continuous toll roads had been created in New York.[17]

In Canada, a company established stagecoach service between Montreal and Kingston in 1808, but the carriage only operated during warm months. The government also started construction on a road between Montreal and

Figure 1. ***Kingston to York: Making a Road.*** A portion of road from Kingston to York. The 150-mile road lined the northern rim of Lake Ontario and provided an alternate route to taking a boat from Kingston to York. The road could not handle heavy equipment most of the year, but it did provide an alternative for Britain when, for short periods, the United States controlled Lake Ontario. The road, however, was only partially complete, and one British general called the route "dreadful." Courtesy of Library and Archives Canada, Acc. No. 1989-255-2.

Kingston, but by 1812, the workers had only completed two sections. Before the war, mail delivery between the two towns took one month to complete the 200-mile trip because of the road's poor condition. The Danforth Road, completed in 1800, connected Kingston to York, but the trail remained in a constant state of disrepair. In 1827, a traveler documenting his trip between the towns wrote that "the horrible corduroy roads again made their appearance . . . by the addition of deep, inky holes, which almost swallowed up the forewheels of the wagon." A British general echoed the traveler's comments, calling the 150-mile road from Kingston to York "dreadful." Another route in western Upper Canada allowed merchants destined for Lake Erie to circumvent the Niagara frontier from Burlington, but the trail could not handle wheeled transport. Indeed, for much of the year, wagons could not traverse most roads in Upper Canada, and they became completely unusable during the spring thaw.[18]

Most fur traders relied on waterways to move goods into the interior. Adventurous merchants followed the Ottawa River, which traversed Lake Nipissing to the French River and entered Georgian Bay on the east side of Lake Huron. Traders relied on this route to carry goods from Montreal to Michilimackinac, even though the dangerous passage required twenty-two to thirty-six laborious portages and Native Americans threatened their shipments throughout the trip. Merchants stowed small, lightweight goods such as furs, firearms, and ammunition in thirty-five-foot-long birchbark canoes to undertake the three- to four-week journey. During the trade's peak, fur exports from Quebec, much of which transited this route, topped 200,000 pounds sterling.[19]

Traveling in America's Old Northwest proved equally difficult. No roads existed between Urbana, Ohio, and US garrisons at Detroit, Chicago, and Mackinac Island. Fort Mackinac, the northernmost military outpost in the United States, sat 300 miles from Detroit and Chicago, and Detroit was located 200 miles from the nearest major settlement at Urbana, Ohio. But no roads had been carved out of the wilderness between Urbana and Detroit, which included a 120-mile section of swamp, to support these garrisons. The Black Swamp, a single contiguous region of standing water, occupied a lake plain in northwestern Ohio. In relatively dry conditions, the swamp would ooze water when walked upon, and only in the driest conditions would the ground remain solid. In 1811, General William Hull created his own makeshift road to Detroit, known as "Hull's Trace," that crossed the swamp. The creation of the wagon-wide path required arduous work by his men, who cut down trees and bridged creeks and swampy areas. "The soil of the land was moist," one of Hull's soldiers recalled, "being in many places a perfect swamp. The weather was rainy and man and horse had to travel mid leg deep in mud." A year later Captain Henry Brush and 200 volunteers set out from Ohio with 300 cattle and 70 packhorses to resupply Detroit after the war had started. His men, who marched through the Black Swamp, lacked potable water while facing the possibility of an attack by Native Americans. "We sleep upon the cold, damp ground without tents," one of Brush's volunteers recalled, "one-third of the company are on guard every night . . . the whole company not on guard 'sleep on the arms' . . . ready for an attack from the hostile Indian tribes."[20]

Transporters used packhorses or wagons to move supplies from Urbana to the Old Northwest outposts. The lack of forage on the route forced many packhorse transporters to carry their own forage, which reduced the amount of available weight for supplies. The decrepit roads damaged wagons and broke horse- and oxshoes. Later in the war, General William Henry Harrison erected a series of blockhouses along the route to hold and protect supplies, including forage for horses. Many of the contractors hired to fill these depots, however, failed to fulfill their contract, which left Harrison's army short of needed provisions.[21]

America's infrastructure further east was more developed than the rugged wilderness of the Old Northwest. A common passage used during the war ran from Albany to Lake Ontario and consisted of a combination of turnpikes, rivers, and canals. Passengers could travel by steamboat from New York to Albany on the North River—now known as the Hudson—aboard the *Car of Neptune*. From Albany, transporters traveled by land to Schenectady, after which they loaded their goods into either Durham boats or batteaux on the Mohawk River. The larger Durham could be loaded with eight to ten tons of cargo on the Mohawk, whereas a batteau could haul around three tons on the waterway. From Schenectady, a transporter followed a series of navigable rivers to the outlet on Lake Ontario at Oswego, New York.[22]

This route was much more developed than the one Hull used to reach Detroit and Mackinac and was critical to America's shipbuilding efforts on Lake Ontario. When the US navy secretary Paul Hamilton tasked Commodore Isaac Chauncey with establishing a base at Sackets Harbor on Lake Ontario, the commodore relied on this route to move more than one hundred pieces of ordnance, thousands of rounds of cannon shot, hundreds of barrels of gunpowder, and shipbuilding materials, such as canvas, rigging, anchors, and cables, among many other provisions. Chauncey benefited from the ordnance and sailors resident at the New York Navy Yard, both of which could travel on the Hudson to Albany and eventually to Sackets Harbor. This waterway route expedited Chauncey's effort to establish a headquarters and dockyard on Lake Ontario.[23]

Chauncey began construction on a shipyard on Lake Ontario because the waterway was on a central section of the 1,700-mile navigable artery that stretched from Halifax to Lake Huron. Britain relied on this maritime route to transport supplies to its outposts in Lower and Upper Canada. The lake itself enabled maritime communication between Kingston, a port on the lake's east side with points west at York, Burlington, and with garrisons on the Niagara River. Land travel from Kingston to York could not substitute for waterborne transport across the lake. The 150-mile road between the two towns could not handle wagons, which made the trail useless for moving ordnance or large amounts of military provisions.[24]

Most of Britain's food rations, cannon, guns, and other supplies originated in England, from where supply ships traveled for ten weeks across the Atlantic Ocean to Halifax. This trip, though safer than the inland journey in Canada, was not always successful. In 1811, the transport ship *Cambo* became lost at sea with 6,000 arms, some of which were destined for British soldiers in Upper Canada. Once a ship arrived at Halifax, and only during the summer, transporters loaded provisions in smaller vessels to travel 700 miles upriver to Quebec. From October to April, this section of the river froze, and floating masses of ice, pushed by rapid currents, made navigation impossible for transport vessels.[25]

From Quebec, transporters navigated almost 200 miles upriver to Montreal. Montreal, a town of 15,000 habitants, lacked major defenses, but water surrounding much of the settlement served as a natural wedge between an invading army and the city. Shippers consolidated goods and supplies at Montreal because the city served as the last point on the river that larger ships could access from Quebec. The stretch of river from Montreal to Kingston, a harbor on the eastern edge of Lake Ontario, averaged 1.3 miles across, with numerous islands that carved channels through the waterway. The river's

Figure 2. *Durham Boat on the St. Lawrence.* Batteaux and Durham boats provided the primary means of maritime transportation on the Great Lakes and St. Lawrence Waterway as well as on navigable rivers in the United States. A typical batteau was thirty feet long and six feet wide, and it required no nails in its construction. Planked elm boards were covered with birchbark and then lined with gum from a fir tree that made the boats watertight. L. H. Tasker described a batteau as a "vessel of wonderful lightness, resonance, and strength, and capable of standing the impetuous torrent of any rapid" (31). Courtesy of Library and Archives Canada, Acc. No. 1981-42-25. Nigel Davies, Gelati, Mexico.

topography created natural choke points, which heightened the danger to captains attempting to avoid shallow channels. In May 1810, a captain entered the wrong channel in the river and his boat capsized, killing seven of his fifteen passengers.

The village of Kingston, located 180 miles west of Montreal, contained Britain's deepest and most accessible harbor on the lake. In 1789, British workers constructed a dockyard west of the town and converted nearby Navy Bay into an anchorage. Kingston's dockyard produced valuable ships during the war, and the town also held stores destined for garrisons in Upper Canada. After this harbor, transporters crossed Lake Ontario and entered the Niagara River, which flowed for thirty-six miles to Lake Erie. Erie provided access to British North America's westernmost areas, including Detroit and St. Joseph's Island, the latter roughly 1,000 miles by water from Quebec.[26]

The preferred method of moving supplies on the St. Lawrence and Great Lakes was a thirty- to forty-foot-long batteau, which hauled corn, flour, and other supplies. A six-foot beam in the boat's center allowed for a mast to be mounted during favorable winds. A typical batteau could carry 9,000 pounds of passengers and freight and remained stable in rapids. A large batteau stretched seventy-five feet long and ten to twelve feet wide and could carry three tiers of barrels on their decks. One writer described a batteau as a "vessel of wonderful lightness, resonance, and strength, and capable of standing the impetuous torrent of any rapid." Starting in 1809, merchants also captained durable sixty-foot-long Durham boats constructed with flat oak-bottom hulls that could deliver seventeen to twenty tons of goods and displaced only four more inches of water than a batteau. Transporters often loaded heavier goods such as grain, iron, and timber into a Durham. In the spring of 1812, 165 batteaux and Durhams operated between Montreal and Kingston, and another 98 negotiated between Quebec and St. Joseph's Island in western Upper Canada.[27]

After Britain's participation in the French and Indian War and the Revolutionary War, British leaders recognized the importance of the St. Lawrence and Great Lakes as a thoroughfare for transporting supplies to their western garrisons. In 1761, Colonel Henry Bouquet began construction of a fort on Lake Erie to protect Upper Canada, and that same year, General Jeffery Amherst dispatched carpenters to the Niagara River to build two vessels. Local officers selected Navy Island (between Lake Ontario and Lake Erie) as the site for the new shipyard, which produced the first decked British vessel on the Great Lakes, the six-gun schooner *Huron*. Later, Navy Island shipwrights completed the schooner *Michigan*, and both ships supported Britain's effort to squash Pontiac's rebellion in 1763, but Britain lost both ships during the violence. In 1780, Britain erected a second shipyard at Detroit, which became the principal dockyard for Upper Canada. There shipwrights constructed the sixty-ton schooner *Hope* and the fifty-ton *Angelica*, each armed with four swivels, which patrolled Lake Erie. The shipyards at Detroit and Navy Island later launched additional vessels that helped secure the line of communication between western Canada and Montreal during and after the Revolutionary War.[28]

During the War of 1812, naval superiority on the lakes depended on the ability of shipwrights to construct and launch decked vessels that could outgun their enemy. The size of the lakes precluded shore batteries from playing a significant role in controlling the waterways, so a fleet's broadside firepower decided maritime superiority. A "ship race" ensued between Britain and the United States on the lakes, with each side seeking to produce vessels that could outgun their enemy. The remote dockyards lacked sufficient numbers of shipwrights, sailors, and supplies, which sometimes forced naval officers to launch a vessel before it was ready. Shipwrights might be forced to plank a hull with green oak, launch a ship without proper manning, or mount different caliber land guns on the ship's deck before a naval engagement.[29]

Great Lakes vessel engineers designed freshwater ships for speed and maneuverability. They sought to lighten a ship's weight by mounting carronades on the deck, rather than long guns, because the lighter carronade was more effective at close range. Shipwrights also built vessels with a high dead rise—the hull's angle from the keel to the widest beam—which allowed ships to cut through water quickly. The short cruises on the lakes also allowed ship captains to load smaller amounts of food and water than was typical for a larger combat vessel, which further lightened the ships. Shipbuilders also converted merchant vessels into warships by adding cannons to their upper decks. These guns made the ships dangerously top-heavy since the new cannons shifted the center of gravity on a vessel designed to carry cargo. Two of Commodore Isaac Chauncey's converted schooners, the *Hamilton* and *Scourge*, sank during a storm on Lake Ontario in 1813, killing eighty-four men.[30]

The Great Lakes could be treacherous for the most experienced seamen. Sudden storms dropped heavy rain and winds that drove ships ashore, forced vessels onto sandbars, or capsized them. Many ocean-going captains remarked that the storms on the Great Lakes were as dangerous as any tempests they faced at sea. Of the five lakes, Lake Erie experienced the worst squalls. With an west–east axis, winds whipped across the lake to create deep swells, gale-force gusts, and heavy downpours. The lake lacked lee side harbors (areas protected from wind) and the loose sand on the lake bottom made anchorage difficult. The lake also contained numerous sandbars, ledges, and points. In 1771, a British ship with a 5,000 sterling worth of pelts sank in Lake Erie, and in 1780, the ship *Snow* perished in the lake, killing forty seamen. One passenger aboard the British sloop *Felicity* recalled the ship's second attempt to cross Lake Erie, after storms forced the captain to return to port: "On Wednesday morning, determined if possible to proceed, we again sailed; and after twenty-four hours of hard labour, were once more sent back with the loss of our top-gallant mast. On this occasion, I was extremely ill, induced by the heavy rolling and pitching of the sloop, and began to fear that we should never succeed in crossing the lake."[31]

Once a vessel was completed, naval officers exercised caution launching new ships. As explained by historian C. Winton-Clare, commanders on each side viewed their engagements like chess players and considered the game lost if one side achieved broadside superiority. Before departing port, officers evaluated their squadron's firepower against the enemy's fleet, and they only sailed if their new craft could outgun the enemy's squadron. The commander of a weaker squadron would retreat to the safety of his harbor and await the construction of more powerful crafts. In some cases, however, circumstances dictated that naval officers launch their fleet before shipbuilders had completed the squadron.[32]

At the start of the war, Britain maintained a modest fleet on the lakes. The country's leadership in British North American understood the importance of the waterways since they had used them to move troops and supplies in the French and Indian War and Revolutionary War. In 1778, the Marine Department was transferred to the army's Quartermaster General's Department and renamed the Provincial Marine. The size of the Canadian Provincial Marine, however, dwindled in peacetime, and the fleet, instead of preparing for combat, conducted maritime law enforcement missions and transported government supplies. In 1803, William Bell, a master shipbuilder at Amherstburg (Ontario), designed Provincial Marine ships to be more capable of combat. The new vessels drew seven feet of water and could clear most sandbars in Lakes Erie and Huron. The shipbuilder also armed the boats with carronades since any hostile engagements would likely occur at short range. The carronade, which contained a shorter and thinner tube than a long gun, could fire twice the shot of a typical cannon. Carronades tripled a ship's broadside firepower compared to the same caliber long gun, but did not increase the ship's weight. A carronade could also be reloaded quicker, required half the crew to operate, and could be swiveled quickly toward a target. The carronade's shortcoming was its distance: the gun could only fire one-third of the range of a similar caliber long gun.[33]

Despite the more capable vessels, the Provincial Marine lacked skilled sailors, shipwrights, and supplies. At Amherstburg, Bell needed skilled carpenters and blacksmiths, and he lacked basic supplies such as rope, which he was forced to take from the village's ropewalk. Also, the Provincial Marine's aging and inexperienced seamen could not operate ships in combat, including one marine captain who was seventy-five years old. Most of the marine's seamen completed only one year of service because of low pay and the boredom during peacetime. One army officer who was later tasked with revitalizing the marine remarked that "the good of the service calls for a radical change in all of the officers, as I do not conceive there is one man of this division fit to command a ship of war."[34]

By the start of the war, the Provincial Marine operated five vessels: three on Lake Ontario and two on Lake Erie. On Lake Ontario, Britain manned the *Duke of Gloucester*, the *Earl of Moira*, and the *Royal George*. In Upper Canada, the western division of the Provincial Marine retained the sixteen-gun *Queen Charlotte*, which was armed with ten 24-pounders and six long guns, and the brig *General Hunter*, which mounted six 6-pounders. By the summer of 1812, the *Lady Prevost* launched with ten 12-pound carronades, and the North West Company provided two boats to the marine, including the 100-ton *Nancy* and 70-ton *Caledonia* that could assist moving supplies.[35]

The Provincial Marine's shipbuilding efforts gave Britain naval superiority on the lakes at the start of the war. Britain's control of Lake Ontario enabled its army to transport heavy supplies and men west from Kingston. The navy's presence on the lake also deterred the US Army from launching a waterborne attack against Kingston and Montreal. An American fleet could cross the lake in three days, but soldiers marching around the waterway to Kingston would be forced to travel for a tiring eighteen days. Further west, British control of Lake Erie permitted the army to shift resources quickly throughout Upper Canada based on circumstances and needs.[36]

This water route also enabled Britain to transport large amounts of food rations during the war. Canada's farmers could not produce enough crops and livestock to support the nutritional needs of a large army. Farmers in Upper Canada produced winter wheat and rye, among other crops, but poor harvests and a scattered population meant that the province could not support the army's massive food requirements. Wheat also had to be ground into flour at a mill, and few commercial-size mills existed in Upper Canada. The commissary general in British North America, who commanded the British Commissariat, estimated that between April 25, 1814, and September 24, 1815, British troops would require 10,612,698 pounds of flour, 8,518,635 pounds of salt pork, and 450,302 pounds of rice, among other food rations, and almost all of these provisions would have to be shipped from Britain to Canada.[37]

To worsen the situation, the bustling traffic on the St. Lawrence and Great Lakes required considerable manpower to keep supplies moving. Local farmers left their homesteads to join these operations, which decreased the land's agricultural output at a time of growing demand. American farmers helped address Canada's food needs by smuggling beef, flour, and salt into Lower Canada before and during the war. In the winter, farmers from New York, Vermont, and Maine drove cattle across the St. Lawrence to sell to intermediaries for the British military.[38]

Transporters also ferried supplies westward for allied Native American tribes. British Indian agents gifted food, knives, liquor, gunpowder, and other goods to local tribes in exchange for their support during the war. In the fall of 1813, a supply shortage in Upper Canada illustrated the importance of these gifts in garnering Native American support. Major General Henry Procter, commander of British forces in Upper Canada, wrote his leadership that "the probable consequences of any further delay in sending an adequate supply of Indian stores to this district are of so serious a nature, that I cannot refrain from urging the necessity of their being pushed forward by every possible means. . . . The long expected supplies cannot any longer be delayed, without the most frightfull consequences. The Indian and his family, suffering from the cold, will no longer be amused with promises."[39]

Britain inherited the practice of gifting from France, which also provided supplies to Native American leaders to garner their allegiance. US independence from Britain threatened to interrupt the latter's relationship with Native Americans in the Old Northwest. American settlers would soon flock to the region, and with their government's support they would begin commercial and political relationships with local tribes. A significant event occurred in the summer and fall of 1796 that would fuel American migration to the Northwest. Under the conditions of the Jay Treaty, Britain evacuated three garrisons at Detroit, Fort Mackinac, and Fort Niagara. The withdrawal raised concerns among local tribes that Britain intended to stop protecting Native American rights in the region. Britain, in part to placate these concerns, sought new locations for these garrisons. They erected or fortified outposts in the region that aimed to control navigation at maritime choke points, especially around rapids or shallow channels where crews portaged around obstacles.

After evacuating Detroit, the British transported their guns and stores to Amherstburg, a small village that emerged across the river the year before. Between 1797 and 1799, they erected an outpost called Fort Malden on the shore above Amherstburg village that could compete with Detroit for control of the 900-yard-wide channel that ran from St. Clair to Lake Erie. The fort underwent numerous improvements leading up to the war, including the construction of four bastions, a redoubt facing the river, a fortified powder magazine, and 150 loopholes for defense. The British also evacuated Fort Niagara and established a new outpost about one mile away on the Niagara River's west bank. By 1799, the structure, called Fort George, overlooked a choke point in the Niagara River at the falls, but the garrison contained few defensive works. The town of York sat between Kingston and Fort George on the northern shore of Lake Ontario, and the village contained a deep harbor, dockyard, and a sizeable ammunition magazine. Fort Erie protected the eastern end of Lake Erie, while Fort Chippawa guarded the Niagara River. Together, Forts George, Erie, and Chippawa protected the line of communication between Lakes Erie and Ontario along the Niagara frontier.

In the upper Great Lakes, British leadership considered locations that could compensate for the loss of Fort Mackinac. The island occupied a strategic position in the Strait of Mackinac that connected Lake Huron with Lake Michigan. Mackinac Island's small village facilitated the fur trade between Lake Superior, the Mississippi River, and Lake Michigan. Britain settled on St. Joseph's Island as a site for the new outpost. The island, located about forty miles northeast from Mackinac, overlooked the St. Mary's ship channel that connected Lake Huron to Lake Superior. St. Joseph's harbors could also provide deep-draft vessels access to its dockyards. Britain began construction on the fort in the summer of 1796, and by 1805 the outpost contained a blockhouse, guardhouse, and palisades, among other structures. Fort St. Joseph became Britain's westernmost garrison and its only one in the northern Great Lakes.[40]

US leaders rejoiced at Britain's evacuation of garrisons on American soil, but the country's broken War Department was not prepared to occupy and fortify the new outposts. The absence of a functional logistics office and the shortage of specie, men, and supplies hindered the department's ability to exploit their new acquisitions. In October 1796, a small American force of sixty-one men occupied Michilimackinac under the command of Lieutenant Porter Hanks. His men erected a fort on the island's south side overlooking the harbor. A customs officer arrived to oversee an Indian trading factory, which doled out goods to local tribes to foster native loyalties.

As war loomed, the Twelfth Congress authorized Madison to raise an army of 25,000 men in five-year enlistments, an authorization that would double the size of the army. Congress also permitted Madison to call out 50,000 volunteers for twelve-month enlistments and muster 100,000 militia from the states to serve for six months. Through these efforts, war proponents in Congress naïvely hoped that they could expand the country's small, broken army into a large professional force in a matter of weeks. They ignored the fact that swelling the army's ranks would only exacerbate the institution's underlying problems.[41]

Since the country's independence from Britain, the United States relied on citizen-soldiers for its national security, and the state militias provided the bulk of the country's forces in the War of 1812. American leaders feared the creation of a strong, standing army because they believed that it would usurp power in the new republic. America's militias, however, existed in law only, since they had rarely been mustered and few governors knew the number of men from their states that would respond during an emergency. This disorganized militia system was incapable of prosecuting an offensive war. During the few instances where the militias had been called out before 1812, the governors, who disagreed with the president's reasons for the request, ignored the call and refused to muster their men. This was an ominous precedent before a war that was opposed by most governors in the Northeast, and yet the Congress, based on the Uniform Militia Act, required New York to provide the second-highest number of men of any state for the conflict. In June 1812, the month that Congress declared war, Acting Inspector General Alexander Smyth told Secretary of War William Eustis that for the month of May, only nine of forty-eight militia districts provided "imperfect" reports regarding the number and readiness of their militia. The inspector general could not assess from these reports the level of training, equipment, and overall readiness for these men, who would soon be dispatched for war.[42]

The United States did possess an undersized standing army in 1812, but public fears of a large military kept it small, poorly supplied, and ill-trained. The service served as a frontier police force, chasing white settlers off Native American lands and enforcing government treaties. Soldiers spent more time hunting, farming, and drinking whiskey than training for combat. Also, the constant contraction and expansion of the service in its early years slowed its development and decimated the officer corps. The Jefferson administration cut the army rolls by 50 percent and discharged eighty-six officers. Without a strong officer corps, the army lacked leaders to guide its men through these difficult years. Instead, older traditionalist generals from the Revolutionary War retained senior positions and failed to prepare the service for military operations.[43]

Jefferson also eliminated the Quartermaster's Department, which procured and transported supplies for the army. He replaced the department with civilian military agents who managed the army's supply depots, and the secretary of war performed the role of a quartermaster general. Starting in 1802, the secretary coordinated the activities of three military agents who conducted quartermaster-type duties. The secretary's new role placed an immense burden on an already overwhelmed War Department. The civilian agents also lacked accountability to the military, and their inefficient operations resulted in wasted government funding.[44]

Secretary of War William Eustis, a physician-turned-politician, knew little about military strategy or management. He was a poor administrator, incapable of fixing the broken department, but few people would have been up to the task. The entire department contained only eight clerks who handled the army's business, including Native American affairs and pensions. In March 1812, just before the war, Congress reestablished the Quartermaster's Department to rectify the ineffectiveness of the agent system. The quartermaster general and his staff procured camp equipment, packhorses, and forage, and the office also transported military supplies. Congress also created a Commissary General of Purchases (the Purchasing Department) that procured arms, ammunition, clothing, and medical supplies, and in May 1812, Congress established an Ordnance Department that was responsible for ordnance, gunpowder, and ammunition, among other items. These departments, however, lacked sufficient personnel and expertise to perform effectively during the war.[45]

The army also continued its practice of hiring private contractors to supply food to the army. The War Department selected the contractor who submitted the lowest bid to deliver a specified number of rations to a destination by a certain date. Unsurprisingly, many of the civilians searched for loopholes to save money at the expense of providing quality food rations, and they often withdrew from contracts without providing the required service. Contractors who avoided their obligations often went unpunished because they did not answer to military authorities. Contractors were divided into regions, and they served customers only within their area of responsibility. This organizational structure became a problem during the war because they lacked the authority to support an army that crossed into Canada.[46]

Before the quartermaster could begin supplying a prewar army, however, the secretary of war had to raise one first. Despite having congressional authorization for 25,000 regulars and 100,000 militia, Secretary Eustis could not find enough men willing to serve. Citizens did not want to enlist in the regular army for five years because of the service's modest pay and difficult lifestyle. New privates were offered a paltry $5 a month, from which one dollar was subtracted for medicine and clothes. Militia recruitment did not fare any better because many governors opposed the war and they would only muster the militia if their state was in danger of being invaded. The governor of Massachusetts, who was supposed to furnish 10,000 men, wrote Eustis that "the militia . . . would undoubtedly prefer to defend their firesides, in company with their friends, under their own officers, rather than be marched to some distant place, while strangers might be introduced to take their places at home." Congress had also not resolved the thorny issue of whether militias could cross international boundaries, an action that most states' laws prohibited. Since the army intended to invade Canada as a first step in his military campaign, this legal problem was debilitating to the war effort.[47]

To finance the war, Congress borrowed $1 million from Philadelphia bankers and raised tariffs to purchase arms and other supplies, but it did not increase internal taxes, which would have been the most effective way to generate revenue for the war. Congress probably remembered that John Adams raised taxes during the Quasi-War with France and was not reelected partly as a result of that measure. Congress also approved money to buy timber for shipbuilding, but it rejected Madison's request to build additional frigates.

The lackluster US military would be pitted against a world power, but by European standards Britain maintained a small army. In 1813, the British Army, expanded for wartime, contained 250,000 men, compared to that of Napoleon, who a year before fielded 600,000 soldiers to invade Russia. Britain usually enlarged its forces during wartime, and the War Ministry reduced them once the conflict ended. The army created new units at the beginning of a conflict and then dissolved them once hostilities ended. The expansion/contraction dynamic undercut the army's tradition and esprit de corps. Most of Britain's resources went to its navy, which was the country's first line of defense against an invader. A large standing navy prevented enemy troops from landing on Britain's shores and protected its maritime trade interests around the globe.[48]

Britain's army in 1812 was more formidable than the one the country fielded in 1776. Between the end of the Revolutionary War and 1812, the army's sustained pace of operations illuminated problems not evident in peacetime. In 1795, Prime Minister William Pitt appointed Frederick Augustus, Duke of York, son of King George III, as commander in chief, and he implemented reforms that overhauled the institution from the command to the field. The Duke of York standardized the army's structure and training and established schools for military education. Each British infantry battalion was organized into ten companies, including eight "battalion" companies, a light infantry company, and a grenadier company. Light infantry and the grenadiers were elite or flank companies.[49]

This training regimen and doctrine produced some of the most disciplined troops in Europe. The British infantry often marched into battle in a two-rank column, after which they formed a two- or three-deep line formation. A line-deployed battalion created an intimidating 200-yard front, two-men deep, all of whom could fire simultaneously at the enemy. Whether advancing or waiting for an oncoming enemy, success often depended on which side could maintain fire discipline and a cohesive formation. The Duke of Wellington's soldiers in the Iberian Peninsula excelled at holding their fire in a defensive position until the last minute, which helped ensure that their inaccurate smoothbore muskets would find their mark at close range. British soldiers also showed discipline and bravery with aggressive bayonet charges to foment panic in the enemy.[50]

An officer's responsibility to maintain the cohesion of an advancing battalion, column, or line was more challenging in North America than in the

Iberian Peninsula. Unlike the rolling hills of Europe, North America's irregular topography challenged efforts to deploy an unbroken battalion line with a 200-yard front. Rock outcroppings, orchards, narrow hills, swamps, and thick woods could dissemble or fragment portions of the line. Narrow terrain could prevent officers from deploying their whole force, or dispatching their cavalry or artillery. During the Revolutionary War, for example, a narrow plain prevented Banastre Tarleton from deploying his Highlanders at the beginning of the Battle of Cowpens, which contributed to his defeat there. British officers adapted to these natural obstacles by deploying their men at larger-than-normal intervals (18 inches), which enabled the men to maneuver through jagged topography.[51]

Another nuance of North American combat was the use of small units of men, armed with rifles, that excelled at "bushfighting," a common method of skirmishing on the frontier. Using tactics adapted from local Native Americans, these men would engage in small, fluid engagements and utilize terrain to reduce casualties and maximize their odds of success. A British soldier who fought in the War of 1812 commented on the American soldier:

> Accustomed to the use of the rifle from his infancy—dwelling in a measure amid forests with the intricacies of which he is perfectly acquainted, and possessing the advantage of a dress which renders him almost undistinguishable to the eye of an European, the American marksman enters with comparative security into a contest with the English soldier, whose glaring habiliment and accoutrement are objects too conspicuous to be missed, while his utter ignorance of a mode of warfare, in which courage and discipline are of no avail, renders the struggle for mastery even more unequal.[52]

The British Army did not integrate skirmishing tactics into their regular units during the Revolutionary War, but starting in the early 1800s, new publications on light infantry tactics rekindled the British military's interest in training and equipping a light corps of soldiers. They created units of light infantry that could fire accurately at a distance, fight independently, and exploit cover to their advantage. Some of these soldiers proved valuable in the Duke of Wellington's Iberian campaign. Wellington incorporated light battalions such as the Ninety-Fifth Rifles who carried Baker rifles, dressed in green, and fought in open and closed order. Light troops fought individually to occupy forests, villages, steep hills, and other cover to harass enemy lines.

The light corps skirmished on the flanks of advancing troops or screened the regular infantry as they marched toward an objective. The British Army employed light units during the War of 1812 where combat often occurred along dense woods, rivers, and hills. Lieutenant General C. W. Robinson, who fought under the Duke of Wellington and transferred to British North America in 1814, noted that "I knew it would be totally different from the open, manly warfare they [his brigade] had been accustomed to, under the Duke of Wellington." In Canada, he directed his men to practice shooting accurately, rather than quickly, and he trained his Light Companies to skirmish in the woods "after the American fashion."[53]

At the start of the war, the regular force of the governor-in-chief of British North America, Sir George Prevost, consisted of around 5,500 regulars, including 420 gunners of the Royal Artillery and five battalions of British infantry. Prevost, recognizing the importance of the St. Lawrence, placed two-thirds of his men above Montreal, with most of them stationed in Quebec. Of those men, Major General Isaac Brock, the administrator of Upper Canada, commanded 1,200 regulars who were scattered in six posts throughout Upper Canada, including 300 regulars at Fort Malden and 400 at Fort George. Prevost and Brock could also count on support from Canadian militia. The 1793 Militia Act for Upper Canada required the entire white male population between the ages of sixteen and fifty to serve in some capacity. The law created a sedentary militia that could be called out during general alarms. An act passed in 1808 by the government in Upper Canada organized this militia by province, with each province providing eight to ten companies of twenty to fifty men each, but they lacked the training and equipment to be effective in war. Brock, aware that sedentary militias were unlikely to perform well in combat, introduced a new clause to the Militia Act in 1812 that authorized the formation of voluntary or "embodied" units. Each militia battalion provided two flank or service companies that the government fully equipped and paraded six times per month. These companies could be "embodied" as necessary to serve beyond the six-month limit. Flank companies proved to be backbone of the militia during the war.[54]

The militia also provided "incorporated" units to the British Army, usually with men drawn from the flank companies. The army permanently embodied and funded the incorporated militia, but the men were still subject to the Militia Act. Some units, known as "Provincial Corps," were enlisted in the British Army and subject to the army's regulations. Prevost authorized the formation of two provincial corps, one in Upper Canada (Glengarry Light Infantry Fencibles) and one in Lower Canada (the Provincial Corps of Light Infantry, or Voltigeurs). The army incorporated one of these, the New Brunswick Fencible Infantry, into the line as the 104th Foot. The overall quality of these Canadian volunteers exceeded their recruited US counterparts. Before the war, Brock believed that 4,000 of 11,650 registered militiamen in Upper Canada were skilled citizen-soldiers worth arming.[55]

These troops required an immense quantity of food, ammunition, clothing, tents, and other supplies, most of which traveled to Canada from England. Governor-in-Chief Prevost needed these supplies to be safely and efficiently distributed throughout the frontier. Prevost engaged with a variety of departments on these complicated logistical matters, such as the Board of Ordnance, which retained responsibility for land and naval ordnance, including muskets, ammunition, and gunpowder, among other items. The commanding Royal Artillery officer, the senior ordnance officer in British North America, reported to Prevost on ordnance issues; the quartermaster general provided camp or field equipment, including tents, canteens, and camp kettles.

The Commissariat, a civil department under the Lords of Treasury, provided a critical service to Prevost during the war. The Commissariat maintained responsibility for procuring, transporting, and issuing food, fuel, and forage for the army, and also storing, transporting, and issuing most other supplies. Based in Quebec, Commissary General William Henry Robinson employed only sixteen officers tasked with the monumental responsibility to transport supplies across 1,700 miles of the Canadian frontier. Robinson's department also conveyed Native American gifts to local governors for further distribution, and provided specie to officers and local officials.[56]

After the United States declared war in June 1812, Madison intended to invade Canada before Britain could prepare their forces. A US assault against Upper Canada would force Britain to concede to American demands by depriving England of vital raw materials, such as lumber. Madison also understood that invading Canada was the only realistic military option because the undersized US Navy could not compete against the British fleet. As Henry

Clay later stated, "When the war was commenced Canada was not the end but the means; the object of the war being the redress of injuries, and Canada being the instrument by which that redress was to be obtained."[57]

During the summer of 1812, Madison adopted a recommendation by Secretary of War Eustis to launch a three-pronged assault into Canada. The center thrust would cross the Niagara River to attack York by land; the eastern prong would seize Montreal. A western assault from Detroit would capture Amherstburg. "Upper Canada," one newspaper optimistically declared, "will fall easy prey to the activity and vigilance of United States troops." Western Americans, most of whom fervently supported the war declaration, volunteered in large numbers to form companies to assault Fort Malden. In their minds, the war allowed them to clear the British and their bothersome Native American allies out of the Northwest Territory.[58] Felix Gundy, a pro-war Tennessee leader, wrote a letter to the *Carthage Gazette* soon after Congress declared war:

> To The Citizens of Western Tennessee: At no time since our independence, has G. Britain failed to use all her exertions to destroy the rising greatness of the Republic. . . . You well know from your contiguity to the scene, that the savage tribes, at the instigation of British agents, are now waging against us a cruel war, unknown among civilized nations. . . . This is no time for temporising. He who is not for us is against us.[59]

2

Conflict in the Old Northwest

Behold the faith of the white men! Tecumseh, you shall avenge the death of your father and appease the spirits of his slaughtered brethren.
—Tecumseh's mother to Tecumseh, quoted in Glenn Tucker, *Tecumseh: Vision of Glory*

Before the war, the northwest corner of the United States occupied a unique place in the minds of many Americans. In 1812, the region contained portions of the Illinois, Indiana, and Michigan Territories and the state of Ohio. Cheap land, productive trapping, fertile soils, and plentiful wildlife drew settlers to the region. The influx of these pioneers put them on a collision course with local Native American tribes and their British allies, who still retained strong commercial ties in the area. The arrival of the Americans followed that of migrants from France and Britain, who had earlier established a presence in the Ohio valley to profit from the fur trade. The Americans, however, pursued a different goal. Many intended to establish permanent lives on farms and homesteads in the region. Local tribes saw these newcomers as a more serious threat than their foreign predecessors, and some Native American leaders sought to evict them from the region. The War of 1812 represented their final effort to retain their land and way of life in the Old Northwest.

The 1783 Treaty of Paris set the Great Lakes, the Mississippi, and the thirty-first parallel as the northern, western, and southern boundaries of the United States. The new territory contained black walnut, ash, bur oak, and sugar maple trees, and vast prairies covered with native flowers and grasses provided sustenance for the area's wildlife. Whitetail deer, elk, and black bear thrived in this vibrant ecological region, which was largely untouched by farmers or land developers. One early British explorer, Christopher Gist, wrote that the area possessed "fine, rich level land, well timbered with large walnut, ash, sugar trees, cherry trees &c, it is well watered with a great number of little streams or rivulets, and full of beautiful natural meadows, covered with wild rye, blue grass and clover, and abounds with turkeys, deer, elks and most sorts of game particularly buffaloes, thirty or forty of which are frequently seen feeding in one meadow." During the war, a soldier described the landscape to his wife: "The country we yesterday passed through is the most delightful I have ever seen. . . . These plains are covered with a most luxuriant growth of grass and herbs, and an endless variety of beautiful native flowers, representing all the hues of the rainbow."[1]

In addition to furs, the region's bubbling springs produced enough salt that the mineral could be commercially mined. Pioneers coated meat with salt to prevent spoilage, so the substance was in high demand in the Old West. Gist described one of the salt licks he encountered in the Ohio valley:

> in the S Side is a very large Salt Lick, the Streams which run into this Lick are very salt, & tho clear leave a blueish Sediment: The Indians and Traders make salt for their Horses of this Water, by boiling it; it has at first a blueish Colour, and somewhat bitter Taste, but upon being dissolved in fair Water and boiled a second Time, it becomes tolerable pure Salt.[2]

Many pioneers encamped around salt springs where merchants traded the mineral for goods and services. The US Congress, whose members viewed salt as a national commodity, took steps to develop and protect the Ohio valley salt springs. In 1797, Congress passed an act that reserved all salt lands within the present state of Ohio for future exploitation by the United States. Congress also provided the president $3,000 to develop salt mines on the Wabash, and they donated some of the territory's salt springs to the newly formed state of Ohio, which profited from renting or selling the mines to entrepreneurs.[3]

Small-scale farmers flocked to the Ohio valley to grow corn, wheat, flax, cotton, and other crops for personal use. They practiced husbandry by raising cattle, hogs, and horses, all of which thrived when eating the region's native grasses. Farmers paid for local supplies, wages, and taxes with corn and livestock, and they sometimes combined their surplus produce with other families and floated their goods downstream to market. Exchange rates based on locally produced goods allowed settlers to barter with each other and with local merchants. Farmers in the region also sold livestock and produce to the US military when the army carried out expeditions in the area. Some immigrants served as tenants on land tracts purchased by large investors. These families worked to improve the land for the benefit of themselves and the landowner, and the landowner paid them in shares.[4]

The growing number of permanent homesteads in the Northwest Territory slowly transformed much of the Native Americans' hunting grounds into an agricultural community. The settlers cleared forests to acquire wood for barns, houses, fencing, and other needs, and they killed native grasses to create arable land for farming. Their actions fragmented deer, elk, and bear habitat and reduced the animals' sources of food. Settlers also hunted local game with dogs, which further harmed populations of whitetail deer and elk. By the early 1800s, hunters had decimated the region's elk and whitetail deer herds. American immigrants, who erected permanent farms and homesteads in the region, disrupted the region's wildlife more than the French or British before them. Native Americans rightfully viewed the newcomers as colonizers rather than itinerant merchants interested in trade.[5]

Not all American settlers, however, were subsistence farmers. Some speculators attempted to establish larger operations, but the absence of labor and the difficulty of transporting goods to market undermined such efforts. Merchants conveyed goods on primitive roads and tempestuous rivers and often lost them to severe weather, Native Americans, or thieves. Labor was also scarce because most able-bodied males focused their energy on creating a successful homestead rather than working for a speculator or local business. Unlike the later migration to California, trans-Appalachian pioneers did not travel to the Northwest to seek quick riches and return home with the profits.

In the Ohio valley, settlements emerged at Cincinnati and Marietta, the latter acting as the economic and social center for the Ohio Company of Associates. In Cincinnati, entrepreneurs provided free lots to attract settlers to the town. Eastern merchants established mercantile stores where they sold trade goods desired by the immigrants. Some of these stores accepted pelts and skins as payment because the pioneers lacked currency to purchase their goods. One storekeeper even resorted to accepting ginseng as payment, but he was not optimistic about his store's financial future.[6]

The Americans' interest in the Ohio valley was no surprise. The region had been a lucrative trading hub before their arrival, and France and Britain had contested ownership of the area for decades. In the early eighteenth century, French traders on the western Great Lakes bartered guns, alcohol, and blankets for beaver, otter, and deerskin pelts. The French established trade centers at Detroit, St. Joseph, and Michilimackinac. They intermarried with Native American women to solidify their commercial alliances, and in 1715, the French constructed their first fort near present day Fort Wayne, Indiana. French merchants cultivated their alliance with the Native Americans by presenting gifts to local chiefs. They donated shirts, hats, combs, mirrors, powder, cloth, shoes, gunpowder, and whiskey as tokens of friendship. At times, however, supplies of these goods became scarce because of the long and perilous journey to the region from the coast. The shortages threatened to unravel the gift-based alliance that bound France and its Native American allies together.[7]

French traders pushed into the Ohio valley from Canada, but British entrepreneurs from the American colonies sought similar riches. A 1732 treaty between Pennsylvania and the Six Nations of the Iroquois codified a commercial bond between Pennsylvanians and western tribes that encouraged merchants to cross the Alleghany Mountains to trade with Native Americans. In 1748, additional agreements between Britain and western tribes gave Pennsylvania traders dominance over the fur trade north of the Ohio River. The Ohio Company, led by prominent Englishmen and Virginians, expanded the new relationships by purchasing 200,000 acres in the upper Ohio River valley.[8]

In 1752, Marquis Du Quesne, the newly appointed governor of French Canada, believed that France must reassert itself in the region to regain commercial dominance. He insisted that Native Americans could trade with Englishmen on British soil, but the Native Americans could not conduct transactions with the British on French territory. Du Quesne dispatched an expedition to erect new garrisons and reestablish France's foothold in the territory. Britain countered by sending Lieutenant Colonel George Washington to the Ohio valley to complete an English fort at Wills Creek, but the French overtook the garrison before he arrived. In the ensuing years, France and Britain fought skirmishes to control the region. Britain prevailed in the contest, known as the French and Indian War (Seven Years' War), and by 1763 the country had solidified its control over the region's profitable fur trade.[9] Benjamin Franklin insightfully explained the differences between American and British pioneers in the region, and he argued that the American colonies retained no equities in a war undertaken to support the British practice:

> The trade with the Indians, though carried on in America, is not an American interest. The people of America are chiefly farmers and planters; scarce anything that they raise or produce is an article of commerce with the Indians. The Indian trade is a British interest; it is carried on with British manufactures, for the profit of British merchants and manufacturers; therefore, as it commenced for the defence of territories of the crown, the property of no American, and for the defence of a trade purely British, was really a British war.[10]

After Britain's victory, the army occupied France's garrisons and constructed new trading outposts where they bartered with Native Americans for pelts. The British governor-general, Major General Jeffery Amherst, stopped the traditional French practice of providing gifts to local Native American leaders because he believed that the native tribes disrupted the region's stability. He also forbade the sale of alcohol. Amherst's new policies strained relations with Britain's allies, and in 1763, Ottawa chief Pontiac incited his warriors to attack British outposts, which resulted in 2,000 British subjects killed or captured. Britain suppressed the rebellion, but the violent outburst prompted the Crown to recall Amherst and appoint a new governor-general, Thomas Gage, who adopted a more conciliatory policy toward the Native Americans.[11]

Britain controlled the region until the 1783 Treaty of Paris granted the lands to the United States at the end of the Revolutionary War. Four years later, Congress passed the Northwest Ordinance, which appointed a governor to the area and established legal protections for settlers' rights. The governor could admit three to five new states into the United States if they met certain conditions for admission. Soon after passage of the ordinance, 20,000 pioneers floated on flatboats down the Ohio River. For $35, a family could purchase a thirty- to forty-foot-long "Kentucky boat," which featured walls and a partial roof to protect the passengers from weather and Native American attacks.[12]

The tide of American settlers into the region set them on a collision course with local Native American tribes. The Six Nations of the Iroquois Confederacy argued that the British king never possessed the land, so Britain had no right to cede the territory to the United States. The American delegation retorted that the Native Americans had allied with their enemy and lost the war, so the lands belonged to the US government. The view of Secretary of War Henry Knox was to demand territory through peaceful land acquisitions, and if that approach failed, to use military force to acquire the land. Once again, the Six Nations Confederacy was embroiled in a power struggle between encroaching powers, similar to its position during earlier hostilities between France and Britain.[13]

The United States and Britain categorized most tribes as allies or enemies, which placed neutral Native Americans in a difficult position when trying to avoid conflict. Some leaders in tribes such as the Wyandots, Senecas, and Delawares, inhabitants of the Sandusky River region, feared that their settlements would be destroyed during the war. Chief Walk-in-the-Water, the influential leader of the Michigan Wyandot, initially planned to remain neutral in the conflict, and Black Hoof of the Shawnees also declared for neutrality. Many neutral chiefs, however, would be forced to side with Britain or the United States during the conflict, and they would switch allegiances as necessary to preserve their way of life. Other Native Americans took a more defiant approach to the American settlers, which led to an unwavering alliance with Britain during the war. "If they [the tribes who sold the land] are fools enough to throw away their hunting ground," remarked one chief, "let them do it; we, however, in this quarter, will do no such thing."[14]

The Shawnee and Potawatomi refused to evacuate their tribal homelands, and charismatic tribal leaders such as Main Pock of the Potawatomi led raiding parties to steal horses, kill livestock, kidnap and murder settlers, and burn frontier villages. Main Pock persuaded warriors to join him on raids through his brilliant oratory and bravery in battle. He and other tribal groups attacked settlers' flatboats from the north shore of the Ohio River to deter new arrivals. They also raided settlements to force recent immigrants to abandon their claims. They targeted livestock because they knew that farmers relied on husbandry for survival. Some of the local tribes also committed violence in response to depredations committed against their own families by the settlers. Frontiersmen then dispatched revenge parties to kill raiding Native Americans, which contributed to an endless cycle of violence in the region. All Native Americans, even peaceful tribes, suffered the wrath of these revenge-seekers, and the courts often acquitted the murderers of their crimes. In one example, a 1782 raid in eastern Ohio killed ninety peaceful Christian Native Americans, and American judges refused to prosecute the raiders.[15]

Most Americans believed that Britain and Spain instigated and supported the Native American raids. Every year Native Americans received knives, hatchets, and other goods from British Indian agents at Amherstburg. Many of the leaders in Britain's Indian Department sympathized with the native's situation. Some Indian agents had led Native American assaults against Americans during the Revolutionary War, and some had married Native American women. British policy encouraged Indian agents to provide gifts to the local tribes, as long as they did not incite them to attack American settlers. Britain gifted guns, ammunition, and gunpowder to their Native American allies, but most of their trade was in other goods. One list of sundries destined for Native American allies in the upper Great Lakes listed blankets, scaling knives, gun flints, scarlet cloth, stitching thread, sewing needles, and ribbons, among other items. Britain also provided food rations to their allies because settlers and warfare in the region had destroyed much of the wildlife that Native Americans relied on for food and fur trading.[16]

The financiers of Britain's North West Company also wanted to rid the region of the new American settlers. The company profited from the fur trade and sought to preserve the economic status quo. New settlers trapped game and hunted their own wildlife, which hurt the company's fur business. North West Company leaders hoped that the British government would demand the reinstitution of the pre-1783 boundaries so the company could control the fur trade from Lake Huron to the Missouri River. The most practical solution, and one that Britain officials endorsed until the end of the war, was the creation of a neutral Native American zone that would serve as a buffer to American encroachment. Britain had proposed a similar arrangement during earlier hostilities with France. They hoped that support for an independent zone would build loyalty among the tribes and shift their allegiance away from France.[17]

After the Revolutionary War, Britain refused to evacuate key garrisons in the region as dictated by the Treaty of Paris. They intended to show their support to the natives, while also furthering the country's commercial interests in the region. Britain refused to depart strategic posts at Presque Isle, Sandusky, Niagara, Detroit, and Mackinac, and they attempted to intervene in negotiations between the United States and regional tribes. American commissioners rejected the British gesture. In the view of American negotiators, British involvement in the discussions insinuated that the Native Americans represented a sovereign nation.[18]

Meanwhile, American settlers requested that its government protect them from the growing number of Native American raids. In 1790, President George Washington sent Brevet Brigadier General Josiah Harmar to the Northwest to subdue the Native Americans, but the Miamis ambushed Harmar and killed 150 of his men. A year later, three allied tribes, led by Little Turtle, surprised Major General Arthur St. Clair, who had established a military post in the region. At the Battle of the Wabash, the Native American alliance killed 629 Americans and wounded 250 soldiers—twice the number of soldiers killed at the Battle of the Little Bighorn one hundred years later.

The British cabinet exploited St. Clair's defeat in an effort to revive the buffer state proposal. They proposed that Britain withdraw from their garrisons in the region in exchange for the creation of a Native American state on American soil. The British minister to the United States refused to forward the proposal to the US government, however, because he knew the government would reject the idea. Meanwhile, British leadership continued to encourage the Native Americans to ally with Britain as hostilities grew with the United States. In early 1794, Sir Guy Carleton, the governor-general of the British North American colonies, delivered a speech to representatives of the Seven Nations of Canada, where he told the warriors that Britain and the United States would likely be at war soon and they must choose sides between the two. His subordinate, Lieutenant Governor Simcoe, repeated the speech at Detroit a few months later.[19]

After St. Clair's defeat, Washington dispatched General "Mad" Anthony Wayne to the Northwest Territory. Wayne organized a new army structure known as the Legion of the United States, which contained four sublegions with 1,280 men each. The sublegions integrated infantry, artillery, and dragoons into a single combined arms unit. Wayne customized his force by directing that each infantry battalion also contain an elite light infantry company for skirmishing and bushfighting. Strong Kentucky horses formed the basis of Wayne's cavalry, and his smaller horses and oxen pulled his supply wagons. In December 1793, Wayne marched to the site of St. Clair's defeat and built a new garrison called Fort Recovery. Wayne selected the site to show the Native Americans that the US military would not be cowed by St. Clair's defeat.[20]

In August 1794, the Shawnees and Miamis planned to attack the force. Blue Jacket's warriors assaulted Wayne's pack train, which sent the general's privateers fleeing to the fort. Wayne's dragoons dashed to the group's defense, but in the confusion a second war party of Chippewa, Ottawa, and Potawatomi warriors killed, wounded, or captured fifty of Wayne's men. Meanwhile, the main force of Native American warriors charged the fort's gate, but the fire from Wayne's men and artillery cut down the attackers. The Native Americans suffered more casualties than expected, and the confederation of 1,200 warriors unraveled. Wayne later pursued the warriors by razing villages and searching for enemy encampments. The Native American confederation, aware of Wayne's approach, selected a battlefield littered by downed trees from a tornado. Wayne waited two days to attack the force, and this delay surprised the Native Americans. Wayne's legion routed the group in a forty-five-minute battle. The Native Americans fled toward the British garrison at Fort Miami, but the commanders refused to allow them into the outpost. After the skirmish, known as the Battle of Fallen Timbers, Wayne forced the renegade tribes to sign the Treaty of Greenville, which required the Native Americans to relinquish more than 10 million acres of land, mostly in present-day Ohio. In return, the US government agreed to withdraw their claim to land north of the Ohio River and east of the Mississippi.[21]

The same year, 1794, American settlement in the region received another boost with the signing of the Jay Treaty, under which Britain agreed to withdraw from its garrisons on American soil. Britain's evacuation of these outposts signaled to the Northwest Confederacy of Native American tribes that Britain valued peace with the United States more than the protection of their Native American allies. The US government assumed control of outposts such as Detroit and Mackinac Island soon after the British withdrawal. As allowed under the treaty, British fur traders continued to trade throughout the Northwest Territory. They established settlements at Green Bay and Prairie du Chien, which gave them access to the upper Mississippi River. The settlements gave the British influence among western Native American tribes in Illinois, Wisconsin, and the northern peninsula of Michigan. The fur traders continued to nurture economic and political ties with the Native Americans in the Old Northwest after the Jay Treaty. At Prairie de Chien, the traders stored 10,000 to 12,000 pounds of gunpowder and musket balls, which could be distributed to the Native Americans should war commence between Britain and America. They also doled out rum, arms, and ammunition to the Native Americans, who traded buffalo and deer meat in return.[22]

One of the most strategic positions transferred under the terms of the Jay Treaty was Mackinac. At the start of the war, Mackinac Island was the northernmost military post in the United States. The strategic garrison sat on a three-mile-long and nine-mile-wide island in the Strait of Mackinac, which connects Lake Huron with Lake Michigan. The waterway, a major fur trading route, served as a launching point for military operations in the area. The Americans erected a fortification on the island's south side overlooking its harbor. The outpost functioned primarily as a Native American trading post and lacked the strength of a fortified garrison.[23]

The US government further established its presence in the region in 1803, when President Thomas Jefferson directed the army to construct a garrison at the entrance of the Chicago River at Lake Michigan (the site would later become Chicago). The government established an agency house at the outpost, called Fort Dearborn, to maintain relations with local Native Americans and trade with the local tribes. The government established other trading houses throughout the region where American Indian agents sold cheap goods to maintain cordial relations with the native tribes. More than twenty-seven trading posts from Georgia to the upper Mississippi doled out annuities to and purchased furs from Native Americans. Many tribes depended on the technology and food provided by these stores for their survival. A severe drought had recently ruined their annual harvest, and the dwindling wildlife population no longer provided enough pelts for trading. Starvation and alcoholism spread throughout many of the region's tribes.[24]

Tecumseh, a Shawnee war chief, and his brother, the Prophet, observed the disintegration of the Northwest tribes with disdain. Tecumseh refused to sign the 1795 Treaty of Greenville and acquiesce to American settlement in the region. Eastern pioneers had cost his family and tribe dearly, and he refused to abandon his native land so easily. White settlers shot Tecumseh's father, a daring and popular figure in the tribe, while he was hunting game. When Tecumseh and his mother found his body, she told him, "Behold the faith of the white men! Tecumseh, you shall avenge the death of your father and appease the spirits of his slaughtered brethren." Shawnee chiefs before Tecumseh tried to reunite the tribe along the Ohio River, where the Great Spirit would protect them. Blackfish, Cornstalk, and Blue Jacket believed that war was the only way to retain their land and defend their way of life. They convinced other tribes to join a loose confederation to oppose the white settlers.[25]

Tecumseh's grand vision reflected his ancestors' legacy, and he sought to unite tribes across the Old West to prevent white encroachment. He told William Henry Harrison, governor of the Indiana Territory, that the chiefs who signed treaties with the Americans would be deposed and their positions filled with warriors. Most of the Shawnee's elder village chiefs were peaceful and had already signed treaties with the United States, including Black Hoof, who signed the Treaty of Greenville. Younger, charismatic war leaders such as Tecumseh threatened the traditional chiefs' fragile hold over the tribe, which was divided between five different descents. Tecumseh chastised men such as Black Hoof who received American annuities of gifts and money in return for relinquishing sacred Shawnee land.[26]

Friend and foe alike respected the Shawnee leader. Tecumseh's infectious personality displayed charisma, wit, and intelligence. British major general Isaac Brock remarked that "a more sagacious or a more gallant warrior does not, I believe, exist. He was the admiration of most people who conversed with him." One Ohio volunteer described Tecumseh's oratory as "concise and impressive." In his early years, Tecumseh became a distinguished soldier, and men flocked to his leadership. In 1791, he scouted for the famous Shawnee war chief Blue Jacket during hostilities with General Arthur St. Clair in the Ohio valley, and he led successful raids against Ohio River flatboats to steal supplies and terrorize settlers.[27]

Tecumseh's efforts to establish a confederacy were unrivaled. He lived on his horse and traveled vast expanses to meet with tribal chiefs, many of whom were drawn to his presence and oratory, even though they usually spoke a different language. "For four years he has been in constant motion," Harrison wrote the US War Department. "You see him today on the Wabash, and in a short time hear of him on the shores of Lake Erie or Michigan, or on the banks of the Mississippi." Native Americans from different tribes across the Old West flocked to Tecumseh and his brother to live a spiritual, nonalcoholic life at Prophetstown, which was located on the Tippecanoe River.

Harrison, the governor of the Indiana Territory at the time, viewed the village as a threat to his region and vowed to disband the Native Americans, either through negotiation or the sword. On November 6, 1811, Harrison and 900 soldiers approached Prophetstown and told an approaching Native American party that he desired peace and that he wanted to negotiate the next day. The Native Americans recommended a campsite two miles north of the village. Tecumseh's brother knew that Harrison would approach Prophetstown the next day to demand that the settlement disband. He decided that his best chance to save the village was to destroy Harrison's army in a surprise night raid. Tecumseh, absent on a recruiting mission, directed his brother to avoid attacking Harrison in his absence, but the Prophet's options were limited. The Prophet and his men attacked the camp that night, but Harrison had organized a strong defensive layout and directed his men to be on high alert. The Americans repulsed the Prophet's ambush at the Battle of Tippecanoe and later destroyed his settlement.

After Harrison defeated the Prophet, Tecumseh vowed revenge. He sought to rekindle the Shawnee's old alliance with Britain in order to resist the Long Knives and save his land. Britain welcomed Tecumseh's offer after the 1807 Chesapeake Affair, which ratcheted up antagonisms between Britain and the United States. More than 10,000 Native Americans resided in the Great Lakes region, including roughly 1,600 in Upper Canada, and their warfighting skills could tip the balance in favor of the British. Sir James Craig, the governor-general of British North America in 1808, believed that Britain should curry favor with these Native American chiefs, because otherwise they would ally with the United States. Later, in December 1811, as hostilities appeared imminent, Major General Isaac Brock, the administrator of Upper Canada, recommended to Sir George Prevost, the governor-in-chief and commander of British forces in North America, that Brock should assault Mackinac and Detroit to gain the favor with the local Native Americans. Brock believed that the Shawnees and other tribes in the region would augment his force if war arose between the two countries. British seizure of the two garrisons would show the local Native Americans that Britain intended to exert its power in support of the tribes.[28] Brock wrote Prevost:

The Indians, I am made to understand, are eager for an opportunity to avenge the numerous injuries of which they complain. A few tribes, at the instigation of a Shawnees, of no particular note, although explicitly told not to look for assistance from us, have already commenced the contest. The stand which they continue to make upon the Wabash, against about 2,000 Americans, including militia and regulars, is a strong proof of the large force which a general combination of the Indians will render necessary to protect so widely extended a frontier.[29]

Sir George Prevost, however, cautioned Brock not to incite the Native Americans or conduct a preemptive assault. Prevost still hoped, as did the British cabinet, that hostilities could still be avoided between the two countries. He did not want Britain actively instigating Native American assaults against US interests in the region. Prevost responded to Brock's letter: "There are too many considerations to allow me to hesitate in saying we must employ the Indians, if they can be brought to act with us. The utmost caution should be used in our language to them, and all direct explanation should be delayed, if possible, until hostilities are more certain."[30]

In June 1812, after Congress declared war against Britain, Brock dispatched Robert Dickson, an influential northwest fur trader, to recruit Native Americans to the British cause. Dickson undertook his task with energy, meeting with numerous Native American chiefs along the Mississippi. "Dickson . . . received the strongest assurances of friendship and support in the cause of their Father the British," an officer on Brock's staff recalled. The British perceived that many of the region's tribes would ally with Britain against the Americans if a conflict arose. Dickson found an eager recipient in Tecumseh, who vowed his tribes' support. "Tech-kum-thai," a British officer at Amherstburg noted, "has shewn [shown] himself to be a determined character and a great friend to our government." The Shawnee chief and his warriors headed to Fort Malden to join the British, and on the way Tecumseh stopped by Fort Mackinac to tell the Americans that he was offering his services to Britain. Tecumseh's alliance with Britain would be his followers' final chance to preserve their native lands.[31]

3

Opening Moves

Michigan Lost

When I detail my good fortune, your Excellency will be astonished.
—Brock to Prevost, August 16, 1812, *The Life and Correspondence of Major General Isaac Brock*

If we judge by his early years, William Hull was an odd choice to be governor of a newly established territory on the fringes of the American frontier. As a teenager, Hull was a standout student. Raised in Derby, Connecticut, he studied at Yale College and later pursued his interest in law. He seemed destined to be a successful merchant or politician, living in the comforts of civilized society. But in 1775, soon after being admitted to the bar, his life took a turn toward military service. Like many men his age, Hull joined the new Continental Army formed to fight Britain for America's independence.[1]

Hull approached military service with the same vigor as he did his academic pursuits. He distinguished himself as one of the war's best soldiers, participating in many of the major battles of the Revolutionary War. He showed competence both in combat and as a staff officer. One of Hulls' finest moments was at the Battle of Saratoga, where his men reinforced and steadied the right flank of a collapsing American line.[2]

After the war, Hull continued in public service, serving as a commissioner to Upper Canada, where he negotiated with the British over Native American rights in the region. In 1805, President Jefferson appointed Hull governor of the Michigan Territory, where his first task was to expand the US footprint in the northwest. In 1807, he negotiated a treaty with the Ottawa, Chippewa, Potawatomi, and Wyandot tribes to purchase 5 million acres of eastern Michigan. The acquisition infuriated many of the region's Native Americans, and they increased raids against settlers in his territory. Hull sought to evict or exterminate any Native Americans unwilling to take up the "mechanic arts," which included farming, blacksmithing, and other modern trades. In 1812, Hull visited Washington, DC, to request additional troops to suppress the renegade warriors.[3]

Jefferson's successor, James Madison, listened to Hull's request, but he had another task for the governor. With war with Britain approaching, Madison needed Hull, one of the most qualified officers available, to raise an army to fortify a garrison on the US-Canadian border. Fort Detroit, acquired from the British under the Jay Treaty, was within Hull's jurisdiction as governor of the Michigan Territory. The outpost sat across from the British fort at Amherstburg and occupied a strategic position along the Detroit River that connected Lake St. Clair with Lake Erie. The fifty-year-old Hull accepted the position because he believed that his force could address the Native American threat in his province. Madison tasked Hull with leading the Army of the Northwest from Detroit to attack Upper Canada, while the army's center thrust under militia major general Stephen Van Rensselaer would launch an assault across the Niagara River from New York State. Regulars would also enter Canada across Lake Champlain to overrun Montreal. US secretary of war William Eustis hoped that coordinated attacks would spread Canada's defenses thin to allow US troops to penetrate deep into its territory. Eustis directed 1,200 Ohio militia and 300 men of the Fourth Infantry Regiment to join Hull's campaign.

Many of the Ohio men possessed frontier combat experience. Some had patrolled the Northwest Territory in January 1812 to combat Native American violence in the region. The three regiments each voted for their own commanding officer, who then assumed the rank of colonel regardless of any previous rank. The Second Regiment selected James Findlay, a major general in the Ohio militia and career politician, to be their commander, and the Third Regiment elected Lewis Cass, a thirty-year-old lawyer and a major general in the Ohio militia, to lead the Third Regiment. The First Regiment chose Duncan McArthur, another major general in the Ohio militia, who was the only one of the three officers who had any military experience: he had scouted for General Josiah Harmar during a campaign in the Northwest.[4]

Hull's British counterpart, Major General Isaac Brock, worried about the state of his troops in Upper Canada. He commanded 1,500 regulars and an unknown number of militia to defend an 800-mile border with the United States. Brock joined the British Army at fifteen, and he rose quickly through the ranks because his family purchased his commissions. The army appointed him lieutenant colonel of the Forty-Ninth Foot, and at the Battle of Alkmaar in Holland, he moved his battalion onto a sand dune to block a French advance. His battalion charged the enemy, who eventually broke ranks. During the fight, a musket ball grazed Brock's throat and knocked him from his horse.[5]

In August 1802, Lieutenant Colonel Brock and the Forty-Ninth Regiment of Foot arrived in Canada amid escalating tension between Britain and the United States. Brock headquartered his men at York, and he worked to stem the growing number of British Army deserters. In 1804, he learned of a plot at Fort George where some men of the Forty-Ninth Regiment intended to kill Lieutenant Colonel Roger Sheaffe, the garrison's commander, and flee into the United States. Brock managed to subdue the mutiny, and afterward the army ordered Brock to take command of Fort George. Once there, he relaxed some of the overly harsh rules implemented by Sheaffe. He supported recreational activities, including sports, hunting, and fishing, which raised the morale of his soldiers. He disciplined his men when necessary, but his soldiers viewed him as a fair and honorable commander. The general's reputation soared when he reportedly told one of his men, "By the Lord Harry, sir, do not tell me it is impossible." He also possessed more combat experience than Sheaffe and was more skilled at commanding a battalion.[6]

Four years later, Brock became the senior British Army officer in Quebec. He fortified Quebec with a new hospital, ramparts, and a grand battery with eight 36-pound guns that could control ship traffic on a channel that ran adjacent to the city. Brock also consolidated command and control of the Provincial Marine under the Quartermaster General's Department to help upgrade and maintain Britain's Great Lakes' fleet. When war arrived six years later, Britain's naval superiority on the lakes gave it a decided advantage over the Americans.[7]

In 1811, Sir George Prevost, who thought highly of Brock, appointed him administrator of Upper Canada, and the army promoted him to major general. With his new position, Brock controlled both civil and military government in the region and could undertake changes to prepare the province for war. He reinforced the 700-man garrison at Amherstburg, later named Fort Malden, with 200 men from York and Fort George, and on the Niagara frontier, he hoped to muster 3,000 militia and 500 Native Americans that could defend against, or at least slow, an American attack into the region. At Kingston, he retained the province's best militia, the Glengarry Light Infantry, which included British officers and reached 600 men by May 1812.[8]

When hostilities commenced, Brock wanted to launch a preemptive strike on Detroit and Mackinac Island to seize the initiative and put the Americans on their heels. Brock believed that British control of Detroit and Michilimackinac would reassure the local population, rally the militia, and solidify the loyalties of the native tribes. Sir George Prevost disagreed with Brock's aggressive stance and ordered the general to undertake only defensive operations. "Our numbers would not justify offensive operations being undertaken," Prevost wrote Brock in July, "unless they were solely calculated to strengthen a defensive attitude." Prevost hoped to exploit America's lukewarm support for the war. He feared that if Britain invaded America first that the attack would unite the country's fractured political parties behind the war.[9]

As governor-in-chief of British North America, Prevost lacked the resources he needed to support Brock and reinforce other parts of the country. Britain retained a small standing army compared to other European countries, and its leadership had already deployed most of Britain's troops to Europe to combat Napoleon. In the spring of 1812, Sir Arthur Wellesley, who was granted dukedom in 1814, initiated new operations in the Iberian Peninsula when he launched an offensive from Portugal and captured two fortresses that opened roads into the Spanish interior. The Duke of Wellington's Anglo-Portuguese army lost 5,000 soldiers in the effort, which was more than twice the number of American battlefield casualties during the entire War of 1812. Wellington continued his offensive into July, landing his most important victory at Salamanca, but the battle cost him another 5,000 men. The bloody British campaign meant that fewer resources would be available for Prevost. On August 10, Lord Bathurst, the secretary of state for war and the colonies, wrote Prevost that he should not expect any more specie from England because of the war in Europe: "The exhausted state of the Military Chest of the Canadas and the impossibility of replenishing it but from England exposes His Majesty's service to serious difficulties."[10]

Prevost understood Bathurst's dilemma and adopted a defensive strategy similar to the approach undertaken by his predecessors. Prevost believed that the United States could not conquer Canada as long as Britain controlled Quebec and the North Atlantic Seaboard. He intended to focus his resources protecting his horizontal logistics line from Halifax to the fortified capital of Lower Canada, Quebec. Prevost sought to avoid war and he hoped that American and British forces, posted along the border, could avoid antagonizing each other: "We must, therefore, use every effort in our power to prevent any collision from taking place between our forces and the American."[11]

The governor-in-chief understood that Quebec served as the most significant entry point and destination for British reinforcements and supplies, should Upper Canada be overrun by American forces. Prevost could assemble reinforcements and supplies in the fortified town to retake the province, while continuing to preserve his line of communications with Britain. Two of Prevost's predecessors in British North America, Sir Guy Carleton (Lord Dorchester) and Sir James Craig, implemented a similar plan. Like Prevost, they retained insufficient troops to guard the entire border. Dorchester and Craig planned to concentrate their forces in Quebec to maintain an open line of communication with England and the West Indies. Eventually, if circumstances permitted, Britain could reinforce Lower Canada with enough troops that the army could retake its western flank.[12]

Though Prevost would evacuate Upper Canada if needed, the governor-in-chief did believe that the region could be defended. He allotted Brock 1,200 men to protect Upper Canada and later dispatched 400 soldiers from Glengarry and 300 new recruits from the Forty-First Foot to fill Brock's outposts. He also planned to strengthen the naval forces and outposts that guarded the province's supply routes along the Niagara frontier and Lake Erie. Supplies consolidated in Montreal, Kingston, and York traveled through this corridor to sustain Brock's garrisons at Detroit, Amherstburg, and Fort Mackinac. Prevost refused to relinquish the province easily to an American invasion force.[13]

In Ohio, General Hull tried to address problems with his militia. At his own expense, he paid armorers to repair muskets, and he acquired gunpowder, blankets, and clothing for his men. Soon, however, a more serious concern emerged. The army's three militia commanders outranked Hull's senior regular officer, Lieutenant Colonel James Miller of the Fourth Infantry. Hull asked Eustis to promote Miller to solve the problem, but the secretary of war refused to become involved. Miller, as a regular soldier, should command the militia, but the three militia officers, who furnished most of Hull's men, refused to be led by a subordinate. The militia commanders thought even less of their commanding general. Lewis Cass sized up Hull before the march to Detroit started: "He is not our man . . . he is indecisive and irresolute, leaning for support upon persons around him." Ohio militia scoffed at being led by a lawyer from the Eastern Seaboard. Upon seeing Hull in Ohio, one militia soldier stated, "He had become old and *quite fat*, and had evidently lost the energy as well as the valor, that thirty-three years previous had given him the post of honor with ANTHONY WAYNE, in carrying the fortress of Stoney Point."[14]

After surveying possible routes to Detroit, Hull decided that his men should follow the most direct route from Urbana, Ohio, to Detroit, a 200-mile journey through woods, swamps, and creeks. Hull's caravan departed Urbana in early June with 300 head of cattle, dozens of wagons, and 120 teams of horses carrying 14,000 pounds of flour, among other supplies. Hull directed his men to build blockhouses for storing supplies along the route. On June 16, the Fourth Infantry built two 20- by 24-foot blockhouses north of Urbana, with a stockade connecting the two structures. Hull left a company of soldiers at the blockhouses to protect them from a Native American attack. The men marched only twelve miles on the first day, and they halted to wait for the wagons to catch up with the group. Hull eventually directed his army's baggage placed onto packhorses, because his wagons could not keep up with the force on the muddy trail. The men cut roads using axes, spades, and any other tool that could cut down trees.[15]

On June 22, the force reached the Black Swamp, which contained an elevated clay basin layered with thick vegetation and forest. Wagons ground to a halt in the muddy morass. Hull's men camped in the swamp and erected another blockhouse. Ankle-deep water chilled the men as they slept. "It was found impossible to distinguish where the road lay," one soldier who encamped at the swamp recalled. "Every man sought for himself a dry place at the root of some tree, where he sat on his knapsack and, leaning against the tree, slept till dawn the next morning."[16]

After the US Army took possession of Detroit and Fort Mackinac, the government did not create passable roads to those outposts, nor did they form causeways through the Black Swamp to aid in navigating that section of the journey. When the trail was dry, the army could use wagons that carried 1,500 pounds each, but a muddy path required the army to rely on packhorses, who could only carry 150 to 200 pounds per animal. The lack of forage on the route forced Hull to ration the amount of food the men gave their oxen and horses during the trip, which further weakened the animals' ability to navigate the makeshift, sludgy road. On future trips during the war, officers directed that the army's horses and oxen carry their own forage, but this decision reduced the amount of space to carry other essentials. These problems left Detroit and Mackinac vulnerable if they required additional supplies or reinforcements. As Hull suggested before the war, Lake Erie would provide a quicker and more efficient route, but the British controlled the lake at the start of the conflict.[17]

On June 29, Hull's army reached the same location where Anthony Wayne defeated the Native Americans at Fallen Timbers at the Maumee River. At the river, Captain Cyrenius Chapin offered to escort Hull's men and supplies to Detroit on his vessel *Cuyahoga* for $60. With his troops and horses worn out from the miserable journey, Hull agreed to the fee and loaded his hospital stores, entrenching tools, invalids, and women onto the vessel. General Hull's nephew accidently loaded the general's chest containing his military papers on the vessel. Hull told the captain to navigate through the western channel of the Detroit River to avoid sailing in front of the British fort at Amherstburg.[18]

On June 18, when Hull's men were approaching Detroit, Madison signed Congress's declaration of war against Britain. Secretary of War Eustis wrote Hull two letters that day, one before the declaration and one after. The first letter reached Hull on June 26 and told him to proceed immediately to Detroit, but the letter did not indicate the reason. In the second letter, Eustis wrote Hull that "war is declared against Great Britain. You will be on your guard, proceed to your post with all possible expedition." This important letter did not arrive until July 2, when Hull was only forty miles from Detroit. For a reason known only to Eustis, he sent the note by ordinary mail.

Fortunately for the Americans, when the message arrived in Cleveland, the postmaster read the dispatch and decided to expedite the communication by express. A young lawyer named Charles Sheeler rode two hundred miles in four days to deliver the news. Before Hull received the dispatch, however, his British counterparts at Fort Malden learned that war had been declared and were prepared for combat.[19]

On July 3, the British garrison at Amherstburg observed the *Cuyahoga* navigating up the Detroit River. The ship's captain ignored Hull's recommendation to avoid Fort Malden by sailing through the western channel. British captain Charles Rolette sailed his armed ship alongside the *Cuyahoga* and called for the US captain to lower its sails. A sailor aboard the *Cuyahoga* demanded to know the reason that the British captain intended to board his ship, in violation of international law. "He replied that an express had reached Fort Amherstburg the night before," the American sailor recalled, "stating that war had been declared." The captain and his men boarded the vessel, ran up the British flag on the *Cuyahoga*, and directed the American band to play "God Save the Queen." The British discovered the sensitive papers in Hull's trunk. "On examining them," one British soldier remembered, "we got a complete insight into all his [Hull's] views: his official correspondence with the Secretary of State was . . . very interesting." The British treated their American prisoners cordially, and the captors promised to release them if the countries were not at war.[20]

Hull's men arrived at Detroit on July 5, exhausted from their 200-mile trek through the wilderness. The general commanded 450 regulars and 1,650 Ohio and Michigan militia. Hull allowed the men to rest for a few days after their arrival. Fortunately for the tired group, they would not need to undertake major renovations at Fort Detroit. Hull, when governor of the Michigan Territory, rebuilt the town after many of its structures had burned in a fire. The outpost sat on a small rise behind the town and formed an oblong shape that covered two acres of ground. Eleven-foot-tall, twelve-foot-thick earthen walls and a six-foot-deep ditch surrounded the structure. The tall, thick walls could shield those inside from direct cannon fire and prevent oncoming soldiers from penetrating the outpost. The fort also contained thirty-four pieces of artillery, including nine 24-pounders. The one drawback of the fort's design was that the town blocked much of the garrison's field of fire from the likely approach of an oncoming enemy. Enemy soldiers could hide inside town as they marched toward the fort. Also, the outpost lacked an unimpeded view of the Detroit River, which allowed British armed vessels to navigate the waterway unmolested. Hull possessed one immobile armed brig, which he ordered to be repaired.[21]

Soon after reaching Detroit, Hull asked the governor of Ohio to send supplies "or this army will perish for the want of provisions." Governor Return Jonathan Meigs assembled ninety-five volunteers under the command of Captain Henry Brush, who agreed to transport food for Hull's troops at Detroit. Brush departed in July 1812 with 70 packhorses loaded with 200 pounds of flour each and 300 cattle. The group eventually halted thirty-three miles south of Detroit because Brush worried that his men would be attacked by Native Americans. He sent a letter to Hull requesting an escort to the outpost.[22]

Hull and Eustis hoped that they would receive assurances from local Native American leaders that they would remain neutral during any future hostilities. US government Indian agents hoped to convince the tribes to avoid siding with the British and augmenting Brock's army with Native American warriors. They scheduled a conference at Piqua, Ohio, with leaders from the region's major tribes, but many of the Native Americans arrived late, so the agents postponed the meeting. The British circulated propaganda that the conference was designed to trick Native Americans into supporting a failing American cause.[23]

Fort Malden, though not as formidable as Detroit, was also a strong defensive work. The fort had been renovated in the spring of 1812. The British commander, Lieutenant Colonel Thomas Bligh St. George, ordered his men to improve the outpost's defenses. His soldiers helped raise the fort's southern and eastern walls, repair cannon platforms, build gun carriages, and erect a log hut in the fort's center to store ammunition. The garrison contained four bastions and a deep ditch, surrounded by fourteen-foot-high pickets with a framed parapet. Each of the fort's faces contained 150 loopholes to conceal British soldiers from incoming fire, and the garrison mounted twenty cannon.[24]

Canadian militia trickled into Amherstburg to fight along side the British. Brock needed these men to augment his small regular force if he hoped to be successful against Hull. St. George commanded 325 regulars, 850 militia, and 400 Native Americans—500 men fewer than Hull, but the American general lacked a naval force. The newly arrived men clamored for guns, clothes, and other necessities. "I am much mortified," St. George wrote Brock, "at the confused state in which I find myself with the men of the militia . . . their wants are many . . . if it is found that we cannot support those who take up arms, I dread the consequences." St. George confiscated ammunition, arms, blankets, and two 3-pounders from the North West Company to equip the militia.[25]

Prevost could potentially command thousands of militia throughout Canada, but like his American counterparts, he was unsure how many men would muster and if they would make good soldiers. Many Canadians settled in the country for free land and they retained lukewarm allegiance to the Crown. In June 1812, Prevost tried to muster militia in Montreal and a riot erupted because the men feared that Britain would send them to the West Indies. Colonel Thomas Talbot, a local land baron and the chief militia officer in the region, expected two hundred men from the Norfolk County (southwest Ontario) militia to muster, but only sixty men turned out. Talbot ordered the group to march to their garrison, but only half of them obeyed, and the remainder deserted. The Oxford County and Middlesex County (southwest Ontario) militias did not turn out in numbers, either, prompting Talbot to exclaim that "the prospect [of raising militia] is dismal—unless there is some other resource that I am not acquainted with." Ultimately Brock collected around 850 militiamen for Fort Malden. "The population is worse than I expected to find it," Brock wrote Prevost.[26]

On July 11, a reluctant Hull decided to cross the Detroit River to begin his part of the campaign. The Americans collected boats and canoes to transport four hundred men to the British side of the river. The general deceived the British into thinking that his men would land below Amherstburg, but they crossed above the town and overran the small village of Sandwich. Hundreds of Ohio militiamen refused to participate in the movement, however, arguing that their state's law prevented them from serving outside the United States. Colonel McArthur chastised the men for their disloyalty. Most of them responded to McArthur's pleas, but 180 stayed at Detroit.[27]

Either out of fear or friendship, the few villagers at Sandwich welcomed the Americans by waving handkerchiefs out their windows and saying, "We like the Americans." Hull made his headquarters in a vacant, two-story brick house in the town and issued a combative proclamation: "If the barbarous and savage policy of Great Britain be pursued," Hull wrote in the widely distributed statement, "and the savages to be let loose to murder our citizens and butcher our women and children, this will be a war of extermination . . . no white man found fighting by the side of an Indian will be taken prisoner—instant death will be his lot."[28]

Hull started to gain confidence. Fifty to sixty Canadian militiamen deserted Fort Malden each day, and Hull's movement to the British side convinced some tribes to remain neutral in the conflict. British lieutenant colonel St. George confirmed Hull's suspicions: "Since that time [the crossing to Sandwich] the Militia have been going off in such numbers, that I have not more than 471 in all this morning—and in such a state as to be totally inefficient in the field." Some local Native American leaders, such as the chief of the Michigan Wyandots, decided to remain neutral after learning about the proclamation. "I am ashamed to find that the words of the Enemy [Hull's proclamation] were so eagerly received & so sincerely obeyed," Richard Dickson, an influential British Native American emissary wrote. The Six Nations of the Iroquois in Upper Canada (the Grand River Iroquois) also decided to remain neutral, despite their traditional alliance with Britain, to the great frustration of Brock and Prevost.[29]

Hull ordered Colonel Lewis Cass's regiment to scout the area between Sandwich and Amherstburg. Cass's men marched twelve miles to the Canard Bridge, where they discovered a detachment of fifty British soldiers. Instead of returning to Hull with a report of his observations, Cass attacked the bridge with an advanced guard and sent some men upriver to encircle the enemy from behind. "They [the British] treated in Such hast[e]," an American recalled, "that we Could not Come up with them." Two brave British privates, John Dean and John Hancock, fired at the intruders. The Americans killed Hancock and took Dean prisoner. Cass requested that Hull send reinforcements to hold the bridge, but the general refused. He directed Cass and McArthur to withdraw from the area. The next morning, Cass and McArthur disobeyed orders by returning to the bridge to fire on British artillery. St. George expected the Americans to hold the bridge and advance on Fort Malden, but Hull removed his troops from the strategic position. "He [Hull] is now the object of their jest and ridicule," an American prisoner of war reported from Fort Malden, "instead of being as he was formerly[,] their terror and greatest fear."[30]

A soggy marsh prevented Hull from transporting the army's two 24-pound cannons between the Canard Bridge and Amherstburg. Hull needed the guns to bombard Fort Malden, so some of his innovative soldiers began constructing floating batteries that could transport the large guns downriver where they could be unloaded on solid ground within reach of the fort. Meanwhile, Hull ordered the completion of the brig *Adams* to guard Detroit's riverfront. He also dispatched Colonel McArthur's regiment into enemy territory to scout for provisions. McArthur's men penetrated seventy miles into Canada and returned in four days to Detroit with 200 barrels of flour, 400 blankets, guns, ammunition, and other military stores. McArthur paid for four days of his men's rations out of his private funds.[31]

British general Isaac Brock, who was still at Fort George, learned of Hull's cross-river movement three days after Hull's advance. Earlier, Brock dispatched his most able subordinate, Colonel Henry Procter, to bring reinforcements and assume command of Fort Malden, but Procter had not yet arrived. Brock began to have doubts about retaining the outpost. Hull had moved a large force across the Detroit River with no casualties before Brock could reinforce Amherstburg with men and supplies, and the British officer continued to have problems recruiting and retaining militia. "Were it possible to animate the militia," Brock wrote Prevost, "to a proper sense of their duty, something might yet be done, but I almost despair." Brock considered a worst-case option where his men would retreat by armed vessel to Fort Erie.[32]

Fortunately for Brock, Hull, who was blind to his advantage, sat paralyzed on the British side of the river. Indecision replaced the leadership that Hull showed when marching his men through the Black Swamp. He held numerous meetings with his officers to determine a course of action. "Should it be [your] . . . opinion," he asked his four senior officers, "that it was expedient to make an attack immediately, and that [you] would answer for your men, I would lead them to enterprise." Lieutenant Colonel James Miller of the regulars told Hull that his men would be "answerable," and that his soldiers would force the enemy from their positions. The three militia colonels replied that they would not be "answerable" for their men's actions, but they hoped their militia would behave well.[33]

Hull ultimately decided to wait for the floating carriages to be completed before launching the assault against Fort Malden. Meanwhile, Lieutenant

Colonel St. George sent men to destroy an important bridge eight miles north of Amherstburg. He posted snipers in the brush and stationed the seventeen-gun *Queen Charlotte* by the mouth of the Canard River where it flows into the Detroit. "I can scarcely think that Genl. H. [Hull] will be defeated but appearances justify such a belief," William Beall, an American prisoner at Fort Malden, wrote in his journal. "I am confident that he will not take Malden though 300 men could do it."[34]

On July 16, Captain Charles Roberts, a British officer posted at Fort St. Joseph, set out with 47 men of the Tenth Royal Veteran Battalion, 180 Canadian militia, and 400 Native Americans to attack the US fort on Mackinac Island. Brock gave Roberts wide discretion to choose whether to assault Michilimackinac or maintain a defensive stance at St. Joseph's. When Roberts learned that the Americans intended to reinforce Michilimackinac, he decided to attack before those troops arrived. He also recognized that his own feeble post could not withstand a serious assault, so he sought to eliminate the nearby American threat.[35]

Roberts's party contained sixty Iroquois Native Americans under John Norton. Norton, an Iroquois leader, ignored the Grand River Iroquois pledge to remain neutral in the war. In 1807, Norton replaced Joseph Brant as the tribe's leader when Brant died. Norton, a Scot by birth, had enlisted in the British Army as a boy when his unit deployed to America. He quit the army and later became an interpreter for the Indian Department and befriended Joseph Brant and his people. In 1811, tired of Native American politics, Norton planned to leave Upper Canada for the Southwest, but Isaac Brock convinced him to stay in Canada to fight the Americans.[36]

Roberts's men loaded two 6-pounders into their watercraft and the war party floated in Native American canoes, flat-bottom boats, and one brig toward Mackinac. Lieutenant Porter Hanks, the American commander at the garrison, heard a rumor of a British attack on the island, but he was unaware that war had been declared. At 3:00 a.m. on July 17, Roberts's men landed on the island's north side and dragged a 6-pounder and scaling ladders through the forest. They planted the gun on a hilltop on the island's north side that overlooked the fort. To Hanks's surprise, he awoke in the morning to find Roberts's men and the 6-pounder aimed at his garrison. Roberts sent a note to Hanks requesting his surrender. The message was the first Hanks had heard that war had been declared. The American lieutenant, faced with the possibility of Native Americans killing his men and the island's few civilians, surrendered his outpost to Roberts and relinquished 700 packs of furs and some military equipment. The seizure of the pelts and the closure of the American trading post placed the North West Company back in control of the region's fur economy.[37]

The fort's demise had an immediate effect on Native American allegiances in the region. Many tribal chiefs in Upper Canada became convinced that Britain would be the likely victor in the conflict, and warriors flocked to St. George at Amherstburg. The Wyandots, whom Hull had earlier convinced to stay neutral, now sided with the British. John Norton recruited three to four hundred Iroquois warriors after the fort's fall. Hull heard that 2,000 bloodthirsty Native Americans joined St. George at Amherstburg after Hank's surrender, and these reports rattled Hull. The British learned of the general's fear through a letter they intercepted between Hull and Secretary of War Eustis. In the letter, Hull declared that "the British can engage any number of Indians they may have occasion for" and that the "situation of this army is critical." The British officer who forwarded the letter to Prevost declared that "the contents [of the letter] appear highly interesting, and lead to the certain hope of the overthrow of the enemy's force in that quarter."[38]

As Hull mourned the loss of Mackinac, the British reinforced Fort Malden. Colonel Henry Procter, Brock's hand-selected commander, arrived with sixty men of the British Forty-First Foot and took command. With these men, Fort Malden contained 300 men of the Forty-First Regiment, 300 militiamen, and a contingent of artillery. Brock would need his regulars of the Forty-First to steady the nerves of the militia and function as the centerpiece of his infantry. One hundred years earlier, the Forty-First foot was formed by collecting a group of injured outpatient soldiers. In 1804, able-bodied men joined the regiment, and the group was transferred to Fort George in Upper Canada. The regiment displayed some disciplinary problems during peacetime in Canada, but they were a disciplined fighting outfit. An inspection officer noted that "the regiment . . . is very creditable in its discipline. The men march well and are steady in the field . . . the regiment is composed of a fine body of young men."[39]

To the east, in Greenbush, New York, the army under US major general Henry Dearborn, sat poised on Canada's border to begin his phase of the campaign. But Dearborn had not yet launched his planned attack on

Montreal. The American assault would have forced Brock to maintain some troops in eastern Upper Canada, away from Hull at Detroit. Dearborn had not even arrived at Albany, New York, however, when General Hull crossed into Canada. Instead, the general spent two months meeting with New England governors rather than preparing his men for war.

On August 9, Dearborn received a message from Prevost requesting an armistice, which he tentatively accepted, but he told the governor-in-chief that President Madison would review his decision. Dearborn's authority did not include General Hull and his area of operations, thus Dearborn could only negotiate for himself. He did not believe, however, that Britain would move troops from Lower to Upper Canada because it would be "incompatible with the true interest of the agreement." Prevost thought otherwise. He wrote to Brock that "a suspension of hostilities . . . has permitted me to move without interruption, independently of the arrangement, both Troops & supplies of every description toward Amherstburg." Brock, though unaware of the terms of the armistice, no longer faced the threat of an American attack along the Niagara frontier. "It now appeared," Hull wrote later, "that the whole war against Canada was to be carried on with the 1,200 Ohio militia, and three hundred regulars."[40]

Hull had thus far been unable to reach Captain Brush's resupply force, which was still located south of Detroit. Hull worried that if his army seized Amherstburg, he would eventually be surrounded by Brock's troops, who would prevent food and supplies from reaching the fort. "The fall of Michilimackinac," Hull wrote another officer on August 11, "the tardy operations of our army at Niagara, and almost all the Indians having become hostile, have totally changed the prospects of this army." Hull probably recalled his own military experience from the Revolutionary War, when General George Washington regularly sidestepped direct clashes with Britain's main force to keep his lines of communication open. "My communication is almost entirely cut off," Hull continued in the letter, "there are but small quantities of provisions, and the most fatal consequences must ensue, unless the communication is soon opened and very strong reinforcements arrive." Hull's men were shocked at his decision to retreat. "To our astonishment, we were ordered to *strike our tents and cross over to Detroit!* [original emphasis]. . . . Great God! . . . A territory which we had invaded without opposition we quit with disgrace." Cass recalled that the retreat was opposed by all of the general's officers, and that the move dispirited the soldiers and lowered the men's confidence in the general.[41]

On August 13, General Brock arrived at Amherstburg with forty regulars of the Forty-First and 260 militia. He reviewed Hull's papers captured on the *Cuyahoga* and learned that the Americans had collected around two thousand men at Detroit. The men cheered Brock's arrival: "Our general was very much beloved," a private in the Forty-First recalled, and "he used to come out and talk familiarly with us." Brock addressed Tecumseh and the other Native Americans who had gathered at the fort: "I have fought against the enemies of our great father, the king, beyond the great lake and they have never seen my back. I . . . come here to fight his enemies on this side the great salt lake [meaning the Atlantic], and now desire with my soldiers to take lessons from you and your warriors, that we may learn how to make war in these great forests."

Tecumseh stretched out his hand to his men and yelled, "This is a man! . . . Their great father from across the Salt Lake had at length awoke from his long sleep." In a private meeting, Brock requested that Tecumseh's refrain from drinking liquor before the battle. Tecumseh promised that his men would not taste liquor until they had humbled the "big knives." "If this resolution be persevered in," Brock replied, "you must conquer." Using a roll of elm bark and a knife, Tecumseh outlined the hills, river, woods, and roads around Detroit, which helped Brock plan his attack on the fort. Tecumseh's charisma impressed Brock. "A more sagacious or more gallant warrior does not, I believe, exist," Brock wrote Prime Minister Liverpool.[42]

Brock directed his militia to wear regular army uniforms to deceive the Americans into believing that his force of regulars was larger than its actual strength. Tecumseh also planned to parade his men in front of the fort to give the appearance that his force was double its actual size. Brock ordered his artillerists to establish a battery at Sandwich from where they could bombard Detroit with their cannon. The *Queen Charlotte* and the *General Hunter* patrolled the river to cover the engineers' efforts.[43]

Brock sent Hull a message asking him to surrender the garrison: "It is far from my intention to join in a war of extermination, but you must be aware that the numerous bodies of Indians who have attached themselves to my troops will be beyond my control, the moment the contest commences." "I have no other reply to make," Hull told Brock, "than to inform you that I am prepared to meet any force which may be at your disposal." Around this time American militia officers discovered a letter where Hull discussed the possibility of surrender, even though Brock had yet to attack Detroit. They believed that the only option to prevent Hull from surrendering was "divesting the general of his command." Circulars known as "round robins" appeared throughout Hull's camp. Signed by Lewis Cass and seventy-nine others, the circular stated, "We signers hereto, agree to seize General Hull and depose him from command, and to defend the fort at all hazards." The men, upset at the retreat from Sandwich, wanted to control their own destiny against the British. Hull decided to dispatch McArthur and Cass, two of the signers of the document, to the River Raisin to retrieve Brush's supplies. The two officers delayed their departure while they were waiting for packhorses from Hull's quartermaster. Hull told the officers that the packhorses would catch up with them, but the drive team became lost on the trail and never arrived. McArthur and Cass departed the fortification with 400 men and camped three miles from Detroit.[44]

On August 15, Brock's engineers completed the battery across from Detroit, and the next day his gunners fired 18-pounders into the fort. They also lit a howitzer that arched a shell downward into the outpost. One eighteen-pound ball landed in the garrison's mess room, killing the recently paroled Lieutenant Porter Hanks, who had stopped at Detroit to meet an old friend. The ball also amputated a surgeon's legs and killed two other officers. McArthur and Cass, on their supply mission, heard artillery fire from the fort, but the officers refused to order their men to the town. Instead, McArthur and Cass directed their soldiers to erect camp and dine on a recently killed ox. If the two regiments had proceeded directly to Detroit, they could have surprised Brock by attacking the rear of his army, which might have changed the outcome of the battle.[45]

Brock, learning that Fort Detroit lacked two of Hull's best regiments, decided to attack the outpost. The assault was a risky one. His men were exposed to cannon fire while crossing the open expanse between the town and the fort. They lacked the heavy artillery that could penetrate the fort's walls and duel with the enemy's guns. Brock's men also lacked scaling ladders to climb the outpost's eleven-foot-tall ramparts. Brock gambled that Hull would capitulate because of his fear that civilians and combatants would be slaughtered by Native Americans once the battle was over. On the night of August 15, Brock ordered an advance party of 600 Native Americans to cross the river south of Detroit. The main body of troops departed just after sunrise. Three hundred and thirty regulars and 400 militia with five cannon (three 6-pounders and two 3-pounders) slipped into river boats and rowed quietly across the river. One soldier recalled, "Amid the little squadron of boats and scows, conveying the troops and artillery, were mixed numerous canoes filled with Indian warriors, decorated in their half-nakedness for the occasion, and uttering yells of mingled defiance of their foes and encouragement of the soldiery."[46]

The next morning the general formed his men into columns and stood at the front. "Pardon me, general," one of Brock's soldiers told him, "but I cannot forbear entreating you not to expose yourself thus. If we lose you, we lose all." "Master Nichol," Brock replied, "I duly appreciate the advice you give me, but . . . I will never ask them to go where I do not lead them." Brock's columns followed the road toward Detroit until they encountered the two 24-pounders manned by American gunners holding a lit fuse. Another 6-pounder loaded with canister was next to them. British officer John Richardson remembered, "When within a mile and a half from the rising ground, we distinctly saw two long, heavy guns . . . planted in the road, and around them the gunners with their fuses burning. At each moment we expected that they would be fired, yet although it was evident the discharge must literally have swept our small, but dense column, there was neither halt nor indecision perceptible [in our column]."[47]

To the surprise of Brock's men, the American gunners did not fire, and Hull's army inexplicably withdrew back into the fort. The preemptive retreat stunned Brock's soldiers. "Whatever the cause," Richardson remembered, "we certainly had reason to congratulate ourselves that we had escaped the threatened danger. I confess that I breathed much more freely when we had left the road." Brock ordered his men to march into an open field and orchard. Some of Hull's officers believed that Detroit's guns could have "in a few minutes [wiped] the whole, British and Indians." One newspaper published a report that the general's officers begged him to attack, to which Hull replied, "Those who live in Glass Houses ought not to throw stones!"[48]

While Brock was advancing on Detroit, the American garrison at Fort Dearborn received orders from Hull to evacuate the post and march to Detroit. After the fall of Fort Mackinac, Hull believed that the isolated outpost at Fort Dearborn was vulnerable to attack and the general wanted to consolidate his forces at Detroit. Hull directed Captain Nathan Heald, commander at Fort Dearborn, to destroy unneeded arms and ammunition and to dole out US government stores to friendly Native Americans who could escort the group. Local Native Americans, mostly Potawatomi, learned about the evacuation order and gathered around the fort to seek their share of the free goods. Heald, despite the possible threat, delayed his departure for seven days as the crowd of Native Americans continued to grow. The courier who brought Hull's orders to Fort Dearborn recommended to the officer that he depart the next morning. Heald, who expected an escort to arrive from Fort Wayne, decided to wait. He knew that his caravan would contain women, children, and the sick, which would slow his travel toward his first stop at Fort Wayne, about 160 miles away.[49]

On August 13, US Army captain William Wells and thirty friendly Miamis arrived to escort Heald's group. In preparation for their departure, Heald distributed stores to the Native Americans gathered outside the garrison, but he withheld the most precious goods, including ammunition, gunpowder, and whiskey. That night, Heald's men poured the whiskey into a nearby river and dumped ammunition inside the fort's well. The Native Americans could hear the clamoring inside the outpost, and they soon learned that Heald's men trashed the gunpowder and rum. The Potawatomis fumed since gunpowder was in short supply and they needed the material for hunting.[50]

Heald, with some money and Hull's order sewn into his undergarments, marched out of the fort with ninety-three Americans at 9:00 a.m. on August 15. The Potawatomi promised an escort, but Heald could not locate them when the group departed. Instead, 500 Potawatomis decided to attack Heald's caravan, despite opposition from some elder chiefs. The Native Americans moved south, two miles behind some hills that flanked Heald's travel route.

As Heald's group approached, the Native Americans showed themselves on the banks, and Heald ordered his men to charge. Heald's soldiers routed the Potawatomis, but the warriors wounded many in the sortie, which left Heald with only twenty regulars to defend the caravan. The Potawatomis pressed their attack, and Heald moved his men away from his wagons and out of range of the Native American's weapons. Heald left some militia and a few regulars to guard the sick, women, and children who remained with the convoy. The Potawatomis advanced on the group and engaged the militia and others in hand-to-hand fighting. They quickly overwhelmed the caravan's passengers, and they began massacring the women and children. One Potawatomi climbed into a wagon and slaughtered twelve children. Captain Wells's Miami Native Americans fled the scene, and Wells fought to save women and children until he was killed. One of the tribal chiefs who opposed the attack, Black Partridge, saved a woman by dragging her away from an assaulting Native American. He acted as if he was drowning her so that the other Potawatomis would leave her alone. She ended up surviving the ordeal. The attack forced Heald to surrender, and despite promises that his men would not be harmed, the warriors killed many of his wounded. They brought a few survivors to their villages where they were abused and mutilated. The Potawatomi killed twenty-six regulars, twelve militia, and captured or killed most of the women and children resident at the fort.[51]

Hull soon received reports of the massacre, which undercut his confidence. The fear of Native Americans killing Detroit's women and children shattered his resolve. His son, daughter, and her two children accompanied him at Detroit, as did hundreds of the town's citizens, many of whom he knew personally. One officer claimed that he observed Hull shivering with tobacco juice splattered across his face and his vest. "I thought he was under the influence of fear," the soldier recalled later. "I had no doubt of it." Hull soon heard reports that Native Americans were flooding into the town. Hull ordered his son to raise a flag of truce from the fort, and another boat departed for Sandwich with a surrender flag. On August 16, Detroit fell to the British.[52]

The decision to surrender puzzled and angered many of Hull's officers, and the general was later charged with cowardice. Hull's decision to capitulate could be traced to his understanding of the outpost's supply lines. Brush's failure to bring provisions to the garrison convinced Hull that no relief would arrive from Urbana, but the British would continue to receive reinforcements and supplies from Lake Erie. Hull believed that he lacked the necessary military provisions to support his army during a prolonged battle or siege, and he could not trust transporters to successfully traverse the swampy woodland route to Detroit. Brock directed Native Americans and small units to intercept supplies and isolate the outpost, and these actions fed Hull's belief that he was cut off from outside support. Without the promise of future supplies, Hull reasoned, the best decision was to surrender the garrison. The general also hoped that if he capitulated before serious combat began, he might save Detroit's civilians from a Native American massacre. "The army would have been destroyed," Hull later recalled at his court-martial, "if not by the tomahawk of the Indians—they must after a defeat have perished for want of supplies." Hull continued, "From the time the army arrived at Detroit, not one pound of provisions had been received—from the moment the declaration of war was known to the enemy, he had intercepted the only line of communication, and thus cut off all supplies."[53]

These factors undercut Hull's confidence, even though he commanded 2,200 men, retained one week's supplies, and possessed plenty of artillery and ammunition. Colonel Cass later remarked that Detroit retained provisions for at least fifteen days and that Hull could have acquired three months additional provisions, including cattle and flour. Brock could not believe Hull's lack of initiative. He thought that Amherstburg would have been overrun once Hull's large force moved into the area, but Hull's ineptitude proved him wrong. "When I detail my good fortune," Brock wrote Prevost, "your Excellency will be astonished."[54]

On August 17, the formal surrender of Detroit occurred. Hull turned over the garrison and relinquished the entire Michigan Territory; the largest concession of land in US history. The surrender was a crippling loss of men and weaponry for the small US Army of the time. The British captured 33 pieces of ordnance, 2,500 small arms, 40 barrels of powder, the *Adams* brig of war, and Miller's Fourth Infantry Regiment. They seized a beautiful brass cannon, which retained the inscription, "Taken at Saratoga on the 27th of October, 1777," in reference to the Battle of Saratoga during the Revolutionary War. The British troops hugged their lost cannon and added the inscription, "Retaken at Detroit August 16, 1812." The US Fourth Regiment refused to surrender its colors, as was customary during a capitulation. Brock's men looked for their flag and they discovered an officer trying to destroy the colors. Shadrach Byfield of the Forty-First, while searching for the flag, slipped on the floor and fell. "My dear man," a fellow soldier told him, pointing toward the source of the Byfield's skid, "that is the brains of a man killed with one of our shots." Brock held a parade within the fort and trumpeted newly freed Private Dean, who had been captured on the Canard Bridge and imprisoned at Detroit. Brock grabbed his hand, complimented his bravery, and declared him an honor to his profession. The general gave Tecumseh his own personal crimson silk sash and wrapped it around the warrior's waist as a sign of gratitude.[55]

The seizure of Detroit and Michilimackinac was a stirring victory for Brock and undermined American influence on the region's tribes. After Hull's surrender, US Indian agents rescheduled the Piqua, Ohio, conference, but only 750 Native Americans attended, not the 3,000 they expected. Hull's defeat prompted neutral tribes to support Britain and skip the conference. "Pleasant weather but unpleasant news," an American prisoner of war at Amherstburg wrote. "We herd [heard] about noon that Hull had given up Detroit and the whole Territory Mitchigan [Michigan]. . . . Shame to him, shame to his country, shame to the world." When word of Hull's defeat reached the editors of the *Nashville Whig*, they refused to believe the validity of the report. "For our own part, we *totally* disbelieve the authenticity of it [news of the surrender]" (original emphasis).[56]

The finger-pointing for Hull's defeat began immediately and mercilessly. Cass blamed Hull for the debacle: "To see the whole of our men flushed with the hope of victory eagerly awaiting the approaching contest, to see them afterwards dispirited, hopeless and desponding, at least 500 shedding tears, to meet their country's foe . . . excited sensations . . . which I trust in God will never again be felt." Thomas Jefferson believed that Hull should be "hanged or shot."[57]

The British did not release Hull until September 1813, in exchange for twenty British prisoners. Hull's court-martial began in January 1814, and the hearing's procedures suggested that the tribunal had already decided on a verdict. They disallowed Hull's attorneys to cross-examine witnesses, and the general had to act as his own counsel against the two best lawyers in the country, Martin Van Buren, a future president, and Philip Parker. The rules regarding the court's testimony also tipped the scales against Hull. The witnesses were not required to testify under oath, and they could listen to the proceeding's testimony, which might influence their views. Secretary of War Eustis recently promoted all of the prosecution's witnesses, who now owed their newfound success to the secretary. "I must say," Hull recalled, "that it appears to me my expedition was more prolific of promotions than any other unsuccessful military enterprise I have ever heard of." The court charged Hull with cowardice, neglect of duty, and treason. In a final twist of irony, General Dearborn, who did not assist Hull in the campaign, led the tribunal.[58]

The court acquitted Hull of treason but found him guilty of cowardice and neglect of duty. The tribunal sentenced Hull to be shot—the only time in US history that a general received the death penalty for his actions in combat. Madison had found his scapegoat. The tribunal did not illuminate Cass and other officers' insubordination to their general, and the tribunal's chairman ignored his own role in the disaster by not launching his promised invasion of Lower Canada. The *Times of London* accurately observed, "Poor General Hull, however, is likely to meet with rather harder measure than General Chatham [who led a failed expedition in the Netherlands in 1809]. Upon his devoted head, will the American cabinet cast all of the odium of their own blunders and miscalculations." President Madison, in a show of kindness to the Revolutionary veteran, commuted Hull's death sentence.[59]

Despite the gloom that emanated from Hull's failure, his attack was the least important of America's three-prong invasion of Canada in 1812. After the surrender, the Americans could still force Brock to retreat eastward by severing the links between his force and supply lines to Lower Canada. If the United States could penetrate and hold territory east of Detroit and Mackinac, Brock would be unable to receive additional supplies from Quebec and other points eastward. Unless Prevost could break the logjam, Brock would be isolated, while the Americans could still move reinforcements—albeit slowly—from Urbana to contest the area. Prevost had already instructed Brock to consider evacuating Detroit, and Brock had even planned an exit route out of the region for his army. If Brock abandoned Fort Malden and Mackinac Island, he could later receive reinforcements from Prevost and attempt to retake the outposts.

America's plan to isolate the British Army in far west Upper Canada depended on the leadership of General Henry Dearborn and Major General Stephen Van Rensselaer, who led the right and center prongs, respectively, of the 1812 offensive. General Van Rensselaer would assault British outposts along the Niagara River, which was a strategic choke point in the movement of supplies from Montreal, Kingston, and York to Upper Canada. American control of the Niagara River and the surrounding regions would isolate Brock and weaken his position. The novice US military, however, faced a difficult test in crossing the Niagara River to assault a British outpost.

4

The Battle of Queenston

The carnage along the shore was shocking.
—A York militiaman at Queenston to his father, October 14, 1812, Library and Archives Canada

In mid-August 1812, US major general Stephen Van Rensselaer reviewed one thousand militiamen posted along thirty-five miles of the Niagara River. General Henry Dearborn had ordered Van Rensselaer to create a diversion along the Niagara frontier to relieve pressure on General Hull's army in Detroit. But Van Rensselaer's men were in no condition to launch a complex, cross-river attack against stout British outposts filled with skilled regulars. For that matter, his untrained citizen-soldiers and crumbling forts could not repel a British invasion, which appeared increasingly likely as fresh British troops and artillery arrived daily at their garrisons. During his inspection, Van Rensselaer found his men in a "very indifferent state of discipline," with most of them lacking basic necessities, including shoes and tents. The men carried a paltry ten rounds of ammunition each—not enough cartridges for a serious fight. "Finding myself in this truly very unpleasant situation," Van Rensselaer decided to concentrate his men at a camp south of Lewistown, New York, where he could train his citizen-soldiers and await reinforcements.[1]

In July, New York governor Daniel Tompkins appointed Van Rensselaer as the militia general in charge of the center thrust of Madison's three-pronged invasion. The administration's war planners hoped that Van Rensselaer's assault would stop supplies flowing from Montreal, Kingston, and York to outposts in western Upper Canada. From Queenston, on the western bank, the Americans could control maritime traffic on the Niagara, which served as a transportation corridor between Lakes Ontario and Erie. A successful attack would hurt the British Commissariat's ability to send food and ammunition efficiently to Major General Isaac Brock at Amherstburg at the far western end of Lake Erie. Britain could also not dispatch shipbuilding materials to the dockyard at Amherstburg, which would curtail the country's effort to strengthen its Lake Erie fleet. The Commissariat could attempt to circumvent the Niagara River by following a route that stretched from Burlington Bay (the headwaters of Lake Ontario) to Long Point on Lake Erie, but the passage could not accommodate heavy provisions, such as artillery. To use the route, transporters trekked for twenty-eight miles from Burlington to the village of the Six Nations on the Grand River. This stretch contained six miles of woods and was described by one observer as "bad travelling." At the village, transporters could load supplies into boats and float down the river to Lake Erie, or they could cross the river and march to Long Point. This portion of the route crossed twenty miles of plains.[2]

Governor Tompkins's appointment of Van Rensselaer surprised observers because the two men were political rivals. Van Rensselaer, a prominent Federalist, clashed politically with Tompkins, a Republican. In 1812, the two would probably run against each other in the gubernatorial election. Van Rensselaer's potential success along the Niagara could elevate his profile and unseat the incumbent governor. Van Rensselaer lacked military experience and training, so he selected his second cousin Solomon Van Rensselaer to act as his adviser. Tompkins agreed to promote Solomon to lieutenant colonel to serve as Stephen's aide.[3]

Despite their familial ties, Stephen and Solomon maintained a distant relationship. Solomon had joined the army at age eighteen and fought with Anthony Wayne at the Battle of Fallen Timbers, one of the few serious battles that occurred after the Revolutionary War. A bullet pierced Solomon's lungs during the fight and he almost died. When Congress and President Jefferson reduced the army in 1802 the army honorably discharged Solomon, just as the service did to so many other promising officers in the young US Army. Solomon then pursued a career in politics, eventually becoming New York's adjutant general, but his hot temper made him ill-suited for the profession.

When a rival politician passed a resolution questioning Solomon's integrity, he beat the man senseless with a cane. Afterwards, the victim's revenge-seeking friends kicked and clubbed Solomon almost to death.[4]

Solomon understood the importance of answering his country's call to service, but he wanted to stay home with his family. His six-year-old child had recently been murdered on the family farm, and his wife was one-month pregnant. A close family friend, Major John Lovett, traveled with Solomon to Lewistown to provide comfort during the campaign.[5]

Stephen had a friendly demeanor, but Solomon showed "tough love" toward his men. He knew they needed rigorous training to be ready for combat because at any moment the British might cross the river to attack the American camp. "The lines are in retched order," Solomon observed, "while the British divided only by a River . . . a mile wide are ready to receive us." His friend Lovett agreed. "I dreadfully fear we shall be convulsed," he wrote a friend, "nothing but a miracle can save us." General Van Rensselaer, under Solomon's advice, directed the men to drill twice per day and maintain proper sanitation by digging their latrines one hundred yards from their tents. The general also demanded that his soldiers dress well and polish their arms and accoutrements. "He [Solomon] is all formed for war," Lovett remarked, "the whole Economy of camp is to him familiar as Pot-boiling." The men felt Solomon's presence during drill and field duty, where he trained them hard and demanded adherence to the rules. "Our little army improves very fast and under his [Solomon] discipline," Lovett observed, "from 4 in the morning until 8 at night, something is constantly going on."[6]

To his men, it appeared that nothing could faze Solomon, but his wife, Arriet, had not responded to dozens of letters he wrote in August: "I have written to you almost every mail since I left home and have not received a single letter from you. . . . what can be the matter of all this, you certainly must be in a situation not to write." He feared the worst and begged a family friend to be honest with him about her fate. He finally received a letter from her, but its message hardly raised his spirits: "The innumerable perplexities in which your absence at this season involves me, with the farm work, she wrote him, "cannot . . . banish from my mind's eye, the awful, the distressing sight of our sweet little 'Van,' when you carried him from the field bleeding and dying in your Arms!"[7]

At Lewistown, General Van Rensselaer required more time to train, discipline, and equip his citizens soldiers, and to his surprise that is exactly what he received. Sir George Prevost sought an armistice with General Dearborn after learning that Britain had repealed the Orders in Council. Prevost believed that news of the repeal would make the war unpopular in the United States, and Prime Minister Liverpool had instructed him to avoid bloodshed if possible. General Van Rensselaer dispatched Solomon to meet with Major General Roger Sheaffe, commander of British forces along the Niagara, to negotiate details of the armistice. During their discussions, Solomon demanded the unimpeded movement of war materials on Lake Ontario, which would allow American forces on the Niagara frontier to be resupplied from Oswego by vessel. After a heated conversation, Van Rensselaer declared the negotiations over because Sheaffe refused to agree to American use of the lake. Sheaffe rose, clapped his hand on the hilt of his sword, and stated "*Sir, you take the high ground!*" (original emphasis). Van Rensselaer rose and responded, "I do sir, and will maintain it." Sheaffe left the room, and when he returned, he told Van Rensselaer that the US Army could use the lake during the armistice. This important concession allowed Lieutenant Colonel John Fenwick at Oswego to bring heavy artillery by ship instead of pulling the cannon across muddy, pock-filled roads toward Fort Niagara. (Britain gained no maritime advantage from the agreement because the Royal Navy already controlled the Great Lakes).[8]

General Van Rensselaer intended to use the cease-fire to train the militia, but in late August camp morale sunk to a staggering low. On August 25, British general Brock marched Hull's captured regulars along Queenston Heights in full view of General Van Rensselaer's men. Hull's surrender "spread great alarm among the inhabitants," General Van Rensselaer recalled, "and produced strong symptoms of distrust among the troops." Soldiers feared that Van Rensselaer might surrender without a fight, and that they would be "*Hulled*" (original emphasis). The citizen-soldiers requested furloughs, and others gained "conscientious scruples" regarding New York State militia laws, which prohibited them from marching into Canada. Before the war, Congress debated, but never resolved, the issue of whether militia could be deployed outside the United States. Some congressional leaders argued that the phrase "repel invasions," embedded in the Article I of the US Constitution, did not indicate that the militia should halt at a specific boundary. Others interpreted the language as prohibiting the militia from being used in a foreign invasion. Without congressional resolution on the issue, local militia commanders alone if they would bring their force into Canada to support Van Rensselaer's plan.[9]

Militia recruitment became so difficult for Van Rensselaer's army that his friend Lovett to resorted to sarcasm to express his despair:

> Are you all astounded & over whelmed at Hull's defeat & surrender? If so, come here and join an army which, last evening, mustered of Rank & File, fit for duty, 691; and all we have to do is to guard a Frontier of 36 miles, on the Niagara, in the very *teeth of Brock and his victorious host*; and within half [ ] point blank shot of their guns. . . . And to cheer our hearts, we have just picked up a Birch Bark, on which is written a Notice from the Soldiers to the Officers of this little army that unless they are paid they will absolutely quit the field.[10]

Just before news of Hull's surrender reached Madison, the president repudiated the Prevost–Dearborn armistice and ordered Dearborn to resume hostilities. Dearborn soon urged Van Rensselaer to attack the British camp since some of Brock's Niagara troops had been sent to Amherstburg. "If the enemy should have detached from Fort George," Dearborn wrote Van Rensselaer, "it may afford you an opportunity to strike a blow." Van Rensselaer crossed the river to meet with Lieutenant Colonel John Macdonell, Brock's provincial aide-de-camp, to formally end the armistice. Macdonell hailed from Glengarry County, Canada, an area with a long and rich history of serving the king. Highland clan warriors in the county's namesake, Glengarry, Scotland, fought alongside the British crown, and in the middle of the eighteenth century, many of these men sought a new life in Canada. Macdonell, who retained vast influence in the county, helped recruit Glengarry men for Brock, and although he possessed no military experience, he provided valuable counsel to the general.[11]

The two men were strolling side by side when Van Rensselaer noticed two beautiful brass howitzers. "These, at all events, are old acquaintances of mine," he remarked to Macdonell. Van Rensselaer recognized the guns from Anthony Wayne's frontier expedition in which he had participated eighteen years earlier. The British captured the guns recently at Detroit and were preparing to ship them to England. "I am partial to those pieces," he joked to Macdonell, "and we must try to take them back." Macdonell replied in the same manner, "And we must try to defend them."[12]

Brock concentrated his men at Forts Erie, Chippawa, and Fort George—strategic points along the Niagara River—but he needed more soldiers to adequately man the garrisons. "I have already afforded you reinforcements to the full extent of my ability," Prevost wrote Brock. "You must not, therefore, expect a further supply of men . . . until I shall receive from England a considerable increase to the present regular force." The governor-in-chief allocated the bulk of his resources to Lower Canada because he did not possess enough men to cover the entire Canadian frontier. Prevost urged Brock to consider withdrawing from Detroit and the Michigan Territory if an American assault along the Niagara frontier appeared imminent. Prevost was concerned that a successful American attack would sever Brock's line of communication between Detroit and Lower Canada. Prevost deployed a company from the Glengarry Light Infantry Fencibles to reinforce Brock's line of communication between Cornwall and Kingston, and he reminded Brock that he could transfer troops from Amherstburg to the Niagara frontier and abandon Detroit.[13]

Queenston, a village located halfway between Fort George and Niagara Falls, occupied one end of the portage road that circumvented Niagara Falls, with the other point in Chippawa. The strategic position contained a 350-foot cliff called Queenston Heights that afforded sweeping views of the river and the American camp at Lewistown. The village contained stone barracks and twenty dwellings surrounded by gardens. The river portage road from Fort Niagara formed the main thoroughfare through the village and intersected the town's single cross street. The Hamilton house, Queenston's largest structure, contained a walled courtyard and several smaller buildings. Brock understood the importance of the position and deployed three hundred regulars and militia to guard the outpost (two flank companies of the Forty-Ninth, the York militia, and some Native Americans). His men also positioned an 18-pounder in a redan halfway up Queenston Heights and a twenty-four-pound carronade placed at Vrooman's Point, one mile downriver. This gun could hit enemy vessels traveling downriver from Queenston, but the carronade's short range prevented its round shot from reaching the crossing point between Lewistown and Queenston.[14]

Van Rensselaer selected the location to assault on the Niagara River. He chose Queenston because he believed that American control of Queenston Heights could establish a foothold on the Niagara, and that the army's presence there would force Brock to dispatch reinforcements from Fort George.

Once Brock deployed those troops, Fort George would be vulnerable to attack by a second American force that would be arriving shortly. A successful assault on both locations would allow Van Rensselaer's men to winter in the comfortable barracks at Queenston and Fort Niagara.[15]

By mid-September, General Van Rensselaer had collected 1,600 men. The newcomers strained the general's finite supplies, and they became impatient with his waiting game. Citizen-soldiers wanted to engage the enemy quickly and return home with tales of glory. The men, who had not yet been paid, drafted a public note threatening to quit the army in eight days unless they received their salary. "The situation of my little army is becoming every day more and more interesting," Van Rensselaer wrote Dearborn, "and I believe existing circumstances would fully warrant me in saying critical."[16]

Van Rensselaer hoped for support from Brigadier General Alexander Smyth, who arrived at Black Rock on September 29 to support the invasion. Smyth, though a US Army regular, had little military experience. Through political connections, he secured an assignment to draft the army's drill manual, and he later became a brigadier general. Cronyism, not experience, helped him secure a coveted officer rank. Lieutenant Colonel Winfield Scott, who would become one of the few bright spots during the war, wrote that Smyth "showed no talent for command, and made himself ridiculous on the Niagara frontier." Smyth reported to Van Rensselaer, but he showed little regard for the Van Rensselaer's citizen-soldier position. Smyth encamped his men at Buffalo instead of marching them to Lewistown to reinforce Van Rensselaer's forces. He wrote Van Rensselaer a rushed letter stating that he could not report in person, as was customary for a subordinate officer, because he needed to attend to duties in Buffalo. In a final show of disrespect, he advised Van Rensselaer where they should attack the enemy, even though Smyth arrived in the area only days before.[17]

General Van Rensselaer, ignoring the slights to his rank, tried to soothe Smyth's ego by writing him that that "I may be, as a citizen soldier, [willing] to surrender my opinion to a professional one." But he also reminded Smyth that he had been encamped along the Niagara frontier for weeks and had formed his plan after serious consideration. Van Rensselaer's diplomatic response should have set the stage for a productive relationship, but Smyth did not react to kindness, and the cordial Van Rensselaer refused to reprimand him for not reporting in person at Lewistown.[18]

On October 9, Van Rensselaer's men received a much-needed morale boost. US Navy lieutenant Jesse Elliot had arrived in Black Rock to refit merchant vessels into warships, and he observed two British vessels, the *Detroit* (captured by the British during Hull's surrender) and the *Caledonia* (owned by the British North West Company), anchored off Fort Erie. Elliot believed that the addition of two vessels could help him strengthen his nascent Lake Erie fleet. Elliot wanted to dispatch a covert party to detach the vessels and sail them to the American side. Lieutenant Isaac Roach, the raid's leader, had no shortage of volunteers from a newly arrived artillery regiment under Lieutenant Colonel Scott.

At midnight, one hundred men filed into two boats and departed from a creek just south of Black Rock. They rowed undetected to the two vessels and boarded and captured the brigs after a brief firefight. The *Caledonia*'s commander, Lieutenant Robert Irvine, put up a spirited defense until an American sword knocked him down and the Americans overwhelmed his small crew. The raiding party rescued thirty American prisoners on the *Detroit* and tried to pilot both vessels back to Black Rock. American soldiers on the river's shore lit torches and lanterns to guide the men home. But the combination of a windless night and fast-moving water swept the vessels downriver in front of four British batteries that rained cannonballs onto them. The vessels withstood the barrage and the men successfully piloted the *Caledonia* to Black Rock under the cover of artillery fire from Scott's men. They did not have the same luck with the *Detroit*, which became stuck on a shoal, and they were forced to abandon and later burn the vessel. The success of the covert raid provided a positive moment for an army that had suffered for two months with nothing to show for it.[19]

Excited by Elliot's success at Black Rock, Van Rensselaer's militia threatened to leave the army if the general did not attack soon. Militiamen were not in the habit of waiting for war. Van Rensselaer complied with their demands and decided to attack the following day. With reinforcements, the general possessed 2,350 regulars and 4,050 militia, compared to Brock's force of 1,230 regulars, 810 militia, and 300 Native American warriors. General Van Rensselaer repeatedly called on General Smyth to join him at Fort Niagara to discuss the invasion, but Smyth ignored his requests.[20]

In early October, American teamsters transported thirteen batteaux from Gill Creek to Lewistown on wagons. Van Rensselaer asked Smyth to send reinforcements and ordered Lieutenant Colonel Fenwick's artillery to march to the embarkation point, which was located at an old ferry landing near Lewistown. Smyth complied with Van Rensselaer's request and ordered his men to march to Lewistown, but because of the horrible conditions of the road—a ten-hour march through ankle-deep mud and potholes—they did not arrive in time for the attack. General Van Rensselaer did, however, command three hundred regulars under Lieutenant Colonel John Chrystie, who had recently arrived in Lewistown. Van Rensselaer directed his men to hire an expert boatman who could navigate the Niagara's treacherous waters. The river was two hundred yards wide, flowed four miles an hour, and contained swirling eddies and whirlpools.[21]

Solomon Van Rensselaer took a moment away from his invasion preparations to write his wife on October 10. He opened the letter by saying that "this letter may be the last you will receive from me; If it is, let me beg of you sometimes to cherish my memory and forget any unkindness you may have received from me. . . . My own and the *patroons* Reputations require that the sacrifice should be made. . . . I must succeed, or you my dear Arriet, will never see me again." For Arriet, who was in the late stages of her pregnancy, this letter probably did little to ease her worries. She knew that Solomon almost died at the Battle of Fallen Timbers and probably believed that she would never see him again.[22]

At 3:00 a.m. on October 11, more than three hundred men under Solomon Van Rensselaer's command marched to the crossing point. Strong winds and cold rains chilled the men; a strong nor'easter had blown in that morning. The frigid men stood on the bank waiting for the boats, when, to their surprise, they watched their hired pilot, Lieutenant John Simms, float past the embarkation point with all of the batteaux's oars, tie his vessel to the shore, and disappear. General Van Rensselaer called off the assault at daylight and sent the wet, tired troops back to their rain-soaked tents. While en route to Lewistown, Smyth received a note from Van Rensselaer stating that he had canceled the attack, and Smyth countermarched his men ten hours back to Black Rock. The militia clamored to attack again as soon as possible. Some of General Smyth's men, including Colonel Chrystie's regulars, needed to recuperate from the long, cold night, but General Van Rensselaer planned to launch the assault in two days anyway. He ordered his men to return the boats to Lewistown and placed them in full view of the British at Queenston.[23]

That same day, General Brock visited Queenston Heights. While there, he probably conferred with Captain James Dennis, who commanded ninety grenadiers in the village and Captain John Williams of the Forty-Ninth Foot, who commanded a cantonment at the summit of the heights. Brock became convinced that the Americans would attack soon. "The vast numbers of troops which have been this day added to the strong force previously collected on the opposite side," Brock wrote Prevost, "convinces me, that an attack is not far distant." But soon Brock had another problem. Some soldiers from the Forty-Ninth threatened to shoot the men that protected the guardhouse. Brock dispatched a staff officer to arrest the guilty parties, but the mutiny suggested that some of Brock's best troops lacked the discipline necessary to defend the heights from attack.[24]

On October 13, General Van Rensselaer organized his second effort. He again called on Smyth to send soldiers from Black Rock, and the general responded that he would dispatch 1,200 men to Lewistown the next day, after they received new uniforms and rested. Van Rensselaer also received two excellent artillery companies under twenty-six-year-old Lieutenant Colonel Winfield Scott, which had arrived at Fort Schlosser on the 12th. By chance, Scott learned about the upcoming attack, and he went to Lewistown to request that his regiment participate. Van Rensselaer told Scott that he could cross the river but that he would need to waive his rank, something that Scott refused to do. Scott decided instead to support the invasion from the American shore with cannon. Another unit, Lieutenant Colonel Thompson Mead's Seventeenth Regiment of Detached New York militia, marched to Black Rock to support the invasion, but they lacked gunpowder and lead for musket balls. General Van Rensselaer told Mead to appear at his headquarters at midnight to be furnished with ammunition, but after a seven-mile march, Mead found the general and his staff absent.[25]

Van Rensselaer's new plan directed that the first wave of soldiers consisted of 150 regulars under Lieutenant Colonel Chrystie, 150 militia, and 40 artillerists, with the entire landing party under the command of Solomon Van Rensselaer. After landing on the Canadian shore, the boats would return to the embarkation point to retrieve Lieutenant Colonel John Fenwick and Captain James Mullany with 550 regulars and several cannon. At this point, however, General Van Rensselaer made a critical mistake: there were at least one hundred batteaux available to his army (fifty of which sat only seven miles away), but he collected only thirteen at Lewistown. With more boats, he could have launched most of his men across in a single wave, but instead he would be relying on the safe, round-trip passage of thirteen boats; all of which would be under fire from British artillery while crossing a hazardous river in the dark. In addition, none of the boats could carry artillery carriages, which would have enabled Solomon to move cannon quickly around the battlefield.[26]

Just after midnight on October 13, on a cold, moonless night, three hundred regulars filed down a narrow ravine toward the embarkation point and clogged the small portage landing area. Lieutenant Colonel Solomon Van Rensselaer had not designated anyone to organize the men at the landing site. The stacked regulars blocked the militia's path to the batteaux. As a result, Solomon allowed 300 regulars to board in the first wave, and half of this group replaced the 150 militia who should have boarded during this crossing. At 4:00 a.m., twenty-five men crawled into each of the swaying boats and prepared to launch. Solomon Van Rensselaer walked down the line of boats and gave the order to push off.[27]

The boat's oarsmen rowed the batteaux into the Niagara's swift currents. The landing zone, located five hundred yards upstream of Queenston, contained a narrow beach of broken sandstone and shale beneath a forty-foot embankment. The boats' pilots had to locate this small beach in the predawn darkness, without any visible features on the Canadian shoreline to guide them. Major Lovett's battery fired their two 18-pounders and two 6-pounders into Queenston, but nighttime prevented the gunners from aiming accurately. The pilots expertly guided the batteaux through swirling currents toward shore. A group of British sentries spotted the invaders and sounded the alarm. British cannon from the redan on the heights and carronades from Vrooman's Point began firing rounds at the vessels, but most of the cannonballs missed their targets in the darkness. British sentries on the shore fired toward the sound of the oars and mortally wounded Lieutenant Samuel Rathbone. "The shore was one incessant blaze of musketry," Lovett remembered. Lieutenant John Beverley Robinson of the Third York Militia maintained a clear view of the action from his perch at Brown's Point, two miles above Queenston. "Day was just glimmering," he recalled, and "the cannon from both sides roared incessantly, shells were bursting in the air, and the side of the mountain above Queenston was illuminated by the continual discharge of small arms."[28]

Within ten minutes, the first batteaux arrived at the landing site. The oarsmen guided all but three boats to the designated point. The batteaux bumped against tree limbs and rocks on the shore, and 225 men slid off to hide under a steep embankment at the river's edge. Lieutenant Colonel Van Rensselaer sent the boats back across the river to retrieve more troops, so without a way to return to the American shore, his men could not retreat. "Now we are here, now we must fight," he told them.[29]

One of the boats that missed the landing area included Van Rensselaer's deputy, Lieutenant Colonel Chrystie. His boat lost an oar-lock which holds the paddle in place. One of Chrystie's officers gripped the oar as the batteau floated off course. The pilot could not change the boat's direction, and the group drifted in front of British batteries. Cannon shot splattered the water around them. One direct hit would have sunk their batteau. "The pilot, panic-struck, turned about," Chrystie recalled, "but being ordered with severity to make the Canada shore at any point, he made another effort literally groaning with fear." Chrystie, recognizing the captain's ineptitude, understood that the boat would not make its destination. He grabbed the steering oar from the oarsmen and navigated back to the American shore to look for another guide. The militia, waiting nervously on the American side, watched Chrystie and his seventy-five regulars paddle frantically back to the shore. The jittery citizen-soldiers, who should have been in the first wave of batteaux and already in Canada, began second-guessing their duty to cross the river into a foreign country. "This pleasant doctrine[,] too [*sic*] the faint hearted[,] soon found almost universal favor," Winfield Scott later wrote.[30]

At Queenston, the Americans began scrambling up the rocky, shrub-strewn embankment toward the heights. Solomon Van Rensselaer ordered the men to halt at the cliff's base. As they waited, British captain John Dennis with sixty grenadiers from the Forty-Ninth Foot, some militia, and a 3-pounder, raced to meet the intruders. Dennis and his men attacked the halted column on its right flank. Soldiers on the heights fired down on the Americans, while Dennis's men fired muskets toward the group. Captain John Wool recalled that "a short but severe contest ensued." A bullet entered the right thigh of Lieutenant Colonel Van Rensselaer just behind the hip bone. He pressed on and another ball penetrated the same thigh. He received a third shot through his calf and a fourth into his heel. Other balls riddled his body, and he dropped to the ground. A musket ball also hit Captain John

Wool and penetrated both of his thighs. He wrapped a coat around his waist and continued to rally the men. Wounded but alive, Van Rensselaer ordered Major Stephen Lush to organize the soldiers on shore and to locate his second-in-command, Lieutenant Colonel Chrystie. Wool found Van Rensselaer below the embankment.

"What can be done?" Wool asked the lieutenant colonel. "I don't know," Van Rensselaer responded. "Something must be done soon or we will all be taken prisoners," Wool replied. "I don't know anything unless we take Queenston Heights," Van Rensselaer responded.[31]

It appeared that the American invasion would be over as quickly as it started. Dennis's men killed or wounded six of the eleven American officers present. "The carnage along the shore was shocking," one York militiaman remembered. But soon more reinforcements arrived from across the river, and the overwhelming number of Americans forced Dennis's party to retreat to a stone guardhouse in the village. From that stout structure, Dennis's men loaded and fired a 9-pounder, which launched spherical case (a hollow iron ball packed with powder and balls that scattered when exploded) and round shot across the river into Van Rensselaer's embarkation point.[32]

By this time, Lieutenant Colonel Chrystie arrived back at the ferry landing, which was a "scene of confusion hardly to be described." No one was directing or organizing the militia into the returning boats, and cannon fire rained down anyone standing at the site. Lieutenant Colonel Fenwick told the men to take cover in a ravine to avoid the artillery fire. Major Lovett, whose vision improved once the sun rose, launched his 18-pounders against the village's guardhouse. After the eighth shot, Lovett hit his mark and "tumbled up a heap of men," as he recalled. The British guns quit firing, and Lieutenant Colonel Fenwick ordered the men back into the ravine to board the boats. He launched four batteaux from the landing site, but the current swept them downriver. Through skillful piloting, they managed to land at Hamilton Cove near Queenston Village. The second landing party contained only 200 men instead of the 550 regulars that the plan called for.[33]

A bugle call brought British captain John Williams and his men down from Queenston Heights to obstruct Chrystie's landing. Williams's men poured a deadly fire toward the waterborne invaders, who were now visible in the daylight. The Americans were "almost entirely cut to pieces," Chrystie recalled. Bullet holes lined Fenwick's boat and water rushed into his batteau.

Figure 3. ***The Battle of Queenston. October 18th, 1813.*** American troops crossing the Niagara River to assault Queenston. The image correctly shows the scattered nature of the landings since many of the American batteaux shifted off course during the crossing. Courtesy of Library and Archives Canada, Acc. No. R13133-387.

They managed to land the boat, and his men clambered onshore to return fire. Lieutenant Colonel Fenwick was "clothed with bullets": he was hit in the eye, the right elbow, and on his side. Major James Mullany and Ensign George Grosvenor tried to retrieve the wounded Fenwick, but stiff fire forced them to retreat; the British recaptured the lieutenant colonel. Some men jumped out of their batteaux to surrender. Major Mullany, realizing that the landing zone was a death trap, waded into the river, grabbed a passing boat and piled six wounded men and five volunteers into the boat. Amazingly, the men rowed to the American side unharmed. The British took four American officers prisoner and killed, wounded, or captured one hundred regulars.[34]

Downriver at Fort George, Isaac Brock had not learned of the invasion until it was underway. In the morning's confusion, the British did not ignite their beacon lights, which would signal that Queenston was under attack. Brock soon learned either by messenger or from the sound of cannon fire that the Americans had marched on the village. Brock mounted his horse and began the seven-mile journey down a mud-coated road toward the action. Lieutenant Colonel John Macdonell and Captain John Glegg, the general's aides-de-camp, followed. Brock believed that the Americans would feign an attack on Queenston to set up their main attack against Fort George.[35]

At Brown's Point, Brock passed a detachment of thirty volunteers from York and waved his hand toward Queenston. He bellowed to the men, "Push on the brave York volunteers." About an hour later, he arrived at Vrooman's Point and questioned the artillerists there, "Why don't you fire that gun?" They explained that the balls from the 18-pounder carronade, which was designed for close combat, fell short of their target. "It can't be helped," Brock admitted, and put his spurs to his horse to head toward to Queenston. Once there, Brock met with Captain Dennis and sent for reinforcements from Chippawa and Fort George.[36]

At the base of the cliff, with Solomon Van Rensselaer out of the action, command devolved to the wounded but walking Captain Wool, who volunteered to lead 160 men to seize Queenston Heights. Captain Wool waved his men forward, and Major Stephen Lush threatened to shoot anyone who retreated from the attack. Lieutenant Wassel Gansevoort, who was familiar with the area's geography, led them up an unguarded precipice. Soldiers grabbed bushes and rocks to pull themselves up, and they eventually located an old fisherman's path that they traversed to the top of the heights. Their route led them directly to the British 18-pounder. British captain Williams's party had been on guard here but descended earlier to stop Fenwick's landing; Wool's men overtook the gun without resistance. He now sought to turn the powerful cannon on Queenston Village to bombard the remaining soldiers there. But before he could do so, he spotted General Brock marching toward his left flank. Brock had gathered thirty to forty men to assault Wool off the heights. The Americans outnumbered Brock, but he rallied his small group by shouting, "Follow me boys!" His men advanced up the steep slope at double-quick time. The tall general, resplendent in his scarlet uniform, waved his sword above his head to urge on the men. Wool's men leveled their muskets at the daring figure, who must be a senior officer. One bullet grazed Brock, but the next one entered his right breast, exited his left side, and he dropped to the ground. Fifteen-year-old private George Jarvis stood next to Brock when he fell. "Are you much hurt, sir?" he asked Brock. The general grabbed his chest, sank down, and died. Soldiers gathered around their beloved fallen leader. A cannonball hit one of the men and he fell on top of the general. The soldiers hid Brock's body in the village. They circulated rumors that their general was only wounded, but many soon learned the truth. Cries of "Revenge the General" echoed throughout the Forty-Ninth Regiment. "To revenge his death," William Merritt of the Provincial Light Dragoons remembered, "and make a determined effort to dislodge the enemy was the general wish . . . although many thought it hopeless."[37]

Lieutenant Colonel Macdonell and Captain Williams rallied seventy men, mostly York militia and infantry from the Forty-Ninth Regiment, to climb the hill and attack the invaders. The men gathered at the base of the hill. "Feel firmly to your right, advance steadily," Williams told his soldiers. "Charge them home and they cannot stand you." Macdonell, mounted on his horse, exhorted his men to charge. The men jogged up the steep slope into a hail of bullets from Wool's party. Despite being outnumbered, the small British group charged Wool's line and forced them backwards. The Americans spiked the 18-pounder and fell back. "The enemy drove us to the edge of the bank," Wool remembered, "when with the greatest exertion we brought the troops to a stand." One man reportedly raised a white handkerchief on the tip of his sword, but Wool pulled it down.[38]

Luckily for the Americans, reinforcements from the Sixth Infantry arrived during the standoff, and soon the American's overwhelming firepower propelled them forward. They discharged a heavy round of musket fire, and one bullet pierced Macdonell's back, exited his stomach, and he fell to the ground. Captain Duncan Cameron, a commander in the York militia, rushed to his colonel to lead him to safety, but a musket ball hit him in the elbow. Macdonell crawled toward his friend Lieutenant Archibald McLean to beg for help. McLean led him a few paces when a bullet pierced McLean's thigh. Cameron then returned and guided Macdonell away from the field. Macdonell, mortally wounded, died the next day at the age of twenty-seven. Captain Williams did not fare any better. A bullet pierced the top of his forehead, giving him the appearance that he had been scalped. Williams collapsed to the ground and his comrades believed he was dead. But not long after he fell, he arose like an apparition and strolled away from the battle site. Williams would later make a full recovery. The remaining men retreated to Vrooman's battery to await reinforcements from Fort George.[39]

After the successful defense, Captain Wool formed his men in a line on the heights fronting the village and sent out flanking parties, including a small detachment of riflemen. He also ordered his soldiers to drill out the spike from the 18-pounder in order to fire shells into the village. By 10:00 a.m. it appeared that General Van Rensselaer's invasion would be successful, despite fierce defense from the Forty-First, Forty-Ninth, and the Canadian militia. His men controlled the heights and had forced the British to leave the village. Lieutenant Colonel Chrystie finally arrived on the battlefield and ordered Wool to recross the river to get his wounds dressed. General Van Rensselaer also permitted Lieutenant Colonel Scott to join the action, and he too arrived on the heights. Upon arrival, Scott found militia Brigadier General William Wadsworth in command, and he cordially offered to split the command with the general. Wadsworth declined his offer and insisted that Scott, the regular, should have command of the whole.[40]

Wadsworth needed American reinforcements to solidify the victory. With more men, the general could fend off counterattacks from the heights and establish an American bridgehead on the northern shore of the Niagara. But no reinforcements arrived. The militia, many of whom should have crossed in the first wave, refused to do so, and Smyth's regulars at Black Rock continued to rest, while waiting for new uniforms. General Van Rensselaer rode through Lewistown exhorting the militia to follow his orders. More than 1,200 men sat idle on the American shore. "I rode in all directions; urged the men by every consideration to pass over—but in vain." He penned a note to General Wadsworth: "I have passed through my camp, not a regiment, not a company is willing to join you. Save yourselves by a retreat if you can. Boats shall be sent to receive you."[41]

Meanwhile, British major general Roger Sheaffe, Brock's second-in-command, collected reinforcements to retake Queenston. Sheaffe, like Brock, was a lifelong soldier in the British Army, but the personalities and backgrounds of the two men were quite different. Unlike his peers, Sheaffe grew up in Boston (instead of Britain) in a low socioeconomic class. His father died at an early age, and he moved to a boardinghouse with his eight siblings. A local British general took an interest in the children and encouraged Sheaffe to join the army. He agreed to the plan, and with the general's financial support, he rose quickly by purchasing his commissions. He served nineteen years in Canada, more than any other British general. In 1811, the army promoted Sheaffe to major general and Prevost directed him to support Brock on the Niagara frontier. Unlike the beloved Brock, the martinet Sheaffe trained his men with excessive rigidity. Sheaffe flogged and confined any men who disobeyed orders, and he rarely allowed his soldiers to leave the garrison to fish or hunt without being in full uniform. He also refused to allow soldiers to use their service weapons to hunt, even when they purchased their own ammunition. Hunting was one of the few enjoyable activities available in the remote Upper Canadian wilderness. In 1803, his harsh manner had contributed to the mutiny at Fort George. Brock said Sheaffe "did not sufficiently study the character of men and his ardent zeal made him seek with eagerness after perfection where it was not to be found."[42]

Sheaffe first dispatched John Norton and his Native American warriors to attack the American position. Norton divided 160 men into five files and directed them to stalk through the woods toward the heights. Canadian militia told the Native Americans that 6,000 Americans occupied the heights, to which some of the Native Americans responded, "the more game the better hunting." Some of Norton's warriors, however, did not possess the same bravado, and many stayed behind, leaving Norton with only eighty followers. "Be men. Remember the fame of ancient warriors, whose breasts were never daunted by odd of number," one of the chiefs told the men.[43]

Around 2:00 p.m., the Native Americans crept up the mountainside and silently approached one of Scott's flank companies. Norton's men gave the "war-whoop" and fired on the surprised company, which fled behind a fence. The Americans returned fire, but most of the bullets passed over the Native Americans, who crouched on the reverse slope. "We saw many brave officers and soldiers fall by the savage band concealed in a thick brush or wood, which prevented our making a due impression in return," remembered one of Scott's men. After the two sides exchanged fire, Norton, believing that Sheaffe's reinforcements were about to climb the slope, ordered his men to press their attack. Some of them bravely approached to within a few paces of the American line. "The Foe raged like a Hive of Bees disturbed," Norton recalled. In his deep voice, Scott bellowed commands, and at six-foot-four, he could be seen across the field by his men. One soldier thought he was going to be made into a "cold Yankee" because of the Native Americans' ferocious fire. Scott ordered a counterattack, and Norton's men fell back into the woods. Some American soldiers followed them into the thicket, and the Iroquois sniped them from behind trees. The Americans, outmatched at bushfighting, discontinued their pursuit and returned to the main line.[44]

While Norton's men were attacking Scott on the heights, reinforcements from Fort George poured into Queenston. By 2:00 p.m., Sheaffe had collected 650 men from the Lincoln Militia, the Forty-First and Forty-Ninth Regiments, and Captain William Merritt's provincial dragoons. Captain William Holcroft with two 6-pounders and Lieutenant William Crowther with two 3-pounders provided field artillery support. The lightweight 3-pounders, known as "grasshoppers," could move with the infantry to pump grapeshot into the enemy's line. Sheaffe placed Holcroft's 6-pounders in an old milk house to fire on any American boats crossing the river.[45]

Sheaffe formed his men into columns and ordered them to march down the portage road to approach the heights from the south. When they arrived at the Phelps farm, Sheaffe tried to order his men into a single, battle-ready line, but the confused soldiers formed a column, facing away from the enemy. Sheaffe called out a command to reverse their position so the men would face the hill. The maneuver caused some confusion, but eventually they lined up in the proper formation, with the Forty-Ninth in the middle, militia on both sides of the Forty-Ninth, and the elite Forty-First Light Infantry and Forty-Ninth Grenadiers on the left and right edges of the formation. Men dragged the two 3-pounder "grasshoppers" to the front of the line. Reinforcements from Chippawa arrived just before the assault, and Norton's Native Americans fell in with the force. The general's army totaled around 900 men, compared to roughly 400 Americans who remained on the heights. Sheaffe ordered his soldiers to follow the path cleared by Norton's Native Americans.[46]

On the summit of Queenston Heights, after receiving General Van Rensselaer's note about the militia's refusal to cross, General Wadsworth and his senior officers discussed if they should retreat. Sheaffe's men arrived below the summit before they reached a decision. The Americans no longer had enough time to organize an orderly withdrawal, and the results would be devastating. "A rapid advance was ordered," one Canadian remembered, "without firing a musket shot on our part, until within a small distance of the enemy." Once within range, the men stopped to halt and fire at Scott's men. The two 3-pounders pumped grapeshot into the American position. Sheaffe's elite Forty-First Light Infantry, situated on his left flank, fired one volley and charged Wadsworth's riflemen with bayonets. The riflemen could fire only one round per minute and possessed no bayonets (bayonets could not attach to rifles), which compelled them to retreat from the field. The withdrawal broke the American line, and Sheaffe's men seized the opportunity by advancing and firing on the Americans. Thick smoke settled across the battlefield and the men could barely see where they were walking. "I have been in many hail storms," wrote one Canadian militia officer, "but never in one when the stones flew so thick as the bullets on this occasion." A group of British soldiers stumbled through the smoke and bumped into Scott's unmanned 6-pounder, which they loaded and turned on the Americans across the river. Lovett, who watched the assault from his battery, recalled that "the mountains seem to shake beneath the stride of death." The panic-stricken men dropped their muskets and fled down the height's steep slopes, grabbing onto bushes and rocks to maintain their balance. Others jumped from the side of the cliff and died on impact, and some dove into the river. "The river presented a horrid spectacle," a Canadian militiaman remembered, "filled with poor wretches who plunged into the stream from the impulse of fear, with scarcely the prospect of being saved." For those who safely climbed down the heights, no boats awaited them to bring them to safety across the river. "Here all were seized with despair," Scott recalled. "No boats had arrived!"[47]

Scott, realizing the hopelessness of the situation, dispatched two men with flags of surrender, but they had not been returned by a British officer (the men carrying the flags were probably killed). Scott carried the third flag himself with the help of two other officers. While they were ascending the heights, two Native Americans sprang from a small culvert and attacked the party. A British regular officer, noticing the commotion, rushed to stop the fighting and escorted the flag to Sheaffe. Despite the surrender, the Native Americans continued firing at the Americans, scalped wounded men, and stripped the dead of anything valuable.[48]

At the Battle of Queenston, Sheaffe captured 958 American prisoners, including one general and six colonels. Wadsworth presented his sword to Sheaffe. "I understand, General, your people have surrendered," Sheaffe asked him. Wadsworth nodded. Sheaffe complimented James Crooks of the York militia for the militia's bravery and gave him the honor of escorting the American prisoners to Niagara.[49]

In their first major battle of the war, the Canadian militia proved as brave and competent as British regulars; the farmers, lawyers, and other citizen-soldiers from York and Glengarry county lived up to their ancestors' heritage. They proved their mettle by charging with Brock and Macdonell in virtual suicide missions against the Americans' larger numbers. In contrast, the American militia performed miserably. Most of them refused to cross the river, and those that did hid below the riverbank to avoid the fighting. Sheaffe paroled the militia and marched the regulars to Quebec to be imprisoned.

The battle should have been Sheaffe's shining moment, but oddly, six months later, Prevost criticized Sheaffe's timid conduct. "After the affair at Queenston," he wrote, "Sir R. H. Sheaffe lost a glorious opportunity of crossing the Niagara river during the confusion and dismay which then prevailed . . . but the eminent military talents of Sir Isaac Brock having ceased to animate the little army, the advantage of that day was not sufficiently improved." Why Prevost waited so long to inform the War Ministry would reveal itself in the spring of 1813, when the governor-in-chief required a scapegoat for British losses that had occurred that year.[50]

On October 17, British soldiers buried Brock and Macdonell in the incomplete York battery at Fort George. The ceremony honoring the death of General Brock was led by a company of regulars while a band played marching tunes, and pallbearers carried the coffins. Militia and Native Americans formed double rows on each side of the street, with their arms resting in reverse in a sign of respect. Soldiers fired their guns every minute throughout the procession. At the end of the ceremony, in a sign of respect, General Van Rensselaer's artillerists fired their cannon to salute the fallen officers. Meanwhile, Solomon Van Rensselaer recovered from his wounds in Lovett's tent. Despite his half dozen wounds, he once again escaped death, and Lovett nursed him back to health.[51]

Brock's decision to charge the heights during the battle is a curious one. As commander of all British and Canadian troops in Upper Canada, he should have been located out of harm's way and providing orders to his officers based on his assessment of the situation. Instead, by charging the heights, he performed a role normally associated with a lower-ranking officer. Brock, whose personality contained a mix of courage, impulsivity, and honor, disliked inaction and preferred to seize the initiative from the enemy, as he did at Detroit. He probably charged with his men because he understood that it would be difficult to dislodge the Americans once they developed a foothold on the heights. The general also led by example, as he showed from his time in Europe with the Forty-Ninth Regiment. Historian Jonathon Riley writes, "Brock was certainly not lacking in courage but on Queenston Heights it may have edged into bravado. But his personal honour—which mattered far more than modern notions of morality in an officer—compelled him to lead the attack in person."[52]

Three days after the battle, General Van Rensselaer resigned. The Federalist politician-turned-soldier became the scapegoat of the Republican administration for the attack's failure. Jefferson, who probably recognized that his predictions of an easy victory against British North America were off the mark, wanted Van Rensselaer "broken for cowardice and incapacity." In his mind, Van Rensselaer's ineptitude, rather than a broken military architecture, led to the loss. Van Rensselaer, in fact, had done his best with the resources given to him. His plan to attack the heights almost succeeded, but he should have waited until Smyth's regulars could participate before launching his assault. Van Rensselaer believed that he had to act or his militia would have deserted en masse, but the general should have waited until he had enough men and boats; a point that Dearborn highlighted to Van Rensselaer's successor. After the Americans attacked Queenston, Sheaffe emptied Fort George's garrison to reinforce Queenston, just as Van Rensselaer predicted he would, in order to save that outpost. General Smyth could have exploited the weakened state of the garrison, but Smyth's men were resting from their long march from Black Rock to Lewistown the day before.[53]

After Van Rensselaer's surrender, Dearborn ordered Smyth to take command of the Niagara frontier. "That you may be so fortunate as to succeed in retrieving our past misfortunes is my most ardent wish," he wrote Smyth. By November, he collected four thousand troops, but many became sick from poor sanitation, and others deserted the camp. Smyth's regulars and militia became frustrated with the lack of pay, clothing, and other necessities, but this did not dampen Smyth's zeal. He wrote Eustis that he would "retrieve your affairs or perish." Smyth issued a bombastic proclamation to the citizens of New York: "Shame, where is thy blush! No! . . . Men of New York! . . . Have you not a wish for fame?" He lambasted Hull and Van Rensselaer: "The cause of these miscarriages is apparent. The commanders were popular men, 'destitute alike of theory and experience' in the art of war." He promised that the American flag would be planted in Canada in two days. Smyth's men mockingly branded him "Alexander the Great." Smyth ordered Colonel William Winder to capture the British batteries across from Black Rock, and he directed Lieutenant Colonel Charles Boerstler to destroy a bridge at Frenchman's Creek to prevent reinforcements arriving from Fort George or Chippawa.[54]

At dawn on 28 November, Winder's men crossed the river and overtook the British outpost across from Black Rock. During the assault one of his detachments became lost near Fort Erie, and the enemy defeated the group. Boerstler captured the bridge, but his men failed to destroy the structure. He lost two boats from artillery fire and he decided to return to the American shore. Smyth dispatched Winder to save the lost detachment, but Winder, upon encountering a large force, decided to retreat. Smyth held a council of war, and his officers decided to discontinue the crossing. Smyth wrote a letter to the British commander at Fort Erie, which must have puzzled the addressee; he demanded that the British surrender in order to "spare the effusion of blood," even though the Americans had been repulsed with ease. Two days later, Smyth tried another assault, but poor planning delayed the crossing for two hours. The British noticed the accumulation of men and artillery on the American side and prepared their defenses across from the buildup. Smyth called another meeting where his officers agreed to postpone the assault until after winter. At this point, Smyth's men and officers became mutinous because of the general's inaction. General Peter Porter, the state's quartermaster general, called him a "scoundrel" and "traitor." Smyth challenged him to a duel, during which each man fired, but neither hit their target. Days later, another soldier fired a pistol at Smyth, barely missing him, forcing the general to surround himself with bodyguards. Smyth, it turned out, was more likely to be killed by his own men than the enemy. Three months later, President Madison dropped Smyth's name from the army rolls.[55]

On November 19, General Dearborn finally decided to attack Montreal. Dearborn had assembled the largest collection of regulars since the war started. He gathered around six thousand men, including seven regiments of regular infantry. The assault on Montreal was the boldest American plan yet, and the operation had the potential to deliver a serious blow to Britain. The British Commissariat stored many of its supplies in the city because large ships from Quebec could advance no farther than Montreal on the St. Lawrence. American control of the town would sever the logistics connection between Lower and Upper Canada. British bases to the west, including those on Lake Ontario, the Niagara, and far west Upper Canada, would suffer shortages of food and ammunition. American control of Montreal would also curtail British efforts to augment their squadrons on Lakes Erie and Ontario because the Commissariat would be unable to send rigging, ordnance, and other shipbuilding supplies to those dockyards. Land and water routes from Montreal to Amherstburg that circumvented Lake Ontario, the Niagara River, and Lake Erie could not handle heavy equipment. Unfortunately for the Americans, the assault proved unsuccessful.

After twenty miles, Dearborn's troops encountered a small enemy force commanded by Major Charles-Michel d'Irumberry, Comte de Salaberry. Some minor skirmishing with Salaberry's men reminded Dearborn's militia of their legal obligations to their state, and they refused to advance further. Dearborn still possessed enough US Army regulars to attack Salaberry, but the general decided to withdraw to Plattsburgh, after which he offered his resignation to Eustis. Eustis refused to accept his resignation. "Fortunately for you," he wrote Dearborn, "the want of success which has attended the campaign will be attributed to the Secretary at War." In this assessment he was right; Eustis resigned on December 3, 1812.[56]

The American armies of the center and the right divisions failed to accomplish anything meaningful in the fall of 1812 other than reveal the broken state of the country's military. The militia provided the bulk of manpower for America's army, but many citizen-soldiers refused to participate in dangerous attacks against British outposts. The few militia that did cross into Canada buckled under the enemy's heavy fire and provided little assistance to American regular officers. America's generals, most selected for their Revolutionary War experience, lacked the ability to organize, prepare, and lead a large combat force into enemy territory. Dearborn and Smyth—each skilled at writing obnoxious letters ridiculing Hull and Van Rensselaer—proved incapable of leading and planning military operations. The only bright spot for the Americans was the brave leadership shown by some of its mid-level officers, including Winfield Scott, John Wool, and James Mullany. A short-sighted and politically minded Thomas Jefferson blamed the defeats on bad generalship, which did play a role, but he probably never considered that his own policies contributed to the army's poor state of affairs. Jefferson and President Madison longed for an effective commander to lead a final attack before winter. Henry Clay had just the person: the hero of Tippecanoe.

5

Harrison Enters the War

For nearly two miles along the road . . . the snow was covered with the blood and bodies of the slain.
—John Richardson, *Richardson's War of 1812*

William Henry Harrison was the logical choice to lead a desperate mission to recover the lost Michigan Territory. His success at Tippecanoe and experience in the Northwest Territory gave him credentials that few generals in the US Army possessed. He understood frontier fighting and could mold an inexperienced army into a disciplined combat force. Residents of the western United States adored Harrison, and they would volunteer in droves to redeem America's honor.

Harrison joined the service in 1791 when poor morale permeated the army. The cunning northwest tribes repeatedly routed US soldiers, who were inexperienced in frontier tactics. Little Turtle and the Miamis defeated Josiah Harmar just before Harrison joined the army. After Harrison arrived at Fort Washington (modern day Cincinnati), local tribes once again annihilated an army under General Arthur St. Clair. The battered survivors encamped in front of Fort Washington, and others straggled in over time, presenting an awful view to new arrivals such as Harrison. Army discipline fell apart in the wake of the defeats—soldiers deserted en masse and drinking, gambling, and dueling became rampant. Ensign Harrison tried to instill discipline in his company, tend the wounded, and muster out the militia in this chaotic and sullen environment.[1]

In 1793, "Mad" Anthony Wayne arrived at Fort Washington determined to protect settlers from Native American abuses and to seek revenge for St. Clair's defeat. He created a "Legion" in the style of the Continental Army and appointed nineteen-year-old Harrison as his aide-de-camp. As Wayne's adviser, Harrison witnessed the general's challenges in commanding an undisciplined frontier army. He observed Wayne dole out court-martials to insubordinates and order the execution of fifteen men.[2]

Harrison also absorbed Wayne's knowledge of frontier warfare. Wayne exercised caution when advancing a force through the wilderness by deploying his men in a way that helped defend against flank attacks and avoid ambushes. Harrison implemented similar practices during his army's march through the Old Northwest to guard against surprise attacks. He also remembered the success of mounted riflemen at the Battle of Fallen Timbers, and he would employ them with success in one of the War of 1812's pivotal battles. Harrison's most important lesson from Wayne, however, involved logistics. He remembered the difficulties that Wayne faced in sustaining an army hundreds of miles from the nearest settlement. Harrison, recognizing these challenges, decided to establish forward supply depots along the route that contractors would fill with supplies before the army's arrival.[3]

Harrison resigned his army commission in 1797, and he later won a seat in Congress. In 1800, President John Adams appointed him governor of the Indiana portion of the Northwest Territory. As governor, he negotiated with Native Americans in the Northwest to acquire more land for the United States, and he led the expedition against the Prophet at Tippecanoe. During that expedition, he gained the trust and loyalty of those who served under him. "Harrison was their favorite," one soldier wrote about Harrison during the war, "and could do more with them [the soldiers] than any other living man." They believed that Harrison would reverse General Hull's failures: "Harrison, at the head of the Kentucky boys—by them respected and revered, will play the Canadians a quite different tune from that of *surrender!*" (original emphasis).[4]

When news reached Kentucky that General William Hull needed reinforcements at Detroit, the state assembled an army to rescue the besieged general. Many of the volunteers for the force hailed from respected families in Kentucky. "Our company was composed of the very Elite of the state young men," one soldier recalled, "of the best familys [*sic*] in Kentucky, young merchants Lawyers and Doctors." Some of Kentucky's most respected citizens became officers in the rescue force, including Colonel John Allen, a rising political star in the state. He studied law in Virginia, later resettled in his home state of Kentucky, and at twenty-eight ran for governor, losing by a small margin. He raised a Kentucky rifle regiment, and his men elected him colonel. Another famous Kentuckian, Captain John Simpson, joined Allen's regiment and his constituency elected him to Congress before the war started. Legally, Harrison could not command these volunteers because he was not a Kentucky citizen. Kentucky governor Charles Scott and governor-elect Isaac Shelby, however, decided to waive the rule and designated Harrison as a major general in the Kentucky militia.[5]

General Harrison was not naïve to the difficulties that would surround his expedition. His men would face the same challenges that Hull had previously: short supplies, late pay for the soldiers, and a grueling march through the Northwest wilderness. His men, who would be advancing in the fall and winter, required woolen clothing to stay warm, but Harrison lacked enough of the material to clothe them properly. Most of his soldiers donned summer cotton linens, which provided little protection against the elements. The force would also be marching during the rainy season. The downpours would turn the Black Swamp into a marshy wasteland and impede the men's ability to move wagons and artillery. The forward supply depots would be critical to their survival in the cold, wet months ahead.

On August 19, Harrison's advance departed Georgetown, Kentucky, toward Detroit. The men learned six days later that Hull surrendered the outpost, and most of the proud Kentuckians were eager to show their mettle to the British. One Kentucky editor wrote, "They seemed indignant at the late news and are anxious to wipe off the stain from the American name." At Piqua, Ohio, Harrison directed his men to march to Fort Wayne to rescue the garrison from a Native American siege. He read the army's regulations and declared that anyone who could not submit to these articles should go home. One man departed the army and his peers dunked the deserter in a river, which "washed away all his patriotism."[6]

Harrison followed the same route to Detroit that Hull created from Urbana, and he also faced the same challenges transporting and receiving supplies in the Old Northwest. Britain still controlled maritime traffic on Lake Erie and could efficiently resupply their garrisons at Amherstburg and

Mackinac, whereas Harrison had to rely on supply depots, filled primarily by contractors, to sustain his force. Contractors were forced to contend with the same difficult terrain en route to the blockhouses. Despite these supply challenges. Harrison told Secretary of War Eustis he would seize Detroit before the onset of winter unless the region received its typical rainfall. If it rained at normal levels, Harrison would wait until winter to move his supplies over the ice on sleds.[7]

On September 1, Harrison's force began its march to Fort Wayne, which sat on the south side of the Maumee River near its intersection with the St. Mary's and St. Joseph Rivers. The men survived on half rations of flour and one ration of beef because Harrison wanted a light army that could move quickly to the besieged fort. The soldiers drank stagnant water that settled in wagon ruts along the road. The grueling conditions of the march, however, did not preclude the men from having fun. Military regulations prohibited soldiers from discharging their weapons unless in combat, but one fellow could not refrain from shooting a fat porcupine sitting in a tree. He leveled his rifle, shot the creature, and yelled "accident" to show that he did not mean to fire. An officer ran to him, raised his sword, and shouted that he did not want any more accidental firings. He apparently did not notice the dead porcupine at the foot of a nearby tree.[8]

Eight days later, the men arrived at Fort Wayne. The Native Americans had burnt cornfields and killed their livestock before they departed, which deprived the starving men of any potential nourishment. Even though they were down to nine ounces of flour per day, most of the men, especially the Kentucky militia, still believed in their cause and their general. "This we can live on, and fight on," one soldier remarked."[9]

While Harrison and his men were at Fort Wayne, rumors circulated that James Winchester, a brigadier general in the regular army, would replace Harrison as commander of the Northwest force. Most residents of the Old West viewed Winchester as an aristocratic snoot. "This will produce a great discontent and murmuring, if not absolute rebellion," one soldier commented. On September 18, their fears became reality when Winchester arrived at Fort Wayne to announce that he had been given command of the army. Harrison refused to serve under Winchester and decided to return to Indiana. Harrison's departure divided the army's loyalty in half between the Kentuckians who refused to serve under Winchester and the regulars who would fulfill their duty to serve their commanding officer. Derisive gossip about Winchester circulated among the volunteer ranks. His men despised him so much in previous commands that they played pranks on him. In one case, soldiers reportedly skinned a porcupine and stretched it over the pole that Winchester regularly sat on and "it liked to have ruined him." They also cut the same pole almost in half and the general fell into a "no [*sic*] very decent place."[10]

On September 20, General Winchester's men set out on the fifty-mile, ten-day march from Fort Wayne to Fort Defiance. Heavy rains turned the trail into muddy slop. The packhorses became mired up to their knees, while wagons sank hub-deep into the ground. Even empty wagons could not traverse the trail. The quartermaster tried to move supplies on frozen ground, but the provisions rarely arrived at their destination before the weather warmed and the ground thawed. The teamsters lost or left behind many horses and packs during the march, and the absence of those supplies were felt in the weeks ahead.[11]

Despite the miserable weather, the men could not resist trying to catch a trophy fish that swam in the crystal-clear waters of the Maumee, but they could not reach the prize with a spear. One enterprising soldier fired his musket at the fish, which unfortunately for him "took off one half of the fools face." Another man swung off a vine to dive for the fish, but the swift current dragged him out of sight, and he was never seen again.[12]

Winchester's men soon reached the intersection of the Auglaze and Maumee Rivers near a crumbling Fort Defiance. The men rebuilt the outpost, later named Fort Winchester, which contained four blockhouses with pickets in between. The new outpost, however, offered little protection from the cold October rains that saturated the men, and typhus fever spread throughout the camp. The sick roll contained three hundred new patients a day, and disease killed one man a day. Some of the men lacked socks, shoes, and basic winter clothing. Winchester moved the men across the river, but this position proved equally cold and wet.[13]

Harrison intended for his forward supply depots to be filled with supplies when the army arrived at the blockhouses. He expected his men to draw on those food rations during their march, but many of the general's contractors failed to provide the purchased provisions. The problems stemmed from the systemic problems with the contractor system, and the difficult terrain and weather did not help. Harrison's quartermaster, for example, did not issue invoices for the army's purchases, so some of the less honorable merchants neglected their duties without fear of legal reprisal. He also lacked sufficient specie necessary to pay many of the contractors, who would not work on credit. The teamsters also had the same problems crossing through the wilderness that Harrison did. They used packhorses to carry supplies, but the lack of forage weakened the animals for the trek through swamps, ravines, and other dangers. Wagons broke and required repairs; horseshoes and oxshoes became damaged and needed to be replaced. Some contractors tried using rivers to move supplies, but winter froze many of the waterways and their boats became lodged in the ice. In November 1812, Assistant Quartermaster Joseph Wheaton departed Pittsburgh destined for the Harrison's army at the upper Sandusky with 133 wagons. Weak bridges, frozen ground, and difficult crossings forced him to undergo constant repairs, and he lost some of his provisions during the journey. In one section, militia had to cut twelve miles of new road because the route was impassable.[14]

The shortage of supplies placed Winchester's men in a perilous situation. The dragoons lacked rifles, blankets, shoes, winter clothing, mounts, and grain for their horses. Soldiers survived on small rations of rancid beef, hickory nuts, and wild fruit. In one location, low food rations prompted soldiers to rename the site Fort Starvation. At one point, a group of three starving soldiers encountered some local deer hunters. They asked the men for food and the hunters obliged them. "It was simply bread and meat," a soldier recalled, "but I thought it the best breakfast I had ever eaten in my life." Winchester's men wrote letters home about their plight, and women in Kentucky formed societies to knit shirts, socks, and blankets for the troops. "We have become acquainted with one much despised in Kentucky," Elias Darnell, a Kentuckian under Winchester recalled, "whose name is *Poverty*."[15]

Soon the volunteers received some good news. On September 17, the War Department assigned Harrison full command of the Northwest Army, but the letter did not reach him until September 24 when he was at Piqua, Ohio. He returned to the army in early October, and after he arrived at Fort Defiance, he informed the men about his new position. The general intended to unite the three wings of the army at the Maumee Rapids, and he appointed General Winchester to command the left wing and spearhead the expedition.[16]

Despite having command, Harrison doubted that he could attack Amherstburg that winter. He hoped to convene four thousand men at the rapids to assault Fort Malden, but sickness and desertion reduced his available manpower. The army's broken logistics system and an unforgiving wilderness had devastated his army. Harrison described these obstacles to Secretary of War Eustis: "The prodigious destruction of horses can only be conceived by those who have been accustomed to military operations in a wilderness in the winter season." Harrison planned to use sleds to cross the strait, but the waterway remained thawed. He would need to construct boats that would take months to complete. He asked Eustis for guidance: Should he continue with the attack even if it was going to fail? The question put the Madison administration in an untenable position, and Harrison knew it. If the administration ordered him to attack and the offensive failed, Eustis would be blamed. If the attack succeeded, Harrison would get the laurels.[17]

The new acting secretary of war, James Monroe, who temporarily replaced Eustis in December 1812 until a permanent secretary could be found,[18] told Harrison that he knew there would be challenges when he accepted the position. He urged Harrison to retake Detroit as soon as practical, but Harrison planned to assault Fort Malden once the strait between the two outposts became frozen. The general was concerned that the British could bombard Detroit with cross-river artillery if he attacked that outpost first. Monroe informed Harrison that the president wanted Amherstburg captured and Detroit retaken, but he would defer to Harrison, the commander in the field, to decide how to achieve the administration's goals. In one of his last letters to Harrison, Monroe finally opined that "the delay of a few months is an evil *not* to be compared with the failure of another expedition."[19]

While Monroe and Harrison were debating, Winchester advanced toward the Maumee Rapids, where Harrison intended to gather his men for an attack on Amherstburg. The men marched six miles through a light snow, and on the second day high temperatures melted the snow into slush and mud, which slowed the soldiers' progress. A few days into the journey, a snowstorm dumped twenty-four inches of snow and halted the expedition. The soldiers cleared holes in the snow, built fires, and waited out the storm. Once the snow stopped, Winchester allocated three sleds per company to carry flour, blankets, and other supplies. The men hacked out roads with axes. Packhorses pulled the sleds, but the bitterly cold weather and lack of forage drained the animals, and they collapsed during the march. Men grabbed the sled lines and towed the supplies through two feet of snow to their destination—an incredible feat for volunteers unaccustomed to the rigors of marching. The soldiers erected new storehouses and expanded old ones along the route.[20]

On January 10, 1813, Winchester's men arrived at the Maumee Rapids, and they constructed a fort on the river's north bank. A few days later two strangers arrived in camp and told Winchester that Native Americans threatened to burn their homes at Frenchtown, a small village on the River Raisin. Other citizens told the general that two British companies had moved into the village. Winchester had no authority to advance past the rapids, but Harrison, sixty miles away, could not be consulted. Winchester met with his officers, and they unanimously agreed to march to the town, even without Harrison's approval. The volunteers' enlistments would expire soon and Winchester believed they would only reenlist if combat was likely.[21]

Winchester ordered Colonel William Lewis with 550 men under Majors George Madison and Benjamin Graves toward Frenchtown, and he later directed Colonel John Allen with 110 men to support their attack. They departed the morning of January 17 and marched eight miles across packed snow to the small village of Presque Isle. The next day they moved along Lake Erie's frozen shores toward Frenchtown. Around noon, they laid their blankets on the snow, ate a quick lunch, and Lewis formed his men for battle. "You have the double character of Americans and Kentuckians to sustain," he told them, "do so, and all will be well."[22]

At 2:00 p.m. on January 18, the Americans crossed the frozen Raisin River and charged up the riverbank into the village. Their stealthy approach surprised the small guard. The Native Americans fled through the town, trailed by their pursuers. They moved to establish a defensive position at a fence two hundred yards from the forest's edge, but William Orlando Butler, an Ohio volunteer, collected ten men, sprinted toward the fence, and arrived there before the enemy. The Native Americans retreated into the safety of the forest.[23]

The Americans, energized by their quick victory, followed the Native Americans into the woodlands. The Kentuckians, armed with their accurate long rifles and knowledge of bush warfare, "gave them Indian play," as one recalled, by using trees and logs for cover to snipe at the enemy. Over 3.5

hours, the two sides skirmished in the dense forest. The Native Americans retreated a mile and a half into the woods, but they inflicted serious casualties among their pursuers. One soldier believed that the Kentuckians were outmatched in the forest. "We fought under great disadvantages," the soldier recalled, "most of us being unacquainted with the Indian mode of warfare." By nightfall, the Kentuckians called off the pursuit and brought their dead and wounded back to the village. Despite the casualties, spirits were high at Frenchtown. The famished men drank cider, dined on apples, corn, and beef, and saw women for the first time in months. The "sight of a women is not the most uncomely object that can be conceived of," one soldier remembered.[24]

Winchester disliked the defensive position there, but he refused to abandon the village. He wanted to honor his promise to protect the townspeople, and he did not possess the means to evacuate his wounded. "The ground I am compelled to occupy," he wrote Harrison, "is not very favourable for defence . . . but it is my only alternative unless I abandon the protection of the village." Harrison, who learned about the victory on January 19, directed reinforcements to Frenchtown. Harrison dispatched Captain Nathaniel Hart, Henry Clay's brother-in-law, to tell Winchester "to hold the ground . . . at any rate."[25]

Winchester did little to prepare the town or his men for a possible attack. He did not order the militia to chop down trees to strengthen the palisade or to build breastworks. The men camped with the frozen river at their backs instead of placing themselves behind the river, which would have provided a better defensive position. Colonel Samuel Wells, commander of the right wing, decided to encamp outside the pickets, and Winchester did not order him to move to a safer location. The campsite contained no natural or artificial structures that the men could hide behind during an assault.

Winchester established his headquarters across the River Raisin from the army's encampment in Frenchtown. The distance of his headquarters to the frontlines would inhibit him from quickly organizing his men if under attack. Inexplicably, Winchester moved his army's cartridges to his headquarters, which would prevent them from being quickly distributed during the battle. The general spoke "contemptuously of an attack from the Indians," Wells recalled, and he did not believe that any preparations were necessary. That evening Wells, despite his crucial position as an officer in Seventeenth

US Infantry, departed Frenchtown to meet Harrison rather than stay with his troops. His soldiers did not build any defenses in his absence.[26]

On January 21, a friendly Canadian from Fort Amherstburg told Winchester that the British intended to attack his position. The general dismissed the story. He believed that it would take British colonel Henry Procter more than two days to collect an army and march on the town. The Kentuckians drank whiskey late into the night. Winchester did not direct any sentries to be placed on the main road or dispatch patrols to scout around the camp.[27]

Procter, in fact, moved with uncharacteristic speed when he learned about Winchester's advance. He decided to march immediately to the village with his entire force to stamp out the right wing of Harrison's split forces. Lieutenant Colonel Thomas Bligh St. George interrupted a dance at Mrs. Draper's Tavern. "My boys," he told the dancers, "you must prepare to dance to a different tune; the enemy is upon us, and we are going to surprise them . . . get ready at once." Early on January 19, Procter's men departed on the eighteen-mile march to Frenchtown. His column included 500 regulars and militia, 800 Native Americans under Wyandot Chiefs Roundhead and Walk-in-the-Water, some marines, and three 3-pounders. He left a handful of men to guard Amherstburg. The men marched across the frozen Detroit River, where the wheels of the artillery and the Native Americans' war chants reverberated across the ice. The long snake-like trail of men marched around ice-covered cliffs as the sun gleamed off their polished weapons. The column crossed the frozen edges of Lake Erie to Brownstown where they received reinforcements, including the small detachment that had escaped from Frenchtown.[28]

A bitter cold, quiet morning dawned on the morning of January 22 at Frenchtown. Thick mist rose from the river and from the snow-covered fields surrounding the town. Concealed within the mist, Procter formed his men into battle and deployed a cannon on each flank and one in the center of his line. At 6:00 a.m., American drums began beating the morning reveille. Sleepy Kentuckians emerged from their blankets to hear the "boom" of British artillery fire. One soldier awoke in a small house, looked out the window, and witnessed cannonballs flying into the village. "To Arms! To Arms!" echoed throughout the camp. An American sentry shot a British grenadier from the Forty-First through the ear in what was probably the first casualty of the battle. Major Madison's men grabbed their guns, darted to the picket fence, and fired at the enemy and "for a considerable time it was one continued roar."[29]

Procter's compact line offered a visible target for the sharpshooting Kentuckians concealed behind a palisade. "Resting their [the Kentuckians'] rifles on the breastwork by which they were covered," one of Procter's soldiers recalled, "the Americans fought under every advantage." They fired at the men operating the British cannon in the center of the line. Some gunners dropped and others fled. Frustrated British private Shadrach Byfield could not locate the hidden Americans, but he soon identified an enemy soldier behind the fence. "There is a man," he told a friend. "I'll have a shot at him." As Byfield pulled the trigger, a musket ball entered around his neck. He collapsed and on the way down accidently cut his friend's leg with his bayonet. "Byfield is dead," his friend said. "I believe I be," he replied. His colleagues carried him to a barn where a doctor wrapped a torn shirt around his neck. He miraculously survived after the surgeon dug the ball out from his shoulder. Like Byfield, American fire wounded other men in Procter's line, and many of them sought cover in nearby woods.[30]

In the turmoil, the British left the 3-pounder unguarded about twenty yards from the fence. Some Americans leapt the palisade to grab the cannon, but stiff fire drove them back. A brave British naval lieutenant, Robert Irvine, sprinted forward amidst heavy fire and grabbed the cannon's drag rope. A musket ball pieced his heel and his boot filled with blood, but he still brought the gun back to the safety of the British line.[31]

While Major Madison's Kentuckians at the palisade were holding off Procter's attack, Colonel Samuel Wells's men struggled to maintain their exposed position in the open field. Kentuckians, armed with slow-firing rifles were no match in an open expanse against smoothbore-armed British regulars who could fire twice as many bullets per minute. Meanwhile, Chief Roundhead's Native American warriors darted past the left flank of Wells's men and soon had them surrounded. The American line began to crumble. Colonels William Lewis and John Allen tried to rally the men behind the riverbank, but the Native Americans surrounded them. Captain James Mead yelled, "My brave fellows, charge upon them," but the Native Americans killed him, and the men began a panicked retreat. At this point General Winchester appeared on his horse. He ordered the retreating men in a "voice not loud," as one remembered, to form under the cover of the river's north bank. Few of the soldiers listened. Chief Roundhead's Native Americans infiltrated the town and blocked passages of retreat.[32]

A haphazard, panicked retreat was the worst choice that the Seventeenth Infantry could have made in the face of Chief Roundhead's warriors. They should have located a defensible position behind the village to organize a last stand, but the scared citizen-soldiers did not have the discipline to execute such a maneuver. The Seventeenth fled down the village's main road, but the Native Americans, who had blocked the exits, shot the men as they tried to escape. Captain James Price and his company of Jessamine Blues ran the bloody gauntlet. Just days before, Price had written his wife: "Teach my boy to love the truth. Never let him run about on Sabbath days, fishing . . . [and] not a day must be lost in teaching him how to work." Price ran his sword through a Native American, but others swarmed and scalped him. Eight men in his company died and thirty escaped.[33]

The men who survived the village retreat arrived at a field behind Frenchtown. Some of them removed their shoes to run "Indian style," but most floundered in the deep snow. "The pursuit was then very hot," as one soldier recalled. Native Americans captured General Winchester, Colonel Lewis, and the general's son just as they cleared the open field. Chief Roundhead stripped the general down to his nightshirt before delivering him to Procter. Another group, under Lieutenant Ashton Garrett, laid down their arms once surrounded by Native Americans. The Native Americans retrieved the guns and killed nineteen of the twenty men who surrendered. Only Garrett survived because the Native Americans could trade American officers for valuable commodities. Meanwhile, an exhausted Colonel Allen, a newly elected Kentucky congressman, sat on a log resigned to his fate. A Native American chief advanced to take him prisoner. But a second man threatened Allen, and the colonel slashed him to death with his sword. A third Native American shot Allen dead. After the carnage, the warriors tied corpses and scalps to their horses and gave the war whoop along the village road. One witness said that in one hundred yards nearly one hundred men died by the tomahawk. "For nearly two miles along the road," a British soldier recalled, "the snow was covered with the blood and bodies of the slain."[34]

The Seventeenth Infantry fled for their lives, but Major Madison's 384 Kentuckians still defended their position at the palisade. They repulsed three enemy charges, but the soldiers ran low on ammunition. Officers darted along the line, distributing the few remaining cartridges. The skilled Kentucky riflemen aimed carefully to ensure that every bullet hit its target. At one point, the British and their Native American allies tried to storm a barn located 150 yards from the palisade. Major Madison, who observed the movement, called for volunteers to burn the barn down. William Orlando Butler grabbed a firebrand, raced to the barn, and set some straw on fire. He returned through a hail of bullets, but he stopped halfway to survey his handiwork. The fire burned too slowly, and Butler returned to the barn to add more straw. Once the fire properly ignited, he fled back toward his line. Musket ball holes covered his clothes but miraculously he survived the daring act.[35]

Procter, who made little headway in dislodging the Kentuckians, moved most of his men to the safety of nearby woods. His artillery continued firing two cannons toward the palisade, but the fire had little effect because the Kentuckians shot anyone who approached the guns. The British also tried to drag a sleigh toward the cannon, but the Kentuckians, believing it was ammunition, fired at the men. A lull in the battle occurred, and Major Madison's men passed bread around the lines.[36]

To Colonel Procter, this small group of Kentuckians proved to be quite a nuisance. He already had the town surrounded and had routed most of Winchester's force, even capturing the general. He wanted to return to Amherstburg quickly in case Harrison attacked that garrison in his absence. He told General Winchester that the Kentuckians should surrender or he would burn the town to the ground.

Major Madison's men cheered when they saw a man carrying a white flag approaching from the British line. They believed that Procter wanted to end the fighting and ask for terms. To their surprise, General Winchester's son carried the flag and told them that the general had surrendered them without conditions to the enemy. "It was like a shock of lightning from one end of the line to the other," one of Madison's soldiers recalled. "A number declared that they would never submit, let the consequences be what they might." Madison, as Winchester's subordinate, should have agreed to the capitulation immediately, but instead he demanded conditions from Procter. He knew the Native Americans would massacre the wounded, and they would probably kill those captured by the British too. Madison refused to surrender. "Sir, do you mean to dictate to me?" Procter responded. "No," replied Madison, "I mean to dictate for myself, and we prefer selling our lives as dear as possible, rather than be massacred in cold blood." Procter eventually agreed to Madison's terms. He promised that his men would be protected from the Native Americans and that he would send sleds the next day to bring the wounded to Amherstburg. The Kentuckians laid down their arms and surrendered their sidearms. "Well, you have taken the greatest set of game cocks that ever came from Kentucky," one man told a British soldier.[37]

Procter organized his men and his 500 walking prisoners of war for the eighteen-mile march from Frenchtown to Amherstburg. The Americans' ragtag look repulsed the British regulars. "The appearance of the American prisoners captured at Frenchtown was miserable to the last degree," one soldier recalled. "They had the air of men to whom cleanliness was a virtue unknown." The Americans wore summer linens instead of wool coats and carried giant knives, which "gave them an air of wildness and savageness."[38]

At Frenchtown, eighty wounded Americans peered out of windows and doors, watching the long column disappear across the river, and an eerie stillness descended in the town. "We passed the night under the most serious apprehensions of being massacred by the tomahawk or consumed in the flames," one soldier recalled. Procter left only one British Indian agent, Captain William Elliot with three interpreters, to guard the prisoners. Elliot told one Kentuckian that the camp's safety did not require guards because the Native Americans had departed, but he also told him that the Kentuckian should stay in a house or the Native Americans might shoot him. Dr. John Todd, a Kentucky surgeon and uncle of Mary Todd Lincoln, remained at the village to treat the wounded as Elliot departed that afternoon.[39]

Despite rumors of an attack, the wounded survived the night unmolested. One hour before sunrise, Dr. Todd observed the three interpreters leave town. At daylight, the wounded men awaited the arrival of the promised sleds to bring them to Amherstburg. Instead of sleds, however, 100 to 200 Native Americans came into view. Dr. Todd recognized a Native American from the day before. "Why are the surgeons and wounded left [behind at the village]?" the Native American asked Todd. "It is the wish of Colonel Procter that we remain here until he can send for us," Todd responded. The Native American shook his head and said that the British were "damned rascals or we would have been taken off the preceding day." He told Dr. Todd to be quiet because the Native Americans were in council and they might decide to kill only the wounded.[40]

The war party let loose on the village. They lit homes on fire and stormed into the flames looking for scalps. "I saw my fellow soldiers, naked and wounded, crawling out of the houses to avoid being consumed by the flames," one man recalled. The men who escaped the flames were tomahawked or thrown back into them to burn to death. Captain Hart, who before the battle carried Harrison's message to Winchester, paid one hundred dollars to a Native American to escort him to Amherstburg. On their way to the garrison, the escort clubbed Hart to death and stole his money. Native Americans killed thirty to sixty Americans and captured some prisoners, which they traded for whiskey and other goods.[41]

Dr. Todd later arrived in Amherstburg where he encountered Captain Elliot. He told Elliot about the situation at the village and begged him to send some men and sleds. "It is now too late," Elliot replied. "You may rest assured that those who are once taken by the Indians are safe and will be taken to Malden, and those who are badly wounded are killed." He also told Todd that "charity begins at home"—meaning that he needed care for his own wounded first—but the massacre troubled him. "It is impossible to restrain the savages," he told him.[42]

Harrison later denied giving permission for Winchester to encamp at the village, and he attempted to avoid blame for the defeat. He wrote Kentucky governor Isaac Shelby, whose citizens had suffered the most in the affair, that "the detachment to the River Raisin was made without my knowledge or consent." Harrison told Monroe that he had not heard from Winchester and believed that the general's force became stuck in the snow. Once he learned about Winchester's intentions, he sent reinforcements to his aid, but they arrived too late. The general understood that the defeat would hurt the morale of his men, who were already living in difficult conditions, and the enlistments of many of his Kentucky and Ohio militia would expire in mid-February. Harrison needed them to reenlist because he could not assault Fort Malden before their enlistments expired.[43]

Colonel Procter probably never intended to honor the agreement with Major Madison. He did not leave the promised guard nor did he send any sleds the next morning. In his report to General Roger Sheaffe, commander of

British forces in Upper Canada, Procter does not mention that he consented to terms with Madison in order to gain the Americans' surrender, only noting that the American army surrendered "at discretion," or unconditionally. He applauded the bravery of his Native American allies but acknowledged that "I had much difficulty in bringing the Indians to consent to the sparing of these lives." He understood that tribal culture called for revenge of fallen comrades and that the only way to prevent this violence would have been to post a strong guard and leave supplies of whiskey, weapons, and other goods that could be traded for the lives of the wounded. But Procter did neither, and he was aware of what the consequences would be. When Governor-in-Chief Prevost learned about the battle, he reminded Procter that he needed to control his Native American allies. Another British official commented, "I wish to god it [the massacre] could be contradicted!"[44]

Despite Procter's heavy casualties (his regulars suffered a 40 percent casualty rate), news of his victory spread through Canada, and Prevost promoted him to brigadier general. General Winchester, who was later paroled, deflected blame for the defeat and massacre. He wrote Acting Secretary of War Monroe that "however unfortunate may seem the affair of yesterday, I am flattered by a belief, that no material error is chargeable upon myself." Of the four hundred men on the right wing, only thirty-five escaped to Harrison's camp on the rapids. Probably 350 Americans died in the action or massacre. When Harrison learned of the defeat, he dispatched 170 men toward Frenchtown to support the stragglers trying to return to his camp. He recalled the men when he learned that everyone had been killed or taken prisoner.[45]

For weeks, the small village at Frenchtown showed the scars of the massacre. Hogs and dogs gnawed at unburied corpses that lay scattered around the village. The animals dashed around the field with arms, legs, and skulls in their mouths. "The hogs appear to be rendered mad by so profuse a diet of Christian flesh," one observer noted. When news reached Kentucky, the state's citizens mourned its lost souls. One newspaper editorial said that "the murders at the River Raisin have excited a spirit that cannot be quelled. To avenge her darling sons, Kentucky is again pouring forth her thousands of volunteers . . . [and] . . . a just revenge will be exacted of the allied assassins." William Orlando Butler, who burned down the barn amidst gunfire, survived the massacre, and wrote a poem to honor those killed at the battle.[46]

Death is his sleep by Erie's wave,
Of Raisin's snow we heap his grave!
Oh many hopes lie murdered here,
The mother's joy, the father's pride,
The country's boast, the foreman's fear,
In wilder'd havoc, side by side.[47]

And a slogan spread through the Old West: "Remember the River Raisin!"

After Winchester's defeat, General William Henry Harrison withdrew his force to the Maumee Rapids. In February 1813, he ordered his chief engineer, Charles Gratiot, to abandon Fort Winchester and construct a new outpost on the south bank of the Maumee River. The new location stood prominently on a hilltop overlooking the water, which flowed three hundred yards away. When Harrison's chief engineer became ill during the construction of the fort, engineer Eleazer Wood overtook the effort. Wood graduated in 1806 from the US Military Academy at West Point and served as an engineer under Harrison. West Point had only been established four years earlier, but the curriculum's emphasis on mathematics prepared many of its students to be successful engineers in the army.

Harrison's men built the fort under trying circumstances. Rain poured on the laborers as they cleared three hundred yards of oak and beech trees in freezing temperatures. Axes could not penetrate the frozen ground, but they still managed to drive 2,500 yards of pickets into the earth. "We fell to work to bury ourselves as fast as possible," Wood recalled. Once completed, the newly christened Fort Meigs contained eight blockhouses and four batteries. After reinforcements arrived, the garrison contained 1,200 defenders.[48]

Harrison's decision to erect a sturdy outpost would play an important role in the US government's plan to regain control of the Northwest. Newly minted Brigadier General Henry Procter, whom Prevost promoted after the victory at Frenchtown, departed Amherstburg in late April to attack Harrison's army. On April 23, Procter's force of one thousand men—half regulars, half militia—crammed on board six vessels to rendezvous at the Maumee Rapids with Tecumseh and 1,200 Native American warriors. They arrived six days later outside of Fort Meigs, where Procter established camp at an old British garrison, south of the American outpost. Procter ordered his soldiers to erect two artillery batteries that could pound the American garrison. On

April 30, British engineers completed the first battery where they placed two 24-pounders and an 8-inch howitzer. The engineers also completed the second position, which contained two 12-pounders and two 5.5-inch mortars.

In response to the British artillery threat, Harrison ordered his men to build a protective earth wall—a grand traverse—that extended the length of the camp. Despite heavy rains, the men erected the dirt shield behind a line of white canvas tents that concealed their activity from the British. On May 1, Procter's gunners began firing at Fort Meigs. Harrison's men removed the tents to reveal the 20-foot-high and 300-yard-long earthwork. Undeterred, Procter's artillerists bombarded the fort from the first two batteries. Procter also ordered a third battery constructed on the east side of the outpost, on the south side of the river.[49]

Cannonballs flew into the garrison day and night. A detail-oriented soldier recorded the number of shots fired by the British each day of the siege:

May 1: 256 during the day, 4 times at night
May 2: 457 times during the day, 4 times at night
May 3: 516 times during the day, 47 times at night
May 4: 207 times during the day and 15 times at night
May 5: 143 times during the day.[50]

Harrison's men climbed into makeshift holes in the traverse and covered them with wood planks and mud. Most of the incoming cannon fire landed in the mud and exploded upwards, over the traverse. When the British fired their cannon at night, sleeping Americans darted from their tents and lay on the ground to avoid the shells. Fatigue soon overcame fear and the soldiers slept through the night alarms. One Kentuckian stood on top of an earthwork to estimate the trajectory of the cannonballs from Procter's guns. He shouted the anticipated impact points of the shells to allow the men in the targeted area to seek cover. He performed this noble duty until, as one observer noted, the Kentuckian stood in silence because he could not identify the direction of one of the shells; it was a direct hit on him.[51]

The Kentuckians sniped at Tecumseh's warriors, who climbed into nearby trees to fire into the fort. "Their [Native Americans] hanging about the camp, and occasionally coming pretty near," one Kentuckian recalled, "kept our lines almost constantly in a blaze of fire; for nothing can please a Kentuckian better than to get a shot at an Indian—and he must be indulged." Harrison, whose gunners lacked ammunition, offered a gill of whiskey to anyone who retrieved an undamaged, 12-pound cannonball inside the fort.[52]

After four days of the bombardment, Harrison's force suffered only ten killed and nineteen wounded, a small number of casualties for such an intense artillery barrage. Harrison awaited the arrival of General Green Clay, whose regiment traveled to Fort Meigs to reinforce the garrison. One of Harrison's scouts volunteered to communicate with Clay, and he successfully eluded Procter's cordon around the fort. The scout found Clay and told him that Harrison requested that Clay's men spike Procter's guns, withdraw across the river, and conduct a fighting advance into the fort.[53]

At 9:00 a.m. on May 5, Colonel William Dudley, who served under Clay, brought his 800-man regiment without detection to the north side of the heights and spiked eleven guns at Procter's northern batteries without losing a man. Procter, who established his headquarters distant from the fort, did not dispatch reinforcements in time to stop Dudley's operation. One of Dudley's three columns, however, loitered around the guns and started a firefight with Native Americans in the tree line. Harrison and his officers signaled to Dudley to retreat, but the men believed that the general was cheering on their victory. "They are lost! They are lost!" Harrison yelled. The Native Americans' fire battered the men, which forced Dudley to deploy his right column to save them. The fighting intensified and shifted from the meadow into the forest. The Native Americans surrounded the column and fired from behind trees and logs, and the Americans haphazardly charged into the woods. Dudley ordered the men to retreat, and the Native Americans pursued them relentlessly. "No human means within the control of this unfortunate officer [Dudley] could save him," engineer Eleazer Wood remembered. The quick skirmish, known as the Battle of the Maumee, resulted in sixty killed from Dudley's group, but the remainder escaped to Fort Meigs. Native Americans killed and scalped Dudley.[54]

The British marched Dudley's men under guard to Fort Miami, located northeast across the river from Fort Meigs, where gunboats would transport them to Amherstburg. As they approached the fort, two lines of Native Americans formed a human gateway into the garrison. The warriors stripped the men of their clothing and whipped, shot, and tomahawked those dashing through the gauntlet. One survivor, Joseph Underwood, recalled that he "dashed off as fast as I was able." He sprinted at an angle through the

Figure 4. ***Tecumseh Saving Prisoners.*** After the Battle of Frenchtown, the British marched American prisoners to Fort Miami, where some Native Americans began killing the survivors. Tecumseh observed the carnage and demanded that the Native Americans desist from the violence. His actions saved many prisoners' lives that day and helped shape a positive and gallant image among Americans. One American officer later stated that "Tecumseh [is] more humane than his ally and employer [Britain]." Courtesy of the Library of Congress, LC-USZ62-46488 DLC.

corridor in the hope that the Native Americans' gunfire would miss him. The man in front of Underwood fell dead and Underwood tripped over the corpse. He raised himself and sprinted into the fort. As Underwood and the other prisoners crammed into Fort Miami, the Native Americans followed them into the outpost, clubbing and scalping the trapped men, until a loud voice echoed over the carnage. "For shame to desist," Tecumseh yelled. "It is a disgrace to kill a defenceless prisoner." Tecumseh rode through the fort with a raised tomahawk, threatening to kill the next Native American who murdered a prisoner. The warriors ceased the bloodletting. American officers praised Tecumseh for saving lives on that day. They believed that the Shawnee warrior possessed more humanity, honor, and integrity than Procter. "Tecumseh [is] more humane than his ally and employer," one American officer recalled, as he "generously interfered and prevented further massacre." The Native Americans killed roughly forty Americans before Tecumseh's intervention. Between the River Raisin and Fort Meigs, the Kentuckians paid a steep price for answering their state's call.[55]

On May 6, Procter tried to bluff Harrison into surrendering. Unlike General William Hull, Harrison refused to capitulate without a fight. "Tell General Procter," Harrison replied, "if he takes this fort, it will be under circumstances that will do him more honor than a thousand surrenders." The British continued the bombardment, but Procter's militia and Native Americans lost interest in the protracted siege and returned home. The next day Procter decided to withdraw to Amherstburg. He branded the campaign a success with his victory at the Battle of the Maumee, but Fort Meigs remained in American hands and Harrison's army threatened Britain's hold on the region.[56]

Throughout the summer, Procter suffered severe supply shortages at Amherstburg. American military success further east had destroyed a significant amount of ordnance, guns, rations, and other materials destined for Procter's men. Thousands of Native Americans and their families gathered outside Amherstburg demanding meat, weapons, and gifts. "In short," Procter wrote Brigadier General John Vincent, commander of British troops in the Niagara peninsula, "our wants are so serious that the enemy must derive great advantage from them alone." Prevost understood Procter's plight, but he had his own supply and manpower concerns. "You cannot be ignorant of the limited nature of the force at my disposal," Prevost wrote Procter in August, "for the defence of an extensive frontier & *ought therefore* not to count too largely upon my disposition to strengthen the right division." Prevost dispatched the Second Battalion of the Forty-First Regiment to Amherstburg, but he told Procter to seize his own supplies from the enemy. Procter eyed the supplies at Fort Stephenson, a thinly defended outpost on the Sandusky River in modern Fremont, Ohio. He could seize American supplies there and also placate his tribal allies who demanded that he attack the outpost. "I thus with all the Responsibility resting on me, was obliged to yield to Circumstances I could not possibly have prevented," Procter recalled.[57]

Twenty-one-year-old Major George Croghan of the Seventeenth US Infantry commanded Fort Stephenson, an old trading post erected in 1806. Since that time, the outpost had undergone numerous improvements, including in 1812 by Colonel Mills Stephenson, for whom the fort was named. In June 1813, Harrison directed that outpost's defenses be further strengthened. Under the direction of engineer Wood, the fort's size was expanded to 300 feet east–west and 150 feet north–south. They left a blockhouse intact that sat protruding from the northern wall of the fort. Croghan added to Wood's work by directing his men to dig an eight-foot trench around the fort and to reinforce the palisades. By July 1813, Fort Stephenson retained clear fields of fire and robust palisades to protect the men from shelling. The major commanded 160 regulars and a 6-pounder named "Good Bess."[58]

Harrison believed that the small outpost could not withstand Procter's assault. He ordered Croghan to set fire to the fort and march to Camp Seneca, Ohio, Harrison's headquarters. When Croghan received Harrison's letter, the Native Americans had already blocked his line of retreat from the fort. Croghan elected to remain in the outpost, rather than withdraw, so his men could fight the enemy from behind a fortification. He correctly reasoned that if they withdrew from the site the Native Americans would ambush and defeat them. The plan was a life-saving, smart decision by a twenty-one-year-old, and one that Harrison, a frontier fighter, should have appreciated. "I have just received your letter of yesterday," Croghan wrote Harrison on July 30, "ordering me to destroy this place and make good my retreat, which was too late to be carried into execution. We have determined to maintain this place, and by heavans [*sic*] we can." Harrison, who expected his subordinates to follow instructions, was unmoved. He relieved Croghan of command and ordered him to Camp Seneca to explain his insubordination: "I had ordered it [Fort Stephenson] to be abandoned. The order was not obeyed."[59]

On August 1, 1813, Procter's 500 British regulars and 400 Native Americans arrived at the fort to demand Croghan's surrender. The major refused to capitulate. Robert Dickson, the British Indian agent, told Croghan's emissary, Second Lieutenant Edmund Shipp, that he could not restrain the savages once they attacked the fort. "When the fort shall be taken there will be none to massacre," Shipp responded. A nearby Potawatomi reached for the lieutenant's sword during the discussion, and Shipp almost killed him before Dickson intervened. "Shipp," Croghan shouted from the fort, "come in, and we will blow them all to Hell."[60]

The next afternoon British gunboats from the Sandusky River and a 5.5-inch howitzer opened up on the outpost. Procter's gunners also mounted five 6-pounders in a ravine north of the stockade. More than 500 cannonballs landed in the garrison over a twenty-four hour period. Wood's design and construction of the fort protected most of the men from the shelling. Procter directed that three 6-pounders fire at the fort's northwest angle to create a breech in the fort's walls. Croghan ordered sand and flour bags stacked at the corner. Cannonballs harmlessly landed against the bags, and the palisade held.[61]

At 4:00 p.m., three 120-man British columns advanced to the fort. Colonel William Short, Procter's brother-in-law, led a column toward the northwest angle and another unit conducted a diversion on the fort's opposite side. Short's men approached within twenty paces of the palisade. Croghan's Kentuckians poured a stream of rifle fire into the group. British soldiers dropped dead and wounded as thick smoke covered the landscape. Short's column wavered and many of his men fled. Colonel Short, undeterred, urged his men to follow: "Cut away the pickets, my brave boys, and show the damned Yankees no quarter!" A bullet hit Short as he descended into the ravine and he died. The remainder of his column leapt into the ditch and chopped at the pickets with axes and sabers.[62]

Unbeknownst to the British, Croghan positioned "Good Bess" inside the blockhouse that protruded from the north wall. His gunners placed the cannon where it overlooked the fort's vulnerable northwest corner, where Procter was likely to attack. They concealed the gunport so the British would be unaware of the cannon's presence, and they loaded a half charge of powder and a double charge of slugs and grapeshot into the gun—a combination that would decimate nearby troops. At this critical moment, Croghan's men unmasked the blockhouse porthole, lit the cannon's fuse, and the 6-pounder unleashed balls and slugs at the packed British soldiers who lined the ditch. The cannon's fire wreaked havoc on Short's men. "The Fort, from which the severest Fire I ever saw was maintained during the Attack, was well defended," Procter reported after the assault.[63]

At 9:00 p.m., after two hours of fighting, Procter ordered a cease-fire. With mounting losses and no sign of progress, he decided to withdraw to Amherstburg. Many of his men, however, remained trapped outside the fort. Some hid under dead bodies in the ditch; others risked sprinting out of the death zone. The wounded called out for water. Some nearby Americans lowered water down to the stricken men. Others chose a less comforting approach toward their enemy. British private Shadrach Byfield, who had been shot at Frenchtown, lay in the ditch with his comrades. "Now we have done the best we could," Byfield told a soldier next to him, and "they [the British officers] are all going to leave us." An American overheard Byfield and responded, "I know your men are going away, but never mind my brave fellows, when they are gone I will come out and take you in and use you well." Byfield decided to try his luck and escape. He darted to the top of the ditch, and muzzle flashes erupted from the fort. He dropped flat, rose again, and darted to the British lines. There he encountered General Procter at one of the British batteries.[64]

"Where are all the rest of the men?" Procter asked Byfield. "I don't think there are any more to come, they are all killed or wounded," Byfield replied. "Good God, what shall I do about the men?" Procter said.[65]

At the Battle of Fort Stephenson, the British incurred ninety-six casualties, and Croghan saved the fort and suffered only one dead and seven wounded. Harrison, furious that Croghan ignored his orders, still appreciated his brave effort. "It will not be among the least of General Procter's mortification, to find that he has been baffled by a youth, who has just passed his twenty first year," Harrison wrote newly appointed secretary of war John Armstrong.[66]

6

America Seizes the Niagara Frontier

*It seemed that the heavans [*sic*] and earth were coming together.*
—Dr. Trowbridge to John Trowbridge, May 1814, *The Trowbridge Genealogy*

Much of William Henry Harrison's success in western Upper Canada depended on American actions further east. Britain still controlled Lake Ontario, Lake Erie, and the Niagara frontier, and could move men and supplies unimpeded across these maritime routes. Harrison, in contrast, received supplies that traversed an unreliable route through swamp and wilderness. One newspaper noted in the fall of 1812, "The British having complete undisturbed possession of the Lakes . . . move their armies with astonishing rapidity."[1] Of the waterways that made up the Great Lakes, none was more important than Lake Ontario.

Lake Ontario occupied a central piece of the 1,700-mile artery that ran across the northern border of the United States. The lake enabled supplies from Quebec, Montreal, Burlington, and York to travel into the Niagara River to Lake Erie, where they would eventually reach Amherstburg and Mackinac Island. The waterway also allowed communication between Kingston, a port on the lake's east side, with points west at York, Burlington, and along the Niagara River. Britain invested in its dockyards at Kingston and York to protect the lake because land travel could not substitute for waterborne transport. The 150-mile road from Kingston to York, which curved along the northern rim of the lake, could not handle wagons most of the year, which made the trail useless for moving ordnance or large amounts of military provisions. British officers could march their men on the road, but they suffered from the journey. Later in 1813, when American ships could travel safely on Lake Ontario, Governor-in-Chief Prevost noted, "The command of the lake enables the enemy to perform in two days what it takes troops from Kingston 16 to 20 days of severe marching; their men arrive fresh, the others fatigued and with an exhausted equipment."[2]

US secretary of the navy Paul Hamilton did little to strengthen the navy's position on the lake. The secretary directed most of his attention to the country's ocean-going fleet, which had provided the only positive storylines for America in 1812. In August of that year, the USS *Constitution* defeated the HMS *Guerrière*, and in October, the *United States* forced the British vessel *Macedonian* to strike its colors. Britain ultimately retained control of the US seaboard, and the two engagements, though they provided nice headlines, did not influence the outcome of the war.

The naval contest that would shape the war's outcome occurred on the Great Lakes, but through 1812, Hamilton retained little interest in the theater. Fortunately for the country, Lieutenant Melancthon Woolsey recognized the need for an American presence on Lake Ontario. He requested military supplies and a full crew for his ship, the eighteen-gun brig *Oneida*, the only US warship available at the start of the conflict. He also bolstered the defenses at Sackets Harbor, New York, and he converted five merchant schooners into gunboats. His small fleet, however, could not compete with the British. The Provincial Marine kept four vessels on Lake Ontario, mounting a total of forty-six carronades, more than enough firepower to defeat the *Oneida*.[3]

After US general Hull's defeat in June 1812, Woolsey received some support for his efforts. President James Madison decided that the country should build fleets on Lakes Erie and Ontario. "The President of the United States," Hamilton wrote Chauncey, "had determined to obtain command of the Lakes Ontario and Erie, with the least possible delay." Hamilton gave Commodore Isaac Chauncey, the American commander in charge of the Great Lakes, wide discretion to hire shipbuilders, buy supplies, and recruit sailors. The commodore's experience prepared him for the task. For the last four years he had commanded the Washington Navy Yard, where some of the navy's best ships had been built or refurbished. Chauncey established his headquarters at Sackets Harbor, and on his first visit there, he was impressed with the condition of the *Oneida*. "I found the *Oneida* in good order," Chauncey wrote Hamilton, "and completely prepared for service." In mid-September, skilled shipwright Henry Eckford arrived in Sackets Harbor with seventy to eighty carpenters to build a supersize lake warship that could contest British control of the waterway. Eckford, a partner in a successful shipbuilding firm, could perform wonders constructing large ships quickly.[4]

As work at Sackets Harbor proceeded, Chauncey directed Lieutenant Jesse Elliot to identify a site on Lake Erie to build two 300-ton ships and convert schooners into gunboats. Elliot selected the harbor at Black Rock, located at the head of the Niagara River, because it was deep enough for larger vessels and the port would protect the fleet in bad weather. American ships, however, would be forced to navigate a treacherous stretch of the Niagara before entering Lake Erie, and British gunners at Fort Erie could fire on ships departing the harbor.[5]

Daniel Dobbins, a longtime Great Lakes merchant captain, soon created a second dockyard on Lake Erie at Presque Isle (Erie), Pennsylvania. Dobbins had been at Michilimackinac when the British captured the fort, and they included Dobbins and his merchant vessel in the surrender terms. The British paroled Dobbins, and he later joined Hull at Detroit, where he was recaptured by the British and sentenced to death as a parole violator. Before he could be executed, he escaped from Fort Malden and arrived safely at his home in Erie, Pennsylvania. After his journey, he traveled to Washington, DC, to advise Hamilton on the situation on the lakes, and the navy secretary, without Chauncey's or Elliot's knowledge, appointed Dobbins sailing master and directed him to build four 40-ton gunboats. Dobbins selected Presque Isle for his harbor because the site could shelter ships from bad weather and its narrow entrance could prevent enemy vessels from sailing into the harbor. Chauncey approved Dobbins's request to build four gunboats and a twenty-gun brig, and he dispatched a master ship designer to Presque Isle. Once Elliot became aware of Dobbins's effort, he wrote angry letters to Chauncey and Dobbins. Elliot now had a civilian competitor on Lake Erie, and Chauncey would be forced to divide the navy's finite resources between them. Elliot also disliked the location at Presque Isle. He believed that its shallow harbors could not admit ships, and he worried that the site could be attacked from British troops at Fort Malden or Fort Erie.[6]

As winter set in, American efforts on Erie became stalled. Transporters could not efficiently transport cannons, guns, and other supplies from New York to Black Rock. The route between the two locations contained navigable riverways from New York City to Seneca Falls, New York, which was 114 miles from the dockyard. Here, transporters unloaded their cargo to trek the remaining distance on a primitive trail. Carts and wagons, loaded with heavy ordnance, could not traverse the 114 miles without significant delays. Eventually Chauncey moved the Lake Erie base to Presque Isle, where supplies from Pittsburgh could reach the dockyard easier than the passage from New York to Black Rock.[7]

Meanwhile, Chauncey focused his efforts on building a fleet to contest British control of Lake Ontario. He ordered ordnance, shipbuilding materials, sailors, shipwrights, and other provisions to Sackets Harbor. Most of his supplies came from the New York Navy Yard, which possessed a large inventory of light and heavy cannons, grape and round shot, arms, and other munitions. Sailors and marines stationed in the yard could also man his ships, and in time more than 700 traveled from New York to Lakes Erie and Ontario. The safe and unimpeded route from the navy yard to Lake Ontario enabled Chauncey to quickly establish an active dockyard at Sackets.

From New York City, men and supplies traveled on the Hudson River to Albany, after which they could travel on land via the Albany–Schenectady turnpike that was completed in 1805. From Schenectady, transporters followed a navigable river system (made navigable by canals) to Oswego, which was located on the shore of Lake Ontario. Once at Lake Ontario, the materials could be snuck into Sackets Harbor using small boats that hugged the shoreline, or Chauncey could send vessels from Sackets Harbor to retrieve the cargo from Oswego.[8]

Eckford and his shipwrights worked quickly at the Sackets Harbor dockyard. In November 1812, they completed the *Madison*, a 590-ton sloop of war with twenty-four 32-pounder carronades, the largest ship on the lake. Henry Eckford's shipbuilding magic constructed the vessel's hull in a remarkable forty-five days. When the sloop launched on November 26, Chauncey gained safe access to the lake. "Nine weeks ago the timber that she [the *Madison*] is composed of was growing in the forest," Chauncey wrote Navy Secretary Paul Hamilton. American superiority on the lake allowed the navy and army to move men and supplies across Lake Ontario. Chauncey could also disrupt the British Commissariat's movements on water and force Britain to use roads to circumvent the lake. In February 1813, one of Chauncey's ships chased a vessel attempting to resupply York from Kingston. One 24-pounder struck the hull, and the ship, which escaped to Kingston, eventually sank in the harbor. The crew tried to salvage the sinking goods, but many were lost or damaged. After the risky attempt, the owner of the provisions noted that "the navigation [on Lake Ontario] was altogether shut to us as nothing would venture out again on the lake." The Commissariat, if unwilling to risk sneaking across the lake, would be forced to use the road from Kingston to York. Merchants charged a steep price to make this difficult journey during the spring or summer, and in the winter, the fee to ship provisions cost more than the goods themselves.[9]

At Kingston, British captain Andrew Gray, an army staff officer, revitalized the Provincial Marine by dismissing an incompetent shipwright and hiring a more capable shipbuilder. His shipyard overhauled the masts of the *Earl of Moira*, and over the winter, the dockyard made progress on a corvette-style craft, the *Wolfe*, which was launched in April 1813, and placed Britain back into the contest for Lake Ontario. Gray lacked the naval ordnance required to properly arm the new ship, so his men mounted cannon from nearby forts onto the vessel. Gray and his successor waited for the arrival of heavy carronades from England to set into the ship's twenty-two gunports, which would enable the vessel to reach its full broadside potential. At Kingston, Gray had access to plenty of local timber, but cannons, round shot, grape, and other materials shipped from Britain. One British journalist described the situation: "Not a shipwright have we, not a seamen, not a bar of iron, not a pound of hemp or pitch or tallow, *nearer at hand than four thousand miles by water, and several hundreds of miles by land* [original emphasis], while the enemy has, the other side of the Lakes, at a distance of a few hundred miles from his Atlantic sea ports, every material for shipbuilding, together with shipwrights and seamen, in abundance." Another Lake Ontario shipyard at York suffered from the mismanagement of a disorganized superintendent. Shipwrights made halting progress on the 30-gun *Sir Isaac Brock*, which was not ready to launch once the ice thawed in the spring.[10]

The new US secretary of war, John Armstrong, who replaced Monroe in February 1813, intended to exploit Chauncey's brief superiority on the lake. With input from General Henry Dearborn and Commodore Isaac

Chauncey, he formed a plan for the army to attack Kingston, a British port on Lake Ontario that served as a harbor for the lake's Provincial Marine. Four thousand troops from Sackets Harbor would march across the frozen St. Lawrence River, thirty-five miles to Kingston to destroy the garrison and the ships wintering there. After Kingston fell, Chauncey and Dearborn would launch a joint army-navy invasion of York (now Toronto), and subsequently the army would overrun British posts on the Niagara River. Armstrong supported the plan because he believed the campaign would force Prevost to choose between abandoning Upper Canada or reinforcing that region with troops from Montreal. If Prevost shifted troops away from that city, their absence would leave Montreal vulnerable to attack. Armstrong correctly believed that a successful attack on Kingston would place Prevost in a "dilemma" where he "either . . . must give up his western posts, or, to save them, he must carry himself in force, and promptly to Upper Canada."[11]

The plan aimed to solidify Chauncey's control of Lake Ontario and the Niagara by destroying the dockyards at Kingston and York and clearing the British from the Niagara region. Chauncey's grip on the lake would be tightened if the army and navy could destroy the ships under construction at York and Kingston. Britain had no alternatives to those shipyards because large-draft combat vessels could not travel from other locations to the lake. Britain needed a shipyard on the lake to build a fleet that could contest Chauncey's squadron.

The American campaign, if successful, would collapse the maritime supply line from Lake Ontario to British posts west of the waterway. The British Commissariat would be forced to circumvent Lake Ontario using the poor road from Kingston that lined the northern rim of the lake to York. Then, from Burlington, they would need to avoid the Niagara frontier by traveling on the route from Burlington to Long Point on Lake Erie. Finally, the road from Montreal to Kingston was only partially complete, so heavy supplies could not be moved by road from Montreal to the Kingston–York road. None of these passages could be relied on to allow the efficient movement of heavy stores, and the presence of a US army in the region would allow its officers to dispatch small units to intercept overland supply movements. The result would be that Britain's outposts at Detroit, Fort Malden, and Mackinac Island would suffer severe supply shortages if the American campaign was successful.[12]

Kingston was the key to the effort. Sir James Yeo, who was en route to assume control of Britain's naval efforts on Lake Ontario, intended to accelerate Britain's shipbuilding operations once he arrived there in May 1813. Armstrong needed to snuff out any chance that Yeo could construct a formidable fleet capable of contesting Chauncey's recent control of Lake Ontario. Kingston, which sat on the confluence of the lake and the St. Lawrence River, also retained a strategic position that controlled access to the lake from the St. Lawrence. Success of the elaborate plan, however, depended on Dearborn, who at sixty-two, and known as "Granny" by his men, showed no talent for generalship. Dearborn had offered his resignation after the failed 1812 campaign, but Eustis refused his offer and ordered him to command the assault in person.

Before Dearborn's troops departed for Kingston, intelligence reports indicated that Prevost had traveled to the harbor with reinforcements and that the garrison now contained 6,000 to 8,000 British regulars. The purpose of Prevost's trip, however, was only to inspect the garrison, which contained 600 regulars and 1,400 militia. Dearborn, concerned that Prevost had reinforced Kingston, began formulating an alternate plan. He believed that his army should instead attack York and afterward assault British forts on the Niagara. Dearborn and Chauncey believed that seizing York and the four ships stationed there would solidify Chauncey's control of Lake Ontario. Chauncey also noted that York contained significant public stores, which would hurt British efforts elsewhere. "By possessing ourselves of these vessels," Chauncey noted to Secretary of the Navy Hamilton, "and taking or destroying all the public stores and munitions of war at York, will give us a decided advantage in the commencement of the campaign." In the campaign's final move, the army would advance on Kingston.[13]

Secretary of War Armstrong agreed with Dearborn's recommendation. In the secretary's mind, York should be easier to seize than Kingston, and the United States could not afford another loss. Prevost's alleged reinforcement of Kingston, Armstrong reasoned, would be at the expense of fortifying posts on the western side of Lake Ontario. "If our first step in the campaign should fail," Armstrong warned Dearborn, "the disgrace of our arms will be complete." Under the new plan, however, American troops would not arrive in Kingston until April or later, which gave Prevost time to reinforce the garrison and finish constructing the harbor's ships in preparation for Yeo's arrival.[14]

Prevost understood that the Americans would likely target York once the ice thawed on the lakes. He hoped that the army could repulse the invasion, but he also wanted his soldiers to be preserved for future operations. "In the event of an attempt at invasion," Prevost wrote Major General Roger Sheaffe in March, "conducted on the principle of his possessing a sufficiency of means for the object, it will be wise to act with such caution as would enable you to husband your resources for future exertion." In other words, Sheaffe should not engage his men in a battle he might lose.[15]

Despite his instructions to Sheaffe, Prevost approved a recommendation by two British lieutenant colonels to launch an assault against the American garrison at Ogdensburg, New York. That garrison had been harassing British ships navigating the St. Lawrence, and American riflemen under Major Benjamin Forsyth launched guerrilla raids into Canada from the outpost. On February 22, 1813, British lieutenant colonel George MacDonnell and five hundred men, dragging three cannon, marched one mile across the frozen St. Lawrence River. Despite heavy snow drifts that obstructed their attack, MacDonnell's men raised bayonets and drove the Americans out of the garrison. MacDonnell's men seized public property, and burned two schooners and two gunboats frozen in the ice. Forsyth retreated to Sackets Harbor, and Ogdensburg never regained an American garrison during the war.[16]

The raid against York would be commanded by Zebulon Montgomery Pike, a household name for most Americans in 1813. Pike's popularity stemmed from expeditions he led into the western United States. In 1806–1807, Pike had led an expedition to locate the headwaters of the Arkansas and Red Rivers in present-day Colorado. His detailed journal, published in 1810, provided readers a glimpse into the beauty, grandeur, and ruggedness of the American West. During the expedition, Pike's expedition discovered "Pike's Peak," which bears his name (though he did not name it himself), but deep snow, tough climbing, and sparse supplies prevented him from ascending it. Pike continued southwest and traveled into northern New Mexico, then Spanish territory, where Spanish troops temporarily imprisoned him.

Though popular as an explorer, soldiering was Pike's real profession. Pike joined the army in 1794 as a private at fifteen. He manned frontier forts in the American West where he displayed bravery and intelligence in leading expeditions from Fort Washington to resupply distant forts. In 1809, the army promoted Pike to lieutenant colonel of the Fourth Regiment, and he trained the forces that fought under Harrison at the Battle of Tippecanoe. In March 1813, the army promoted him to brigadier general under General Dearborn, and Dearborn assigned him the critical role of leading the attack against York.

By April, Lake Ontario's ice flows began to thaw and Chauncey's vessels could depart Sackets Harbor for the first time in months. On April 20, Dearborn's men began loading cannon and soldiers onto his fleet for the attack on York, the first phase of Dearborn's revised plan. The arduous task called for each gun to be dissembled from their caissons and limbers, rowed out in boats to the anchored vessels, and heaved onto the ships. Pike's men boarded in platoons, each man carrying a musket, bayonet, and haversack, among other items. More than 1,600 soldiers and sailors eventually boarded Chauncey's ships, with 600 alone aboard the *Madison*, four times the ship's capacity. Chauncey's fleet—one ship, one brig, and twelve schooners—departed the next day to undertake the first major amphibious operation in US history. Before leaving Sackets Harbor, General Pike wrote his father, "I embark to-morrow in the fleet at Sackett's Harbor at the head of a column of 1,500 choice troops, on a secret expedition. If success attends my steps, honor and glory await my name—if defeat, still shall it be said we died like brave men, and conferred honor, even in death, on the AMERICAN NAME."[17]

At the request of Dearborn, Chauncey ordered the fleet to depart, even though he believed they should remain in port because of a looming storm. As Chauncey predicted, at 2:00 p.m. a giant squall arrived and dumped heavy rain on the fleet just outside the harbor. The windy storm prevented the fleet's further movement and made life miserable for the troops crammed into the vessels. Aboard the schooners, only half of the seamen could fit below the decks, which left many of them without cover from the pelting rain and wind. Chauncey eventually withdrew the fleet back into the harbor to wait out the storm. On April 25, the squadron resumed their journey to York.[18]

The city of York held strategic and symbolic importance for Prevost. York was the provincial capital, and its dockyard was outfitting the thirty-gun frigate *Sir Isaac Brock* and the ten-gun *Duke of Gloucester* in the port. The town also served as a depot for supplies destined for Fort Erie and other parts of Upper Canada. York, however, contained few natural defensible positions, and General Roger Sheaffe required additional cannon and men to fortify the town. The garrison contained only two hundred men. Lieutenant Colonel Ralph Bruyeres, commander of the Royal Engineers in Canada, inspected garrisons throughout Upper Canada and provided recommendations for defensive improvements. When he inspected York in February, he wrote Sheaffe: "I wish I could say as much in favor of the position at York, but I do not think it possible to do anything there with advantage at present. It will require immense labor and expense to make it a strong post, for it does not possess any advantageous feature of ground to work upon. It must be all art, without any assistance of nature." Fortunately for Sheaffe, in late April, two companies of the Eighth Regiment of Foot, including a company of elite grenadiers, stopped at York on their way to Fort George and were in town during the attack.[19]

Prevost knew about York's shortcomings, but he refused Sheaffe's requests for more ordnance and soldiers. In the spring of 1813, Prevost faced difficult decisions in allocating his finite resources between Upper and Lower Canada. Lord Bathurst, secretary of state for war and the colonies, wrote Prevost in June that the Prince Regent, who acted on behalf of the king, approved Prevost's cautious, defensive strategy. "The measures which you have adopted for the defence of the Province," Bathurst told Prevost, "under your command . . . have met with the Royal Highness's approbation. The Prince Regent has been pleased equally to approve of the instructions which you have given to General Sheaffe for the defence of the Upper Province."[20]

In the spring of 1813, British major general Roger Sheaffe was at the peak of his military career. He received a baronetcy after Queenston, and he served as the acting administrative-military leader of Upper Canada. One of Sheaffe's officers recommended that Sir Roger launch a cross-river assault before the enemy became organized, but Sheaffe disagreed. He disliked sending troops on bold, risky missions, and Prevost had instructed him to save his manpower. Sheaffe's methodical, cautious mindset helped him achieve victory at Queenston, and there was little reason to change tactics now.[21]

General Sheaffe eventually collected seven hundred men at York that included two companies of the Eighth Infantry, the Glengarry Light Infantry, and flank companies from York militia, among others. He also possessed three dozen cannon, but few functioned at the time of the battle. One 18-pound battery guarded the main landing, and two 12-pounders covered the Government House. Sheaffe also lost some Provincial Marine sailors who departed for Amherstburg on April 15, which further challenged his manning needs. He lacked enough soldiers to man his cannons and still form a capable infantry force. Surveyor General Thomas Ridout, concerned that the town might be overrun, received Sheaffe's permission to move government papers to a safe location outside of town.[22]

On April 26, 1813, the American fleet approached York. Dearborn and Chauncey gathered the senior officers in the *Madison*'s wardroom to review the plan of attack. Pike, who would command the landing, detailed his plan of attack and expectations in a brigade order. "Every corps will be mindful of the honor of the American army," his order read, "and the disgraces which have recently tarnished our arms." He directed Major Benjamin's Forsyth's riflemen, who would arrive on the beach first, to maintain their ground at all costs. Any man who left his post without orders would be put to "instant death." Pike directed that no soldiers besides the riflemen load their guns because the men would charge the landing with bayonets, "thus letting the enemy see that we can meet them with their own weapons." Pike's order also discussed the importance of respecting private property in York, an issue that would assume more importance than he probably anticipated. Many of the citizens of Canada are "our own countrymen," his orders read, and because the provinces had been forced into the war, their property "must be held sacred." Any soldiers who pillaged private property "shall be punished with death."[23]

At daylight on April 27, a British picket spotted fourteen American ships moving toward York harbor. The morning dawned with a strong breeze, and the soldier peered through his spyglass to observe ships' decks crowded with troops. By 8:00 a.m., Forsyth's 170 riflemen and portions of the Fifteenth and Sixteenth Regiments embarked in two large batteaux and three or four other boats. High winds forced Forsyth's boats west of their preselected site toward a large open field. General Sheaffe dispatched Major James Givins and his Native American warriors to obstruct the landing. The Native Americans followed the boats down the shoreline, stopping occasionally to fire their rifles. "The English blazed away at us," Ned Myers, one of the rowers recalled, "concealed in a wood."[24]

Forsyth ordered his men to lay on their oars, and the helmsmen kept the boats parallel to the shore, about two hundred yards away. He waited to land his men until the first boats carrying Fifteenth Infantry arrived near him. He identified a new landing site and the helmsmen changed course and headed for shore. Major Givins and his Native American allies stood at the waterline and poured a vicious fire into the oncoming craft. Bullets pelted the water like hail. "I confess frankly I did not like the work at all," Myers admitted. "It is no fun to pull in under a sharp fire, with one's back to the enemy, and nothing but an oar to amuse himself with." They landed at a shrub-covered embankment west of town, near an old French fort. Forsyth's crack North Carolinian sharpshooters primed their Model 1803 Harpers Ferry rifles and fired from their boats as they approached the landing site. Chauncey's schooner launched grape and canister shot over Forsyth's men toward the enemy. The riflemen slid off the boats into three feet of water, waded to shore, and rushed up the bank.[25]

Major Givins's Native American warriors greeted the landing with heavy fire, but the Glengarry Light Infantry, ordered to reinforce the Native Americans, became lost on the outskirts of York. Forsyth's men repulsed the unsupported Native Americans and the warriors sought cover. The new landing site, dotted with shrubs and trees, provided the perfect concealment for Forsyth's sharpshooting riflemen to guard the beachhead.[26]

Soon after Givins's assault, Sheaffe ordered the grenadier company of the Eighth Regiment, an elite force of 120 men, to march double-time toward the Americans. The Eighth Regiment, known as the "King's Regiment," had a storied history that included valiant service in Egypt in 1801, where the regiment led an assault against a stout French position in Alexandria. During the War of 1812, the Eighth had already participated in the successful assault on Ogdensburg where it captured two stands of American colors. Donald McClean, a legislative clerk with no military experience, joined McNeal's group with a musket, but he probably could not load his gun. Captain Neal McNeal, an officer beloved by his men, led the regiment.[27]

As the regiment approached Forsyth's riflemen, the sharpshooters sought cover in the nearby woods. The Eighth Regiment, wearing scarlet uniforms, provided visible targets in the forest for the skilled American riflemen. The men aimed with precision, and their guns, accurate up to three hundred yards, rarely missed their mark. The British, armed with inaccurate muskets, could not hit the green-clad North Carolinians, who dodged fire from behind trees and logs.[28]

As the American riflemen and the Eighth Regiment exchanged fire, some companies of the Fifteenth and Sixteenth Infantries landed on the beach and charged the embankment to support Forsyth's men. "Nothing could be heard but the shouts of the rival combatants," one soldier remembered, "the war-whoop of the savages, and the echo of bugles, mingling with the scattered reports of musketry." As the men crested the bank, the grenadiers fired at the approaching enemy and surged with a bayonet charge. The infantrymen dashed below the embankment to seek cover. Bullets whizzed over their heads. As the grenadiers closed within arm's length, the Americans rose and fired into the regiment. British soldiers dropped to the ground, dead and wounded, and the unit stumbled backwards. A bullet hit British captain Neal McNeal, radiant in his officer's uniform, in the head. A bullet also killed McNeal's master sergeant, and another killed the legislative clerk that had joined the regiment. Of the 120 men of the brave company, only 30 survived the fight.[29]

As the grenadiers fell near the landing site, Sheaffe organized three to four hundred men into column, including a second company of the Eighth Regiment and the Newfoundland and York militias, to prepare for an assault. Sheaffe waited patiently to gather his men together, just as he did at Queenston, and he probably expected similar results. He placed the Newfoundland Fencibles in the center, a company of the Eighth Regiment on the left, and some militia on the right, with the whole under the command of Major Rowland Heathcote. As the column marched across the clearing toward the beachhead, Chauncey's schooners, twelve of which had moved within range of the enemy to provide covering fire, launched grape and canister shot at Sheaffe's newly formed columns. The Eighth Infantry, being closest to the lake, suffered the brunt of the fire. The schooners, armed with 24- and 32-pounders, also fired at York's three batteries.[30]

Meanwhile, on the *Madison*, US general Pike shouted to his staff, "By God I can't stay here any longer. Come, jump into the boat." Pike and the remaining companies of the Fifteenth Infantry headed toward the landing site. The boats landed east of Forsyth's location, and Pike organized his men into platoons. The Sixteenth Infantry and the Third Artillery Company with two field guns arrived soon after. Unlike the chaotic and disorganized landing at Queenston the previous year, Major Charles Hunter skillfully organized every platoon as it landed, even though the wind and waves brought each boat to a different point along the beach. Hunter eventually organized 1,800 men and eight guns, an enormous undertaking and a testament to the effective coordination between the army and navy.[31]

At 10:00 a.m., Pike's platoons marched in open column toward Sheaffe's men in the clearing. The Fifteenth Regiment's colors flew and drummers played "Yankee Doodle." They dragged one 6-pounder and a howitzer across the streams and ravines west of the city. The column arrived near Sheaffe's men and fired into the group. Chauncey's schooners pumped grape and canister shot into enemy troops visible in the clearing. The combined land and naval fire pummeled the compact British column. Sheaffe ordered his men to withdraw.[32]

Many of Sheaffe's soldiers, including the survivors of the McNeal's company, gathered around the western battery, the site of two dilapidated 18-pounders, to await orders. A few officers climbed the battery's bastion to determine if the gunners could hit one of Chauncey's ships. The retreating men from the dissolved column piled into the battery, and in the confusion one soldier moved an open box of cartridges near the guns—a major break of artillery protocol. One British officer walked to the platform with a lit match behind his back, awaiting orders to light the cannon fuse. The officer accidently dropped the flame into the open cartridge box. "Every man in the battery was blown into the air," recalled one observer, "and the dissection of the greater part of their bodies was inconceivably shocking." More than a dozen men died, and the wounded soldiers looked like zombies, with blackened faces, frizzled hair, and clothes that emitted a putrid odor. An American surgeon aboard the *Oneida* observed the explosion and believed that he saw forty men flying through the air.[33]

Most of Sheaffe's men retreated to the Governor's House and the safety of its two 12-pounders. British gunners fired grape and canister at Pike's men and temporarily halted the Americans. Pike ordered six additional cannon brought up, and their fire eventually silenced the British battery. The Americans expected to see a surrender flag. Pike sat down on a stump to interrogate a captured British soldier as American cannon continued to fire into the Governor's House.

Sheaffe convened a meeting with his staff, and they agreed to retreat. He ordered his men to burn the *Sir Isaac Brock*, the shipyard, and the storehouse. As Prevost had instructed, Sheaffe wanted to save his two hundred regulars to fight another day. His soldiers began the dangerous and important operation to burn the *Sir Isaac Brock* and the fort's other stores. During the operation, a soldier lit York's grand magazine, an underground room that contained two hundred barrels of gunpowder, buckets of iron shells and shot, and cartloads of stone. A massive explosion shook the town that could be heard for thirty miles. One observer recalled, "At first it was a great confused mass of smoke, timber, men, earth, &c, but as it rose in a most majestic manner it assumed the shape of a vast balloon. When the whole mass had ascended to a considerable height, and the force by which timber, &c, were impelled upwards became spent, the latter fell from the cloud and spread on the surrounding plain."[34]

The American surgeon on the *Oneida* wrote, "It seemed that the heavans [*sic*] and earth were coming together." Debris fell more than five hundred yards from the site, and large stones catapulted in the air and sank deep into the earth upon impact. The blast probably had the same power as an explosion produced by seven tons of TNT. US colonel Cromwell Pearce recalled that "the earth shook and the sky darkened, while the crashing of the rocks, high in the air, and the groans of the wounded, rendered it one of the most awful sites in nature." General Pike sat on a stump two hundred yards away from the magazine, interrogating the British sergeant, when a large rock landed on his spine. "I am mortally wounded," Pike uttered to a companion, "my ribs and back are stove in." The British sergeant died, as did Captain Benjamin Nicholson, who was interviewing the sergeant with Pike. By a miracle, Pike's nearby aide survived because a British soldier's body shielded him from the blast. The men carried Pike to a schooner for treatment, and during the trip he asked what the loud huzzas were for. "The British Union Jack is coming down, General," the soldier replied, "the Stars are going up." Pike survived long enough for his soldiers to hand him the captured British flag. They later transferred Pike to the *Madison*, where Chauncey stayed with him in his last hours. Pike died around sundown. His men buried Pike and Captain Nicholson, Pike's pupil and friend, at Fort Tompkins.[35]

The blast spread confusion among the survivors. The explosion killed 38 Americans and wounded 222. Major Heathcote recommended that the British charge the Americans in the confusion around the explosion, but Sheaffe decided to withdraw his army to Kingston. He ordered his militia officers, Major William Allan and Colonel William Chewett, to attain the best terms possible with the enemy. Sheaffe's retreat "left us all standing in the street like a parcel of sheep," York's sheriff remembered.[36]

The surrender negotiations started poorly. The American officers appointed to conduct the talks, Lieutenant Colonel George Mitchell and Major William King, refused to negotiate with militia officers since the Americans had defeated British regulars. Reports also trickled into the delegation that British soldiers exploited the parlay to buy time to destroy the *Sir Isaac Brock* and other military stores. King stopped the negotiations. Eventually cooler tempers prevailed and King and the militia officers settled on terms, which still required Dearborn's approval to become official. Colonel Pearce's men secured public buildings and stores.[37]

General Dearborn stalled ratifying the articles because he reportedly disliked the conditions. Reverend John Strachan, an anti-American rector of York, became so frustrated with Dearborn's dallying that he decided to row to the *Madison* to meet the general. As Strachan made his way to the boathouse, he encountered Dearborn and showed him the terms. Strachan demanded to know when the militia would receive their paroles and when American medical officers would tend to the wounded. Dearborn told Strachan that the British gave a false return of officers in the original terms, which invalidated the articles. In reality, Dearborn was concerned that the articles listed Colonel Pearce, rather than himself, as the commanding officer of the successful attack. Strachan tried to challenge him, but Dearborn told him "to keep off [and] not to follow him as he has business of more importance to attend to." Strachan later found Chauncey and complained that the Americans would plunder the town before ratifying the document's terms.[38]

Indeed, Dearborn's men began to loot private property, contrary to Pike's order that such offenses would be punishable by death. Forsyth's riflemen were probably the biggest offenders. They stood guard in the city and carried a grudge from their defeat at Ogdensburg in February. They also had a reputation for plundering private property, and Forsyth rarely punished the offenders. American soldiers looted Major Givins's house and stole another resident's furniture, bed, table linen, kitchen utensils, silverware, books, and musical instruments. Ely Playter of the Third York Militia hid in the woods as American soldiers broke into his house: "They came to my house, broke the door, and took many things away. We watched them till dark and supposing they staid [*sic*] all night at fathers we went back to the M. Rideouts where we staid [*sic*] all night."[39]

Other young soldiers sought excitement after their first wartime action. Ned Myers, a sailor aboard the *Scourge*, admitted to stealing private property. Liquor, he claimed, drew out his mischievous side. He made a few runs from the schooner *Scourge* into York, where in one instance his fellow looters held a shopkeeper hostage as they stole tea, sugar, and ten gallons of whiskey. "For myself," Ned admitted, "I was influenced more by the love of mischief, and a weak desire to have it . . . than from any mercenary motive." Meanwhile, wounded British soldiers suffered on the battlefield without treatment, and the Americans crammed others into a squalid garrison under armed guard. Sheaffe departed the city with his two surgeons and medical supplies, which left the remaining militia with no means of treating the casualties.[40]

The morning after the battle, Dearborn approved the surrender terms, but the American plundering continued. Three days after York's capture, someone ignited the Provincial Parliament building, the adjoining clerks' offices, and the library. The fire burned books, papers, records, and furniture from the Upper and Lower Houses. Dearborn's men probably started the fires, perhaps in anger after discovering a scalp hanging over a mace behind the speaker's chair. With the River Raisin massacre fresh on their minds, the men might have burned the chamber in retaliation. Regardless of the reason, the blame for the wanton destruction lay at Dearborn's feet, who did little to maintain control of York following the capital's surrender. Granny Dearborn, aroused from his slumber by reports of looting, apologized for the depredations and sent Lieutenant Colonel Eleazer Ripley of the Twenty-First Infantry Regiment to regain order. He also allowed York's magistrates to deputize citizens to enforce rules, but Dearborn's tardy measures could not save the city.[41]

General Sheaffe, for his part, did not escape blame either. Frustrated local leaders criticized the general's dismal efforts to defend the city. "They [the British army] were sent to defend, not to lose, the Canadas. They might be required not unnecessarily to irritate the Americans," one militia leader wrote, "but surely they can never be justified for not anticipating the attacks that the enemy were preparing for our destruction." Sheaffe should have sent a stronger contingent to contest the Americans' landing, but he maximized the fighting power of his few men by organizing them into column.

Ultimately, the American navy and army outgunned Sheaffe, in a town with poor defenses. Sheaffe did as Prevost ordered him and saved his men to fight another day. Nevertheless, Prevost removed Sheaffe in June and replaced him with Baron Francis de Rottenburg.[42]

The Americans seized more than $1 million in stores and public property, including £2,000 and twenty-eight cannon destined for the Niagara and Amherstburg. "The loss of stores at this place will be an irreparable one for the enemy," Chauncey told Secretary of the Navy Hamilton, "for independent of the difficulty of transportation, the articles cannot be replaced in this country." The Americans confiscated cases of ammunition, shells, and shot labeled for Niagara and Amherstburg, and also took large stores of flour, beef, and peas, likely destined for Amherstburg. The men captured the *Duke of Gloucester*, which was in such poor condition that Chauncey could only use the ship for storage. The British, before their departure, destroyed the *Sir Isaac Brock*, and they burned cables, cordage, canvas, and other materials destined for Britain's dockyard at Lake Erie. At York, the Americans found Sheaffe's baggage and papers, and Dearborn took a personal interest in Sheaffe's musical snuff box—and the scalp found hanging in Parliament. Dearborn promised to send the scalp to Secretary of War Armstrong with an account of the story behind it. A shocked Armstrong refused to allow the scalp to be a "decoration to the walls of the War Department," as Dearborn intended.[43]

As the Americans inventoried their confiscated goods, Sheaffe's men began their 150-mile walk to Kingston on the dilapidated road that lined the north rim of the lake. Thawing snow and heavy rains turned the roads into a muddy mess. One soldier recalled, "The snow had just thawed . . . which, with the heavy and copious rains usual at this season, rendered the roads, that are bad at best, almost impassable." Inhabitants hid supplies and horses from Sheaffe's troops, and some appeared happy that the Americans won the battle. If there was a bright spot for the British, it included a single act of bravery from a sergeant in the Eighth Infantry Regiment, who, despite the possibility of becoming a prisoner of war, snuck into York to retrieve his regiment's knapsacks, firelocks, and a drum from the battlefield.[44]

Following the campaign's blueprint, Dearborn planned next to assault Fort George. The outpost, described as a fort in a "ruinous and unfinished condition," was located at the intersection of the Niagara River with Lake Ontario. Responsibility to protect Fort George fell to British brigadier general John Vincent, who defended the fort with 1,000–1,200 regulars and 500 militia. Vincent also held six detached batteries between the fort and Lake Ontario, but they lacked rear palisades to protect the gunners from a flank attack. Prevost directed Yeo to survey the American fleet to determine if he could safely transport 300 men from Quebec to reinforce Fort George, but they would not arrive in time for the American attack. Without control of Lake Ontario, Prevost could not move his troops quickly into the region.[45]

On May 8, Isaac Chauncey and his fleet arrived at Four Mile Creek, four miles east of the American garrison at Fort Niagara (across from Fort George), to disembark troops for the upcoming attack. Dearborn's men camped and rested to recuperate from illness, hunger, and fatigue. Chauncey returned two weeks later with 350 additional men for the assault, giving Dearborn a total of 2,500 troops. The American army would be led by skilled men such as Colonel Winfield Scott, who relinquished his staff position for a battlefield command in order to participate in the assault. Scott was assisted by Lieutenant Oliver Hazard Perry of the US Navy, whom Chauncey had dispatched to command at Presque Isle on Lake Erie. Chauncey assigned Perry the hazardous task of landing troops on the enemy's shore. General Dearborn, who became ill before the attack, relinquished command to General Morgan Lewis, a former governor of New York.[46]

At Fort George, British brigadier general John Vincent divided his army into three commands. He placed troops under Colonel Christopher Myers and John Norton's Native Americans near the lakefront on the British left, where Vincent anticipated the American landing. Lieutenant Colonel John Harvey protected the river on the British right, and Colonel William Claus guarded the fort with 130 soldiers, including a company of the Forty-Ninth Regiment. General Vincent hoped for a stronger turnout from the local militia, but many refused to join his force and some had already deserted the garrison. "I can neither report favorably of their numbers, nor their willing cooperation," he wrote Prevost in May. Vincent established a supply depot sixteen miles southwest of Fort George at Beaver Dams that would serve as a rally point for his troops if they were forced to retreat.[47]

On May 25, American gunners at Fort Niagara began a devastating cannonade against Fort George. More than twenty-five cannon, many firing "hot shot," propelled balls into the log-framed garrison, which soon caught on fire. "We have been cannonaded since Day light," Colonel Harvey wrote Colonel Baynes. "The Enemy's fire has been wholly (& most successfully) directed hitherto against the Fort which is made a compleat example of— every Log Barrack in it being burnt down." One 18-pounder ball crushed the carriage of the fort's 12-pounder. Flames and shells exploded in every direction. At 2:00 p.m., the Americans ceased fire since most of the fort was in flames.[48]

The next day, Chauncey's men placed buoys in the river to mark his ships' positions during the attack. The buoys would ensure that the commodore's vessels could find their positions at night and during bad weather. The schooners *Scourge*, *Asp*, and *Hamilton* would float close to the shore to provide covering fire for the disembarking troops. The *Julia*, the *Ontario*, and the *Growler* would enfilade a battery near a lighthouse, while the *Governor Tompkins* and the *Conquest* would fire at an artillery position near the mouth of Two Mile Creek. The largest vessels, the sloop of war *Madison*, the *Lady of the Lake*, and the brig *Oneida* drew too much water to approach the shore, but their guns could still target Vincent's troops. The flotilla's total broadside battery included fifty-one guns, which when combined with the batteries from Fort Niagara, totaled seventy guns and mortars.[49]

On May 27, around 1:00 a.m., the men awoke, ate an early breakfast, and boarded the vessels. One soldier spotted Dearborn leaving his headquarters for the fleet and described him as "old roman-like, though then an invalid, looking General." Scott's advance led the attack, with 400 select light infantry, including Forsyth's riflemen and the flank companies of the Fifteenth Infantry. Scott was followed by three waves from the Sixth, Fifteenth, and Sixteenth Infantry Regiments, with around 1,500 men each. Chauncey could also lead 400 seamen ashore if necessary.[50]

Around sunrise, the troops sailed toward Fort George and Chauncey's schooners took their positions. Captain Ephraim Shaler of the Twenty-Fifth Infantry recalled that it was a lovely morning, with Lake Ontario unusually smooth and a thick fog blanketing the water. The cold damp weather shivered the men in Scott's boats, but the fog concealed the fleet's advance. Vincent's sentries could see little in the mist, but a stiff breeze soon dissipated the fog to reveal ninety to one hundred batteaux, each loaded with fifty or sixty men, heading toward the shore. "The enemy," an American soldier wrote, "if he were not before apprised of our intentions, had them now in clear development before him."[51]

In twenty boats, Scott's advance neared the beach. Two of Chauncey's schooners fired over Scott's men into the landing site. British colonel Christopher Myers directed the Glengarry Light Infantry and John Norton's Native Americans to seek cover in a ravine. When Scott's boats arrived within 150 yards of the shore, Myers's men sortied out of the ravine to fire at the approaching enemy. "In a twinkling as it were," a First Brigade soldier observed, "as if raised . . . from the ground, a line of soldiers made conspicuous by the glowing scarlet of the British uniform, was exhibited along the whole crest of the bank." Scott's crewmen quit rowing, and his infantrymen tried to load their muskets in the chaos of a small boat crammed with soldiers. Myers's men fired accurately at the craft, prompting one of Scott's soldiers to refer to the enemy as "duck-shooters." The rain of bullets pelted the water like hail. "All appeared to be in confusion," an officer under Scott recalled. Some of the boats swung parallel to the shore and the men landed haphazardly along the beach.[52]

Despite the heavy fire, by 9:00 a.m. most of Scott's boats landed on a narrow beach with a seven- to eleven-foot-high bank, near Two Mile Creek. Scott and his select light infantry jumped from their boats and charged up the bank to secure the landing spot. Two companies of the Glengarry Light Infantry, later joined by the Royal Newfoundland Regiment and the Lincoln Militia, fired and charged with bayonets. "The action was very close and warm," an officer under Scott recalled. Colonel Scott stopped a bayonet thrust with his sword but fell seven feet backwards toward the beach. General Dearborn, who watched from the river, broke into tears because he thought that Scott was dead, but the officer only suffered minor bruising from the fall.[53]

Around this time, General John Boyd's First Brigade landed to the left of Scott's men while under a withering fire from the British. A bullet hit one soldier and he fell dead into the water like "a stone thrown overboard." Bodies piled up along the waterline. Colonel Myers brought the remainder of his brigade into action and personally led a charge against the embankment. Three hundred men from the King's Regiment, the Glengarry Light Infantry, and the Royal Newfoundland charged the beach. Chauncey's schooners launched a barrage of grape and canister shot that decimated the approaching British force and saved the American landing. Myers's troops continued to harass Boyd's Sixteenth Regiment, who tried to form ranks on the beach.[54]

Winfield Scott's line regrouped from the chaos and charged the enemy a second time. "For fifteen minutes the two lines exchanged a rapid and destructive fire," Boyd recalled, "at a distance of only six or ten yards." Clouds of smoke enveloped the embankment. The cries of the wounded and the boom of artillery shattered the normal tranquility that blessed the river each morning. More American reinforcements arrived, and they began to decimate Myers's smaller force. Scott received three wounds, and his men fell back to the main body of troops, located near Fort George. "The contest soon became unequal," a British captain recalled, "more from the destructive fire from his [Americans] craft than from his troops." Myers's outnumbered men admirably performed their duty in harrowing conditions.[55]

Once Scott established a beachhead, 3,000 to 4,000 Americans landed with eight cannon. Scott organized the men into columns and they marched toward Fort George. One of Scott's officers recommended that the riflemen follow a circuitous path through woods to gain the enemy's flank. Scott already had witnessed the success of attacking the enemy's rear at Queenston, when Lieutenant Wassel Gansevoort led the men up the unguarded fisherman's path. Scott's riflemen edged their way through the woods, following a trail of muskets, knapsacks, and cartridges dropped by Myers's retreating men.[56]

Colonel Harvey, who succeeded the wounded Myers, brought up the British right division with the Forty-Ninth Regiment and some militia. Major William Holcroft supported Harvey's line with a 6-pounder and a 5.5-inch howitzer, which pumped grape and canister shot into Scott's advance. But soon Harvey spotted American riflemen in the woods trying to turn his left flank. Concerned that his men would be surrounded, he withdrew to the fort. Soon after Harvey's retreat, Colonel Vincent decided on the same course of action for his entire force. He ordered the fort evacuated, guns spiked, and ammunition and other valuables destroyed. "I could not consider myself as justified in continuing so unequal a contest," he later wrote Prevost, "which promised no advantage to the interests of His Majesty's service."[57]

Colonel Scott intended to seize valuables from the flaming fort before it burned down. Occasional small shells popped off in the flames. As Scott approached, a magazine exploded, knocking him off his horse, and a large

Figure 5. ***Capture of Fort George (Col. Winfield Scott Leading the Attack).*** General Winfield Scott and his men storming into Fort George. The British had already evacuated the fort once the Americans entered the garrison, so there was no fighting at this point. Scott did rush into the burning fort to cut down a flagpole to gain the British colors. He also received a shoulder wound during the assault, which was one of many injuries Scott received in the war. Courtesy of the Library of Congress, LC-USZ62-48156.

splinter embedded itself in his collarbone. Despite the pain, he found an axe buried in the fort's flagstaff where British soldiers tried to cut down the pole. Scott, with a damaged collarbone, hacked away at the pole until he acquired his trophy. His men removed lit matches from two magazines on the verge of exploding. A naval officer raised the Star-Spangled Banner on a makeshift mast on top of one of the bastions. At 1:00 p.m., General Lewis wrote to Dearborn, "Fort George and its dependencies are ours." Meanwhile, Vincent and his men withdrew further inland. He ordered Forts Chippawa and Erie destroyed and all of his units to rendezvous at Beaver Dam, a supply depot near Queenston. Scott wanted to pursue the retreating army, but Boyd, the senior officer, denied his request.[58]

The Battles of York and Fort George represented the first significant joint army-navy operations in the short history of the United States. The success of the effort, however, rested with Chauncey and Dearborn, not the War Department. The War Department issued an ambiguous order before the campaign which explained that the commanding officer for each service would manage his own people. The document did not address which service would be in overall command of the mission, which left open the possibility that the navy and army would pursue their own plans during the mission. Navy Secretary William Jones understood that interservice problems could develop since the War Department did not assign a single commander over both forces: "There is no difficulty in settling the subject of relative rank between naval and military commanders; but that of *command* is a subject of great delicacy and can be approached but with great caution." Chauncey and Dearborn, however, set aside personality and politics to achieve their objectives without the need for an overall commander. The navy's fire killed oncoming enemy infantry, which allowed the army to establish a foothold on the beach with little loss of life. Without the navy's support, the infantry would have perished on the shore from the withering fire from Myers's men. Oliver Hazard Perry's participation in the successful joint landing likely fostered a positive image of army-navy collaboration that would spill into the fall of 1813, when Perry would cooperate with William Henry Harrison to retake Michigan and the Northwest Territory.[59]

By June, the Americans controlled Lake Ontario and the Niagara frontier. The raid on York led to the destruction of the *Sir Isaac Brock*, which temporarily halted Britain's efforts to contest Chauncey on Lake Ontario. If that ship had launched, British naval forces on Lake Ontario would have equaled the American squadron, and Yeo's fleet could have challenged Chauncey for control of the lake. The Americans also seized vital food rations destined for Procter at Fort Malden, and soon after the attack, Procter suffered serious supply shortages. He lacked enough gifts for his Indian allies, and his men ran short of food at Fort Malden. The dockyard at Amherstburg was also short of key materials required to complete new vessels.

Not only would Procter soon be short of military provisions, but the US Army's temporary control of Lake Ontario and the Niagara frontier forced the British Commissariat to rely on land and riverine routes to circumvent Lake Ontario and the Niagara frontier. These routes traversed damp woodlands, and carts or wagons loaded with heavy supplies did not use these trails most of the year. The Commissariat was thus challenged to provide Procter the large amounts of provisions he required, and the shortage was felt quickly because of the destruction of provisions at York destined for Fort Malden.

America's control of Lake Ontario, however, would be temporary because the army failed to overrun Kingston. American forces should have exploited their naval superiority on Lake Ontario to destroy Britain's largest dockyard on the lake. The destruction of Kingston would have retarded Britain's efforts to build larger ships and ensured continued American control of the lake. In May 1813, Sir James Yeo assumed control of Britain's naval operations on the lake. His arrival heralded the start of a historic shipbuilding race, headquartered in North America's remote frontier, whose result would shape the war's outcome.[60]

7

Britain Strikes on Lake Ontario

The hill was a continual sheet of fire.
—British soldier at the Battle of Stoney Creek, quoted in William Merritt, *A Desire of Serving and Defending My Country*

On May 15, 1813, thirty-one-year-old Sir James Yeo arrived at Kingston to assume command of the Provincial Marine. Yeo, an experienced seaman and fighter, possessed the daring and resolve needed to reinvigorate Britain's shipbuilding efforts on Lake Ontario. During the Napoleonic Wars, Yeo led a fifty-man assault against an outpost in northwest Spain and routed the garrison. The next year, he commanded an undersize Anglo-Portuguese force in Cayenne, French Guiana, against a fortified position and defeated the enemy after heavy fighting. Portugal and Britain knighted him for his valor in combat. Yeo later commanded the frigate *Southampton*, and in 1812, his ship blockaded the southeastern coast of the United States. In November of that year, he captured the US brig *Vixen*, but both ships wrecked on a shoal en route to the Bahamas.

The Great Lakes proved to be a different kind of challenge for Yeo. His greatest assets on the lakes were skilled shipwrights and a productive shipyard, which together could produce vessels that could outgun enemy ships. Yeo would need to balance his impulse for combat with the broader goals of controlling the lakes and preserving his fleet, because scarce resources inhibited Yeo from rebuilding a defeated squadron. While at Kingston, Yeo, a career naval officer, reported to Governor-in-Chief Prevost, rather than to the Admiralty, which offended his service sensibilities. The command structure contributed to a rift that soon developed between the two men.

The state of Kingston's shipyard concerned Yeo. He wrote Secretary of the Admiralty John Croker that Kingston's ships were in a "very weak state" and that "the Enemy's squadron are very superior, both, in number, and the complete way they are equipped." By August 1813, however, his fleet grew and could challenge US commodore Chauncey on the lake. In April 1813, shipwrights launched Yeo's flagship, the twenty-three-gun *Wolfe* (formerly the *Sir George Prevost*), armed with fourteen carronades and nine long guns. Yeo's fleet also contained the twenty-gun *Royal George*, the largest ship on the lakes at the start of the war, which was armed with eighteen carronades and two long guns; the sixteen-gun *Earl of Moira* armed with fourteen carronades and two long guns; the fourteen-gun *Lord Melville*, armed with twelve carronades and two long guns; the twelve-gun *General Beresford* (formerly the *Prince Regent*) armed with ten carronades and two long guns; and the twelve-gun *Sir Sidney Smith* armed with ten carronades and two long guns. Yeo recommended that his ships engage Chauncey before the American flotilla grew any bigger. He also requested "more grown up young men" from the Admiralty to serve as midshipmen.[1]

Yeo would soon get his first taste of Great Lakes combat. In late May 1813, while Chauncey's fleet was attacking Fort George, Prevost decided to assault Sackets Harbor, New York. He learned that an American attack was underway against Fort George, and he wanted to divert those forces away from the Niagara to relieve pressure on Brigadier General John Vincent. Prevost tried to send reinforcements to Fort George, but without control of Lake Ontario, the troops, forced to march, would not arrive in time to support Vincent. With the American ship *Madison* away from Sackets Harbor, Prevost could destroy the dockyard at Sackets Harbor and set back Chauncey's shipbuilding efforts. Yeo agreed with Prevost's plan and readied his ships to support the invasion.[2]

Chauncey feared that Prevost would attack Sackets Harbor while his fleet was away at York and Fort George. The twenty-six-gun *General Pike* was under construction at the dockyard, and once launched, its twenty-four-pound long guns would outshoot any ship on the lake. The commodore ordered his brother, Lieutenant Wolcott Chauncey, to defend and destroy the *General*

Pike if necessary. "If this place should be attacked," he wrote his brother, "let the defence of the new Ship be such, as to do yourself credit." Lieutenant Colonel Electus Backus, a regular US Army cavalry officer, defended the harbor with only four hundred men because Colonel Alexander Macomb's Third Artillery Regiment, which typically protected the garrison, accompanied General Henry Dearborn at Fort George. On the night of May 27, Backus asked New York militia general Jacob Brown to assume command of the garrison. By the next day, Brown commanded nine hundred men at Sackets Harbor, roughly half militia and half regular army.[3]

Colonel Edward Baynes commanded the British assault force with almost nine hundred men, including two companies of the King's Foot, the Canadian Voltigeurs, the elite grenadier company of the 100th Foot, four companies of the 104th Foot, and some British Native American allies. Commodore Yeo's flotilla contained an additional seven hundred seamen on nine ships, including the twenty-three-gun *Wolfe* and twenty-gun *Royal George.* The British hoped to surprise the Americans on May 28.

That morning, Lieutenant Chauncey sailed into Sackets Harbor firing alarm guns. He spotted Yeo's fleet, which contained "a very liberal supply of boats," approaching the garrison. Pickets fired signal guns to muster local militia, and messengers and officers darted to nearby towns to collect citizen-soldiers. Chauncey's warning gave Brown time to prepare for the attack. He gathered his senior officers, including Colonel Backus, Lieutenant Chauncey, and others, and held a short council of war. They correctly predicted that the enemy would land on Horse Island, a small, twenty-four-acre plot of land that was connected to the mainland by a 400-foot-long, partially submerged causeway. Colonel John Mills's Albany Volunteers, armed with a 6-pounder and muskets, stationed themselves on the island to fire a few shots at the landing force and retreat. On the mainland, six hundred men were stationed behind a gravelly ridge where the causeway intersected with the shore. This ridge was to be the Americans' primary defensive line, and Mill's men would gather here after withdrawing from Horse Island. If the American line broke, Colonel Backus's regulars were to conduct a fighting retreat toward Fort Tompkins. At Navy Point, Lieutenant Chauncey would be responsible for burning the *General Pike* and the outpost's naval stores if the British force overran the garrison.[4]

The sound plan depended on the fortitude of militiamen, whose boasts

Figure 6. *South-East View of Sackett's Harbour.* The American garrison at Sackets Harbor on Lake Ontario. Shipwright Henry Eckford produced some of the largest ships during the war at the dockyard. In May 1813, Britain attempted to destroy the garrison, including the twenty-six-gun *General Pike*, which was under construction. Courtesy of the Library of Congress, LC-DIG-pga-13780.

of bravery often disappeared once bullets started flying. Daniel Morgan and Nathaniel Greene used a similar arrangement in the southern campaign of the Revolutionary War, when each commander placed militia in their front and demanded they fire two rounds before retreating. After the militia fled, the regulars could advance against a softened enemy, while the officers regrouped the fleeing militia with the regulars.

Yeo's fleet tried to approach Sackets Harbor on May 28, but the wind forced the flotilla off course. British officers, concerned that they lost the element of surprise, recommended returning to Kingston. Prevost agreed. Yeo, who was accustomed to planning his own amphibious invasions, fumed at the decision, but Yeo reported to Prevost and could not contest his orders. Soon after the discussion, a British officer spotted an isolated group of boats rowing to Sackets Harbor with American reinforcements. Colonel Baynes dispatched three canoes loaded with Native Americans to intercept the boats. After a short skirmish, the Native Americans captured twelve of the twenty boats, 115 soldiers, tents, and equipment. Based on the raid's success

Figure 7. ***The Troops Disembarking to Attack Fort Oswego, under the Command of Genl. Drummond and Sir T. Yeo, Lake Ontario, May the 6th 1814.*** This image shows an amphibious British assault that occurred in May 1814 against Fort Oswego on Lake Ontario. The approach of the British fleet and the disembarkation of soldiers shown in the image would have been similar to the British attack on Sackets Harbor in 1813. At Sackets Harbor, transports filled with soldiers landed at Horse Island on the causeway, while being protected by the navy's ships. Courtesy of the Library of Congress, C-DIG-ppmsca-23090.

and the emergence of favorable winds, Baynes decided to press the attack. The landing boats would assemble around the *Wolfe* at midnight to embark on the two-mile journey to Horse Island. Meanwhile, Yeo's gunboats would sail into the harbor to silence the batteries there.[5]

At midnight, 870 soldiers from the British flotilla piled into batteaux and gunboats. Cold rain chilled the soldiers who huddled at the bottom of the boats. A gunboat's stern light guided the batteaux toward Horse Island, but heavy rains and winds pushed the boats off course. The delay forced the men to approach Horse Island at sunrise, which revealed their approach to the Americans. The batteaux pilots tried to approach the island's western side, but heavy fire from Brown's and Mill's troops forced them to disembark on the north side. The Albany volunteers fired rifles and their 6-pounder at the approaching landing craft. "They opened a well directed fire from their field pieces and rifles," one British seaman recalled, "that almost every shot did execution." One batteau suffered fifteen killed and wounded, forcing the soldiers to man the oars. The landing party tried to return fire, but they could not spot the camouflaged enemy, who wore green clothes that blended into the island's foliage. The gunboats fired grape and canister shot into the shoreline, but the defenders, hidden behind logs and trees, avoided the fire.[6]

Once the batteaux neared the shore, the grenadiers of the 100th Foot splashed into the water, followed by Royal Scots, the King's Eighth, and four companies of the 104th. The Albany volunteers abandoned their 6-pounder and splashed across the causeway to join their comrades on the mainland. Brown's 450 militiamen, lying prone behind the ridge, waited for the British to approach. According to Brown, his untested men believed that they were ready. "All anxious for the fight," Brown recalled, "were you to believe their professions." The British soon appeared, advancing in perfect discipline down the causeway, trudging through three feet of water. The 100th Foot led the way with fixed bayonets.[7]

Brown exhorted the militiamen to restrain their fire until the enemy closed. Despite the command, the frightened volunteers fired too early. Few of their bullets harmed the enemy, and the men panicked. "To my utter astonishment my men arose from their cover," Brown recalled, "broke, and before I could realize the disgraceful scene there was scarcely a man within several rods of where I stood." Brown waved his sword topped with a handkerchief to rally the men, but his dramatics did not stem the retreat. Lieutenant Colonel John Mills urged his men on until a musket ball struck him in the chest.[8]

Once Colonel Baynes overran the American position, he ordered his force to march northeast along a lakeshore road that led to Fort Tompkins. Major William Drummond, sword above his head, led the 104th and 100th Regiments down the wagon road. Baynes ordered the 104th with some Native Americans and Canadian Voltigeurs to cut through the forest to cover the right flank of the main body. A few Albany volunteers, encouraged by Backus's arrival, fought behind the cover of trees and bushes to slow Drummond's advance. They inflicted steady casualties, but the British charged with bayonets and chased them out of the forest. One American sharpshooter waited for an opportunity to shoot the man who led the enemy force. When Drummond was twenty yards away, the American fired and the British officer dropped to the ground, seemingly dead. His men darted to the sharpshooter and bayoneted him. Luckily for Drummond, his soldiers convinced him to place his epaulettes in the front pocket of his overalls, and the musket ball struck its pad and steel plates. He suffered only a bruise. "Tis not mortal . . . charge on men!" he extorted.[9]

Beyond the tree line, an open field expanded into Fort Tompkins. Here, Brown found Captain Samuel McNitt of the Jefferson County (New York) militia, one of the few militia officers who had not fled the battlefield. McNitt rallied some men behind a stack of logs on the eastern edge of the field. Brown complimented McNitt's group on their bravery and cursed the others who had fled the field. He galloped off to look for additional troops.[10]

The Voltigeurs and Native Americans, who had followed the path through the woods, emerged from the tree line. The Native Americans let out a war cry and raced toward the McNitt's position. His men fired one shot and retreated. "I never saw in my life people better hamstrung and using their legs better," Captain Jacques Viger of the Voltigeurs recalled. "It was fun to see them clear out!"[11]

Major Drummond, with the main body of the British force, arrived near the Americans' final defensive position at Fort Tompkins. A two-story building, protected by a thirty-two-pound cannon, formed the central defensive point of the outpost. Two barracks extended outward from the fort and a ditch connected the two facilities. Backus's light dragoons manned the trench; Major Jacint Laval's soldiers occupied the loophole-lined buildings. At the edge of the forest, Drummond organized three hundred men into two columns to advance on the blockhouses. His men lacked artillery so they would need to dislodge the Americans by bayonet. Drummond organized three hundred men into two columns to advance on the fort.

As the British columns emerged from the woods, the American 32-pounder discharged a vicious barrage of round shot and grapeshot at the columns. Trees and branches snapped in every direction. Dense smoke settled along the forest line and throughout the field. "I do not exaggerate when I tell you, that shot, both grape and musket, flew like hail," recalled a British soldier. Another soldier said that "cannonballs and grapeshots dropped on the forest like rain."[12]

The column on the left advanced through the fire and assaulted one of the stockades. John Le Couteur of the 104th and his comrades lay flat against the buildings, and Laval's men stuck their muskets out of the loopholes. "It was really an uncomfortable position," Le Couteur remembered. "There was neither glory nor pleasure in being riddled, or rather fringed, with balls." The 104th Regiment cleared the stockade and advanced toward one of the blockhouses, but stiff fire kept them at bay. Lieutenant George Jobling with twenty men charged the 32-pounder, but he lost half of his group in the effort and retreated. During the contest, British fire mortally wounded Lieutenant Colonel Backus, who heroically led the fort's defense. Backus survived for eight days before succumbing to his injuries.[13]

General Brown galloped to the 32-pounder and located Lieutenant Thomas Ketchum, who had quit firing the gun. "General," the lieutenant told Brown, "I cannot fire this piece again, the flame from the marine barracks is so hot my men cannot remain here." Brown told him to do the best he could, and he dashed to Navy Point, where he observed clouds of smoke ascending from the area.[14]

At Navy Point, American Lieutenant John Drury and his men observed a red flag hoisted from Lieutenant Chauncey's schooner that signaled that the men should burn the *General Pike*. Drury gave the order. Panic spread throughout the area as the men began trying to burn the vessel while readying boats to make their escape. General Brown rushed to the chaotic scene to explain that the fort still remained in American hands. Major Samuel Brown, the general's brother, assured him that the ship remained intact and that Drury's men had panicked. General Brown ordered his brother to locate Lieutenant Chauncey and relay to him that the battle continued. Fortunately for the Americans, the green timber that Henry Eckford used to construct the *General Pike* burned slowly, and the men doused the flames before they destroyed the ship. After the battle, a court of inquiry charged Drury with cowardice, but the tribunal acquitted him when other witnesses testified that Chauncey raised and lowered a red flag.[15]

Prevost, standing on the edge of the forest line, peered through a spyglass to assess the situation when a shower of grape covered his party and a cannonball fell within yards of him. "The opposition [was] so great," remembered a British soldier, "that our men were constantly falling back on the rear where we were, and balls were whizzing about us in all directions." Baynes told Prevost that his troops could not seize the blockhouses because his men had taken heavy losses from the earlier assaults. And the short-range carronades from the British fleet could not reach the fortified buildings to assist in the raid. Prevost allowed Baynes to withdraw his troops out of artillery range and re-form for another attack.[16]

Under a flag of truce, Drummond walked to the blockhouse to demand the Americans' capitulation. Laval met Drummond and his aides: "Why do you retreat, if you wish us to surrender?" Laval asked him. "Only to form a fresh attack and to save a further effusion of blood," Drummond responded. "Then tell Sir George Prevost, we will await the issue of his attack," Laval replied.[17]

Despite the confidence of his officers, Prevost, concerned that Chauncey would arrive from Fort George with Dearborn's troops, feared that the British expedition would be cut off from Kingston. Prevost also observed giant dust clouds in the distance, which he believed were reinforcements moving toward the garrison. Drummond told Prevost that he could capture the barracks, but the governor-in-chief ordered him to retreat. The Americans' stiff defensive stand led to high casualties in Prevost's force, especially among officers. Baynes's men methodically withdrew from the mainland, and the Americans did not molest them during the movement.[18]

Yeo blamed Prevost for the loss. He revealed his frustration in a letter he wrote to the Admiralty. "Then the troops, after gaining decided advantages," Yeo wrote Croker, "were reluctantly ordered to re-embark and leave a beaten enemy, having obliged them to set fire to their stores and retire within their enclosed forts and blockhouses." The battle fueled Yeo's anger at being commanded by a nonnaval officer, and one that he believed to be incompetent on the battlefield. The animosity between Yeo and Prevost hindered army-navy operations throughout the remainder of the war.[19]

Meanwhile, at the western end of Lake Ontario, British general John Vincent, after his defeat at Fort George, withdrew his forces toward Queenston. He ordered Forts Erie and Chippawa evacuated and directed his men to rendezvous at Beaver Dams, after which he would march his force to Burlington. After the American army seized Fort George, Dearborn refused Winfield Scott's offer to chase Vincent's force on May 27. The general stalled until June 1 when he finally directed General William Winder to pursue the retreating army. General John Chandler with 1,000 men and a regiment of dragoons joined Winder's 1,400 soldiers.

Winder learned that the British army erected camp at Forty Mile Creek, halfway between Forts George and York. The American soldiers carried six days of provisions and marched toward Vincent's force. Colonel Vincent withdrew to Burlington Heights and left a small advance seven miles forward at Stoney Creek. Here, twenty-foot-high hills surrounded a horseshoe-shaped meadow owned by James Gage, a local farmer. A swamp flanked the position on the left and a small mountain anchored the right. A road ran from Burlington Heights to Fort George through the middle of the hill. Winder's men seized Stoney Creek from the small British contingent on June 5.

General Chandler placed the Fifth, Sixteenth, and Twenty-Second Regiments on the hills facing the meadow. The men concealed themselves behind a natural abatis of bushes and tree stumps that the Gage family had cut down but had yet to clear. Chandler posted two companies of artillery on the brow of the hill overlooking the main road. Three 6-pounders and a howitzer, loaded with round shot and canister, faced Vincent's likely approach from Burlington Heights. A small advance under Captain Jacob Hindman encamped in the meadow next to the artillery.[20]

General Chandler placed the Twenty-Fifth Regiment in the plain, 150 yards from the hill, where they could not be supported by the main line. At 11:00 p.m., Chandler's able adjutant, Major John Johnson, convinced Chandler to reposition the vulnerable regiment to a location where artillery could cover the troops. American infantrymen on the hill loaded buckshot into their muskets to improve their ability to hit the enemy at close range. Winder's cooks built fires on the meadow's north side to illuminate the likely approach of a British attack. That evening Winder and Chandler discussed the exciting prospects of defeating Vincent's troops the following day.[21]

News of the Americans' arrival concerned Vincent. His vulnerable position at Burlington Heights could be approached from three directions, and low morale and illness permeated his ranks after the defeat at Fort George. British lieutenant colonel John Harvey, the deputy adjutant general to Vincent, recommended that his army conduct a surprise attack on the American position at Stoney Creek. A night assault was risky, but Vincent, desperate to avoid a pitched battle at Burlington Heights, agreed to the plan. Harvey was to lead 750 regulars, including five companies of the King's Regiment and five companies of the Forty-Ninth Regiment. Lieutenant James Fitzgibbons of the Forty-Ninth reportedly disguised himself as a suttler selling butter and strolled into the American lines to note their positions. His report highlighted the Twenty-Fifth Regiment's vulnerable location in the meadow, but Chandler later rectified the mistake.[22]

On June 5, 1813, at 11:30 p.m., the British troops departed into a moonless night toward the enemy. A light shower fell on the men as they began their seven-mile march. The King's Regiment walked on the right side of the road, the Forty-Ninth Regiment on the left. Harvey ordered the columns to maintain complete silence. He wanted to surprise the sleeping American camp with a bayonet attack. Harvey ordered the flint removed from his men's muskets because he did not want their guns to misfire. A local man, Billy Greene, had learned the American countersign from his brother-in-law. The countersign would allow Harvey's troops to approach American sentries without causing alarm. Harvey asked Greene to lead the column toward Chandler's position.[23]

A little before 2:00 a.m., the British advance encountered the first American pickets. Greene gave the countersign and demanded to pass. The sentry, unaware that Greene was a British sympathizer, allowed him to approach, after which Greene stabbed him with his sword. The British advance party continued, led by John Norton and his Native Americans, to an open field. Alert American sentries, hearing the groans of their dying comrade, fired their muskets at the charging warriors. The Native Americans shot one sentry as the other galloped away. American captain Ephraim Shaler recalled hearing "one of the most dreadful shrieks that ever fell on mortal ear" from one of the speared sentinels.[24]

Harvey ordered his men to remain silent, but the front columns yelled huzzas and charged. They advanced down the road that intersected the meadow below the heights. They speared the American cooks and tripped over clanking camp kettles and mess pans. Harvey's men encountered the Twenty-Third Regiment and the two groups engaged in a bloody melee. Swords, bayonets, and guns clashed in the pitch darkness where men could not identify friend or foe. Chandler's Second Artillery fired into the melee and probably wounded and killed some of the American advance. Vincent's men bayoneted dozens of Americans in the fracas.[25]

The attackers stopped at a rail fence, and the officers tried to reform their soldiers, but their commands could not be heard over the noise of musket and cannon fire. "Our men never ceased shouting. No order could be heard," one soldier recalled. "Everything was noise and confusion." The cooks' fires illuminated the British formation to the right wing of Chandler's line. Chandler's regiments waited for the British to march within gunshot, and they launched scattering buckshot against the enemy. "The Hill was a continual sheet of fire," one British officer recalled. For a half mile, muzzle flashes illuminated the slope. The Americans repulsed repeated British attempts to ascend the hill. Harvey's force fractured and sought shelter at a forest on the edge of Gage's farm. An American victory appeared imminent.[26]

As Harvey's line withdrew, an enterprising officer of the Forty-Ninth Regiment called for volunteers to rush the American artillery. Major Charles Plenderleath solicited volunteers to participate in the daring mission against the American guns. Nineteen-year-old Sergeant Alexander Fraser volunteered to join the major, as did about twenty others. Plenderleath, mounted on his horse, encouraged his volunteers to advance down the road. His soldiers stabbed horses and men along the way. Sergeant Fraser recalled bayoneting seven Americans; his brother speared four. The Forty-Ninth charged the position. Fortunately for Plenderleath, Major Nathan Towson of the Second Artillery received an order to cease firing his cannon, and he was in the process of hitching his artillery horses to their caissons when Plenderleath's men attacked. The US Twenty-Third Regiment fired volleys at the incoming group. Bullets struck Plenderleath's horse six times and two balls passed through his thigh. The British group pressed the position, and stiff hand-to-hand fighting ensued. Plenderleath's group overran the gunners and seized four cannon.[27]

General Chandler heard the commotion and went to investigate. As he approached the position, four musket balls pierced his horse, which bucked Chandler to the ground. The fall damaged Chandler's hips and shoulders, but he continued toward the artillery to ensure that the Twenty-Third Regiment supported his gunners. When he arrived, he observed confused men darting around the position. He believed that Adjutant John Johnson was trying to reform the Twenty-Third Regiment. He stepped among the men and called for his adjutant: "Where's the line? Where's the line?" To his surprise, Johnson did not respond, but Major Plenderleath of the Forty-Ninth did. His soldiers pointed their bayonets at Chandler and made him a prisoner. Minutes later, US general Winder approached. "Come on my brave fellows, they are routed," Winder exclaimed. Winder looked around the position and he soon realized that he was among the enemy. He pointed his pistol at Sergeant Alexander Fraser, who responded, "If you stir, sir, you die." Winder dropped his gun and Plenderleath mounted Winder's horse. The Forty-Ninth Regiment also captured Major Nathan Towson of the Second Artillery, but Towson daringly escaped by zigzagging away in the darkness as the British fired muskets at the shadowy figure.[28]

Despite Plenderleath's success, the British could not overrun the American position. But the raid salvaged the attack by capturing two general officers, spiking two guns, and seizing two cannon. The British monarchy awarded Plenderleath the Companion of the Order of the Bath for his role in the assault at Stoney Creek. "I am of opinion," a senior British officer wrote, "that had not Major Plenderleath made the dash he did the Americans would have kept their ground and our ruin would have been inevitable." Colonel Vincent had been absent for much of the battle. A horse threw Vincent to the ground, and he became lost in the woods. Harvey dispatched scouts, who located the general the next morning. At the Battle of Stoney Creek, the British suffered 23 men killed, 135 wounded, and 52 missing. American losses officially stood at seventeen killed and thirty-eight wounded, but the casualties were probably higher for both sides. The Twenty-Fifth Infantry alone reported forty-five killed and wounded.[29]

After the British captured the two American generals, command of the US force devolved to cavalry officer James Burns. Burns, despite commanding most of the force, decided to retreat to Forty Mile Creek. Critics later chastised Burns's decision to withdraw, but he could not locate his two senior officers and some of his army had deserted into the woods. Dearborn blamed Burns, a cavalryman, for the fiasco: "If either of the general officers had remained in command, the enemy would have been pursued and cut up, or if Colonel Burns had been an officer of infantry." At dawn on June 6, he ordered his men to withdraw to Fort George. The Battle of Stoney Creek was a moral and strategic victory for the British. The British halted Dearborn's plan to destroy Vincent's army, and Plenderleath's charge changed the course of the campaign along the Niagara.[30]

The Americans stayed at Fort George until June 23, when General John Boyd ordered 500 men under Lieutenant Colonel Charles Boerstler to destroy the De Cou house at Beaver Dams, which was located eighteen miles from Fort George. General Vincent was allegedly storing munition and supplies at a stone house there that belonged to a Canadian militia captain. His men spent the first night of the advance in Queenston, and two of Boerstler's officers, staying in the house of a Canadian militia officer, openly discussed the attack. The owner of the house, James Secord, received grievous injuries at the Battle of Queenston, and his wife, Laura, nursed him back to health. Because of his wounds, James could not warn Fitzgibbon of the Americans' advance, but Laura Secord determined to relay the message herself. Laura had proven her courage the year before when she searched for her husband among the dead and wounded at Queenston. She found his unconscious body, brought him to safe quarters, and tended to his injuries.[31]

Laura Secord resolved to take a circuitous nineteen-mile route to Fitzgibbon in order to avoid the American lines. She departed early on June 22. Her rigorous seventeen-hour hike took her through swamps, dense woods, and rivers. She avoided American patrols and Native American parties, and safely arrived at De Cou's house. She begged a Native American chief to escort her to Fitzgibbon. "Woman! What does Woman want here?" he asked her. She told him that she had urgent news for the lieutenant, and he finally allowed her to see the officer. Fitzgibbon questioned Laura intensely to confirm that she told the truth. Once convinced, he dispatched his men to receive the invaders.[32]

On June 24, as Boerstler's men neared De Cou's house, Native American parties under John Brant, Colonel William Kerr, and Dominque Ducharme attacked the rear of his column. Boerstler formed his men into two lines to meet the assaults from front and rear. The infantry repulsed the Native American attack, but the warriors dissolved into the woods, leaving the Americans no visible targets. The Native Americans attacked the column's front, and the American infantry drove the warriors back into the forest. "After this [attack]," one of Boerstler's men recalled, "every exertion was made to draw the Indians from the woods, to the open ground, but without much effect. The few [Native Americans] who were bold enough to venture, were handled so roughly that they soon returned to their lurking places." The Indians surrounded the left and right flanks of the column, and continued to fire into Boerstler's stacked column, clearly visible in the open road. Fitzgibbon formed his men in the road in front of the Americans.[33]

After four hours of fighting, the contest left Boerstler's men exhausted, low on ammunition, and frustrated they could not reach the Native Americans. Fitzgibbon demanded Boerstler's surrender. He informed Boerstler that his soldiers were the advance for Major Peter William De Haren's flank companies of the 104th Regiment, which was located nearby. Boerstler refused Fitzgibbon's demand and requested to see De Haren's troops for himself. Fitzgibbon's captain portrayed the colonel and told the American officer that he could not reveal his force to the enemy. The ruse worked, and Boerstler agreed to surrender as long as the officers could keep their arms, baggage, and horses, and the British would release them on parole.[34]

The arrival of the flank companies concerned Boerstler, but not as much as the possibility that the Native Americans would massacre his force if he did not surrender his men to British custody. Just as William Hull before him, Boerstler refused to leave his wounded to the mercy of the Native Americans. The Caughnawagas stole the soldiers' clothing and sidearms, but they left the men unharmed.[35]

After the defeat, the American army withdrew to Fort George. Most of the troops were later transferred to Sackets Harbor to protect that base, which left the commanding officer at Fort George, Brigadier General George McClure, with 100 regulars. McClure, a politician with little military experience, rightfully feared that the British would recapture Fort George in its weakened state. When he learned about a British advance on the garrison, he ordered his men to burn the nearby village of Newark, which contained more than one hundred dwellings, a library, a church, and 400 inhabitants. The men undertook the operation with ferocity. McClure's men burned at least eighty dwellings. The soldiers carried one immobile woman out of her house before burning her home. The operation left the village's citizens in freezing weather without shelter or supplies. "*The village of Newark* is now in *flames*," McClure proudly wrote Secretary of War Armstrong. "The few remaining inhabitants in it, having been noticed of our intention, were enabled to remove their property."[36]

McClure believed that he was following Secretary Armstrong's orders. In October, Armstrong permitted McClure to destroy Newark if such an action was necessary to achieve better fields of fire. McClure, however, planned to leave the fort, so there was no need to destroy the village. McClure also did not give the town's citizens enough time to pack their belongings and evacuate. One of McClure's officers resigned in protest, and the government disavowed McClure's actions. On December 10–11, 1813, McClure's force withdrew from Fort George to Fort Niagara.[37]

British lieutenant general Gordon Drummond intended to retaliate against McClure's barbarous deed. He seized Fort George and then he planned to cross the river to attack Fort Niagara. On December 18, 560 British soldiers under Lieutenant Colonel John Murray climbed into batteaux to cross the river. Once landed, they formed three columns, fixed bayonets, and crept quietly up to the fort, hoping to catch the guards by surprise. They learned the password from a captured sentry, and a few of Murray's men approached the fort's open gate. They relayed the password to the guard, killed him, and rushed into the fort. The Americans fired cannon into Murray's men, but the British soon overwhelmed the American gunners.[38]

The defeat at Fort Niagara was another stinging loss for the Americans. The British captured 14 American officers and 330 men, and they killed 65 soldiers. Murray seized 29 cannons, 7,000 musket and rifles, 7,000 pairs of shoes, and the clothing of the Eighth and Forty-Ninth Regiments, which had been stolen by the Americans in June. McClure fled for Buffalo before the fighting started. Secretary of War Armstrong, realizing McClure's failings, replaced him with Brigadier General Amos Hall.[39]

On the same day as the attack on Fort Niagara, Major General Phineas Riall, who replaced Vincent as commander of British troops west of Kingston, crossed the Niagara with 1,000 British regulars and 400 Native Americans. He intended to seek retribution for McClure's wanton destruction. His army burned and pillaged Lewistown, Youngstown, and Manchester in New York State. On December 29, Riall seized Black Rock and destroyed four schooners there. His troops then advanced on Buffalo and overran General Hall's militia, who fled at the sight of the British army's approach. Riall's men plundered and burned the town. Only the onset of a harsh winter brought Riall's pillaging expedition to a stop.

The defeats at Stoney Creek and Beaverdam, and the American evacuation of Fort George, signaled the end of campaigning in 1813 on the Lake Ontario littoral. The American army, in an effort to destroy Vincent's force, were routed twice by the enemy, and Vincent's effort reversed Britain's string of losses along the lake. McClure's departure from Fort George marked the end of the Niagara campaign and ended the army's ability to obstruct Britain's maritime movement of supplies from Lake Ontario to Lake Erie. Britain, in contrast, exploited the withdrawal and attacked American garrisons and dockyards to destroy and seize vital supplies, including muskets, schooners, and cannons.[40]

After the failed campaign, Dearborn resigned from his position, and Armstrong appointed another incompetent crony as his replacement. James Wilkinson, whose biography contained a lifetime of treacherous plots, became the commander of the Ninth Military District, which encompassed Vermont and parts of New York and Pennsylvania. Armstrong had other viable choices for the position, including Jacob Brown, who showed skill defending Sackets Harbor, Alexander Macomb, or promising lieutenant colonels such as Winfield Scott. After Armstrong appointed him, Wilkinson held numerous celebratory dinners as he traveled to Sackets Harbor, arriving there in late August 1813.

Changes were also afoot for the British officer corps in Upper Canada. In June 1813, Baron Francis de Rottenburg replaced General Roger Sheaffe as the commander of Upper Canada's forces. Rottenburg possessed an extensive military resume that outshined Wilkinson's conspiratorial antics. Born in Poland, Rottenburg entered in the French Army in 1782 and served for a decade under Louis XVI, after which he fought in the Polish rebellion. When Russia crushed the revolt, he joined the British Army and deployed to Canada in 1810 as a brigadier general. His men viewed Rottenburg as a caring and capable leader. In his new role, Rottenburg commanded three divisions, including the Right Division of troops under Colonel Henry Procter in the west, the Central Division at York and Niagara, and the Left Division at Kingston. "There is a vast deal to be done in this Province," Rottenburg wrote Governor-in-Chief Prevost in July. "Everything is unhinged and requires my utmost exertions to keep affairs in some shape or other."[41]

The fate of Procter and the Northwest Territory, however, would not be decided solely by clashing armies. On Lake Erie, British and American shipyards under the command of R. H. Barclay and Oliver Hazard Perry, respectively, engaged in an unprecedented shipbuilding race to gain superiority on the waterway. The navy that regulated maritime traffic on Lake Erie would control western Upper Canada. Overland routes that circumvented Lake

Erie to Michilimackinac were dangerous and slow, and Amherstburg's survival depended on resupply through the lake. As a result, Barclay and Perry raced to build ships to seize control of Lake Erie and decide the contest for the Northwest.[42]

8

America Retakes the Northwest

Father! Have a big heart!
—Tecumseh to Brigadier General Procter, quoted in William Coffin, *1812: The War, and Its Moral*

In the winter of 1812–1813, US Navy commodore Isaac Chauncey visited the shipyards at Black Rock and Presque Isle (Erie) on Lake Erie. At Presque Isle, Chauncey found four gunboats under construction by Sailing Master Dobbins, but the commodore worried that the small boats could not safely navigate Lake Erie. Chauncey also lamented Dobbin's lack of carpenters, and the few woodworkers he did employ were house carpenters, not skilled shipbuilders. Chauncey did approve of the harbor's location, but he was concerned that a sandbar that crossed Presque Isle's outlet would pose a problem for departing vessels. He also knew that Presque Isle could benefit from the foundries at Pittsburgh that produced ordnance, anchors, and other shipbuilding materials. Chauncey directed Dobbins to build a brig, and he sent for skilled carpenters to assist him. He also wrote numerous letters requesting additional resources for Presque Isle to reinvigorate the shipbuilding efforts there, and he eventually moved the Lake Erie base to the harbor.[1]

Presque Isle's dockyard did indeed retain a significant advantage over Black Rock. Many of the harbor's shipbuilding supplies could be transported year-round from Pittsburgh and Philadelphia to Presque Isle. A well-maintained road existed between Philadelphia and

Pittsburgh, after which supplies could travel on the Allegheny River to French Creek to be unloaded and traverse a sixteen-mile stretch of road to Presque Isle. Pittsburgh contained three foundries that could provide cannon, round shot and grapeshot, and other materials to the dockyard. Philadelphia housed a navy yard where Perry could acquire ordnance, sailors, and other materials.[2]

The route to Black Rock from New York City, in contrast, contained serious logistical challenges. New York contained a navy yard that could supply Black Rock, but carts and wagons loaded with heavy ordnance could not cross the passage for most of the year. From New York, transporters followed navigable rivers until they were within 114 miles of Black Rock, after which they unloaded their provisions on land. Wagons hauling the heavy ordnance required by ships could not traverse this trail most of the year. Black Rock also retained another disadvantage. Ships could not leave the harbor without coming under fire from British guns at Fort Erie, which sat across from Black Rock on the Niagara River. The Americans would need to seize that garrison before ships departed Black Rock to ensure they were not damaged or destroyed in route to Lake Erie. The Americans could try to sneak the vessels out of the harbor at night, but if British gunners were alerted to the commotion, they could fire cannons within short range of the vessels and likely damage or sink a number of them.

Chauncey's renewed interest in Lake Erie was supported by his new boss, William Jones, a successful merchant and shipbuilder, whom President Madison appointed secretary of the navy in early 1813. Jones intended to assume a greater role in the development of the Great Lakes fleet than his predecessor. Unlike Paul Hamilton, Jones refused to delegate complete authority and decision-making to Chauncey. He rightly believed that American naval superiority on the Great Lakes would be the foundation to successful operations in the region. "It is impossible to attach too much importance to our naval operations on the lakes," he wrote Chauncey. "The success of the ensuing campaign will depend absolutely upon our superiority on all the lakes —and every effort, and resource, must be directed to that object." Jones directed Chauncey to build a second brig at Presque Isle (Chauncey already told Master Dobbins to build one brig), and at Chauncey's request, Jones dispatched Master Commandant Oliver Hazard Perry to Presque Isle to revive the country's shipbuilding efforts on Lake Erie.[3]

In the summer of 1813, Britain also sought to breathe energy into its efforts on Lake Erie. The Royal Navy dispatched Commander Robert Barclay to Amherstburg to assume command of the British naval forces on the lake. Barclay, a skilled and brave seaman, had participated in naval combat before. He lost an arm during a skirmish in the English Channel, and he also served aboard a ship of the line during the Battle of Trafalgar in 1805. His naval skills would be tested at Lake Erie, but his success would depend more on a productive shipyard than advanced naval tactics.

Barclay arrived at Amherstburg on June 6, 1813. He first assessed the condition of the twenty-gun sloop of war *Detroit*, which, when completed, would be the largest on the lake. Barclay, however, lacked the shipwrights and necessary materials to finish the sloop. The American raids against York and Fort George had resulted in the loss of cannons, round shot, grape, canvas, rigging, rope, and other materials destined for Amherstburg. Unlike Perry's situation at Presque Isle, Barclay faced an insurmountable logistics challenge. New cannons would need to be sent from Montreal if Governor-in-Chief Prevost had any to spare, or more likely they would be shipped from England. Barclay intended to forge ahead by any means necessary. He cannibalized the *Queen Charlotte* by stripping her sails, cables, and anchors for use on the *Detroit*. He transferred some of Fort Malden's cannons to the *Detroit*—including some of those captured at Detroit—but he lacked enough gunpowder to conduct the preferred amount of live fire exercises. Prevost did send twelve 24-pound carronades to Burlington Bay, but the ordnance, because of the poor condition of the road, could not travel farther than Burlington to reach Long Point on Lake Erie. American naval activity on western Lake Ontario and the Niagara during the summer prevented Britain from using the river as a maritime route to resupply Barclay. The commander also received matches and tubes that were so damaged that he directed his men to use pistols to ignite his ship's cannons.[4]

Barclay also required 300 more seamen to man the vessel. Barclay pled with Sir James Yeo, commodore of the British squadron on the Great Lakes, for additional men and cannon, but Yeo's focus remained on Lake Ontario. Yeo did dispatch around fifty seamen aboard the transport ship *Dover*, which arrived three days before Barclay engaged Perry's fleet. Without a full complement of sailors, Barclay was forced to rely on soldiers who lacked knowledge of sailing operations to operate the *Detroit*. Without additional ordnance and sailors, Barclay doubted that he could defeat the Americans' growing fleet at Presque Isle. Without the proper armaments and manning, his squadron's poor condition "renders the prospect [of defeating Perry] rather gloomy," he wrote Colonel Vincent on June 17.[5]

Barclay proposed that the British execute a combined army-navy assault on Presque Isle. Major General Baron Francis de Rottenburg, who assumed command of Upper Canada from Major General Sir Roger Sheaffe, rejected the idea. Rottenburg's priority was to retake Lake Ontario from Commodore Chauncey and to collaborate with Yeo to ensure that his dockyard produced combat-ready vessels quickly. In fact, in July 1813, Rottenburg advised recently promoted Major General Henry Procter, commander of the British right division, that if the Americans gained superiority on Lake Erie, the commander should withdraw his forces to Montreal. General Rottenburg, as was instructed by Governor-in-Chief Prevost, was prepared to relinquish his western flank to fortify eastern Upper Canada if needed.[6]

Meanwhile, General William Henry Harrison awaited word from Perry that his ships were ready for combat. Kentucky governor Isaac Shelby, who later joined Harrison with reinforcements, understood the importance of the lake. "Without the command of Lake Erie," Shelby wrote Harrison, "it is evident to every reflecting mind, that no decent [descent] upon upper Canada by way of Malden, can promise a favourable issue, and it will be madness in the extreem [*sic*] to put to hazard the best blood & interest of our country to attempt it until that event is effected."[7]

At Presque Isle, Perry rushed the completion of his two brigs, the *Lawrence* and *Niagara*, with the help of renowned New York City shipbuilders Noah and Adam Brown. The Brown brothers performed shipbuilding miracles at Erie and were unsung heroes in the war. One newspaper reported that an eighteen-gun war vessel was built in fifteen days by the Brown brothers. "This looks like energy," the editor wrote. Perry also retained another advantage over Barclay. In April he traveled to Pittsburgh and reported to Chauncey: "I have just now returned from Pittsburg. Most of the articles, we shall want, can be procured there." Pittsburgh's three foundries provided Perry galley stoves, cables, anchors, and shot. In 1812, Pittsburgh's Eagle Foundry advertised that the company produced smith's anvils, rollers for rolling iron, and forge hammers, and "generally every kind of castings." Other factories produced anchors for Perry's fleet, and one of the foundries could bore cannon. Perry also received support from the Philadelphia Navy Yard, and he also purchased canvas in the city.[8]

Perry closely managed the shipbuilding effort at Erie, and his involvement energized the dockyard. He managed the purchase and distribution of supplies for Presque Isle, as was illustrated by his visit to Pittsburgh. Perry, however, could be easily frustrated by any delays in the production process. When he learned that anchors for his brigs would not be ready until July 20 instead of the original deadline of May 1, he called the contract an "abominable deception." He then requested that Chauncey provide him spare anchors because he would not be delayed "for the misconduct of the anchor maker at Pittsburgh." Despite the delays, by July 1813 his dockyard had built six warships in less time than it took Barclay's shipwrights to build the *Detroit* and two gunboats.[9]

Like Barclay, Perry needed more sailors to man his new fleet. He blamed Commodore Chauncey, his senior officer, for his manpower shortages. "For God's sake, and *yours*, and mine," he wrote Chauncey in July, "send me men and officers, and I will have them all in a day or two . . . the vessels are all ready to meet the enemy the moment they are officered and manned." When Chauncey did not send reinforcements, Perry sought intervention from Secretary of the Navy Jones, and he violated navy protocol by writing to the secretary directly: "I cannot describe to you, sir, the mortification of my situation." Perry's impatience with Chauncey ignored the commodore's situation on Lake Ontario, where he also lacked skilled sailors to operate his fleet. Perry, frustrated with his fleet's slow preparations, requested leave from Lake Erie to assume command of a ship in the Atlantic. Perry's frustration with Chauncey and repeated requests to be reassigned to the Atlantic probably hurt Perry's relationship with his inexperienced subordinates, who looked to their squadron commander for guidance and leadership.[10]

In July 1813, the Brown brothers completed the *Lawrence* and *Niagara*, but transporting the vessels onto the lake would risk their capture or destruction. Barclay's fleet blockaded Presque Isle to prevent Perry's ships from departing the harbor for the lake. To cross into the lake, Perry would need to float his new brigs, stripped of their guns, across a sand bar in front Barclay's fleet. His new ships drew nine feet of water, but the sandbar in front of Presque Isle only allowed passage for ships drawing four to five feet of water. If

Barclay caught Perry trying to move the vessels across the shallows, he could easily capture or destroy them.[11]

On July 31, Barclay withdrew his blockade from Presque Isle to resupply his ships. Once his fleet disappeared across the horizon, Perry decided to make his move. Noah Brown and his foreman planned to float the brigs across the sandbar. They placed long pontoons, known as "camels," under each side of the bridge. The camels contained valves to pump water in and out of the containers, which raised and lowered the ship. Perry decided to move the *Lawrence* onto the lake first. Over four nervous and laborious days, his men removed the ship's guns and pumped water into the camels. They drove wooden beams through the sides of the *Lawrence* in order to lift the brig as water was being pumped out. Even with these efforts, the brig became stuck on the bar. The Americans removed the ship's masts and yards to lighten it further. On August 3, the *Lawrence* successfully floated onto Lake Erie. The men then performed the same procedure with the *Niagara*, but while it was crossing the bar, Barclay's fleet appeared on the horizon. The *Niagara*, absent her guns, would have been an easy target for the British. Perry, who had already moved his smaller ships onto the lake, formed his vessels into a battle line. A thick haze prevented Barclay from observing the *Niagara*'s defenseless state on the bar. Barclay was also apprehensive about risking battle until his shipyard completed the *Detroit*, so he ordered his squadron to return to Amherstburg. This event, considered the first instance of "Perry luck," seemed to follow the commander throughout his Erie operations. After Perry floated most of his ships across the bar, he wrote Harrison: "I am of [the] opinion that in two days the naval superiority will be decided on this lake. Should we be successful, I shall sail for the head of the lake immediately to co-operate with you, and hope that our joint efforts will be productive of honour and advantage to our country."[12]

Seven days later, Lieutenant Jesse Elliot arrived with 102 sailors and became Perry's second-in-command, but Elliott believed he should lead the fleet because he had once commanded American forces on Lake Erie and he also assisted in the capture of the *Caledonia* and *Detroit*. Perry assigned Elliot to the *Niagara*, and the lieutenant selected the fleet's best sailors for his own vessel—seamen who should have manned Perry's flagship the *Lawrence*. Perry showed unusual patience with Elliot and did not contest the assignment of the men to the *Niagara*.[13]

Perry's force now totaled 400 men, but he lacked enough time to train the young sailors. Most of Perry's officers had not conducted fleet maneuvers or participated in combat, and many of them received their officer's rank only weeks before the battle. Perry, Elliott, and the other captains established rigorous training regimens since combat could arrive at any moment. The gun crews trained by firing at empty barrels, and sailors practiced operating the vessels and firing muskets. The compressed and demanding training schedule helped foster esprit de corps among the young sailors, and the regimen also nurtured trust in their commander, whose sailing skills they respected.[14]

Once on the lake, Perry established a base at Put-in-Bay, Ohio, a well-protected natural harbor on the lake, located southeast of Amherstburg. From the new location, Perry's fleet could observe the British squadron and interfere with Barclay's supply lines. On September 2, Perry sailed to Sandusky, Ohio, to meet with General Harrison. Harrison and Perry, like Procter and Barclay, maintained a strong interservice relationship, despite answering to different chains of command. Referring to Harrison, Perry wrote that "he is the only officer we have of enterprise." Both officers understood the importance of working together in the remote region. They needed to coordinate naval and land operations to achieve success against Procter. Harrison outranked Perry, but he showed respect for Perry's naval acumen and engaged him as a peer, not as a subordinate. The general also provided 130 Kentucky riflemen to help man the American flotilla. After Perry departed Presque Isle, Harrison, referencing upcoming operations, wrote Perry that "it will be a subject for our joint consultation, whether we should take the whole of the troops to the island's nearest Malden." In his letter, Harrison did not demand a certain course of action, but he instead sought Perry's advice and consultation. The two men shared a mutual acquaintance in Harrison's nephew Richard Randolph, who lived in Perry's hometown of Newport, Rhode Island, which probably helped the two officers build rapport.[15]

In early September, Perry met with his subordinates to plan for combat with Barclay's fleet. Perry predicted the likely British order of battle on the lake, and he assigned each of his ships an enemy vessel to target. He stressed the importance of engaging in close action with the British so the American fleet could use its carronades. The *Lawrence* and *Niagara* contained two-thirds of Perry's total broadside power. Perry needed to close with the enemy quickly to utilize the close combat guns.[16]

At Amherstburg, Procter's situation became desperate. The American victory that summer at Fort George and Britain's withdrawal from Fort Erie gave the United States control of the routes across the Niagara frontier. And Chauncey's cruises on Lake Ontario, along with Perry's recent appearance on Lake Erie, disrupted the British Commissariat's ability to send supplies across those lakes. Chauncey and Perry lacked complete control of either waterway, but they could safely navigate the lakes and intercept enemy supply ships. The Commissariat's alternative was to transport the goods overland from Burlington to Long Point, after which the supplies could be snuck onto Lake Erie and covertly brought to Amherstburg. Or the Commissariat could use a primitive overland route from York that bypassed Lake Erie altogether. Food rations could be sent on these routes, but the trek would be filled with delays and lost goods, and the roads could not sustain Procter's garrison for the long term.

Procter's dire situation resulted in part because Upper Canada's substandard agricultural production could not locally address his army's needs. Most farmers in the province practiced subsistence agriculture, with no surplus crops to sell at market. The settlers grew enough wheat to support their flour needs at the homestead. Also, local livestock owners did not raise enough animals to address the army's considerable requirements for beef and pork. During the war, the situation deteriorated as farmers enrolled to work on boats on the St. Lawrence.[17]

Beef and flour dwindled to a point where Procter believed his hungry Native American allies would turn on his army. These warriors had been important ingredient for Major General Isaac Brock's success at Detroit, but their loyalty depended on the British providing a regular stream of gifts to tribal chiefs. "The Indian and his Family, suffering from Cold, will no longer be amused with Promises," Procter observed. "I do not hesitate to say that if we do not receive a timely, and adequate Supply of Indian Goods and Ammunition, we shall be inevitably subjected, to Ills of the greatest Magnitude." Indeed, Procter understood the "ills" that the Native Americans could inflict based on his own operations against the Americans.[18]

By September 9, Procter placed his men on half allowances of food, and his supply of flour dwindled to a day's worth for his men. The supply crisis forced Barclay to engage Perry one month before he was ready. Yeo later claimed that he believed Barclay could have waited longer, even though Yeo had rejected Barclay's requests for support. The British needed to clear Perry from Lake Erie so they could receive supplies dispatched by Rottenburg. Barclay had two difficult choices: he could burn his fleet and retreat with the army, or prematurely fight the enemy. "I therefore instantly decided," Barclay recalled later, "on that which appeared the most honorable and determined to risk everything rather than abandon my Post without a struggle." Procter agreed with Barclay's decision.[19]

Barclay's fleet contained 364 crewmen, but only 50 were British sailors. Landsmen, unfamiliar with ship operations, completed his crew. In total, the crews of the *Queen Charlotte* and *Detroit* contained only 10 experienced seamen out of 130 men. These landsmen desperately needed gunnery training, but the gunpowder shortage limited the number of live fire exercises they could execute. Procter donated seventy men from the Forty-First Foot to help man the *Detroit*, and he also stripped cannon from Fort Malden to arm the fleet.[20]

At sunrise on September 9, Barclay's fleet hoisted anchors and sailed toward Perry's armada. Barclay's flagship, the *Detroit*, retained seventeen long guns and two carronades. The *Queen Charlotte*, his second strongest ship, mounted three long guns and fourteen carronades. Barclay's squadron also contained the brig *General Hunter*, two schooners (the *Lady Prevost* and *Chippawa*) one small sloop (the *Little Belt*), and two other smaller vessels. The American squadron contained Perry's flagship the *Lawrence* with two long guns and eighteen carronades, and the *Niagara* mounted the same complement of guns. Other ships in his fleet included the *Scorpion*, *Ariel*, *Caledonia*, *Somers*, *Tigress*, *Porcupine*, and *Trippe*. In total Barclay's fleet contained nine more guns than Perry's, but the American fleet retained more carronades. Carronades possessed triple the broadside firing power of a long gun, but their limited range meant that Perry would need to close with the British squadron quickly. The American's total cannon weight was 645 pounds heavier than the British (1,528 to 883), thus giving Perry's flotilla more firepower than Barclay. In addition, Barclay's men transferred cannons from Fort Malden to the *Detroit*, which varied in caliber, without knowing how the guns would perform aboard his ships. Barclay lacked enough gunpowder to perform live fire exercises to test the accuracy of the newly mounted guns, and his men had to use pistols to fire the fleet's cannon because of the poor condition of the matches sent to Amherstburg.[21]

Seamen aboard Perry's flagship observed Barclay leaving port. "Sail oh! Enemy in sight, Get under Way!" spread across Perry's fleet. "All hands, all hands, all hands to quarters." Perry unfurled a large blue banner with white lettering that read "Don't Give Up the Ship" to pay homage to Captain James Lawrence's dying words on the USS *Chesapeake.* Lawrence's ship had been defeated by the HMS *Shannon* in June 1813 off the coast of Boston. "My brave lads," Perry told the crew of the *Lawrence*, "this flag contains the last words of the brave Capt. Lawrence. Shall I hoist it?" "Aye, Aye!" rang across the deck. The entire fleet cheered once the flag became visible. Perry inspected each station and asked his crew if they were ready for battle. A light wind slowly moved the two fleets closer to each other. Despite Perry's intent to close quickly with the enemy, he instead set a course that would more gradually approach Barclay's fleet. The action may have confused his commanders, who believed that he would sail directly toward the British line. "We neared the enemy very slowly," one seaman recalled, "which gave us a little time for reflection . . . it seemed like an awful silence that precedes an earthquake."[22]

Barclay formed a battle line with the *Chippawa* in front, followed by the *Detroit*, *General Hunter*, *Queen Charlotte*, *Lady Prevost*, and *Little Belt.* Perry placed his two schooners in front (*Scorpion* and *Ariel*), followed by the *Lawrence*, which would engage Barclay's flagship, and the *Detroit*, which would be trailed by the *Caledonia.* The *Niagara*, captained by Elliot, followed the *Caledonia* and would attack Barclay's second largest ship, the *Queen Charlotte.*

As the American line of ships approached the British squadron, Perry directed his sailors to close in on the enemy. The ship behind Perry, the *Caledonia*, was too slow to keep up with the *Lawrence.* The *Niagara*, which trailed the *Caledonia*, possessed enough speed, but the vessel needed to take an indirect route around the *Caledonia* to follow Perry into battle. The result was that Perry's three schooners and one sloop lagged far behind his flagship as he sailed alone toward Barclay's squadron. Before Perry made his maneuver, he should have signaled his intentions to the fleet. His officers likely wondered if they should stay in the battle line or follow Perry on a more direct course toward the enemy. Perry had recently received a new set of signals from the Navy Department, but he did not employ them at this critical time.[23]

Barclay's long guns targeted the approaching *Lawrence*, which, armed primarily with carronades, could not return fire. For thirty agonizing minutes, cannonballs tore the brig's rigging and decks. Flying splinters and cannonballs killed and wounded some of Perry's crew. The masts and spars of the *Lawrence*, however, remained undamaged. Some observers attribute the captain's successful approach to another instance of "Perry luck," but in this case, Barclay's inexperienced gunners, firing a multitude of calibers, had difficulty hitting their target. If Barclay could have damaged the *Lawrence*'s masts before it closed in, he probably could have captured or destroyed the brig before the remainder of the American fleet lent assistance to the damaged vessel.[24]

The *Lawrence* sailed within 250 yards of the *Detroit*, and Perry ordered his gunners to unload their carronades. Without a signal, Elliot was unsure whether he should follow the *Lawrence* or stay in the battle line. He chose to stay with the battle line, a decision he was later be criticized for. Elliot's critics believed that he was a coward who should have closed with his assigned enemy ship, the *Queen Charlotte*. That ship joined the battle and closed on the *Lawrence*. Perry was on his own.[25]

The *Queen Charlotte*, *Detroit*, and other ships from the British fleet pounded the *Lawrence* for two hours. Surgeon Usher Parsons recalled, "Little could be heard but the deafening thunders of our own broad-sides, the crash of balls dashing through our timbers, and the shrieks of the wounded." Parsons worked feverishly to tend to the wounded, but too many men sought treatment. The *Lawrence*, a shallow draft vessel, did not contain sufficient space below the waterline for a sick bay where the wounded could be treated in relative safety. Parsons chose the wardroom as his hospital, and its location above the waterline made his surgery harrowing work.

During the fight, Parsons applied a splint to the hand of one midshipman. The sailor eased back once Parsons completed his work. A cannonball shot through the hull, hit the man, and sent his lifeless corpse to the other side of the room. Parsons carried out six amputations during the action and cared for dozens of sailors. Amidst the carnage, Parsons recalled some humorous moments. Lieutenant John Yarnell, Perry's first lieutenant, came below the deck with blood streaming from his scalp. The surgeon applied lint to the wound and wrapped his head in a bandage. Yarnell descended again later with another injury, and this time the wounded gathered in the wardroom began laughing. Cannonballs had destroyed the ship's hammocks and pieces of reed floated around the deck like snow. Some of the material had settled on Yarnell's scalp, which made his head look like an owl. The men joked that the devil had arrived. Perry regularly appeared in the wardroom to request spare men who could fight on the upper deck. After Perry's seventh visit, Parsons explained that he had no more men to offer him.[26]

The British fleet's intense broadsides destroyed the *Lawrence*'s rigging, masts, and spars, causing the brig to float aimlessly. Cannonballs knocked the *Lawrence*'s guns off their carriages; corpses, blood, and body parts littered her deck. By 2:30 p.m., the *Lawrence* suffered twenty-two killed and sixty-four wounded during the two-hour exchange. By destroying the American flagship, the British fleet appeared close to victory. Perry, however, remained unhurt, and he asked Lieutenant William Taylor for a boat to ferry him to the undamaged *Niagara*, which had finally sailed closer to the action. Taylor told him that the *Lawrence* possessed only one functioning boat and that the hull suffered serious damage during the firefight. The oarsmen would need to lean to one side to prevent the boat from sinking. Perry, undeterred, directed a private to haul down the *Lawrence*'s blue banner, and he, along with four other seamen, climbed into the boat to begin their harrowing journey to the *Niagara*. Barclay's gunners, who observed Perry's escape, trained their guns on the departing crew. Balls splashed around the boat, but none of them hit their target. Perry arrived at the larboard side of the *Niagara* and boarded the vessel. Perry instructed Elliot to depart the *Niagara* and bring a schooner into battle. Aboard the *Lawrence*, Yarnell, as Perry had instructed, lowered the ship's colors to surrender.[27]

At 2:45 p.m., Perry bore down on the British fleet in the undamaged *Niagara*. He planned to break through the British battle line and deliver a broadside to the *Detroit*. The *Queen Charlotte* and *Detroit* tried to counter the move, but the two vessels became entangled with each other. The *Niagara*'s broadside hit both ships. The *Caledonia* trailed the *Niagara* and also executed a raking fire. The *Niagara* turned and launched more broadsides at the entangled vessels. A splinter lodged in Barclay's thigh and incapacitated him—his eighth wound in the service of the Royal Navy.[28]

Barclay's fleet had suffered serious damage even before the *Niagara*'s attack. Early in the fight, American fire killed Captain Robert Finnis of the *Queen Charlotte* and his first lieutenant. Cannon fire from the *Caledonia* also killed the *Detroit*'s first lieutenant. Barclay had no choice but to surrender his flagship. Other vessels in his fleet also surrendered, except for one schooner

Figure 8. ***The Battle of Lake Erie, Commodore O. H. Perry's Victory.*** The Battle of Lake Erie, with Master Commandant Perry in a small boat after evacuating his flagship, the USS *Lawrence*, seen in the foreground. Perry's flagship came under fire from multiple British ships because the speed varied among ships in his battle line as they approached the enemy fleet, and Perry did not signal to his officers to change the position of the ships. "Perry's luck" was evident at the battle, however, as Perry departed his flagship under fire and safely arrived at the *Niagara*, from where he commanded his fleet to victory. Courtesy of the Library of Congress, LC-DIG-pga-02289.

and sloop that tried to escape but were quickly captured. Aboard the *Lawrence*, Yarnell raised the colors back to their proper position on the shattered vessel. At 4:00 p.m., Perry penned his historic words to General Harrison, which became etched into America's memory: "We have met the enemy and they are ours; two ships, two brigs, one schooner, and one sloop."[29]

Perry returned to the *Lawrence*. Her deck presented a morbid scene. "I am not hesitant to say there was not a dry eye on the ship," Sailing Master Taylor recalled. The screams of the wounded echoed throughout the ship; corpses littered the upper deck. The sailors able to stand greeted Perry's arrival in shocked silence. "Those of us who were spared and able to walk," Parsons remembered, "met [Perry] him at the gangway to welcome him on board, but the salutation was a silent one on both sides; not a word could find utterance." The British captains boarded the *Lawrence* and gave Perry their swords. He accepted them, told the officers to retain their sidearms, and inquired about Commodore Barclay. When he learned of his wound, Perry directed his men to tend to Barclay, a gesture that probably saved his life. Barclay's fleet suffered forty-one killed and ninety-four wounded; Perry's casualties included twenty-seven killed and ninety-six wounded. Chauncey, Perry, Elliot, and the crews of the American fleet received $255,000—the estimated value of the British fleet—from the US Treasury Department for their victory.[30]

Soon after the battle, recriminations against Elliot's conduct abounded. Critics contended that Elliott should have followed Perry into the battle, but the commodore did not signal for him to trail the *Lawrence*. Perry, basking in the victory, ignored the criticisms and directed his officers to stay silent on the issue. Perry feared that an endless cycle of recriminations would emerge if his men engaged in the debate. Indeed, Perry had enough to be proud of—his victory was a national sensation.[31]

With Barclay's fleet destroyed, General Procter debated his options. He could fight Harrison, defeat him, and capture supplies from Americans outposts in the region, or he could withdraw toward the center division of the British army at Burlington Heights. Many of his allied Native American warriors returned home after the battle or indicated that they would ally with the United States. Procter convened a council of war with his officers and 200 remaining Native American warriors, including Tecumseh. He told the group that he intended to retreat toward the Niagara and burn the stores at Detroit and Amherstburg. The chiefs remained divided on whether they should agree to Procter's suggestion. Then Tecumseh spoke. The Shawnee chief wore a deerskin dress with a handkerchief wrapped around his head. A plume of white ostrich feathers protruded from the bandana, and his piercing black eyes danced around the room. "You always told us you would never draw your foot off British ground, but now father we see that you are drawing back," Tecumseh declared. "And we are sorry to see our father doing so without seeing the enemy. We must compare our father's conduct to a fat animal, that carries its tail upon its back, but when affrighted, it drops it between its legs and runs off." Tecumseh reminded Procter that Britain had abandoned their Native American allies after the Revolutionary War, and that by retreating from the Northwest, they were doing so again. The Shawnee chief would leave his bones at Amherstburg before he would retreat. The chiefs raised their tomahawks and began shouting. Procter, in order to appease his Native American allies, told the chiefs that he would make a stand at Moraviantown, a village halfway between Burlington Heights and Amherstburg. He directed his men to burn the garrison at Amherstburg including navy yard, barracks, and public store houses. Harrison, who respected Tecumseh and despised Procter, wrote that Tecumseh's strategy showed "the talents of the former [Tecumseh], and the great defect of them in the latter [Procter]." On September 24, Procter's army, with women, children, baggage, and artillery, departed Amherstburg. He marched his force along the south shore of Lake St. Clair to the Thames River, after which he planned to advance upriver to Burlington Heights on the western tip of Lake Ontario.[32]

After his victory on the lake, Perry turned his attention to assisting Harrison. The general intended to attack Fort Malden with the commodore's assistance. Perry's fleet would transport Harrison's soldiers to a landing point three miles south of Amherstburg and provide covering fire as the troops debarked. Harrison deferred to Perry on how the navy would support the operation. Perry, armed with his experience from the joint army-navy assault against Fort George, decided to tow batteaux behind his warships to assist with disembarking troops. Harrison organized his men in preparation for an expected counterattack by Procter's force, but despite the preparations, the Americans landed unopposed. Procter had departed Amherstburg five days earlier. Harrison arrived at that garrison on September 27.[33]

Harrison soon proceeded to Detroit, where he waited for Colonel Richard Johnson's 1,000 mounted riflemen to arrive from Fort Meigs. Harrison required mounted infantry to gain on Procter's retreating army, which Harrison believed had more than 1,000 horses. He also probably recalled the importance of mounted infantrymen during Anthony's Wayne campaign, where at the Battle of Fallen Timbers mounted infantry rolled up the enemy's flanks. Colonel Richard Johnson, commander of a regiment of mounted Kentucky riflemen under Harrison, marched his men toward Detroit and through the battlefield at the River Raisin. Johnson had sent a detachment of men to join General Winchester on that campaign, and most of the men died during the battle, so the area had special meaning to his soldiers. They walked to the locations where their friends had been killed and mourned their loss. "They looked in grief and reverential awe," one soldier recalled, "on the spot where the noble and gallant Allen had fallen, where the handsome and brilliant Hart had gone down, and where the chivalrous Woolfolk had been butchered." A Native American guide showed some of Johnson's men where Captain John Simpson had been killed. His comrades could identify his remains because of his height. They buried the bones, and the group proceeded to Detroit where they arrived on September 30.[34]

On September 21, Harrison also received Kentucky reinforcements under the command of Governor Isaac Shelby, who followed Hull's road from Urbana to Detroit. General Shelby renounced his rank and subordinated himself and his men to Harrison. Shelby's men constructed a six-foot-high fence out of trees and brush on a peninsula to confine their 3,000 horses so they could graze on its pastures. For an unknown reason, the horses became frightened and stampeded toward the camp. They darted between the camp's huts and tens, killing and wounding some of Shelby's men. Some of the horses ran into water and were lost; others became stuck in the river's sandbank. The men calmed the remaining animals and extracted them from the sand.[35]

Harrison, after some delays, departed Detroit on October 1 to pursue Procter's force. He intended to move his soldiers across three bridges that stood between him and Procter's army, but he feared that the British had destroyed them to slow his pursuit. His army arrived at the first two crossings before they were destroyed. The third bridge was only partially ruined, and Harrison's men quickly repaired it. Meanwhile, Perry supported the land movement by carrying the army's baggage from Detroit and covering the force as it crossed over the Thames River.[36]

Meanwhile, Procter's unwieldy caravan trudged northeast toward Moraviantown. Poor roads and a shallow Thames River slowed his force's progress. Some of his supply boats trailed the caravan on the Thames River, and many of them became stuck on sandbars while trying to navigate the river's many curves. Procter destroyed the stuck boats and abandoned others. American dragoons also caught up to some of the slower boats and overtook them. Procter lost much of his artillery during the journey, including two 24-pounders, which illustrated the difficulty of moving heavy ordnance on Upper Canada's unimproved roads and trails.[37]

Harrison's army closed in on the British on October 5, and prepared to engage the enemy force. Procter, aware of the American approach, halted on the north bank of the Thames River, one and a half miles west of Moraviantown. The village offered a strong defensive position, but Procter chose instead to fight in the woods outside of the town. He stationed the Forty-First Foot on his left flank among some tall trees, and he posted a 6-pounder on a road that ran through the middle of the position. Procter dispatched his remaining cannon—a 6-pounder, two 3-pounders, and a howitzer—to Moraviantown.[38]

Tecumseh located a strong defensive position for his warriors between two small swamps. The swamps contained moss-lined trees, fallen logs, and overgrown vegetation that his warriors could utilize for cover. The thick mud would also prevent Harrison's horsemen from penetrating the area. Tecumseh's Native American force consisted of Shawnees, Ottawas, Delawares, and Wyandots, among other tribes, but Tecumseh commanded fewer than 500 warriors by the time of the battle. Tecumseh believed that his men could defeat the Americans. He walked along the lines, shook the hands of his men, and shouted words of encouragement in Shawnee. He shook Procter's hand. "Father! Have a big heart!" he told the British general.[39]

Two hours later, the American force approached Procter's lines. Harrison intended to send Lewis Cass's brigade of regulars (Cass had been promoted to brigadier general) down the road against the Forty-First Foot and keep Colonel Richard Johnson's mounted infantry in reserve. Johnson learned, however, through observation and prisoner statements, that Procter had formed the British in open column at intervals three feet apart, which would make them vulnerable to a cavalry charge. Colonel Johnson directed 500 men to charge the British Forty-First, and Harrison's infantry, under the command of Colonel Isaac Shelby, was to follow the mounted militia into combat. At what would be known as the Battle of the Thames, or Moraviantown, Harrison's army outnumbered Procter's three to one.[40]

Colonel Johnson arranged his men into four, double-file, charging columns. Even though his Kentucky militia marched seventy miles in three and a half days, they were eager for action. Cries of "Remember the Raisin!" echoed throughout the formation. They sought revenge against Procter and the Northwest Native American tribes for massacres at Fort Dearborn, Fort Miami (after Fort Meigs), and Frenchtown.[41]

The horsemen galloped down the road and quickly overran the 6-pounder. The British fired a round, but most of their balls flew overhead of the charging horsemen. The horsemen passed the second line of infantry, wheeled about, and fired into the line with their rifles. The Forty-First broke ranks. "For God's sake, men, stand and fight," a sergeant exclaimed, but his plea went unanswered. Procter also tried to rally the soldiers, but they did not respond to his pleas. "I cannot but observe," he later wrote, "that the Troops do not seem to have had that Confidence in themselves, that they have shewn, on every former Occasion." The Americans captured most of the Forty-First and turned Procter's flank. On this day, the Forty-First did not live up to their reputation, and the men's faith in Procter must have been at an all-time low. He left most of his artillery in the village rather on the battlefield, and he placed his men in an open expanse instead of the more defensible position in Moraviantown. General Procter galloped off once the Forty-First broke and did not join Tecumseh's warriors in the swamp.[42]

After the Americans routed the Forty-First, the mounted rifles charged Tecumseh and his warriors, whose left flank was now open. A group of twenty Americans nicknamed the "Forlorn Hope," which included Colonel Johnson, rode in the column's front to attract the enemy's fire in order to reveal the Native Americans' position. As the vanguard neared the swamp, the Native Americans fired on the group and killed or wounded fifteen of the twenty men. Johnson, who survived the charge, ordered his men to dismount since their horses could not trot through the marsh. The Kentuckians, armed with long rifles, pressed into the swamp, fighting tree to tree and log to log, to rout the Native American force.[43]

Despite their flank being turned by the retreat of the Forty-First, Tecumseh and his band of followers continued to fight. At some point during the battle, a bullet killed the gallant Native American chief, but it is not clear who fired the fatal shot. Colonel Johnson fired at one chief, but no one could confirm that the man was Tecumseh. The location of the warrior's body also remained a mystery. Some accounts claim that British soldiers identified the body and showed it to some American officers, who stripped it of clothing and cut strips of skin for souvenirs. Other accounts suggest that his warriors retrieved the hallowed body from the battleground and buried it somewhere in the swamp. Either way, Tecumseh's demise sapped his followers' morale and they retreated deeper into the marsh.[44]

At the Battle of the Thames, Procter lost 606 enlisted men and 28 officers captured or killed, but 200 escaped with him. Prevost ordered a court-martial, and the court suspended Procter's rank and pay for six months. At

Figure 9. *Battle of the Thames—Death of Tecumseh.* Colonel Richard Johnson, who led the forward vanguard known as the "forlorn hope" at the battle. In the illustration, Johnson is firing at Tecumseh, but no evidence supports the claim that Johnson killed the Shawnee chief. Also, at this point in the battle, Johnson had ordered his men to dismount from their horses because the animals could not wade through the marsh. Courtesy of the Library of Congress, LC-USZ62-16868.

the battle, Harrison captured six brass artillery pieces, two 24-pounders, and he reclaimed the famous Revolutionary War cannon surrendered by Hull at Detroit, along with boats, wagons, artillery, arms, and other military stores. For the Kentuckians, the battle of October 5, 1813, eliminated the Native American threat in the Northwest Territory and ended twenty years of British intervention in the region. The editor of the *Kentucky Gazette* wrote, "The War in the North-West has closed, peace is now sealed with the blood of the Kentuckians. Our exertions have at length ended a war of *twenty years* duration. Let Kentuckians exult! Let the whole western people rejoice. . . . Thanks to the Almighty we have at length destroyed the cause of war to the west and north-west." After the battle, Harrison issued a proclamation to the people in Upper Canada, which allowed for the continuation of their local governments, and he promised protection of their private property. Harrison, in a gesture of respect for Perry, allowed the lower-ranking officer to co-sign the document.[45]

Harrison returned to Detroit to wait for provisions that would allow him to march toward Michilimackinac, but a violent storm destroyed two American schooners on Lake Erie, one of which contained the men's baggage, along with provisions of salt and flour. Harrison held a meeting with his commanders, who explained that they needed more supplies to undertake the campaign because they would not arrive before fall. At that time of year, storms on Lake Huron would prevent Perry from safely navigating the lake, so the group postponed their raid until the following year. Procter's and Barclay's actions, even in defeat, had forced the Americans to delay their attack on the island. "At any rate," Harrison wrote Secretary of War Armstrong, "it is not a matter of much importance to have that place in our possession during the winter, cut off as it is from a communication with the rest of the world."[46]

Indeed, the British commanding officer at Mackinac, Captain Richard Bullock, lacked enough food to feed the garrison's one hundred men. His isolated position at the far end of Britain's logistics line made his garrison vulnerable to any disruptions in his overextended supply lines. He normally relied on provisions from Amherstburg via Lake Erie, but Harrison and Perry had severed that line of communication. Food rations could be moved through a series of road, rivers, and portages from York to Mackinac, but the journey would be difficult in the winter with creeks and rivers frozen. This unmapped and dangerous route extended from York to Lake Simcoe, then to Matchedash on Lake Huron, where Bullock would send canoes to retrieve the supplies. Bullock, in an effort to survey the trip to Matchedash on the lake, tried to send two large canoes and a batteau to the bay in October, but they returned unsuccessfully because of the thick snow and ice on the lake. Bullock also hoped to send the schooner *Nancy* to Matchedash, but the ship's poor sails and cables made it unfit to attempt the dangerous journey. In October, Bullock retained sixty-eight pounds of salt meat and enough flour to feed the garrison for one month. Bullock purchased provisions from the island's few inhabitants and reduced the amount of rations his men received. On November 1, he slashed the issue of beef to one-half pound per day, and on Christmas, he reduced it further to one-half pound per four days a week.

In October, Bullock and his men finally received something that raised their spirits: some newspapers arrived at the isolated garrison: "The newspapers . . . was a welcome treat to us here as we seldom hear anything of passing events."[47]

Despite Harrison's success, operations outside the region could decide the fate of the Michigan Territory and western Upper Canada. Prevost and Yeo still controlled the eastern half of Upper Canada. American failures to destroy Kingston enabled Yeo to continue building a fleet that could contest control of the lake from the Americans. If the British succeeded, Prevost could reinforce his western flank and attempt to retake Amherstburg and Detroit. American leadership, however, understood the importance of Lake Ontario and intended to retain control of the waterway. In late 1813, American war planners focused on eastern Lake Ontario, with the aim of seizing Kingston and wresting the remainder of Upper Canada from Britain. With control of Montreal, Kingston, and Lake Ontario, the United States could slice the logistics corridor from Quebec to Upper Canada. But the US Army, fraught with leadership and institutional pitfalls, had yet to prove that it could conduct a successful cross-border operation.

9

The Montreal Campaign

As the enemy advanced, I plainly saw we had nothing to trust but every man doing his duty.
—John Harvey, Canadian militiaman at Crysler's Farm, quoted in Matilda Edgar, *Ten Years in Upper Canada in Peace and War*

In February 1813, President Madison replaced Secretary of War William Eustis with John Armstrong. The new secretary brought a different perspective and management style to the war in Canada. Armstrong served in the Revolutionary War, and when hostilities with Britain commenced in 1812, he rejoined the army as a brigadier general in command of New York City's defenses. Armstrong understood British North America's logistical vulnerabilities. In early 1812, as a private citizen, he highlighted a sound war strategy to Secretary Eustis: "In invading a neighboring and independent territory like Canada, having a frontier of immense extent; destitute of means strictly its own for the purposes of defense; separated from the rest of the empire by an ocean, and having to this but one outlet—this outlet forms your true object or point of attack; because, if gained, every thing depending upon it is gained also."[1]

After his appointment, Armstrong set out to organize the War Department. He issued a new directive that divided the United States into nine military districts and shifted the army's focus from fortifications and militia to a stronger regular force. He also issued the "Rules and Regulations of the Army of the United States," which, for the first time, outlined the duties of various staff offices and codified promotion rules and other army procedures. Armstrong also benefited from a bill passed by Congress in 1813 that provided additional personnel to the new Quartermaster Department and the Commissary of Ordnance. The army's broken logistical machinery, established in early 1812, lacked enough staff to function effectively. Armstrong failed to centralize the supply architecture during his tenure, however, and an inadequate logistics system continued to plague the army in 1813–1814.[2]

Many of Armstrong's generals resented the secretary's detail-oriented approach. He often provided guidance on issues that would normally be handled independently by his officers, and he circumvented the chain of command by communicating with his officers' subordinates. His overreach into his subordinates' activities angered many of his generals, who resented his involvement and lack of trust in them.

During his tenure, Armstrong's focus remained on Kingston and Montreal at the expense of the Lake Erie theater. In the spring and summer of 1813, the secretary had directed Dearborn and Chauncey on the campaign that resulted in the attacks on York and Fort George. Since assuming office, the secretary largely ignored Harrison's and Perry's efforts further west. Some of his inattention to the region could be attributed to personal feelings. Armstrong disliked General Harrison's reliance on militia troops, and he disapproved of the general's casual appearance (he often donned a hunting shirt).[3]

Armstrong proposed that the army and navy conduct a joint attack on Kingston in the winter of 1813. Two brigades could move from Lake Champlain via Châteauguay with sleighs, cross the St. Lawrence, and seize Kingston, after which the army's main body would rendezvous with that force to conduct future operations against Montreal. He directed Major General James Wilkinson to assault Kingston directly from land or cut the harbor's supply line from Montreal. "In conducting the present campaign," Armstrong wrote Wilkinson, "you will make Kingston your primary *object*, and that you will choose (as circumstances may warrant) between a *direct* and *indirect* attack upon that post" (original emphasis). The secretary believed that a combined army-navy pincer movement would force the British to surrender Kingston or retreat to Montreal.[4]

The general in charge of the campaign, Wilkinson, served in the Revolutionary War and rose quickly to the rank of brevet brigadier general. Conspiracies and quarrels, however, rather than sound generalship, marked Wilkinson's career. He discredited himself in a coup to overthrow George Washington, and he illegally negotiated a trade agreement with Spain in a plot known as the Spanish Conspiracy. Wilkinson joined Anthony Wayne at the Battle of Fallen Timbers and became the army's ranking officer upon Wayne's death in 1796. In 1805–1806, he served as the governor of the Louisiana Territory, and at the start of the war he commanded the Seventh Military District in New Orleans, where his troops remained undersupplied and poorly trained. Despite his inability to prove himself as a competent officer, Wilkinson was promoted to major general of the Ninth Military District, which included parts of New York, Pennsylvania, and all of Vermont.

For the campaign to be successful, Wilkinson needed to collaborate with the officer in command of the Lake Champlain region, Major General Wade Hampton. Hampton, a pompous southern plantation owner, despised Wilkinson and refused to report to him. Armstrong, replicating the convoluted command structure that had existed before between Stephen Van Rensselaer and Alexander Smyth, allowed Hampton to report to him on matters relating to the training and organization of his army. Hampton would later obey Wilkinson once the two armies joined together to assault Montreal.[5]

The command arrangement undercut the expedition before it began. Ambition and popularity, more than duty and mission, motivated Wilkinson and Hampton. Hampton was disinclined to join Wilkinson's army, a critical aspect of the plan, because Hampton would then be forced to report to Wilkinson, something his fragile ego would not allow. When Wilkinson arrived at Albany, New York, he penned a letter to Hampton, suggesting that Hampton transfer his force to Plattsburgh for the upcoming campaign. The directive incensed the prickly Hampton. "I am taught," Hampton wrote Armstrong, "that even my local movements are to depend upon orders issuing from an individual 200 or 400 miles distant. In a word I am permitted to do nothing but that which that individual may think proper to permit me to do." He asked to be discharged from the army, a request Armstrong denied. Wilkinson, infuriated that Hampton ignored his order, wrote Armstrong: "I hear not a word from Hampton. I hope he does mean to take the stud, but if so we can do without him and he should be sent home."[6]

On August 26, 1813, Wilkinson convened a council of war with Commodore Chauncey and other officers in the region. The council debated options for the "reduction of Kingston" by an indirect or direct attack, as Armstrong had instructed. The council agreed to make a feint against Kingston and advance down the St. Lawrence to cut Kingston's line of communication with Montreal and starve the garrison of supplies and reinforcements. Kingston's garrison would be forced to evacuate to reopen their line of communications, after which the American army could fight them outside of the town's defenses. Governor-in-Chief Prevost might also choose to reinforce Kingston with troops from Montreal, which would leave that city vulnerable to attack by Hampton. After conducting the feint against Kingston, the force would combine with Hampton's army assembling at Plattsburgh, New York.[7]

The campaign was the boldest plan yet endorsed by the War Department. The destruction of Kingston and its dockyard would curtail Yeo's efforts to control the lake, and likely give control of the strategic waterway to the United States for the remainder of the war. The more important target, however, was Montreal. British deep-draft vessels could not navigate the river above the city, so Montreal served as a vital storage and distribution point for supplies. If the Americans seized Montreal, Britain could not sustain its garrisons or dockyards west of the town, including posts on Lake Ontario, the Niagara frontier, and Lake Erie, because overland routes could not substitute for waterway transport. Only two sections of a road from Montreal to Kingston had been completed, and another alternate route required significant work to be usable. The proposed passage started at the Ottawa River, which branched off from the St. Lawrence west of Montreal. The proposed route, destined for Kingston, would be considerably longer than the St. Lawrence, and it would require the creation of multiple canals and portages to become a viable passage. (The route was not completed until 1828). The American operation, therefore, had the potential to sever Upper from Lower Canada.[8]

In September, Armstrong pressed Wilkinson to prepare for operations, but many of Wilkinson's troops fell ill, and so did the general himself. By mid-September he recovered and announced that he would advance to Kingston with a force of 8,000 men. Wilkinson believed that his army would be successful. "All things are working well," he wrote Armstrong, "and it would seem that nothing short of an act of God or a betrayal of my plans can prevent our success." Armstrong, excited at the prospect of his Revolutionary War comrade's success, wrote Wilkinson that if he seized Kingston, "you will thus literally fulfill the orders you have received and merit the baton of a field marshal."[9]

Commodore Isaac Chauncey's fleet was an important ingredient in the campaign. His ships would prevent the Royal Navy from landing reinforcements at Kingston during the attack, and he could protect the army flotilla as it floated down on the St. Lawrence. In August and September 1813, just weeks before the operation, the two fleets engaged each other to control Lake Ontario. Sir James Yeo, commander of the British fleet on the Great Lakes, and Chauncey spotted each other off the Niagara in August, but they did not close in for battle. That night, on August 7, 1813, a storm sank the US schooners *Hamilton* and *Scourge*, and two days later, the schooners *Julia* and *Growler* became separated from the American squadron and were captured by Yeo. In three days, Chauncey lost four ships. The commodore later added a new schooner, the *Sylph*, and the American squadron again sailed from Sackets Harbor to find Yeo's fleet. On September 11, the two squadrons met near Amherst Bay, but neither officer would commit to battle. Yeo and Chauncey, concerned with preserving their fleets, refused to engage the other unless assured of success.[10]

Two weeks later, on September 28, the two flotillas encountered each other south of York in gale-force wind conditions. The two squadrons closed, and the flagships traded fire from 1,500 yards away. During the exchange, round shot from the *Pike*'s long guns damaged Yeo's flagship, the *Wolfe*. Chauncey sailed toward the *Wolfe* to finish it when British captain William Mulcaster, recognizing the *Wolfe*'s disabled state, skillfully sailed the *Royal George* between the *Wolfe* and the *General Pike*. He slowed his ship to a halt and initiated a broadside exchange with Chauncey's flagship. While the *George* was exchanging broadsides with the *General Pike*, Yeo's crew repaired the *Wolfe* and sailed toward Burlington Heights. Mulcaster's brilliant move saved the British flagship from destruction and likely prevented the Americans from gaining enduring control of the lake. As Yeo's fleet sailed to Burlington Bay, Chauncey chased the flotilla in gale-force winds. The pursuit was known as the "Burlington Races," and the American squadron eventually retired when it neared the British port and became threatened by land-based artillery. For the moment, the Americans could travel safely on Lake Ontario, and Yeo would not molest Wilkinson's assault on Kingston.[11]

Despite Chauncey's ability to navigate safely on the lake, Secretary of War Armstrong began to doubt his original plan to assault Kingston after he learned that Governor-in Chief Prevost fortified the garrison with 1,500 troops. He decided that Wilkinson should attack Montreal instead. "I call it [Montreal] a greater and safer object," Armstrong wrote Wilkinson, "because at Montreal you find the weaker place and the smaller force to encounter." Wilkinson, who favored attacking Montreal from the beginning, supported the change, but both men began to worry about the onset of winter. Cold temperatures would soon freeze the St. Lawrence and prevent Chauncey from supporting the expedition. Ice and snow would cover Lower Canada's wilderness roads, challenging the army's ability to move wagons, pack animals, and artillery. These realizations prompted both men to doubt that the expedition could succeed in the cold months ahead. Wilkinson, who earlier said that only God could stop his invasion, now believed that more earthly impediments would challenge him. He demanded written proof from the Madison administration that they still wanted him to assault Montreal, in place of Kingston, in the upcoming campaign. "It is necessary to my justification," Wilkinson wrote Armstrong, "that you should, by the authority of the president, direct the operations of the army under my command, particularly against Montreal."[12]

Neither Armstrong nor Wilkinson, however, relayed the news to Commodore Chauncey that Montreal, rather than Kingston, was now the target. Not until October 29 did Wilkinson inform Chauncey about the plan to bypass Kingston and seize Montreal. The commodore was "mortified" at the decision. Chauncey believed that seizing Kingston and destroying its shipyard should be the campaign's priority. He also feared that if his squadron sailed up the St. Lawrence, Admiral Yeo would assault a defenseless Sackets Harbor. Nevertheless, he agreed to assist Wilkinson, but he told Secretary of the Navy William Jones that his fleet would vacate the St. Lawrence by November 1 to ensure that his ships would not be trapped in ice and destroyed. Chauncey's unwillingness to support the effort cast doubt on its success. The army, divided between Hampton and Wilkinson, now faced an interservice crisis with Chauncey, who was a critical ingredient of Armstrong's plan.[13]

In mid-October, Hampton's army began its march to the Châteauguay River to hold the enemy in check and await his rendezvous with Wilkinson. On October 21, Hampton crossed into Canada with 4,000 infantry and ten guns. Prevost, learning about Hampton's advance, worried about Montreal's defenses. He mustered 8,000 sedentary militia to help fortify the city and transport supplies. He also directed Lieutenant Colonel Charles-Michel d'Irumberry, Comte de Salaberry, a Canadian born British regular, to attack Hampton's approaching force. Salaberry received the dispatch while dining at a tavern. "D— it," he exclaimed, jumping up from his seat, "Hampton is at Four Corners, and I must go and fight him!"[14]

Salaberry, a French Canadian, had served with distinction in the British Army. In 1793, at fourteen, he joined the Forty-Fourth Regiment. Promotions came slow to Salaberry, who lacked the funds to purchase his commissions. In the West Indies, his company of grenadiers covered a bloody British withdrawal from a fort, and in 1803 the army promoted him to captain in the Sixtieth Regiment of Foot, a colonial service regiment. In 1809, the unit deployed from Ireland to Canada.[15]

Salaberry retained a reputation for bravery and courage. In the West Indies, he agreed to duel a skilled Prussian swordsman, even though Salaberry lacked skill with the weapon. The Prussian slashed Salaberry's face, and instead of quitting, Salaberry patched himself with a handkerchief and continued the bout. (Reportedly Salaberry mortally sliced the Prussian at the waist.) Though brave in a duel, Salaberry, a temperamental martinet, often exploded on his senior officers, which prompted some of his best leaders to leave the regiment. In the spring of 1812, Prevost asked Salaberry to raise a Provincial Corps of Light Infantry, known as the Canadian Voltigeurs, which was a full-time unit paid for by the Province of Lower Canada. The soldiers would be equipped, armed, and trained like British Army regulars. Salaberry selected his men from prominent families within Lower Canada.

Anticipating Hampton's approach, Salaberry chose a strong position on the left bank of the Châteauguay River, thirty-five miles from Montreal. A road ran parallel to the river 300 yards away, and four ravines extended from nearby woods across the lane. Salaberry directed his men to create breastworks along the ravines with stacked logs. He also ordered his militia to construct an abatis two miles in front of the main position. In total, Salaberry commanded around 400 Canadian militia. Lieutenant Colonel George R. J. "Red George" MacDonnell reinforced Salaberry with 1,400 additional militia.[16]

Hampton's troops marched through dense brush and woods to Salaberry's location, arriving on October 25. Scouts told Hampton that the enemy's position could be turned by crossing the river's ford. Hampton divided his army into two brigades. The First Brigade commanded by Colonel Robert Purdy and the Second Brigade led by Brigadier General George Izard. Hampton directed Colonel Purdy to cross the ford and flank Salaberry's position.

Purdy's brigade departed on a pitch-black night, relying on guides to navigate 1,500 men through fifteen miles of marsh, fallen logs, and thick woods. After fourteen hours, the column advanced only six miles. The delay caused Purdy to order his brigade to halt and sleep. The men slept on the ground; cold drizzle covered their bodies. That night, Hampton received a message from Armstrong to establish winter quarters in Four Corners, New York; Armstrong had decided to call off the expedition. Hampton considered recalling Purdy, but he could not relay the message to the colonel's distant brigade. Hampton resolved to commit his forces to battle.[17]

At dawn, Purdy's men awoke and continued their march. Hampton's hired scouts mistakenly led the men away from the ford. "We were led out, after marching the whole of the night," Alexander Neef recalled, "without rest, in difficult woods, and thro' almost impenetrable swamps, two miles above the ford, and nearly opposite the enemy's encampment." The next morning the First Brigade emerged in a thick cedar swamp directly in front of Salaberry's position, rather than at the ford as expected. They startled Captain Jean Baptiste Bruguiére's company of sedentary militia and a sharp skirmish ensured. Salaberry ordered MacDonnell to support Bruguiére with Captain Charles Daly's Third Battalion militia.[18]

Meanwhile, US general George Izard waited for orders from Hampton to engage Salaberry's main position. Around 2:00 p.m., Hampton, hearing gunfire from Purdy's direction, ordered Izard to advance. They approached Salaberry's position. "Give yourselves over," one American officer under Izard reportedly yelled to the Canadians. "We do not wish you any harm." Salaberry, disinclined to accept the American's offer, fired his musket at the man, knocking him off his horse. Izard's men pressed forward toward the abatis. "On the brink of a deep ravine," Izard remembered, "we are met by a volley of musketry." He formed his men into columns, and they fired into the right side of the enemy's line. The fusillade took a toll on Salaberry's Canadians, and Izard's men began shouting for victory. Salaberry, sensing the Americans would overrun the position, ordered bugles sounded and directed his men to shout. Lieutenant Colonel MacDonnell also ordered his men to sound their bugles, which portrayed a larger force than actually existed. "After these mutual cheerings," an aide to the Voltigeurs remembered, "volleys were for some time exchanged on both sides." Izard's men slackened their fire, awaiting the results of Purdy's assault.[19]

At Purdy's position on the south side of the river, the Americans engaged Salaberry's advance in a swamp. Salaberry directed Daly to hold his position. Daly, despite being gravely outnumbered, advanced his men into some underbrush to find cover. They knelt behind the greenery and fired rounds against Purdy's 1,500-man brigade. The Americans returned fire, but most of their balls flew over the heads of the Daly's soldiers. After a prolonged exchange, Daly ordered a bayonet charge. A bullet wounded the captain, but he bravely pressed on. Another bullet injured him and he collapsed near the American line. The second-in-command organized a retreat and retrieved his wounded captain from the field.[20]

MacDonnell, recognizing Daly's predicament, reinforced his position and fired into Purdy's brigade from nearby bushes. The stiff fire, combined with the damage he had taken from Daly, convinced Purdy to withdraw from the field. He countermarched his men three miles into the wilderness, and once again they slept on the ground without food. Heavy rain pelted the tired soldiers, and shouts from Native American warriors kept them awake through the night. Salaberry's men collected 150 flintlock muskets, knapsacks, and other items dropped by Purdy's fleeing brigade. The next day, Hampton, who learned about Purdy's failure, ordered Izard to withdraw.[21]

At the Battle of Châteauguay fewer than 400 Canadians had thwarted an attack by 4,000 American soldiers. Salaberry's victory, fought mainly by Canadians, stirred a sense of national pride. "A determined perseverance in this honorable conduct cannot fail of crowning the brave and loyal Canadians with victory," British officer Edward Baynes wrote in a general order. Militiamen such as Daly performed with courage and skill, and Canadian newspapers published accounts of the glorious victory. Prevost praised Salaberry in letters to Lord Bathurst, the secretary of state for war and the colonies, but the prickly officer wanted even more accolades. "It grieves me to the heart to see that I must share the merit of the action," he wrote Baynes. "Methinks that if any merit is to be obtained I am entitled to the whole." Nevertheless, Salaberry lavished praise upon his subordinates. "Capt. Daily [Daly] of the

3rd Batt[allion], in gallantry cannot be surpassed," he wrote in his official report. "He contended with 50 men against a force ten times in number."[22]

After withdrawing his troops from the field, Hampton convened a council of war. The officers shouted at each other about the campaign's failure, but they eventually agreed to retire to Four Corners for winter. Of the American officers that participated in the battle, only General Izard performed well. His organized and disciplined men capably executed their role in the attack, but Hampton recalled them after Purdy's failed river crossing. Hampton, for his part, hoped to avoid combat once he read Armstrong's note to withdraw to winter quarters. The cautious officer, fearing failure, refused to commit his entire force to destroy Salaberry's army. General Purdy, meanwhile, lost control of his men after a short skirmish against a much smaller force. Major John Wool remarked that "no officer who had any regard for his reputation would voluntarily acknowledge himself as having been engaged in it." Following the council, Hampton's army undertook a miserably cold three-day march to Four Corners.[23]

In mid-October at Sackets Harbor, Wilkinson's first units began transferring from the base to a staging point on Grenadier Island, which sat halfway between Kingston and Sackets Harbor. Chauncey's ships could protect soldiers on the island, and its harbor provided a safe landing point for boats transporting Wilkinson's army to Grenadier. The transfer from Sackets Harbor to the island occurred in stages, and during one movement, a storm overtook the army's boat transports as they traveled to the island. The winds pushed many of the boats off course toward the mainland or onto islands scattered through the eastern part of the lake. The gusts also ruined or moved many of the boats anchored at Grenadier. From Sackets Harbor to Grenadier, observers could see bonfires dotting the horizon that had been lit by stranded soldiers. Wilkinson's men began to clean up the mess, but the damage had been done. He lost half of his rations for the campaign, a significant amount of ordnance, ammunition, and medical supplies, and the storm damaged about one-third of his army's water transport.[24]

On November 3 at Grenadier Island, 8,000 of Wilkinson's soldiers climbed into more than three hundred boats to navigate the St. Lawrence. Wilkinson, unaware of Hampton's defeat, planned to continue his part of the campaign toward Montreal. Chauncey brought his ships to the mouth of the St. Lawrence in preparation to escort the boats to French Creek on the St. Lawrence. Before his departure from the island, Wilkinson wrote Armstrong that he had attempted to communicate with Hampton regarding a location where the two armies could join, but Hampton had "treated his [Wilkinson's] authority with contempt." He went on to tell Armstrong "how radically destructive it is to a military enterprise, for a subordinate to resist or neglect the orders of a superior." Wilkinson's force entered the St. Lawrence, and Chauncey's fleet sailed down the south channel of the St. Lawrence to protect the floating army. On November 5, Yeo's squadron appeared in the river's north channel with only an island separating the two squadrons. The Americans tried to engage Yeo, but the British fleet retreated to Kingston the next day.[25]

Chauncey remained in the St. Lawrence briefly, but he soon decided to withdraw back to Sackets Harbor. The commodore feared that his fleet would become trapped in the river and he would be forced to winter in the waterway. Yeo could park his ships at the mouth of the St. Lawrence and prevent Chauncey from leaving until the river froze. Chauncey's fleet departed in stages, with his first ships protecting the entrance to the river. The entire squadron arrived at Sackets Harbor on November 11. Meanwhile, Wilkinson's unwieldy caravan of 328 boats continued toward Montreal through a treacherous section of the St. Lawrence known as the Thousand Islands. Strong currents, whirlpools, and rapids separated his flotilla, which was strung out for five miles in the river. The site of the ships moving through the river prompted one Canadian soldier to remark that "I have never witnessed such a beautiful site as the army going down the rapids."[26]

Wilkinson's flotilla continued to a point just below Ogdensburg, New York. Here, the men would need to pass by the British guns at Prescott. Wilkinson ordered his men to load their ammunition into carts and every man not operating a boat to disembark on the US side of the river. The soldiers on land marched safely at night past Prescott's guns, but Wilkinson's boats needed to run the gauntlet. For three hours British guns fired at the dimly lit shapes from 1,800 yards away. Surprisingly, none of the cannon hit any of the boats, but one sailor was killed and two boats ran aground during the float.[27]

Prevost directed that a "corps of observation" follow the American army along the riverbank. He charged Lieutenant Colonel Joseph Morrison's Eighty-Ninth Foot with the task. Morrison, respected by his men, had witnessed little combat during his fourteen-year army career, but his subordinates could compensate for his lack of combat experience. Lieutenant Colonel John Harvey, the officer who ordered the successful night assault at Stoney Creek, was Morrison's second-in-command. Newly promoted Major Charles Plenderleath, who executed the daring raid against the enemy's artillery at the same battle, led a regiment of the Forty-Ninth Foot. On November 7, Morrison embarked in sixty batteaux with 800 men destined for Prescott on the St. Lawrence. Naval officer William Mulcaster accompanied the group with two schooners and seven gunboats.[28]

On November 9, Wilkinson paused his flotilla before a set of rapids, which were reportedly protected by British guns. He dispatched a small force to clear the bank of any enemy so his boats could continue toward Montreal. That force successfully cleared the area and encamped downstream, and then waited for the flotilla to proceed. Wilkinson, however, aware of the trailing British force, changed his mind, and decided to disembark his troops to address the threat in his rear. Morrison received reports about the Americans coming ashore, so he looked for a strong defensive position to station his men. His vanguard crossed John Crysler's farm, which contained split rail fences that intersected a field east of the farmhouse. The field stretched almost one mile to the eastern woods, and a swamp protected Morrison's northern flank; Mulcaster's gunboats on the St. Lawrence guarded his southern flank. The likely approach for the American force toward the farm was from the east, across the field, where the enemy was vulnerable to artillery fire. Morrison positioned his advance in the gullies and ravines that traversed the field.[29]

The morning of November 11 dawned with grey skies but no precipitation. Wilkinson ordered General John Boyd with 2,000 regulars to attack Morrison's army. Wilkinson wanted Boyd to protect his rear flank and deter Morrison from following the Americans to Montreal. Boyd organized his men into three brigades. Brigadier General Robert Swartout commanded the Fourth Brigade, which was to attack the enemy's right flank through the woods—opposite the river. Brigadier General Leonard Covington led the Third Brigade, which was to assault Morrison's left flank along the river. The two brigades were on opposite sides of the field, unable to provide mutual support during the battle. The First Brigade under

Figure 10. ***The Battle of Crysler's Farm.*** At the Battle of Crysler's Farm, Lieutenant Colonel Joseph Morrison achieved a brilliant victory against a larger American force commanded by General Wilkinson. Wilkinson disembarked his men before arriving at Montreal to deal with Morrison's trailing army. Morrison selected a strong defensive position, and his men inflicted serious casualties on the American force. Notice the ravine in the middle of the field and the split rail fences located to the right side of the image. Courtesy of the Upper Canada Village.

Brigadier General Isaac Coles lagged behind the Third Brigade at such a distance that his men would not play a significant role in the battle.[30]

Wilkinson, bedridden with a fever, stayed onboard a schooner during the preparations. He reportedly imbibed large doses of whiskey laced with laudanum to deal with the pain. A few days earlier, his men found Wilkinson "abominably intoxicated" from opium and/or liquor, and they assisted the general off the boat into a nearby house. The general fell asleep near a fire, where his men, concerned that he would fall into the flames, removed him from the danger.

Around 2:00 p.m., US colonel Eleazer Ripley's Twenty-First Infantry advanced into the woods east of Crysler's farm. The Canadian Voltigeurs, skilled light infantrymen, darted into the forest and fired into the mass of

men moving in their direction. The sharpshooting delayed Ripley's advance and gave Morrison's men time to form a two-rank line in the clearing. The 2,000 marching Americans formed an imposing sight to the 800 British soldiers. "As the enemy advanced," John Harvey recalled, "I plainly saw we had nothing to trust but 'every man doing his duty.'"[31]

Captain Henry George Jackson from the British Royal Artillery opened fire with his three 6-pounders. His gunners fired shrapnel shells loaded with twenty-seven musket balls that burst into the American advance, killing men and throwing the columns into disarray. Mulcaster's gunboats also fired their long guns toward the Americans. "The enemy had judiciously chosen his ground among the deep ravines," Boyd wrote in his official report, "which everywhere intersected the extensive plain, and discharged a heavy and galling fire upon our advancing columns."[32]

Covington's brigade, moving near the river, was the hardest hit. The Americans advanced across a ravine while under fire from British gunboats and cannon. "On ascending from the ravine," a soldier in the Third Brigade recalled, "our troops were brought within pistol shot of the enemy." Morrison's men, concealed around the small village of Williamsburg, poured a devastating fire into Covington's brigade. A rifle shot mortally wounded General Covington as he tried to lead his men forward. A musket ball fractured the hip bone of Covington's second-in-command while another bullet wounded the third officer in line to command the brigade, and he also retired from the field.[33]

On the American's right side (opposite the river), the American Third Brigade marched through dense pine woods and swamp to attack the left of Morrison's line. The Voltigeurs and the Mohawks fired at the advance, softening up the brigade before the main exchange. Morrison, observing the American flanking movement, swung the Eighty-Ninth Regiment backward to protect his left flank. They formed a two-rank line that faced the forest at a 45-degree angle, where the American force would exit the forest. General Swartout, commander of the Third Brigade, tried to form his men from a marching column into line, but his force became disorganized in the woods. His soldiers, observing the readied British line, streamed piecemeal out of the forest, firing irregularly at the British battle line. The British waited until the Americans were within range and fired their muskets. The disciplined, devastating fire destroyed the front of Swartout's column. American cavalry then charged the Forty-Ninth. The British opened their files to allow the horsemen to pass harmlessly through their ranks. The Forty-Ninth wheeled about, a skilled and difficult movement, and dispensed a destructive fire into the cavalry. Thirty horses returned to the American lines without riders. The Third Brigade recoiled backwards, and Morrison ordered his men to advance against the retreating Americans.[34]

During the affair, Boyd's gunners brought only two pieces of American artillery into action. One American artillery lieutenant encountered an impassable ravine while withdrawing from the field with his 6-pounder. The British Eighty-Ninth charged the group, captured the gun, and killed the officer and his men. After 4:00 p.m., Boyd, observing defeat, ordered his men to withdraw to their original position. The British had decimated his force.[35]

At Crysler's farm, Morrison achieved a brilliant victory with a small number of disciplined regulars. His success delayed Wilkinson's advance toward Montreal and gave Prevost's militia more time to fortify the city. The American army paid a steep price for the rearguard action. The British killed 103 of Boyd's men, including General Covington, and they wounded 237 more. The British lost only 22 killed and 148 wounded.[36]

Even after the failure, Wilkinson still intended to attack Montreal, but he lacked the necessary supplies to survive through the winter. He expected Hampton to rendezvous with his force, bringing food, provisions, and 4,000 men. On November 12, the day after the battle, Wilkinson received a message from Hampton stating that he would not march to the designated rendezvous point to join Wilkinson's force. He further told him that he did not possess the supplies that Wilkinson's army required. Wilkinson was livid. He wrote Hampton that he could not find "language to express my sorrow" at Hampton's lack of support. Wilkinson decided to abandon the attack on Montreal, and he established winter quarters at French Mills. The 1813 campaign for Montreal was over.[37]

At the end of the 1813, Governor-in-Chief Prevost could take measure of Britain's success defending Canada. The army and navy had protected their most vital assets at Kingston and Montreal, but they had lost Detroit, Amherstburg, and Lake Erie. The British Army also regained control of the Niagara frontier after the American evacuation of Fort George, and they inflicted damage on American garrisons along the Niagara and Lake Erie. At the end of 1813, Britain still retained control of Lower Canada and portions of Upper Canada, and Britain's line of communications between Canada and England remained intact.

Prevost would soon benefit from the changing momentum of the war in Europe. In 1812, the French Grand Army suffered greatly during its invasion of Russia. Napoleon lost perhaps 570,000 men, 1,000 cannon, 200,000 horses, and veteran soldiers from his elite Imperial Guard. Momentum further tipped toward the Allies on June 21, 1813, when Wellington defeated Joseph Bonaparte at the Battle of Vitoria and the French army withdrew back across the Pyrenees. Soon after this victory, Austria joined the Allies, and for the first time since 1795, all of Europe's major powers were united against France. On October 16–18, the allies defeated Napoleon at the Battle of the Nations, where the emperor lost 68,000 men killed, wounded, or captured at the battle, and his army withdrew to France. Napoleon escaped to Paris, but the battle signaled the end of his reign. On March 30, 1814, the allies entered Paris. Napoleon abdicated his throne and the allies exiled him to Elba. Madison learned of the emperor's abdication in May 1814. With Napoleon's demise, Madison lost a critical piece of his war strategy.[38]

With the Napoleonic threat fading toward the end of 1813, Prime Minister

Liverpool intended to reassert Britain's influence in North America. Britain planned to reinforce Prevost and undertake a new offensive to strengthen Britain's position at the negotiating table. "Are we prepared to continue the war for territorial arrangements," Foreign Minister Castlereagh asked Prime Minister Liverpool in August, "to take the chance of the campaign, and then to be governed by circumstances?" The extent of Britain's demands would be based on the success of the military campaign. From the outset, Liverpool sought an Indian buffer state in the northwest, protection for Canada, and unimpeded access to the Mississippi. A *Times of London* editorial demanded a more extreme concession from the traitor Madison: "The present American government must be displaced or it will sooner or later plant it's poison dagger in the heart of the parent state. It must be displaced by the powerful effect of great military success to our arms, continued and connected until they enable us to dictate the terms of an honourable peace."[39]

In February 1814, Bathurst asked the Duke of Wellington's opinion concerning Britain's strategy in North America. Wellington, skeptical of forcing an American surrender, told Bathurst, "I do not know where you could carry on such an operation which would be so injurious to the Americans as to force them to sue for peace." Wellington's assessment of the war, despite his self-acknowledged ignorance of American topography, proved remarkably accurate. He believed that Britain must first control the Great Lakes since land operations depended on the country's ability to move troops and supplies by water. "That which appears to me to be wanting in America is not a General, or General officers and troops, but a naval superiority on the Lakes," Wellington later told Prime Minister Liverpool. The *Times of London* believed that Wellington should assume command in America: "We have often said, and we repeat it, that America is a scene which the Duke of Wellington's talents might be displayed far more beneficially to his country than they can possibly be in the courtly circles of the Tuileries [in Paris]?"[40]

Lord Bathurst, secretary of state for war and the colonies, communicated his new strategy to Prevost in June 1814: "The intention of His Majesty's government [is] to avail themselves of the favourable state of affairs in Europe in order to reinforce the army under your command." Bathurst dispatched 13,000 troops to the North American theater, with 3,000 men designated for a diversionary campaign in Chesapeake Bay and 10,000 for Prevost's upcoming offensive. With the new forces, Liverpool expected results from Prevost.

Bathurst told the governor-in-chief that the new army should destroy Sackets Harbor, capture or destroy the American navy on Lakes Erie and Champlain, recapture Fort Niagara, and reoccupy Detroit and the Michigan Territory.[41]

Despite the change in British policy, reinforcements would take weeks to arrive in North America. Many of the new soldiers would not land in Halifax until the summer of 1814. In the interim, the United States would again try to invade Canada in its last major northern assault of the war. Skilled officers would lead the campaign, and they would help the nascent US regular army form into a viable military force. For the campaign to be successful, however, the United States would need to defeat the British army and hold territory in Canada. Such a move could prevent Prevost from using land routes to move supplies, but the United States had yet to prove that its military could win and hold territory.

10

Seeds of a Disciplined American Army

We did not baulk him.
—Brown to Secretary of War Armstrong, July 6, 1814, *Documentary History of the Campaign Upon the Niagara Frontier*

Before the prime minister, the Earl of Liverpool, implemented his new strategy in North America, Secretary of War Armstrong intended to strike Kingston in the summer of 1814. The secretary detailed a plan to newly promoted Major General Jacob Brown in a letter on February 28, 1814. The message directed Brown to assault Kingston if the general could meet certain criteria, including "practicable roads, good weather, large detachments (made westerly) on the part of the enemy, and a full and hearty co-operation on the part of our own naval commander." Armstrong, in a failed effort to spread misinformation to the enemy, also included a second letter to Brown, which he directed that the general should use to "mask your object." That letter contained realistic details about a second American campaign on the Niagara frontier, but the secretary provided no guidance to Brown on how the general should leak the information to the enemy.[1]

To make the message more confusing, the bogus directive was a real expedition, where Brigadier General Winfield Scott's army would assault British garrisons along the Niagara frontier. Armstrong's letter directed Brown to support Scott's effort to clear the Niagara frontier and proceed toward western Lake Ontario. Commodore Chauncey and General Brown, evaluating the first letter, agreed that since recent reinforcements arrived in Kingston, they could not meet Armstrong's conditions. So Brown began making preparations to move his troops to the Niagara to join Scott, which he likely viewed as an alternative plan to Armstrong's original directive.[2]

When Armstrong learned that Brown planned to move west, he criticized the general for misunderstanding him, but he agreed that since the mistake had been made, Brown should proceed to the Niagara anyway. Madison's cabinet later affirmed the guidance. The Lake Erie squadron, under Commodore Arthur Sinclair, was directed to deposit one force to assault Mackinac, which the British still controlled, and later sail to Matchedash on Lake Huron, where Britain was reportedly building a small shipyard. Sinclair would also transfer Brown's and Scott's troops to the north shore of Lake Erie to assault Burlington, York, and eventually Kingston. The final piece of the plan included guidance to Major General George Izard to build and launch fifteen gunboats into the St. Lawrence to disrupt supply movements and create a diversion from Brown's assault to the west.[3]

Armstrong, even after his bungled letters, supported the plan because US forces controlled Lake Erie and he wanted to exploit the navy's ability to move troops and supplies on that waterway. He believed that the campaign would hurt Britain's efforts to reinvigorate their alliance with Native American tribes that resided in western Upper Canada. Armstrong also wanted to clear the British from Mackinac, where they had successfully remained since its seizure in 1812, and he intended for the army to destroy the fur trading outpost at St. Joseph's Island and assert US power on the Upper Great Lakes.[4]

The secretary's plan focused on the Lake Erie region because during the spring and early summer of 1814, Yeo launched new ships on Lake Ontario that bottled up Chauncey's fleet. Chauncey's squadron remained bottled up at Sackets Harbor by Yeo's fleet, which had recently launched new ships. Chauncey predicted that he could move onto the lake in June, after he launched the fifty-eight-gun *Superior* and the forty-two-gun *Mohawk*. Armstrong, anticipating that the commodore could support Brown in June, told the general to commence his initial operations without the navy's support. Brown should first overrun Fort Erie and seize the bridge at Chippawa. Once Chauncey emerged from Sackets Harbor, the commodore would support Brown's campaign to assault Forts George and Niagara, and later Burlington and York.[5]

The campaign retained one advantage over previous American efforts. Armstrong finally placed capable officers in senior army positions to lead the offensive. The War Department promoted Winfield Scott, Jacob Brown, and Eleazer Ripley, with an average age of thirty-three, to brigadier general in early 1814. For the first time in the war an American army would be led by skilled, brave leaders who proved to be an enormous improvement over past leadership.[6]

During the winter of 1813, Chauncey's shipbuilding efforts lacked the energy and determination of the year before. A mild and wet winter turned the roads into sludge and challenged the transporters' efforts to move supplies to the harbor. The resulting supply shortage included kedges, anchors, cannon, rigging, and other materials. Carronades transported by wagon from Baltimore to New York had difficulty making the trip. Chauncey complained that "we have had to transport, from Baltimore, Philadelphia, and New York, our heavy ordnance and stores, over roads almost impassable during the whole winter . . . [and] the state of the roads [are] . . . almost insurmountable."

Henry Eckford did not start building ships until January. By April, Eckford had completed the *Jefferson* and *Jones*, but the *Jones* contained no guns or iron ballast to keep the vessel upright, nor did it have a crew. Eckford also continued his work on the massive fifty-eight-gun frigate *Superior*, a ship larger than the USS *Constitution*. Meanwhile, Chauncey fretted over Yeo's efforts at Kingston. "The enemy is driving on with great force," he wrote Navy Secretary Jones, "with his large ship at Kingston which is intended to be an 80-gun ship upon two decks but will mount 100 guns or upwards."[7]

Indeed, Yeo's shipwrights worked feverishly throughout the winter. In January 1814, the Admiralty gave Yeo a command independent from the army, so he reported directly to the Admiralty rather than Prevost. The Admiralty promoted Yeo from commodore second class to commodore first class, which gave him the pay and much of the status of a rear admiral. These moves meant that Yeo could request support directly from the Admiralty, rather than asking for resources through Prevost. With Yeo's promotion, the commodore would need to consider Britain's fleets on other waterways besides Lake Ontario. During the winter, Yeo possessed a larger labor force than he did during the spring and summer because the region's farmers could work in the dockyard rather than tend to crops. Yeo, however, still lacked ordnance and ship stores, and his men required more food rations at Kingston. The Admiralty recognized Yeo's dilemma, but its leaders also believed that he retained sufficient ordnance to execute his mission. By the spring 1814, Yeo possessed twenty-five 24-pounders, fifty-six 18-pounders, and one hundred and thirty-six 32-pound carronades, among other guns. Despite Yeo's logistical challenges, shipmasters finished construction on the fifty-eight-gun *Prince Regent*, the forty-gun *Princess Charlotte*, and three gunboats launched in the spring of 1814, which blockaded Chauncey's fleet at Sackets Harbor. The American base remained blockaded until May 1814, when Yeo withdrew to Kingston to await the completion of the most ambitious Great Lakes shipbuilding project to date—the three-deck, ship of the line, 102-gun *St. Lawrence*. The ship was the only first-rate line-of-battle ship that the Royal Navy would sail exclusively on freshwater. The vessel, operated by a crew of 600–700 men, gave Yeo control of the lake starting in mid-September.[8]

A key ingredient of President Madison's sweeping campaign was Commodore Isaac Chauncey's fleet, which would prevent enemy reinforcements from departing Kingston for Fort George across the lake. His ships could also support assaults on Forts Erie and George by transporting troops and supplies across Lake Ontario. Chauncey continued to wait for guns and stores in order to finish the fifty-eight-gun *Superior* and the forty-two-gun *Mohawk*. General Brown, who was in command of the expedition, anxiously waited to hear from Chauncey regarding the status of his fleet. In April he wrote to Chauncey: "It is very unkind in you to remain so long silent . . . you never intimated to me, a doubt of your ability to face the enemy, at any moment after the ice was out."[9]

General Brown asked for advice from his two brigade commanders, Winfield Scott and Eleazer Ripley, regarding the army's course of action if Chauncey declined to support the mission. Scott, who rarely declined an opportunity for combat, recommended they continue with the invasion. Ripley disagreed, arguing that they should wait for Chauncey's fleet to support them. Brown agreed with Scott, and he readied his 3,500-man force to execute the first phase of the new campaign.

That summer, Lieutenant General Gordon Drummond prepared Upper Canada's defense. He knew that the Americans would probably attack his region, but he did not know where they would strike along the 1,000-mile frontier. He decided to disperse most of his troops across the Niagara frontier so they could reinforce each other at the point at which the Americans attacked. He stationed 1,500 regulars at posts between Forts George and Erie. He also reinforced Burlington and York, and 600 men from the Forty-First guarded Fort Niagara.[10]

On July 3, Brown crossed his men upriver from Niagara Falls. He still had not heard from Chauncey, and was becoming anxious. "Upon receipt of this [letter]," Brown wrote Chauncey in June, "will you have the goodness to let me know by *Express*, when you will be out; and if I may expect you in the neighborhood of Fort George, by the 10th of July? Or what day?" Chauncey's response did not put Brown at ease. The commodore replied that his operations depended on Yeo's movement from Kingston. Chauncey worried that Prevost would attack Sackets Harbor while his squadron was away supporting Brown's operation, and he refused to leave the harbor unguarded.[11]

Scott's First Brigade landed north of Fort Erie, and Ripley's Second Brigade disembarked south of the garrison. The outpost, which contained only two companies of British regulars, quickly surrendered. The following day, Scott led the American advance toward Chippawa. General Phineas Riall, commander of the Niagara area under Drummond, learned of the Americans' landing at 8:00 a.m., and he ordered five companies of the First Foot of Royal Scots from Fort George to the area. Riall hoped the outpost would stall the American advance as he consolidated his reinforcements. Lieutenant Colonel Thomas Pearson, stationed at Chippawa with the flank companies of the 100th Foot, selected a strong defensive position north of the Chippawa River. The river, 250 feet wide and 20 feet deep, ran through the middle of the village of Chippawa. A high, narrow, wooden bridge, protected by a redoubt and fortified bridgehead, crossed the ravine.[12]

Winfield Scott's First Brigade led Brown's army along the Niagara toward Lake Ontario. The British stripped wooden planks off nearby bridges to slow Scott's advance. Heavy rain prevented Scott's men from fording the swollen creeks. His men repaired bridge after bridge over a twelve-hour period. By sunset, the brigade reached the Chippawa River. Pearson's vanguard fired at the group from the far bank. The river could only be crossed by the narrow bridge in front of Pearson's position. Scott understood that his fatigued men would likely be decimated trying to cross the bridge, so he ordered them to withdraw two miles and camp for the night. The brigade's cooks prepared a

Fourth of July feast for the soldiers. At 11:00 p.m., Generals Ripley and Brown joined Scott with siege guns and other artillery.[13]

The next day, General Riall received 300 reinforcements from the King's Regiment, bringing his force to 1,350 regular infantry, 200 militia, and 350 Native Americans. With the additional men, Riall decided to go on the offensive. He believed that Brown's men, occupied at Fort Erie, could not assist Scott in a confrontation, though in reality that garrison folded quickly to the American assault. Lieutenant Colonel John Harvey, Drummond's adjutant general, encouraged him to act. "Lieut.-General Drummond feels confident that," Harvey wrote Riall, "an opportunity will be afforded you of effecting, by one action, the defeat, capture, or destruction of a considerable part of the enemy's disposable force." Riall had witnessed undisciplined American forces retreat without a fight in his expedition against Black Rock and Buffalo the year before. This enemy force would undoubtedly not be any different.[14]

Unbeknownst to Riall, Scott, since his promotion to general, had been relentlessly training his brigade. In April, while Brown's troops were waiting for the spring campaign, Scott exercised his men for ten hours a day. He adopted the French system of infantry tactics and taught his officers to shift from a marching column into a two-rank line. He personally observed the training and repeatedly held conferences with his officers to discuss areas of improvement. The soldiers disliked the strenuous training at first, but, as Scott recalled, they "began to perceive why they had been made to fag so long at the drill of a soldier . . . confidence . . . inspired the whole line." Drummer Jarvis Hanks called Scott "the most thorough disciplinarian I ever saw." For Scott, July 5 was another day to exercise his men. He intended to parade them on the plain north of his campground that afternoon, unaware that Riall's entire force was encamped nearby.[15]

At 4:00 p.m. on July 5, Riall ordered his men to advance forward in three columns. They crossed the bridge at the Chippawa River and advanced toward the American position. One American picket rashly fled the scene, leaving a wounded soldier on the field. General Brown, disgusted with the cowardly effort, relieved him on the spot. Brown ordered Brigadier General Peter Porter with militia and Iroquois warriors under Red Jacket to sneak through the woods to attack Riall's right flank. Porter's men overran a small enemy advance in the forest and raced forward until, as he recalled, "we found ourselves within a few yards of the British army." The British fired at Porter's skirmishers, who retreated behind Scott's brigade. Meanwhile, Riall dispatched John Norton and his warriors to advance through the woods to approach the rear of the American camp. They snuck through the forest and exchanged fire with Porter's force. Men ducked behind fallen logs and trees while firing at the enemy. "We shouted and closed with them without firing till we reached them," Norton remembered.[16]

Brown heard the commotion on the left flank and concluded that Riall's main force was trying to flank them. He ordered Scott with Captain Nathan Towson's artillery to engage the enemy on the plain south of the Chippawa River. Captain Towson was no stranger to combat. He had participated in the battles of Queenston, Fort George, and Stoney Creek. At the latter battle, the British captured him during the Forty-Ninth's assault against his artillery, but he escaped by darting away from his captors.

Despite being called forward, Scott did not believe that Riall's main force awaited him. After dinner, he marched his men toward the field, "without expecting a battle, though fully prepared for one," he remembered. Scott formed his brigade into column and led them north along the river road. Brown galloped by Scott and shouted, "You will have a battle!"[17]

When Porter withdrew, Riall ordered his artillery officer to place two 24-pounders and a 5.5-inch howitzer along the river road and three 6-pounders west of the road. Scott's brigade condensed itself to cross the narrow Street Creek Bridge and Riall's guns opened up on the appetizing target. Bodies piled up on the little bridge, and Scott became convinced that a major battle was in the offing.[18]

On the north side of the plain, Riall advanced two battalions forward, the First Foot of the Royal Scots under Lieutenant Colonel John Gordon and the 100th Foot, commanded by the Marquis of Tweeddale. These troops faced the center of Scott's line. From a distance, Riall's men opened a scattering fire on Scott's force. Lieutenant Richard Armstrong of the Royal Artillery moved two 24-pounders four hundred yards from Scott's men and began firing on the brigade. Scott ordered his soldiers to move from column into a two-rank line, but stiff musket and artillery fire caused confusion among his men. Captain Towson, positioned on Scott's right flank, fired his two 6-pounders and 5.5-inch howitzer against Armstrong's battery. He scored a direct hit on an ammunition wagon, which ignited in flames. Scott's men, seizing the moment, formed an organized, two-rank line. Riall believed that Scott's men, dressed in grey uniforms, were Buffalo militia, until he observed their disciplined movements under fire. "Why, these are regulars!" Riall reportedly exclaimed.[19]

Scott placed his flanks obliquely forward, which allowed his men to concentrate their fire against the British center. The soldiers stood in three-foot-tall grass, ready for battle. General Scott reminded his men that they just celebrated the Fourth of July. "Let us make a new anniversary for ourselves!" he shouted. "A little arrogance near the enemy," Scott recalled later, "when an officer is ready to suit the action to the word, may be pardoned by his countrymen." Meanwhile, Brown ordered Ripley to advance with the Twenty-First Regiment through the woods and attack the British rear and right flank. His men marched through chin-deep water into the forest to protect the First Brigade's left side.[20]

Brown rode forward with thirty dragoons to direct the movements of his men and energize their efforts. The two lines on the plain approached within sixty paces of each other. Thick smoke smothered Towson's cannon and his gunners could not see the enemy. Scott galloped to Towson on his right flank. "Captain," Scott told him, "more to the left; the enemy is there!" The captain shifted his fire to the left and pummeled the British line. The outgunned American artillery maintained a continuous fire throughout the afternoon.[21]

From one hundred yards away, Scott ordered his men to fire. The British soldiers recoiled, but the men quickly filled the gaps caused by their casualties. The two lines exchanged fire at close range. After five minutes, the Americans began to push the British line backwards. The British, however, still threatened Scott's left flank. Ripley's Twenty-First Infantry did not arrive in time to support Major Thomas Jesup's Twenty-Fifth Regiment, leaving Scott's left side exposed. British Native American warriors fired on Jesup's men from the woods, while light infantry skirmishers shot at them from behind a rail fence. British cannonballs from three 6-pounders tore through Jesup's group, wounding and killing many men. The regiment lost an astonishing fifty men in ten minutes. Jesup's soldiers could not hit the concealed enemy, and he ordered his men to cease fire. Jesup understood that if he withdrew from the position, Scott's vulnerable left flank could jeopardize the battle's outcome. Jesup's only option was to move forward. "Support arms and advance," he yelled to his men. His men halted, fired, and dashed toward the rail fence. Jesup's men closed so quickly with the British that the charge "brought us within grinning distance." The two sides exchanged a light fire and the enemy scrambled away, leaving Scott's left flank secured.[22]

Scott's brigade continued to fire disciplined shots at the center of the British line, which began to crumble. Tweeddale and Gordon, mounted on their horses, tried to compel the elite grenadiers to undertake a bayonet charge, but American fire had already killed or wounded most of the officers from the First and 100th Foot. Musket balls injured Tweeddale and Gordon shortly thereafter. Of the 100th Foot's fourteen officers, only three remained unharmed after the battle. Scott later reported that the enemy's flanks "mouldered away like a rope of sand." He pressed his men forward across the bloody plain, through 700 dead and wounded men. Scott reached the south side of the Chippawa River, but artillery fire forced his men to lie prone to protect themselves from the guns. Porter's men established themselves on Scott's left flank. Engineers advised Generals Scott and Porter that the strong British position at Fort Chippawa could not be overrun without heavy casualties. Since only a few hours of daylight remained, Brown ordered the brigade to withdraw to the main camp.[23]

At the Battle of Chippawa, the American army could take pride in its performance. They exhibited discipline and courage shown by few American soldiers during the war. "In a fair field fight," one boastful American soldier recalled, "we have flogged nearly double our number of the Enemies choicest troops . . . hurrah for Scott's Brigade." In his official report, General Riall acknowledged that his battalions "suffered so severely that I was obliged to withdraw them." William Merritt of the Canadian Provincial Dragoons stated that "we candidly confessed, we were beaten without prevarication, which was never the case with the Americans in the like situation." Brown, in his first report to Secretary of War Armstrong, wrote that when the enemy advanced "we did not baulk him." At the Battle of Chippawa, Riall lost 148 killed, 321 wounded, and 46 missing—roughly 25 percent of his total force. The First and 100th Foot took the brunt of the casualties. More than 50 percent of their men were killed, wounded, captured, or missing. On the American side, Scott's brigade suffered for its newfound discipline. The general lost 41 killed and 219 wounded.[24]

After the battle, Brown intended to seize Forts George and Niagara, but he abandoned the idea because his force lacked the heavy cannon necessary to bombard the outpost. Brown decided to wait in Queenston for Commodore Chauncey, who he hoped would bring two 18-pounders and a rifle regiment from Sackets Harbor. Brown also needed a logistics line opened between his position and supply depots at Genessee and Sodus on the southside of Lake Ontario. Brown's supplies from these depots currently had to travel part of the way by land on one of two routes, and both of which contained poor roads and were monitored by the enemy.[25]

Brown's army spent most of July waiting at the village, where sickness spread through the ranks and reduced his force to 2,660 effectives. On July 23, Brown received unwelcome news: Chauncey would not be coming to his aid. For the first time in the war, Chauncey refused to support the army. He told Brown that if Yeo avoided engaging him on the lake that he would need to remain near Sackets Harbor "to prevent his [Yeo] doing mischief." Yeo had also received reinforcements at Kingston, and Chauncey worried that Yeo might try to lure his fleet from Sackets, after which Yeo's reinforcements might assault his base using army transport boats. By late July, Chauncey had launched both the *Superior* and the *Mohawk*, but he still refused to support the operation. Chauncey had been sick with a fever, and he possibly still resented Wilkinson's earlier decision to assault Montreal instead of Kingston. Whatever the reason, the commodore would not support Brown, so the general decided to withdraw his army to Chippawa. Without Chauncey's help, Brown's army would wither as Drummond's men received supplies from their open logistics lines.[26]

General Riall needed intelligence regarding Brown's objectives. The Americans might retreat to New York or they could continue the campaign. John Norton's men captured an American deserter who revealed that Brown's army departed Chippawa for Burlington Heights. Riall directed Lieutenant Colonel Thomas Pearson to follow Brown's force and observe its movements. Pearson moved his 1,100-man force toward Chippawa, and on July 25 encamped his army along a road called Lundy's Lane, one mile from Niagara Falls. Pearson dispatched a scouting party under John Norton and William Merritt, who observed American pickets.[27]

Drummond and Riall agreed to consolidate their army at Lundy's Lane. Drummond ordered Morrison with the Eighty-Ninth Foot and detachments of the Royal Scots and King's Regiment (the Eighth) from Forts George and

Mississauga—800 men total—to advance toward Lundy's Lane. The central location would allow Riall to shift soldiers toward the Niagara garrisons or Burlington Bay, depending on the movements of the American army.[28]

On the same day, General Brown heard reports that the British had overrun Lewistown on the American side of the Niagara. From Lewistown, the British could capture the supply depot at Fort Schlosser. Brown directed General Scott to advance toward Queenston in hopes of diverting the British away from Fort Schlosser. He ordered Scott to request support if he encountered the enemy in force. General Scott, who had been itching for action since Chippawa, remembered Brown's order differently: "Find the enemy and beat him," he later recalled. Major Eleazer Wood expressed Scott's sentiment by telling a comrade that if they encountered the enemy, "we shall probably feel his pulse."[29]

Scott's four infantry regiments of 1,100 men marched with 70 of Towson's gunners toward Chippawa village. At 5:00 p.m. on July 25, the brigade crossed the Chippawa Bridge, and its advance spotted British dragoons outside Wilson's Tavern. One British soldier stayed behind while his comrades fled. The gentlemen saluted the approaching American officers, who returned the salutation, and then he departed. Scott's men questioned the tavern's hostess, Mrs. Wilson, who was an American by birth. "Oh, Sirs!" she told them, "if you had only come a little sooner you would have caught them all." She explained that Riall had encamped his 800-man army near the tavern. Scott dispatched an officer to notify Brown about the enemy's location, and he ordered his brigade to march north toward the British position.[30]

When he learned of Scott's approach, Riall ordered his men to withdraw to Queenston, where they could join forces with Drummond, Morrison, and Colonel Hercules Scott. Drummond, however, marched toward Lundy's Lane, and when he arrived there, he immediately realized the topographic advantage of posting men at the position. He countermanded Riall's order and sent Morrison's men back to Lundy's Lane.

At the strong position, the British line occupied a mile-long hill spread east to west, with the sunken lane along its top. General Drummond placed two 24-pounders, a Congreve rocket detachment, two 6-pounders, and a 5.5-inch howitzer on the slope's right side, which could fire down on an approaching enemy. British artillery could batter American forces from a distance before they reached the bottom of the hill. A cleared farm area, intersected by rail fences, sat in front of the ridge. The Americans would need to cross this open expanse to assault the British position. Morrison's best unit, the Eighty-Ninth Foot, occupied the center of his line. He placed the Eighth Regiment behind his artillery park on the reverse slope to serve as a reserve. The slope would protect the Eighth Regiment from incoming fire, and they would be ready to engage as necessary.[31]

At Lundy's Lane, Drummond expertly stationed his men to exploit the natural advantages of the position. Disciplined British infantry excelled when posted in a defensive posture, especially on a ridge or hilltop. Their discipline, training, and skilled officer corps would enable them to hold their fire until the last minute, as the Eighty-Ninth did at Crysler's farm. General Scott, upon reconnoitering the British position, considered retreating from the field, but he believed that a withdrawal would cause confusion in his ranks, and he also hoped that if he held his position, the sight of his force would convince Drummond that the entire American army would soon arrive.[32]

At 7:15 p.m. on July 25, thirty minutes before sunset, Scott marched his 1,200-man brigade out of the woods. He ordered the Ninth, Eleventh, and Twenty-Second Regiments to form a two-rank line, and Towson placed his two 6-pounders and a 5.5-inch howitzer close to the portage road. British artillery Captain James Maclachlan fired his two 24-pounders and two 6-pounders downward on Scott's force. Shot and shell devastated the First Brigade from five hundred yards away. As they advanced closer and emerged from the forest, grapeshot slashed fencing and branches, which crashed onto the men's heads. "The cannon balls, grape shot, & musket balls flew like hailstones," Drummer Jarvis Hanks remembered, "and yet we were not firing a gun." Scott's men sprinted across the open plain and tried to jump over the rail fences, but many fell dead while climbing over them. The British killed more than half of Scott's men during the approach. Riall's rocket detachment also fired Congreve rockets, but they exploded harmlessly in the air, forming a novel spectacle for Americans. Towson tried to hit the British guns with his cannon, but most of his fire embedded in the hillside. Drummond's larger guns trained on Towson's men, killing soldiers, horses, and artillery. One shot hit an American ammunition wagon, which exploded in a fiery ball. The Americans lost twenty-seven out of the thirty-six men serving their three guns.[33]

While Scott's brigades were marching toward the slope, Major Jesup's Twenty-Fifth Regiment tried to flank the British left and drive into the rear of Drummond's position. Jesup's men crept silently through thick undergrowth as the sun fell behind the horizon. His soldiers exploded into the First Battalion of the King's Regiment and the Upper Canadian Incorporated Militia. The unexpected assault fomented panic among the soldiers, who fled without firing a shot. The Twenty-Fifth pressed forward to the Queenston Road in the rear of the British position. Jesup directed Captain Daniel Ketchum and his company of Connecticut light infantry to secure the thoroughfare. In the darkness, the Americans encountered small groups of British soldiers moving down the lane. They captured a dozen officers, including Major General Riall and Drummond's aide-de-camp. Jesup's stunning success boded well for Scott's plan. If Jesup could hold his position in the rear, he would force the British to divert men off the hilltop to the Queenston Road.[34]

Scott's brigades, however, never came closer than four hundred yards from the enemy line. "The first brigade was . . . suffering very severely from the continued and destructive fire poured in upon them," General Ripley recalled later. Scott's distant fire could not reach the enemy. They soon expended their ammunition and causalities mounted. The First Brigade's officers expected the enemy to charge down the slope with bayonets to finish the job, but the British remained on the ridgetop.[35]

Major Jesup learned about the brigade's situation and decided to return to the main line. During his return, Jesup's soldiers encountered a group of British regulars, who, in the ensuing firefight, freed some of his prisoners, but Jesup retained Riall and Drummond's aide-de-camp. Word spread through the American army regarding Jesup's high-ranking prisoner, and cheers erupted as his men brought Riall back to Scott's main position.[36]

Around 9:00 p.m., General Scott received reinforcements. Generals Brown, Ripley, and Porter arrived with the Second and Third Brigades and artillery under Major Jacob Hindman. Around the same time, British colonel Hercules Scott's 1,500 regulars and 250 militia also arrived on the scene, which gave Drummond 3,700 men and eight cannon. Hercules's men marched an astonishing twenty miles under a simmering sun to arrive at the battlefield around 9:00 p.m.

One of General Brown's engineers, Colonel William McRee, recommended that Brown assault the British artillery park on the hill. Brown called

Colonel James Miller of the Twenty-First Regiment to his side: "Col. Miller, take your regiment and storm that work and take it." "I'll try Sir!" Miller replied. Miller, a brave and disciplined soldier, showed his mettle in 1812 at the Battle of Maguaga outside Detroit and again at Fort Meigs. Brown also ordered Ripley's brigade forward to relieve Scott's men.[37]

At 9:15 p.m., Miller's Twenty-First Infantry, along with the First Infantry and portions of the Seventeenth and Nineteenth Infantry, marched quietly up the slope in two lines toward the guns. American artillery poured cannon fire over the soldiers' heads toward the British armaments. Each regiment chose different paths once on the slope. The First Infantry advanced straight into British artillery fire, and they recoiled backwards and sought shelter against the slope. The Twenty-Third Infantry advanced on the right of the First and British fire killed and wounded many of its men. General Ripley reformed them on the south side of Lundy's Lane where they sought cover from British artillery fire.

Colonel Miller's Twenty-First Infantry approached the guns more stealthily. They crept down a small ravine, camouflaged by small bushes and thickets. When twenty yards from the British guns, they encountered a fence lined with bushes and trees. Miller ordered his soldiers to steady their guns on the fence, take aim, and fire. The accurate discharge caught the British gunners by surprise. The Americans darted into the artillery park and seized seven guns, including a 24-pounder. The colonel's toehold on the ridge gave Brown a vital position where his men could repulse enemy counterattacks from a defensive position. General Ripley, and later General Scott, arrived to reinforce Miller and hold the ridge.[38]

General Drummond intended to retake his artillery park. He ordered the Eighty-Ninth Foot to advance and fire at the hilltop intruders. The Americans could hear the British approach their position in the darkness: "Halt, dress, forward," the officers exhorted. Scott, rather than form a traditional battle line, moved his men into column and advanced double-time into the center of the enemy line. Scott's 250-man column pierced the British line and caused confusion among the enemy's ranks. The brigade haphazardly continued their advance and encountered a second line of British soldiers. In the confusion, Ripley's brigade, seeing muzzle flashes beyond enemy lines, fired on the rear and left of Scott's column. The First Brigade quickly withdrew from the action.[39]

Figure 11. ***Battle of Niagara from a Sketch by Major Riddle*** (Battle of Lundy's Lane). This sketch shows the American advance toward the British guns on the hill that intersected Lundy's Lane. At the Battle of Lundy's Lane, the British line was roughly one mile long, and most of its guns sat on the British right flank. At this point in the battle, the Americans, led by General Scott, had already crossed a farm in front of the hill and had been decimated by British artillery fire. The battle was one of the few during the war that the American army could be proud of. Courtesy of the Library of Congress, LC-DIG-pga-12905.

The Eighty-Ninth Foot advanced and unleashed a powerful discharge against the Twenty-First. Ripley's men responded with their "buck and ball" cartridges, which contained a musket ball and three to six pieces of buckshot. The ammunition's wide dispersal maximized the chance of hitting an oncoming target. "There appeared a perfect sheet of fire between the two lines," Ripley recalled. The Eighty-Ninth charged Miller's men with bayonets, and bloody hand-to-hand combat ensued. American fire wounded Colonel Morrison in the attack, and a musket ball entered below General Drummond's ear and lodged in the back of his neck. He wrapped a handkerchief around the wound and refused to dismount his horse. The Twenty-First held their position, and the British withdrew from the area.[40]

Just before midnight, Drummond organized a third attempt to retake his guns. Once again Scott's battered brigade participated in the fight. Scott moved his men north in column and passed to the west of Drummond's line, but the British had anticipated such a maneuver. "When within short musket shot," Scott recalled, "there was an unexpected halt, instantly followed by the crack of small arms and the deafening roar of cannon." At that point, Scott's force ceased to exist as a brigade. His 900-man force only retained 100 effectives, with more than half of the brigade's officers killed or wounded. A musket ball shattered Scott's left shoulder, passing through his body. Major Jesup dragged the general from the field and placed him behind a tree. British fire also wounded Scott's aide-de-camp, William Jenkins Worth, who would fight with Scott thirty-two years later during the Mexican War. A musket ball lodged into General Brown's inner thigh, but he refused to dismount his horse and continued to observe the battle. General Ripley had thus far escaped harm, with two musket balls piercing his hat.[41]

In the darkness, the men could not see each other's uniforms. A noncommissioned British officer approached American engineer David Douglass, saluted, and said, "Lieutenant Colonel Gordon begs to have three hundred men, who are stationed in the lane, below, sent to him, as quick as possible, for he is, very much pressed." Douglass grabbed his musket and hoisted it above his horse mount. The shocked soldier exclaimed, "And what have I done, Sir? I am no deserter." The poor British soldier had no idea he was talking to an American officer.[42]

The fighting became ferocious along the ridgeline. Muzzle flashes revealed each side's positions in the darkness. Bayonets, clubs, and muskets clanked, and the groans of the wounded and dying echoed across the ridge. "Both armies fought with a desperation bordering on madness," a surgeon in the Twenty-First recalled. "Neither would yield the palm [give up] but each retired a short distance wearied out with fatigue. Such a constant and destructive fire was never before sustained by American troops without falling back." After multiple charges and countercharges, British bugles sounded across the hill, a signal for them to withdraw. General Brown and his men had won one of the bloodiest battles of the War of 1812.[43]

The American brigades, wounded, exhausted, and thirsty, could not solidify their victory. The men needed water, and the wounded, scattered across the hilltop, required medical attention. Brown directed Ripley to withdraw from the ridge in order to rest and hydrate. Ripley did not possess enough horses to pull the captured cannon down the slope, and his fatigued, wounded men could not undertake the arduous task. Despite concern over leaving the captured artillery, Ripley obeyed Brown's order and returned to camp around 1:00 a.m. Brown later claimed that he ordered Ripley to return to the battlefield at dawn, and that Ripley ignored the directive. At sunrise, General Drummond, observing no Americans on the hill, sent men to recover the two 24-pounders and an American 6-pounder. The American troops rested until late morning, and Ripley refused to engage a reinforced enemy a second time. General Porter, astonished at the order to retreat, complained that "our victory was complete, but, alas, this victory gained by exhibitions of bravery never surpassed in this country was converted into a defeat by a precipitate retreat, leaving the dead, the wounded and captured artillery, and our hard earned honor to the enemy." Brown should have directed his men to remain on the hard-fought hill and erect defensive breastworks.[44]

The outcome of the battle, one of the bloodiest of the war, revealed itself the next morning. An American surgeon recalled that "the dead had not been removed during the night, and such a scene of carnage I never beheld, particularly at Lundy's Lane, red coats and blue and grey were promiscuously intermingled, in many places three deep, and around the hill where the enemy's artillery was carried by Colonel Miller, the carcasses of 60 or 70 horses disfigured the scene." The Americans lost 171 killed, 572 wounded, and 110 missing; the British suffered 84 killed, 559 wounded, 193 missing, and 42 taken prisoner, including a major general. Scott's brave and disciplined First Brigade showed its mettle, but the group no longer existed as a functioning unit.[45]

For the Americans, the Battle of Lundy's Lane, more than any other fight during the war, planted historic seeds for a disciplined regular army. American soldiers fought like seasoned soldiers, marching up a slope into oncoming fire and quitting the field only after British fire had decimated their brigades. Drummond's soldiers also performed bravely in the chaos of the moonlit night, charging and recharging the artillery position until American fire killed or wounded most of their officers. As one British officer noted after the battle, "The firmness that was there displayed on the part of the British Army certainly entitled every officer present to be *knighted*." The Americans claimed victory at Lundy's Lane, but they did not retain possession of the hill, and their depleted force could not continue the campaign.[46]

Following the battle, Ripley, who retained command because of wounds to Scott and Brown, sent his injured soldiers across the river to Buffalo. He wanted to withdraw to the American side of the Niagara because he believed that the battle-worn army needed to recover and resupply, but his generals disagreed with him. Brown, though convalescent, intervened and ordered Ripley to remain in Canada. Ripley, adhering to the order, withdrew his force to a location above the British garrison at Fort Erie, where his men began to strengthen the outpost to await the possibility of a siege. After learning about Ripley's interest in withdrawing across the river, General Brown lost confidence in the commander, and he asked General Edward Gaines to travel from Sackets Harbor to assume command. Gaines arrived on August 4 with two hundred men.[47]

Fort Erie, a crumbling wreck of a garrison, required a thorough overhaul to be transformed into an effective defensive post. Lieutenant David Douglass of the engineers, working under Major Eleazer Wood, oversaw the completion of the walls and constructed two bastions on the north side, each mounting six guns. They also erected a stone tower on the fort's lakeside called the Douglass Battery, which mounted two guns. A seven-foot-high earthwork connected the battery with the northern bastions and another 650-yard earthwork jutted west from the fort and curved toward the lake, ending at Snake Hill. Snake Hill contained a twenty-foot-high redoubt and five guns, which the men named "Towson's Battery" in honor of the artillery captain. Douglass's comprehensive measures to fortify the garrison would play a crucial role in the upcoming battle.[48]

General Drummond, upon arrival near Fort Erie, decided to isolate the Americans and starve out the garrison. He sent a detachment to overrun Buffalo and Black Rock to destroy supplies destined for Fort Erie. American major Lodowick Morgan of the First Rifles with 240 riflemen repulsed Drummond's raid and forced the enemy to recross the Niagara. After the defeat, Drummond directed his men to erect two artillery batteries to fire on Fort Erie. The cannon fired their first shots on August 7. The general planned to execute a three-prong night assault against the stout structure. The first column under Lieutenant Colonel Victor Fischer would penetrate the weak point between Snake Hill and the lakeshore. The second column under Lieutenant Colonel William Drummond would assault the fort directly. And a third column under Colonel Hercules Scott would attack the right of the American position, including the Douglass Battery. On August 14, the British halted their bombardment and prepared to attack. General Gaines, believing an attack was imminent, ensured that his sentinels were awake, armed, and at their stations.[49]

Two hours before daylight, the first British column with 1,300 men tried to penetrate the area between Snake Hill and the lakeshore, but stiff fire from the American Twenty-First Regiment cut down the British soldiers. The British troops, under Lieutenant Colonel Fischer, attacked their objective five times, and the Twenty-First repulsed each advance. Some of Fischer's men accidently walked into the fort, where the Americans took them prisoner. Colonel Drummond's second British column assaulted the fort's walls and also suffered heavy casualties. American fire also repelled Hercules Scott's third column, but Scott shifted his men northward and successfully penetrated the fort's northeast bastion. Drummond directed his men to support Scott's lodgment. American reinforcements poured into the small area. Bloody, close-quarters fighting ensued. "Give the d—d Yankees no quarter," Colonel Drummond screamed. An American soldier shot Drummond in the heart, and he collapsed. Colonel Hercules Scott assumed command, but an American soldier fired at his head, hitting him, and he too fell incapacitated. As the melée raged on, ammunition stored underneath the bastion caught fire, exploding pieces of wood and metal two hundred feet into the air. The detonation killed many of Scott's men, who retreated shortly thereafter. At the first battle of Fort Erie, the British army suffered a steep 40 percent casualty rate. Drummond lost 905 men killed, wounded, or missing of the 2,250 men of his force.[50]

On August 30, Drummond's soldiers constructed two additional batteries, and in early September he received two fresh regiments, including regulars from Europe. Three batteries continued to fire on Fort Erie, and one cannonball exploded in General Gaines's quarters, seriously wounding him. Drummond held the fourth battery in reserve because he lacked sufficient round shot. His men suffered during the siege. Cold rain soaked the soldiers, who lacked tents or shelter to protect them from the weather. Poor sanitation practices also led to disease, which rapidly spread throughout his force, further depleting Drummond's number of combat-ready soldiers.[51]

In mid-September, Brown, who assumed command after Gaines's incapacitation, decided to undertake a daring offensive to destroy the batteries. He organized a 1,600-man assault force under General Porter and a second column under Brigadier General John Miller that contained 400 soldiers. At noon on September 17, the Americans departed the fort. Heavy rainfall drenched the men, but the precipitation disguised their movement from the

British. Porter's men advanced west along the main road and veered onto a small forest path. The path ended 150 yards from the third British battery. At 3:00 p.m., Porter's men exploded out of the forest into the first battery and caught the British by surprise. "They seemed to be thunderstruck," Drummer Hanks recalled, "and surrendered at pleasure." The Americans captured the blockhouse, spiked the guns, and exploded the ammunition. They captured 400 men and 13 officers. Miller's soldiers combined with Porter's force to assault the second battery. Some Americans charged with bayonets; others fired their muskets. After heavy fighting, the Americans captured the blockhouse and disabled the cannon. The two units then attacked battery number one, but British reinforcements arrived and forced the Americans to withdraw. During the fight, a British soldier shot General Ripley in the neck. Few expected him to live, but he survived after three months of convalescence. In the second battle of Fort Erie, General Drummond's force suffered 609 men killed, wounded, or missing, and the Americans disabled three of his six siege guns. Brown's force lost 511 killed, wounded, or missing.[52]

On September 21, Drummond withdrew his army to new positions at Chippawa, Lundy's Lane, and Queenston. On the same day, American major general George Izard departed Sackets Harbor to reinforce Fort Erie with 4,000 men. In late July, Chauncey, with the addition of the *Superior* and *Mohawk* in his fleet, could safely protect army transports across the lake. Izard arrived on September 28 to assume command at Fort Erie. He decided to march against Drummond's force at Chippawa in the hope that the general would leave the fortified position and fight the Americans in the open. Drummond refused the bait and his men stayed entrenched in their lines. Shortly thereafter, Izard learned that Chauncey withdrew his fleet to Sackets Harbor in response to Yeo launching the mammoth, 102-gun *St. Lawrence* on September 10. On November 5, 1814, Izard, lacking Chauncey's support and unwilling to risk another bloody engagement at Lundy's Lane, abandoned Fort Erie. The sacrifices undertaken by Scott, Miller, Brown, and their men failed to influence the war's outcome once Izard made the decision to withdraw from Erie. The general resigned two months later.

During the summer of 1814, the second part of Secretary of War Armstrong's plan went into effect. The secretary tasked the US Army, in conjunction with the navy, to overrun the remaining British outposts in the upper Great Lakes and assert control in Lake Huron. Britain still controlled Mackinac Island after American victories on Lake Erie and at the Battle of the Thames. General William Henry Harrison and Commodore Oliver Hazard Perry had decided not to attack the outpost in the fall of 1813 because they lacked the supplies required for the effort. They agreed to postpone the assault until the spring of the following year, by which time Perry, who was promoted to captain, had been transferred to Newport, Rhode Island. In early 1814, Jesse Elliot, who inherited the Lake Erie command from Perry, prepared the *Niagara* and *Lawrence* to enter Lake Huron once the ice thawed in the spring. Elliott directed Captain Arthur Sinclair to lead the expedition, which would be supported by soldiers under the command of Lieutenant Colonel George Croghan, who in 1813 had successfully defended Fort Stephenson from British assault. Croghan dispatched five companies of regulars under the command of Major Andrew Holmes with two artillery pieces to support Sinclair. Holmes's regulars, combined with militia and the fleet's marines, brought Croghan's total force to 700 men.

On July 12, 1814, Sinclair entered Lake Huron with three brigs (the *Lawrence*, *Niagara*, and *Caledonia*) and two gunboats (the *Scorpion* and *Tigress*). After entering the waterway, Sinclair decided to locate a British supply base that reportedly existed in Georgian Bay at Matchedash. After spending two weeks searching for the depot, he proceeded to Fort St. Joseph's, which the British had abandoned in 1812 after they seized Fort Mackinac. Some of Croghan's men also raided a North West Company trading post at Sault Ste. Marie. They killed cattle, ruined gardens, and imprisoned civilians, but they eventually released the employees.

Without control of Lake Erie, the British Commissariat could not provide adequate supplies to the garrison at Mackinac Island. In February 1814, Lieutenant Colonel Robert McDouall with 200 men departed York with supplies for the outpost. The force crossed a frozen Lake Simcoe and halted on the banks of the Nottawasaga River. They built huts and constructed twenty-nine batteaux while waiting at the river for the ice to break up. On April 22, they navigated the river in batteaux until they reached the waterway's mouth in Lake Huron two days later. They crossed the lake and arrived at Mackinac Island on May 18. McDouall's journey was perhaps one of the most difficult resupply feats of the war.[53]

Since Britain seized Fort Mackinac in 1812, British soldiers had improved the garrison's defenses. The soldiers built a new blockhouse on the same rise where in 1812 the British had posted the 6-pounder that prompted Lieutenant Porter Hanks to surrender Fort Mackinac to the British. They also strengthened the pickets surrounding the fort. Sinclair's delay in approaching the island allowed McDouall, who assumed command upon his arrival at the outpost, to be aware of Sinclair's incoming squadron and collect additional militia and Native American warriors, which grew his strength to around 650 men.[54]

On July 26, 1814, Sinclair's fleet approached Mackinac Island. He and Croghan reconnoitered the island and debated where they should land the soldiers. They learned that the *Lawrence*'s and *Niagara*'s 32-pounders could not elevate high enough for their shot to reach the fort, but the cannons could still protect the soldiers during a landing. Croghan, after evaluating McDouall's position, believed they could not directly assault the fort without serious casualties. He decided that his men should land on the island's north side and locate a defensible position to place their two 6-pounder field guns. He believed that McDouall would be forced to leave the fort and attack the American position, because McDouall's Native American allies would compel him to engage the Americans.[55]

Sinclair's ships formed a battle line and raked the shoreline with their cannon. The men rowed ashore and advanced toward a farm on the northern end of the island, which contained a clearing suitable for Croghan's 6-pounders. As Croghan's men entered the clearing, they met a torrent of cannon and musket fire. McDouall had decided to meet the intruders at the farm rather than wait inside the fort. He advanced the bulk of his force with a 3- and a 6-pounder and posted Native American warriors in the woods along his rear and flanks. The British cannon fire did little damage to Croghan's men, and the lieutenant colonel formed his soldiers into two lines and ordered them to advance toward the British. His gunners moved the two 6-pounders into the clearing and fired on McDouall's troops, but without much effect. Croghan directed his militia to outflank the British right, but McDouall, observing the maneuver, withdrew men to address the threat. Croghan also dispatched Major Holmes and his regulars to assault McDouall's left.[56]

Around this time, McDouall heard a false report that Americans were landing between his position and the fort, and he dispatched men to investigate the alleged intrusion. Major Holmes and his regulars stumbled into this group, along with a group of Native American concealed behind trees. The fire from the British regulars and their Native American allies killed Major Holmes and many others. The Americans withdrew from the scene without retrieving their wounded, and they rejoined the main body of troops. McDouall, after learning that reports of the American landing were false, regrouped his men back at the clearing. Croghan directed his main line to charge, but the effort drove McDouall's men deeper into the thicket-laden woods lined with ravines. "I determined no longer to expose my force," Croghan later wrote Secretary of War John Armstrong, "to the fire of an enemy deriving every advantage which could be obtained from numbers and a knowledge of the position." Croghan, who had showed so much poise in 1813 at Fort Stephenson, decided to withdraw to the ships, rather than assault the British position in the woods. "Though the enemy formidable as they were in numbers," McDouall wrote Prevost, "have made so very poor a business of their attack, yet still I must ever regret their not being more effectually punished." The clash resulted in sixty-six American casualties.[57]

Following the failed assault, Sinclair departed Mackinac and raided a British supply base at Nottawasaga, where he destroyed the British schooner *Nancy*. He then returned to Detroit, but he left the *Tigress* and *Scorpion* with twenty-five regulars to block the flow of supplies to Mackinac. Sinclair also directed the *Tigress* to conduct short cruises around St. Joseph's to intercept fur canoes passing between Sault Ste. Marie and French River. "I think they will be starved into a surrender," Sinclair wrote Secretary of the Navy William Jones. Already one fleet of boats from Montreal, filled with supplies for Mackinac, turned around when the commander learned of the American presence on Lake Huron. Another small group of British soldiers from Mackinac tried to retrieve seventh barrels of provisions concealed in a nearby bay, but the presence of the two American ships forced them to unload the goods before they reached the island.[58]

Lieutenant Miller Worlsey, who had led that expedition, requested permission to attack the two American gunboats. McDouall agreed, and he dispatched four large rowboats, one armed with a 6-pounder and another with a 3-pounder, to seize the two vessels. Around 76 British soldiers manned the rowboats, with another 200 Native American warriors riding in nineteen canoes. As the group approached the *Tigress*, the British officer directed some of the Native Americans to stay behind, which reduced the attacking group to ninety-two men. The four rowboats snuck quietly toward the *Tigress*, with two boats lining each side. The soldiers climbed aboard the American schooner, surprising the crew and quickly capturing the vessel. The raid resulted in eight American casualties and with British control of the vessel and its thirty-one crewmen. Worsley believed that the *Scorpion*'s crew, located miles away, probably did not hear the shooting. He continued to fly the US colors and the next day approached the *Scorpion* without arousing suspicion. Once he neared the ship, Worsley's crew fired a 24-pounder into the *Scorpion*'s hull, after which his men swung grapples onto the ship's rails and boarded the vessel. Worsley's men captured the *Scorpion* and its crew of thirty seamen, soldiers, and five officers. Two of the *Scorpion*'s crew died in the attack. The capture of the two gunboats returned control of the upper Great Lakes to Britain and reopened the supply line from York to Lake Huron.[59]

At the end of 1814, Britain retained control of the upper Great Lakes, the Canadian side of the Niagara frontier, and Lake Ontario. The American campaign, the last major invasion of the war, returned no results that would influence the peace negotiations toward the favor of the United States. Prevost's officers once again repulsed the American army, but they suffered a few costly defeats. No American force occupied Canadian soil, and any disruptions to Canada's supply line were temporary. The Madison administration should have remained focused on Kingston, because destroying the dockyard and the ship *St. Lawrence* would have given Chauncey sustained control of Lake Ontario.

Chauncey's failure to support the army greatly disappointed General Brown. The commodore could safely traverse Lake Ontario starting in July, and American success in 1814 depended on Chauncey transporting fresh soldiers, cannons, and other supplies to the American force. Chauncey, however, refused to leave Sackets Harbor, which ultimately sealed the campaign's fate. Brown's frustration boiled over in a letter to Chauncey written on September 4: "The exception you take at my letter to the secretary [where Brown complained about Chauncey's lack of support], would be very reasonable and proper, provided the fleet of Lake Ontario was your private property . . . but I have been induced to believe that it was the property of the Nation."[60]

Despite the failed effort, the 1814 invasion carved a place in US military history. The country's disciplined troops, led by elite officers, stood equal to British firepower on the battlefield for the first time in the war. The grey uniforms observed by Riall at Chippawa became the standard for West Point cadets in honor of the battle. Most importantly, the victories demonstrated to the American public that a disciplined, standing army could defend the interests of the young republic. Americans, many fearful of a powerful military force, witnessed the army accomplish more in a few months in 1814 than the militia had in two years. The country's attitude toward a standing army began to change as many realized that the militia could not defend America's growing interests. The country's postwar standing army would be led by men who served during the War of 1812, including Jacob Brown, John Wool, and Winfield Scott. Scott became one of the most successful generals in US history, and the Battles of Chippawa and Lundy's Lane served as the formative moments in Scott's career. Jacob Brown earned the Congressional Gold Medal in November 1814 for his actions in Canada, and in 1821, he became commanding general of the US Army.[61]

The country needed its best soldiers in late 1814, when Prime Minister Liverpool's war strategy changed from defense to offense. He wanted to secure territorial concessions that could help protect Canada and its Native American allies from future attacks. Liverpool's new approach forced Madison to feel the full weight of America's decision to declare war against a superpower. America's military strategy, which had focused on seizing land to influence the negotiations, transitioned into a defensive effort to preserve US territory. The year 1814 was a defining moment for the country's future.

Prevost Invades New York

I see no end to this war of Broad Axes.
—Jones to Macdonough, July 5, 1814, quoted in *Naval War of 1812: A Documentary History*

In the summer of 1814, Master Commandant Thomas Macdonough faced a daunting task. In 1812, the navy appointed him as the commander of US naval forces on Lake Champlain, a strategic waterway on the US-Canadian border. The lake served as a north–south thoroughfare between Lower Canada and New York. Lake Champlain stretched 125 miles long and 14 miles wide, offering efficient transport in the rugged, wilderness-filled region.

Macdonough was a veteran seaman. He entered the navy as a teenager, and by 1814 had served fourteen years in the service. In the early 1800s, he was a midshipman aboard the USS *Constellation*, and during the Barbary Wars, he joined Stephen Decatur in a bold raid to burn the captured *Philadelphia*. At the beginning of the War of 1812, Macdonough, an officer aboard the *Constellation*, requested an independent post, and the navy transferred him to Portsmouth, New Hampshire, to command a gunboat fleet. In October 1812, Macdonough became the commander of naval forces at Champlain, and in July 1813, the navy promoted him to master commandant.[1]

First Navy Secretary Paul Hamilton and then Navy Secretary William Jones, preoccupied with controlling Lakes Erie and Ontario, largely ignored Lake Champlain and provided Macdonough few supplies and men. Macdonough armed three merchant schooners, which added to his fledgling fleet, but on June 3, 1813, the British captured two of them, the *Growler* and the *Eagle*. His remaining squadron—two gunboats and a sloop—sought shelter at Burlington, Vermont.

In 1814, Lake Champlain was vital to the war's outcome. In June 1814, Lord Bathurst, secretary of state for war and the colonies, wrote Governor-in-Chief George Prevost that it is the "intention of this majesty's government to avail themselves of the favourable state of affairs in Europe in order to reinforce the army under your command." And he was going dispatch "twelve of the most effective Regiments of the Army under the Duke of Wellington." Bathurst directed Prevost to destroy the US naval ports at Sackets Harbor and Lake Erie and to occupy the Lake Champlain corridor. British control of the Lake Champlain region would deter an American assault against Montreal and secure the crossroads at Albany, New York, that led west to Ontario, east to Springfield and Boston, and south to New York City.[2]

Even with the reinforcements, Prevost doubted that he could undertake offensive operations until the British regained supremacy on Lakes Ontario and Champlain. Prevost understood the importance of waterway transport in the region, but Bathurst disliked his reluctance. "I am bound in fairness to apprize you," he wrote Prevost in August, "that if you shall allow the present campaign to close without having undertaken offensive measures against the enemy, you will very seriously disappoint the expectations of the Prince Regent and the Country." Bathurst wanted no excuses from the soon-to-be reinforced leader.[3]

Prevost also requested that Admiral Alexander Cochrane, the commander of the West Indies and North American stations, conduct amphibious operations along the Eastern Seaboard to divert American attention from the New York campaign. Cochrane's raids, conducted in July and August 1814, destroyed towns and villages throughout Chesapeake Bay. Later, Major General Robert Ross joined Cochrane with 4,000 troops, and the army under Ross attacked and burned much of Washington, DC, in August 1814. Cochrane and Ross then attempted to assault Baltimore, where an American sharpshooter killed Ross, and the Americans repulsed the British assault.

With Cochrane's diversion underway, the stage was set for Prevost to achieve his first victory as a battlefield commander during the war. Prevost, heeding Bathurst's warning to start the campaign before winter, decided to invade the Champlain valley before seizing US ports on Lakes Erie and Ontario. Commodore Yeo had lost naval superiority on those lakes, so Prevost decided to postpone attacks on those waterways. The Champlain valley corridor also offered the shortest route into the United States, and the attack would help protect Montreal's southern flank. The governor-in-chief also knew that he could rely on American smugglers in the Champlain valley to supply his troops during the expedition. Vermont's farmers sold flour, beef, and produce to the British throughout the war, and they even provided lumbar, spars, and other materials for Britain's shipbuilding efforts on Lake Champlain. Vermont's citizens had traded with Canada for decades and most maintained a peaceful coexistence with the country during the conflict, a relationship that valued money over politics. Prevost understood his army's reliance on these goods, and he intended to avoid antagonizing the locals and disrupting the flow of supplies from the state.[4]

With these factors mind, Prevost determined to march on the western side of Lake Champlain, and he selected Plattsburgh, New York, in the eastern Champlain valley as the army's first target. He planned to advance south from Montreal to seize Plattsburgh and possibly press farther down the New York-Vermont border to destroy American outposts. Even as Bathurst pressured Prevost to undertake offensive operations, he cautioned the governor-in-chief not to extend his line too distant from Montreal and thus make his supply line vulnerable to American irregulars.[5]

Prevost's plan depended on the British seizing control of Lake Champlain. Prevost needed the British fleet to destroy the small American squadron on the lake so he could safely move men and supplies on the waterway during the invasion. The force, which reached more than 10,000 men, would require a daily allotment of forty-five tons of food and provisions. The lake provided a faster and safer alternative than moving provisions over land along the western shore of Lake Champlain. An overland logistics train would be subject to raids from American irregulars and would be delayed by steep ravines and the road's poor condition. British control of the lake would also enable Britain's fleet to support the army's attack on the city of Plattsburgh with their naval guns.[6]

In July 1813, Sir James Yeo had charged Captain Daniel Pring with organizing the dockyard and assuming command of the small fleet on Lake Champlain at Île aux Noix on the Richelieu River. Prevost later dispatched a master shipbuilder to Île aux Noix to assist Pring in building a frigate, later named the *Confiance*, which when launched would be the largest ship on the lake. The governor-in-chief also permitted Pring to build the sixteen-gun brig *Linnet*. Yeo later replaced Pring with Captain Peter Fisher because he believed that Pring, due to his lower rank, should not oversee construction of such a large ship. Yeo also did not want Pring commanding a squadron during battle, but Pring continued to manage the dockyard as Fisher's second-in-command.[7]

In December 1813, Macdonough moved his small fleet to a more secure harbor near Vergennes, Vermont. The new dockyard, located seven miles into Otter Creek, occupied a deep, narrow waterway that could be defended by land batteries. Macdonough moved to Vergennes because he believed that cannons could be moved easily to the town on snow (using sleighs), and he knew that the village's foundries could produce round shot and other shipbuilding necessities. The falls at Vergennes provided waterpower for local foundries, which reportedly forged a thousand 32-pound balls before the battle. At or near Vergennes, other useful industries contained blast and iron furnaces, rolling mills, and a wire factory. Monkton, a few miles away, contained usable veins of iron. In 1807, Monkton Iron Company Store (Monkton Iron Works) in Vergennes advertised nail rods, rolled iron, and German steel for sale. The land around Vergennes also possessed plenty of timber for shipbuilding. Navy Secretary Jones noted to Macdonough that he planned to move supplies from New York to Albany before the Hudson froze so that Macdonough could build fifteen galleys. From Albany, heavy ordnance could be shipped on the Hudson River, then portaged to Lake George and into Lake Champlain.[8]

In the winter of 1813, Secretary Jones became increasingly concerned about the state of affairs on the lake and dispatched expert shipbuilders Adam and Noah Brown to assist Macdonough in constructing a larger fleet. The Brown brothers had built Perry's squadron from scratch at Presque Isle and could perform similar miracles at Vergennes. They arrived in February 1814 and embarked on an ambitious project to build six gunboats and a twenty-six-gun sloop of war, the *Jones*. The shipwrights required four hundred yards of canvas for the *Jones*'s main topsail, and they also needed anchors, cables, and cordage sent to the dockyard. Most importantly, Macdonough needed guns for the ship and sailors to operate the new vessels. He requested soldiers from Major General George Izard, but Izard only gave him a small contingent.[9]

In early April, Pring sailed his squadron of six sloops and ten galleys, including the twenty-gun *Linnet*, toward Vergennes. He wanted to destroy the *Jones* before Macdonough's shipbuilders completed the vessel. On May 14, the British squadron approached Otter Creek. American shore batteries pelted Pring's fleet, which also returned fire. After a ninety-minute exchange, Pring's ships could not subdue the batteries, and he withdrew to Île aux Noix.[10]

The failed attack gave Macdonough a new sense of urgency to complete the *Jones* before the British returned with a larger force and destroyed the American dockyard. For six anxious days, Macdonough waited for his new sloop of war to be launched before Pring returned to the harbor. On April 11, Macdonough's men cast the *Jones* into the water (Secretary Jones later renamed the *Jones* the *Saratoga*). The remarkable shipbuilding enterprise exhibited by the Brown brothers allowed them to take wood "from the stump" (green wood from freshly cut trees) and complete the vessel in only forty days—a tremendous feat. On May 26, Macdonough sailed his squadron into Plattsburgh Bay. He trapped Pring's fleet at Île aux Noix and sought out General Izard to plan a joint attack against Montreal.[11]

Macdonough understood that his supremacy on the lake would be short-lived because the British were nearing completion of the *Confiance*. Macdonough, wanting to keep pace with Fisher's efforts, requested permission from Secretary Jones to build another brig. The secretary, frustrated with the constant demand for shipbuilding resources, told Macdonough that he was tired of the "irksome contest of shipbuilding." Jones eventually agreed to Macdonough's request, but he voiced his displeasure in a letter he wrote to Macdonough in July. "I see no end to this war of Broad Axes," he wrote the master commandant. On August 27, shipwrights completed the twenty-gun *Eagle*, which joined Macdonough's fleet in Plattsburgh Bay.[12]

As the shipbuilding race continued, on August 31, 1814, Prevost marched his army across the US-Canada border toward Plattsburgh. Prevost's force benefited from the experience of Iberian Peninsula veterans who fought under the Duke of Wellington. Prevost's overseas reinforcements consisted of forty-four total units of cavalry, artillery, and infantry units; twenty-two of these units originated from the Peninsula. Six of the seven divisions of Wellington's Peninsular Army dispatched troops to British North America, as did the cavalry division, but only four of the six Peninsular units available to Prevost fought in the upcoming battle.[13]

Three of Wellington's generals also accompanied the force. Major General Frederick Robinson commanded the First Brigade, Major General Thomas Brisbane the Second, and Major General Manley Power the Third. They each brought capable staffs who had conducted multidivision, complex operations in Europe. Prevost, unlike these generals, had not campaigned in Europe, so the newly arrived officers retained little familiarity with Prevost's capabilities as a military commander. They disliked Prevost's constant reviews of their troops, a practice that Wellington had not required in Europe. They were also frustrated by the staff department's poor organization and the confusion that resulted when supporting the needs of a large body of troops.[14]

To combat these veterans, US Army brigadier general Alexander Macomb commanded only 1,500 men at Plattsburgh. Earlier in April, General Izard reinforced Plattsburgh, and Macomb's force grew to 5,000 men by July. But Secretary of War John Armstrong inexplicably ordered Izard to transfer two-thirds of his army to Sackets Harbor to support Major General Jacob Brown's assault on the Niagara. Armstrong, aware of Prevost's build-up in Montreal, issued the directive anyway. A frustrated Izard warned Armstrong that "Plattsburgh . . . will, in less than three days after my departure, be in the possession of the enemy." Despite his protests, on August 29, 1814 Izard departed the Champlain valley with 4,000 men, leaving Alexander Macomb to face the British army with only a small contingent of regulars.[15]

Macomb's troops encamped outside of the village of Plattsburgh. The Saranac River flowed through the middle of the town, and its southern bank rose fifty feet above the water. Plattsburgh's defenses required serious repair. One observer noted in late 1813 that "we were left so destitute of the means of defense, that one thousand British troops might have carried the place with all ease." The town contained three redoubts along the Saranac River, and the strongest fortification, Fort Moreau, occupied the line's center, while Forts Brown and Scott flanked Moreau. When Macomb assumed command, he organized his soldiers by redoubt and challenged them to defend their garrison to the last man. He hoped that his order would create "emulation and zeal" among the novice troops. Macomb also mustered New York and Vermont militia who trickled into Plattsburgh and grew his force to 4,000 soldiers.[16]

On August 31, 1814, Prevost's soldiers advanced for five days down the wilderness road to the village of Chazy, fourteen miles north of Plattsburgh. At daybreak on September 6, the brigades formed into two attack columns. Prevost dispatched the first column under General Robinson to advance along the lake road, while General Power's force marched inland through Beekmantown. Power's army contained four companies of light infantry and a formidable artillery train that included two 24-pounders, three 6-pounders, one 8-inch howitzer, and three 24-pound carronades.[17]

After Prevost's force advanced toward Plattsburgh, Sir James Yeo made a surprising decision. Just days before the planned attack, Yeo ordered Captain George Downie to replace Captain Peter Fisher. During his time at Île aux Noix, Fisher had befriended Prevost and his family, and Yeo resented Fisher's familiarity with someone that he disliked. Yeo also blamed Fisher for the *Confiance*'s slow construction and sought a more aggressive commander to support the invasion. Fisher and Pring, however, had managed the shipbuilding effort well in spite of the shortage of men and supplies required to build the vessel. Fisher's and Pring's shipbuilding efforts suffered because Yeo and Prevost allocated most of their resources to Kingston to support construction of the first-rate, 102-gun *St. Lawrence*. Pring lacked the necessary number of sailors, cannon, and ammunition to complete the *Confiance*.[18]

The curious move placed Downie in command of four ships, including the *Confiance*, which was launched upon his arrival at the shipyard. Downie toured the vessel on August 25 and had little time to become acquainted with his new flagship. Downie also lacked Pring's and Fisher's knowledge about the lake and the enemy fleet. His appointment caused anxiety among the sailors, who now reported to a new captain on the cusp of a major naval battle. Pring assumed second-in-command of the fleet aboard the *Linnet*.[19]

As Prevost's force approached Plattsburgh, US general Macomb convened a council of war with his officers. The leaders correctly assessed that the British force would approach Plattsburgh from the lake road and through Beekmantown. "Let it not be said that Erie was better defended than Plattsburgh," the general told his men. He dispatched Major John Wool (who served nobly at the Battle of Queenston) with 250 regulars and Captain Luther Leonard with two cannon to Beekmantown. General Benjamin Mooers's detachment of New York militia joined Major Wool's regulars at Culver's Hill, a good defensive position on the road north of Beekmantown. When scarlet-clad New York militia appeared on the hill, frightened Americans mistook the New Yorkers for British regulars and fled south to Beekmantown. British troops arrived at the hill around 7:00 a.m. on September 6. In the brief skirmish there, a musket ball killed the Duke of Wellington's nephew.[20]

The British force continued advancing toward Plattsburgh. Wool's regulars fired at the group as they marched down the Beekmantown Road. Captain Martin Aikin's rifle company joined Captain Luther Leonard at Halsey's Corner. Luther's men placed two pieces of light artillery in the road, and Wool's regulars formed in front of the guns to conceal them from the enemy's view. When the British approached, the regulars dashed to a nearby stone wall, and Leonard's gunners opened fire with cannonballs, grapeshot, and canister, while Aikin's riflemen and Wool's regulars fired on General Power's vanguard. The combined attack ravaged the front of the British column. One cannonball mashed the legs of sixteen British soldiers, according to one observer. The disciplined British troops filled the gaps left by the dead and wounded and continued to press forward. Aikin signaled his men to fire from behind a nearby fence "which was instantly done & as quickly returned," one militiaman remembered. After the third volley, British bugles sounded the charge. The British soldiers dropped their knapsacks and sprinted toward the wall. The Americans fled at the intimidating sight of charging British soldiers. They crossed the Saranac River and regrouped along the south bank of the waterway. The men shredded the upper and lower bridge and used the timber to create another redoubt on the south bank.[21]

British light infantry, concealed in a house near the riverbank, fired at the Americans in their redoubts. Macomb directed his gunners to fire "hot shot" at the house, which caught fire and forced the snipers to retire from the position. Undeterred, British light infantry advanced toward the river. American soldiers, some armed with accurate rifles, poured a deadly fire into the advance and repulsed the British with serious loss. Prevost ordered his men to place his formidable array of cannon throughout the village in preparation for an assault with his main force. He ordered his gunners to fire on

Figure 12. ***Battle of Plattsburg.*** This illustration shows the fighting within Plattsburgh and the naval engagement on Lake Champlain. Prevost arrayed a formidable arsenal of cannon on the east side of the riverbank and waited for the British squadron to engage the Americans. Prevost's decision to withdraw after the navy's defeat was heavily criticized by his generals. Courtesy of the Library of Congress, LC-DIG-pga-14060.

the Americans once Downie engaged the US fleet on the lake. The British squadron, however, languished in port, where Downie's men feverishly tried to finish the *Confiance.* Prevost dispatched a cavalry officer to wait at Île aux Noix and return to him with news of the squadron's departure.[22]

Prevost wrote numerous letters to Downie urging him to finish the *Confiance*, which was afloat but not ready for combat. Downie told Prevost that the *Confiance* would be ready for battle on September 8 or 9. The response did not satisfy Prevost, who explained that the squadron should depart immediately. "In the [prior] letter," an agitated Downie responded, "I stated to you that this Ship was not ready. She is not ready now, and, until she is ready, it is my duty not to hazard the Squadron before an Enemy who will be superior in Force." Prevost, who was fixated on the navy's arrival to begin the attack, replied that "I need not dwell with you on the Evils resulting to both Services from delay."[23]

On September 8 shipwrights completed enough of the *Confiance* that the ship could sail to combat, but Downie required a strong north wind to navigate to Plattsburgh. Prevost wrote Downie: "I ascribe the disappointment I have experienced to the unfortunate change of wind, & shall rejoice to learn that my reasonable expectations have been frustrated by no other cause." The British force waited three days for Downie's squadron to arrive in Plattsburgh Bay. The Americans exploited the delay to fortify their positions and collect additional New York and Vermont militia. During the pause in hostilities, Captain George McGlassin of the US Fifteenth Infantry requested permission from Macomb to attack a rocket battery opposite Fort Brown. Around midnight on September 10, McGlassin and fifty men surprised three hundred British defenders and destroyed the battery.[24]

Downie finally weighed anchor from Chazy and sailed toward Plattsburgh Bay. The *Confiance*'s crew towed gunpowder behind the flagship because the ship's incomplete magazine could not hold explosive material. The crew continued to work on the magazine and other parts of the ship as they sailed toward battle. Downie's sailors also lacked experience. Many of the men were recent draftees who had boarded his ship only six days before the *Confiance*'s departure, and the remainder joined at Chazy, two days before the battle. The novice gunners had practiced only two or three times on their cannon, which cast doubt on their ability to operate the guns under fire. A carpenter aboard the ship later said that "the ship was in an unfinished state altogether." Despite its flaws, the *Confiance*, with its thirty-one 24-pound long guns and six 32-pound carronades, was still the largest ship on Lake Champlain.[25]

At daylight on September 11, Downie scaled his guns (fired them with cartridges only) to clear the barrels and to signal to Prevost that his squadron would soon engage the enemy. Around 7:30 a.m., Downie rounded Cumberland Head and observed American masts north of Crab Island on the southern end of Plattsburgh Bay. "There are the Enemy's ships," Downie told his crew. "Our Army are to storm the Enemy's works at the moment we engage, and mind don't let us be behind." His crew cheered and returned to their posts. Downie embarked in a gig to reconnoiter the American position. He observed the American fleet anchored in a stationary battle line, north to south, with ships one hundred yards apart, beginning with the *Eagle*, *Saratoga*, and *Ticonderoga*. The *Preble*, positioned far southwest, would prevent Downie from flanking the southern side of the flotilla.[26]

Macdonough anchored his fleet in the bay because the small cove would force Downie to fight him in close quarters. Downie's squadron contained mainly long guns, which would be less effective inside a small bay than in open water. Macdonough's ships, in contrast, mounted primarily carronades, whose greater firing power at short distances could devastate an enemy fleet. Downie could approach the American squadron from two directions. He could sail south around Crab Island and navigate his ships between the shore and island, but this course would leave his squadron exposed to Fort Scott's cannon and dangerous rock outcroppings. He could also enter the bay in front of Macdonough's ships, but this approach would make his fleet vulnerable to American broadsides as it moved into position. While Downie was considering his options, Prevost convened his senior officers to discuss their land assault. They agreed that Brisbane's soldiers should create a diversion at the Plattsburgh Bridge while Robinson's troops advanced into the rear of the American position at Pike's Ford. Prevost told General Robinson, "It is now nine o'clock, march off at ten."[27]

Macdonough, meanwhile, made last-minute preparations. He understood that anchored ships required some mobility because stationary fleets could be destroyed by a more mobile enemy under sail. To ensure that his fleet could change directions, he directed that spring lines be placed from the bow anchors to the stern. When seamen wound the springs in, they could pivot the ships to the port or larboard side. Macdonough placed the springs in underwater loops of rope where they would be protected from enemy fire. His men also retained another advantage over the British fleet. The anchored American squadron freed most of the crew from their sailing duties, allowing them to man the guns instead. Macdonough's diligent preparations would ultimately decide the outcome of the battle.[28]

After 9:00 a.m., Downie's fleet sailed into the bay. He decided to approach the American squadron from the north, where his fleet would cross in front of the stationary American squadron. Downie ordered the *Finch* to lead the British line, followed by *Confiance*, *Linnet*, and *Chubb*. The *Linnet*, assisted by the *Chubb*, would engage the *Eagle*; the *Finch* would contain the *Ticonderoga* and *Preble*. Downie hoped to place the *Confiance* across from Macdonough's largest ship, the *Saratoga*. The British fleet crossed in front of the American battle line, and Macdonough's flagship unleashed a withering broadside. Downie ordered his gunners to hold fire until the squadron positioned itself across from the American fleet. The bay's changing winds and currents forced Downie slightly off course, and he anchored only two cable lengths away from the *Saratoga*, closer than he originally intended. The captain, standing on the *Confiance*'s deck, observed Prevost's inactive troops and questioned why the soldiers sat idly. Downie expected Prevost to attack Macomb once the British squadron began battle. Prevost could seize Fort Scott's batteries and turn them against the American fleet to give Downie an important edge in the upcoming fight.[29]

Within minutes the two fleets exchanged vicious broadsides from three hundred yards away. "The *Saratoga* suffering much from the heavy fire of the *Confiance*," Macdonough recalled, but "I could perceive at the same time, however, that our fire was very destructive to her." Macdonough darted throughout the ship, shouting encouragement and assisting his men. He was sighting in a gun when a ball from the *Confiance* cut the *Saratoga*'s spanker boom and the mast fell on top of Macdonough, knocking him to the deck. His crew believed that he was dead. Macdonough revived himself and resumed command of the ship. Another ball smashed into a gun being sighted in by Macdonough's first lieutenant, Peter Gamble, instantly killing him.

Causalities also mounted aboard the *Confiance*. Fifteen minutes into the exchange, a cannonball hit the muzzle of a 24-pounder, dismounting the gun and driving the weapon into Downie, killing him. Lieutenant Joseph Robertson wanted to signal Pring, the next in command, that Downie was dead, but he could not locate the captain's signal books. The American ship destroyed the *Confiance*'s two gigs, and Robertson could not dispatch a seaman to the *Linnet* with the news. For the time being, Robertson would command the fleet, and he inherited the job at a most desperate time.[30]

Around 10:30 a.m., British fire cut the *Eagle*'s spring and the ship began to turn west, making it vulnerable to a raking fire from the *Linnet*. Captain Robert Henley decided to cut the other springs, and the ship floated safely behind the *Saratoga*. The movement, however, exposed the *Saratoga*'s left side to the *Linnet*'s guns. The combined fire from the *Linnet* and *Confiance* destroyed most of the *Saratoga*'s starboard cannon. Macdonough directed Sailing Master Philip Brum to use springs to wind the ship around, so its undamaged larboard guns could fire on the *Confiance*. A cannonball pierced the ship's side and a splinter hit Brum, ripping off his clothes and sending him flying to the deck. Brum rose, placed a handkerchief over the wound, released the stern anchor, and cut the bower cable. The ship wound around and gave Macdonough a fresh side of guns.[31]

The *Saratoga* unleashed a withering broadside fire that ravaged the *Confi-*

ance's fore, main, and mizzen masts, her bowsprit, spanker, and jib boom. One shot ripped a seven-foot hole in its hull and it began listing dangerously too starboard. More than 105 shots pierced the vessel's hull. The crew worked tirelessly to cork the holes with shot plugs. "The ship was making water very fast," Robertson remembered. "The Rigging, Spars, and hull completely Shattered; upwards of forty men killed, and the wind from that quarter as not to admit of the smallest prospect of escaping, had the ship been in a condition." Eight feet of water poured into the ship's hold. The British crew shifted supplies to the port side to raise the starboard hole upward past the waterline. They moved the wounded throughout the ship's cockpit to prevent them from drowning. "The vessel was absolutely torn to pieces," Judge Hubbel recalled. "The decks were strewn with mutilated bodies lying in all directions, and everything was covered with blood." Robertson had no choice but to strike his colors. He did so at 10:50 a.m. "The havoc on both sides was dreadful," Midshipman William Lee on the *Confiance* recalled. "Were you to see my jacket, waistcoat, and trowsers, you would be astonished to know how I escaped as I did, for they are literally torn all to rags with shot and splinters." Lee claimed that a Trafalgar veteran aboard the *Confiance* told him that Nelson's famous battle at Trafalgar was a "flea bite" compared to the fight on Lake Champlain.[32]

After the *Confiance* surrendered, the USS *Saratoga* turned on the HMS *Linnet* (the *Chub* and *Finch* had already been captured). The *Linnet* could not continue the fight alone. Water flooded the ship's hold and cannon shot destroyed its sails and rigging. Its captain struck her colors. Macdonough received the British officers aboard the *Saratoga*. They offered their swords, but he told them, "Gentlemen, your gallant conduct makes you worthy to wear your weapons, return them to their scabbards." He allowed the officers to roam the deck of his flagship. After two hours and twenty minutes of fighting, Macdonough wrote Secretary Jones that "the Almighty has been pleased to grant us a signal victory on Lake Champlain in the capture of one frigate, one brig, and two sloops of war of the enemy." Macdonough retrieved the wounded from both sides and dispatched them to Crab Island, where a makeshift hospital had been established. "I have much Satisfaction in making your acquainted," Pring wrote Yeo after the battle, "with the humane treatment the wounded have received from Commodore Macdonough . . . his generous and polite attention also to myself, the Officers and Men, will ever hereafter be gratefully remembered." Unfortunately for Downie, he died instantly in the battle, only seventeen days into his command.[33]

Before the British ships surrendered, Prevost's troops moved into position to assault the American defenses. Robinson's force, which would attack the rear of Macomb's position, advanced toward a ford in the Saranac River. His troops followed the road until it disintegrated into a series of into small logging paths. Prevost did not send scouts to map the area, and Robinson marched blindly into the woods. The troops retraced their steps, and after one hour they reached the ford, where thick woods lined a high bank overlooking the river. Power's brigade crossed first. His light infantry dashed down the steep bank and "forded the river like . . . foxhounds, driving the Doodley [Americans] in all directions." Robinson recalled that his men rushed through galling enemy fire "with an impetuosity that nothing could check." The general crossed the remainder of his force and formed his regulars into columns. His troops marched through thickets, crossed a ridge, and reached a road in the rear of Macomb's position. Without guides, Robinson managed to position his army one mile behind the enemy's force, poised for a devastating assault. In Plattsburgh, Brisbane's force moved in column toward the destroyed upper and lower bridges, ready to attack the front of the American position.[34]

Around this time, Adjutant Edward Baynes, one of Prevost's aides, delivered a message to Robinson from Prevost. The letter stated that the *Confiance* and *Linnet* had struck their colors and that the army should withdraw. Robinson shared the shocking information with General Power, who was "equally astonished at its contents." Power begged Prevost to cancel the order to retreat, and Brisbane told Prevost that he would have possession of the fort "in a few minutes." Prevost reportedly told Brisbane that "my orders must be obeyed." The directive stunned Robinson. "Never was anything like the disappointment expressed in every countenance," Robinson wrote later. "The advance was within shot, and full view of the Redoubt, and in one hour they must have been ours." Robinson's men rarely retreated from a fight. On the Iberian Peninsula, his brigade had faced some of France's best troops and fought them at close range in bloody melées. The Vermont and New York militiamen, citizen-soldiers mustered during the crisis, lacked the fighting prowess of Napoleon's soldiers. They would have given Robinson a spirited fight, but they likely would have yielded to Wellington's veterans.[35]

Prevost feared that an attack against Plattsburgh's stout defenses would have resulted in steep casualties for his force. The loss of the navy's fleet also imperiled his ability to be resupplied by the lake. As Bathurst had instructed, Prevost refused to overextend his supply line, which could be disrupted by American irregulars. American possession of the lake would also enable American troops to advance into the rear of his army. Prevost's prudent decision was consistent with Bathurst's warning that he should protect his supply line. Robinson complied with the Prevost order, as did the rest of the men, who withdrew around 3:00 p.m. on September 11. Rain poured on the soldiers as they withdrew north toward Montreal. Wagons bogged down in muddy roads and compelled Prevost to leave some stores and ordnance behind. Robinson, frustrated with Prevost's timidity, called the campaign a "disgraceful and unfortunate affair."[36]

British newspapers mercilessly criticized Prevost's decision to retreat. "We had an army of 14 to 15,000 regular and brave troops," one letter in the *Times of London* read, "who only wished to be allowed to storm the enemy's fort, and which everybody says would easily have been accomplished had any other person had the command that Sir G. Prevost." The letter further stated that "we have suffered more disgrace from the incapacity of this man [Prevost] than we will retrieve for months to come, let our exertions be ever so great." A disillusioned Prime Minister Liverpool commented: "He [Prevost] has . . . managed the campaign as ill as possible," he wrote Castlereagh, "and if he cannot redeem himself with some brilliant success, he must be recalled." The Duke of Wellington, commenting on the campaign from Europe, sympathized with Prevost's predicament. "Whether Sir George Prevost was right or wrong in his decision at Lake Champlain is more than I can tell, but of this I am certain—he must have . . . retired . . . after our fleet was beaten, and I am inclined to believe that he was right."[37]

To some degree, the criticisms were unfair. Prevost excelled as a defensive strategist, distributing limited resources throughout his extensive area of operations and ensuring that his primary strongholds in Lower Canada—Montreal, Quebec, and the St. Lawrence—could withstand attack. As a battlefield commander, however, Prevost's track record in North America was more mixed. Some observers acknowledged that others besides Prevost deserved blame, especially Yeo: "We have almost uniformly been unsuccessful; and yet, Sir George Prevost is *blamed*, while every other commander, though keeping in harbour while the enemy dares him to the fight; though defeated, though captured, though driven back in disgrace before inferior numbers, is *praised*."[38]

Prevost, for his part, attributed the attack's failure to the navy. "The melancholy fate of our vessels blasted these [the assault's] intentions," he wrote General Gordon Drummond after the battle. Pring, second-in-command of the fleet, underwent a court martial for his actions during the naval exchange. The panel disagreed with Prevost's assessment and declared that Prevost forced Downie to engage the American navy before his squadron was ready. Most of the officers testified that Downie believed Prevost would seize the American batteries and turn them on Macdonough's fleet to assist Downie during the engagement. Yeo, for his part, also shifted blame to Prevost, chastising him for the naval defeat, even though Yeo himself had not supplied Downie's squadron with the necessary men and materials. A court that examined Pring's actions at the battle found that "the Capture of His Majesty's said late Ship *Confiance*, the brig *Linnet*, and the remainder of the said Squadron, by the said American Squadron, was principally caused by the British Squadron having been urged into Battle previous to its being in a proper state to meet its Enemy by a promised Co-operation of the Land Forces which was not carried into effect."[39]

The year 1814 came to a close with the United States celebrating New York's defense. Macdonough's victory and Prevost's withdrawal convinced Americans that they could defeat Britain on US soil. The success helped return some credibility to the isolated Madison administration, which was under pressure from Congress to produce victories or settle the war. In late October, news reached London regarding the British failures at Plattsburgh and the unsuccessful British assault on Baltimore that occurred in September 1814. Prime Minister Liverpool asked Wellington, who was serving as ambassador in Paris, if he wanted to assume command in North America or assist Foreign Minister Castlereagh at Vienna. Wellington believed that he was needed more in Europe, and Wellington reiterated to Liverpool the importance of British superiority on the Great Lakes. He explained to the prime minister that "if we can't [gain naval superiority on the Great Lakes] I shall do you but little good in America." He also highlighted his skepticism that Britain can force America to surrender on Britain's terms: "I confess I think you have no right from the state of war to demand any concession of territory from America . . . you have not been able to carry it [the war] into the enemy's territory . . . and have not even cleared your own territory of the enemy on the point of attack . . . the state of your military operations, however creditable, does not entitle you to demand any." One newspaper editor believed that the time had arrived for Britain to concede the frontier to the United States: "It appears to me to be downright madness, by a continuation of the war, to regain what we have lost upon the lakes."[40]

The British public, surprised by the failures and tired of war, questioned the continuation of the conflict. For a decade, British citizens read bloody accounts of war at places such as Cuidad Rodrigo, Badajos, and Talavera, all clashes that were necessary to rid Europe of the Napoleonic threat. Britain lost a generation of men during this time, and many Britons believed they should enjoy the fruits of their hard-fought European peace. The two failed attacks at Plattsburgh and Baltimore tested Britain's patience for more bloodshed, and many members of Parliament shared their sentiment. Englishmen were also tired of paying the property tax that the government levied to pay its war debts.[41]

Liverpool was aware of the public's shifting mood, and events unfolding outside of England demanded his attention. In Europe, the Congress of Vienna, which aimed to redraw the Continent's boundaries after Napoleon's defeat, was proceeding poorly, and the Allied-restored French monarchy was on the verge of collapse. The combination of these domestic and international concerns prompted Liverpool to send new instructions to his delegation in Ghent, which had continued negotiations through the winter of 1814. Liverpool told Castlereagh that the British commissioners should consider the most recent American proposal for peace. That proposal, which the British delegation eventually accepted, restored the status quo ante bellum. The treaty called for any territory and prisoners acquired during the conflict to be returned to the respective country. The agreement ignored the thorny issue of navigation rights on the Mississippi and fishing claims in Newfoundland. The treaty also did not address any of the war's causes, including impressment and Britain's seizure of neutral shipping. Madison, however, after suffering financial, political, and military anguish from the conflict, was eager for peace. On Christmas Eve 1814, the commissioners signed the Treaty of Ghent. The document still needed to be ratified by the US Senate (and signed by the president), and by Parliament, but the stage was set for peace. Hostilities ended once both sides ratified the treaty, which occurred on February 16,

1815. The next day the delegations enjoyed Christmas dinner with each other, but news of the accord would not reach North America for weeks.[42]

In a letter to George Canning, Liverpool cited his reasons for seeking peace with the United States. The prime minister highlighted the population's aversion to the property tax and the challenges emerging at the Congress of Vienna. He also noted Wellington's thoughts on the conflict, when Wellington explained that Britain should seek peace because there is "no vulnerable point of importance" that Britain could seize to force the United States to make concessions. Finally, he commented on the state of the Canadian frontier: "The continuance of the war for the purpose of obtaining a better frontier for Canada, would I am persuaded, have been found impractical . . . no additional frontier which you [Canning] could possibly expect to obtain would materially add to the security of Canada." Liverpool further wrote that "the frontier must in any case be of such prodigious extent, that it never could be made, as frontier, defensible against the means which the Americans might bring against it."[43]

In his comments, Liverpool acknowledged the country's difficulty in protecting the US-Canadian frontier. Governor-in-Chief Prevost would require an inordinate number of soldiers, sailors, and fortifications to prevent American incursions along a 1,700-mile horizontal line. Liverpool noted that if Prevost seized additional territory, as the army attempted to do in the Champlain valley, the move would not necessarily improve the frontier's security. American troops could circumvent the occupied area to attack the flanks, or they could advance into the rear and cut off the supply line. The frontier, in essence, was indefensible, given America's natural advantages.

The Duke of Wellington, from his position in France, believed that the defense of the region started with British control of the Great Lakes. When Liverpool suggested that Wellington assume command in Canada, Wellington responded, "That which appears to me to be wanting in America is not a General, or General Officer, and troops, but a naval superiority on the Lakes . . . the question is, whether we can acquire this naval superiority on the Lakes. If we can't, I shall do you but little good in America." At the end of 1814, Britain retained control of Lake Ontario, but its fleet had lost naval superiority on Lakes Erie and Champlain.[44]

Prevost understood these perspectives more than most. Overland routes could not substitute for transportation on the Great Lakes, and the British army in North America could not guard the entire frontier. He relied on the British Commissariat to convey supplies to remote locations quickly and safely. Prevost depended on these transporters to converge men and supplies to points of an American attack, and he also needed them to support troops withdrawing eastward. The Americans also depended on transporters to support their activities, but their supply lines were much less vulnerable. America's lines of communication ran perpendicular (north and south) to the Canadian border, and if Britain occupied one of these corridors, the Americans could develop alternative routes. There is no location that Prevost could attack that would force multiple outposts to fall from shortages in supplies.

During the war, transporters on both sides overcame major logistical obstacles to deliver supplies, and their actions often decided the victor in land and naval battles. Armies, marching through remote wilderness areas, could not sustain themselves without adequate supplies, and soldiers garrisoned at remote fortifications, hundreds of miles from the nearest supply depot, could not survive without the regular delivery of food and other necessities. Civilian and military transporters also supported an unprecedented freshwater shipbuilding race by delivering a myriad of materials—canvas, cables, anchors, cannon, round shot—across primitive roads, shallow rivers, and snow to isolated dockyards. The number of long guns and carronades required by these shipyards tested the logistics capabilities of the United States and Britain. Their deliveries helped fulfill the ambitious plans of expert shipwrights, such as Henry Eckford and William Bell, who proved themselves as valuable to the war effort as any naval officer.

The war along the US-Canadian frontier was a testament to the importance of logistics when waging war. Britain possessed an exceptionally vulnerable line of communication that lay along its front, while the US Army fought battles 200 miles from the nearest supply depot where no roads existed before the war. The British Commissariat and the US Quartermaster Department faced seemingly insurmountable obstacles to maintain these supply lines and deliver flour, pork, cannon, and other military provisions to armies and fortifications. Military and civilian transporters traversed rapids, ravines, woodlands, swamp, muddy roads, and frozen waterways with carts, oxen, sleighs, and packhorses to deliver their goods. These efforts ware reflected on the battlefield and showcased the importance of logistics in the most extreme conditions.

Epilogue

The shipbuilding contest on Lake Ontario did not end with the launch of the *St. Lawrence*. In January 1815, Commodore Chauncey returned to Sackets Harbor where Henry Eckford had begun to lay the keel for a 120-gun, three-decker. And later that year, the Brown brothers, who had transferred to the area from Vergennes, started building a second 120-gun ship. The two ships, named the *Chippewa* and *New Orleans*, were among the largest warships in the world. Sir James Yeo likewise started construction on two additional triple-decked ships.[1]

Toward the end of 1814, the British Admiralty criticized Yeo for his lack of communication with his leadership. They were aware of Yeo's role in the defeats on Lake Erie and Lake Champlain through court-martial testimony. The Admiralty understood that both fleets had been incomplete when launched, and its leadership probably believed that Yeo had not provided sufficient resources to those dockyards. The Admiralty, however, ignored those issues when it recalled Yeo, and only referred to his lack of communication with his superior officers. Yeo learned about the recall a few weeks after the peace treaty was signed, and his replacement arrived in mid-March 1815.

For his return trip home, Yeo planned to travel to Britain from New York, so he accepted an invite from Commodore Chauncey to spend time at Sackets Harbor, which was on the way to the city. Yeo and two of his officers enjoyed their time with the commodore. He entertained them so well that they extended their stay. As noted by historian

Robert Malcolmson, "Left unrecorded were the private conversations between the two commodores or the after-dinner toasts and discussions about the tense days spent hiding out in the forest near the Harbour or waiting for consistent breezes near the Head of the Lake."[2]

The Admiralty, though critical of Yeo for his lack of communication, did not censure him for his conduct in British North America, and they gave him a reputable assignment commanding the HMS *Inconstant* and directed him to disrupt the slave trade in West Africa. Yeo's Lake Erie commander, Robert Barclay, underwent a court-martial for his defeat. The panel determined that Barclay possessed an incomplete fleet and that he bravely engaged the enemy with inadequate ships and crews. "The court was cleared and agreed," the panelists decided, "that the Capture of His Majesty's late squadron was caused by the very defective Means Captain Barclay possessed to equip them on Lake Erie," and his gallantry "entitled him to the highest praise." Unfortunately for Barclay, because of a reduction in forces in the Royal Navy, Barclay went on half pay for most of a decade.[3]

After the war, Oliver Hazard Perry commanded the *Java* in the Mediterranean, and during the cruise he got into a physical altercation with the commander of the ship's marines. The US Navy reprimanded both men for their conduct, and the two eventually fought a duel in October 1818. Perry refused to fire during the exchange, and the marine captain missed his shot. After the war, rumors persisted that Lieutenant Jesse Elliott, angry at not being placed in command of the fleet, intentionally held his ship back. Perry tried to ignore the issue, but Elliot continued to criticize Perry's conduct in public. Perry eventually pressed charges, but a trial was never held. Perry died in Venezuela in 1819 of yellow fever while commanding a ship during a diplomatic mission to the country.

After the Battle of Lake Champlain, the US Congress gave Thomas Macdonough a gold medal for his actions on the lake, and the navy promoted him to captain. Macdonough remained in the navy until his death at sea in 1825. General Winfield Scott, who participated in most of the major battles on the Canadian frontier, later become one of the country's most successful generals. During the Mexican War, he was accompanied by fellow War of 1812 officers John Wool and William Worth. Shipbuilder Noah Brown was elected as an assistant alderman in New York in 1815, and he retired from ship construction in 1833. He apparently became destitute and was found working in a shipyard as journeyman. In 1817, Henry Eckford became the chief of naval construction at the New York Navy Yard. He later retired and served in the New York State legislature, during which a court indicted Eckford in a major fraud scheme. A hung jury could not convict Eckford, so he was free to accept an offer from the Ottoman Empire to build ships for their navy. He arrived there in 1831, and after one year in the country, he contracted a disease and died.

Governor-in-Chief Prevost, despite his success defending Canada, was recalled to England in March 1815. He faced a court-martial inquiry regarding the failed Champlain valley invasion. Yeo submitted charges against Prevost, which alleged that the governor-in-chief forced the British fleet to sail before it was combat ready. Yeo, of course, refused to acknowledge his part in changing commanders just before the battle or his lack of support for the British dockyard at Champlain. The inquiry was scheduled to occur on January 15, 1816, but Prevost's health deteriorated and he died on January 5, 1816.

Prevost, in fact, excelled as a military strategist during the conflict. As an administrator, Prevost efficiently disseminated limited resources, raised a robust militia to defend the country, and refortified garrisons between Montreal and Kingston. He judiciously shifted his finite resources throughout Canada to repulse American attacks and protect the country's logistical arteries. He kept the bulk of the army in Quebec to defend Canada's supply line to Halifax and England, and he allocated as many troops and supplies to Upper Canada that he could spare. Prevost's success, in some ways, is remarkable. His soldiers successfully protected Kingston and Montreal, and his army never allowed the Americans to maintain a permanent hold on Canadian soil (with the exception of Amherstburg). The longest period of time that American troops remained on Canadian soil was for eight months during 1813 when they garrisoned themselves at Fort George until December. Without holding territory, the American army could not permanently disrupt the land and waterway supply movements that sustained garrisons in Upper Canada.

Prevost also understood the importance of the Great Lakes as a channel to move troops and supplies throughout his area of operations. He managed the Provincial Marine in the beginning of the war, and he supported William Bell's efforts to develop his fleet at Amherstburg. Starting in 1813, however, Prevost depended on Yeo to maintain control of the lakes. Yeo's arrival at

Kingston, combined with the influx of new resources and shipwrights, heralded the start of a major shipbuilding race on Lake Ontario.

Yeo's attention to Kingston, however, especially the resource-intensive 102-gun *St. Lawrence*, came at the expense of his squadrons on Lake Erie and Lake Champlain. Yeo largely ignored Barclay's fleet, even when the commander begged Yeo for more sailors. Chauncey was similarly focused on Lake Ontario, but unlike Yeo, the United States had multiple navy yards and ironworks industries that could support shipbuilding activities at more than one dockyard. Because of this industrial advantage, Chauncey's focus on Lake Ontario did not greatly affect shipbuilding efforts at other dockyards. The New York Navy Yard reinforced Sackets Harbor; the Philadelphia navy yard supported Presque Isle. Macdonough's dockyard relied on local industry in Vergennes to meet many of its needs. Navy Secretary Jones also ensured that Lakes Erie and Champlain received cannon, sailors, and shipwrights.

Indeed, America's naval accomplishments could be traced to the country's industry. Perry owed much of his success to the businesses that provided materials to his shipwrights at Presque Isle. Companies such as Pittsburgh's Eagle Foundry produced anchors, round shot, and other materials, and Philadelphia navy yard provided cannon and other materials. From Philadelphia, transporters could efficiently move supplies to Pittsburgh and then north to Presque Isle on a combination of maintained roads and navigable rivers. Macdonough's efforts at Vergennes benefited from the local industry in that town, including businesses such as Monkton Iron Works that powered itself from the waterfall on Otter Creek. Macdonough also received provisions from outside Vergennes that transporters conveyed from New York City on a route that consisted primarily of navigable waterways. Finally, Chauncey's headquarters at Sackets Harbor profited from its proximity to the New York Navy Yard, from where an efficient combination of roads and rivers enabled supplies to be moved for most of the year.

Barclay and Pring, in contrast, suffered severe shortages that hamstrung their ability to produce viable squadrons quickly. Most of their shipbuilding materials, apart from timber, originated in England. Any disruptions to the concentrated supply line from Halifax, including enemy raids on supply depots, could have serious ramifications for rushed shipbuilding efforts, since Barclay and Pring had only months, not years, to build a combat-ready fleet. In 1813, for example, American operations on the Niagara frontier and the navy's temporary control of Lake Ontario forced the British Commissariat to rely on an overland route that circumvented the Niagara River. Transporters could not move cannons destined for Barclay on this route (from Burlington to Long Point), so the commander cannibalized guns from Fort Malden and other ships. The American attack on York, which occurred during the same campaign, also affected Procter's army and Barclay's fleets. The seizure of the town and resulting destruction of ammunition, foodstuffs, and other provisions produced cascading effects deep into western Upper Canada.

One of the most strategic waterways during the war was Lake Ontario. The lake protected the western flank of Lower Canada, and it also served as a means for Kingston to support York and Burlington. The 150-mile stretch of decrepit road that traversed the northern side of the lake could not handle heavy equipment most of the year, and the march delayed and fatigued any soldiers who undertook it. If the US Navy controlled Lake Ontario, all points wests would suffer supply shortages, and the US Army could freely advance up the St. Lawrence toward Montreal.

American war planners, however, never fully exploited the periods when they controlled the lake. The country's forces repeatedly battered western Lake Ontario and the Niagara frontier, instead of focusing their campaigns against Kingston or Montreal. The United States did attempt assaults against the town. In 1812, the right wing of the American army conducted a feeble attempt against Montreal, and in 1813, Wilkinson's campaign never reached the settlement. In the interim, American war planners remained focused on the Niagara frontier, including in 1814 when attacking the region served no real purpose. Britain had already retreated from Amherstburg, so outposts along the Niagara frontier, and also York and Burlington, had no garrisons to support to their west. The only significant remaining British outpost in the Upper Great Lakes was on Mackinac Island, and the Commissariat could not rely on the long and difficult passage from York to Lake Huron to support that garrison year-round.

In 1813 and 1814, American war planners regularly proposed assaults on Kingston and Montreal, but those targets were often relegated to the final—and unfulfilled—phase of a campaign. Commodore Chauncey pressed the army to destroy Kingston and extinguish Yeo's fleet, but twice the commodore and other officers refused to attack the dockyard because it had been reinforced by additional troops (in one case, the report of reinforcements was false). Chauncey also became paranoid after Yeo's attack on Sackets Harbor, and he worried that the British would strike the harbor when his fleet was away from the dockyard. In the summer of 1814, he refused to cruise the lake to provide men and cannon to General Brown, which prematurely ended the expedition.

Chauncey's 1814 mindset was reflective of a handicap in American war planning: the Madison administration and its generals feared defeats on the battlefield. Madison retained weak support for the war, and he needed victories to bolster his fragile political base. The administration, often under advisement of its generals, called off campaigns against Kingston or Montreal because of the real or perceived reinforcement of troops. They preferred instead to assault areas that offered likely success rather than locations that promised to turn the tide of the war. Armstrong's generals wanted to preserve their reputations and not be tarnished by defeat, and the administration worried about the negative publicity associated with failed campaigns. Bad publicity fueled criticism from state and federal leaders who opposed the war, and the defeats softened support from Madison's allies.

Throughout the war, the army's and navy's reliance on supply routes influenced the outcome of the conflict's land and naval battles. When the United States temporarily controlled the Niagara frontier in 1813, the British Commissariat could not transport cannons to Barclay at Amherstburg through Lake Ontario and the Niagara River. And once Perry defeated Barclay on Lake Erie, the Commissariat could not supply Procter with enough food and gifts for his Native American allies, which factored into his decision to retreat. General Harrison also refused to chase Procter after the British defeat at Moraviantown because he worried that he would overstretch his supply line to Detroit. He had already witnessed Procter's difficulty trying to traverse the same road and river with cannon and other supplies. Poor road conditions also affected Chauncey during the winter of 1813 by delaying the arrival of cannons to Sackets Harbor, which postponed the launch of his new ships. As a result, Chauncey, in 1814, could not support the initial phase of General Brown's campaign. And once Chauncey launched his ships onto the lake in July, he still refused to support Brown, which forced the general to curtail the campaign's goals.

These examples highlight the interdependencies that existed on the US-Canadian frontier during the war. Land or naval engagements in one theater often produced ripple effects in other regions. These effects highlighted the vulnerabilities of Canada's supply line and showcased the importance of logistics in the war along the frontier.

NOTES

ABBREVIATIONS USED IN NOTES

AO	Archives of Ontario
ASP	*American State Papers*, Class 5, Military Affairs (unless otherwise noted)
DHCNF (*Year*)	*Documentary History of the Campaign Upon the* Niagara Frontier
DRIC (*Year*)	*Documents Relating to the Invasion of Canada and the Surrender of Detroit*
HCHC	Historic Cherry Hill Collections
NARA	National Archives and Records Administration
NW	*Naval War of 1812: A Documentary History*
NWR	*Niles Weekly Register* (bound volumes)
LAC	Library and Archives Canada
LCMGIB	*The Life and Correspondence of Major General Isaac Brock*
LOC	Library of Congress
MLWHH	*Messages and Letters of William Henry Harrison*, ed. Logan Esarey
OHPP	Oliver Hazard Perry Papers, University of Michigan, William Clements Library Special Collections
Samuel Bates Papers	Samuel Bates Papers, Lawrence Lee Pelletier Library, Allegheny College
SBD	*Select British Documents of the Canadian War of 1812*
TNA	The National Archives, Kew, United Kingdom
WHHP	W. H. Harrison Papers, 1800–1815, Indiana Historical Society, ed. Douglas Clanin

PREFACE

1. Robinson to Prevost, August 27, 1814, in *DHCNF 1814*, 1:181.
2. *Cobbett's Weekly Political Register*, November 5, 1814; Hull to Eustis, April 3, 1809, and June 15, 1811, in William Hull, *Memoirs of the Campaign of the North Western Army of the United States, A.D. 1812* (Boston: True & Greene, 1824), 19–20.

CHAPTER 1. ORIGINS OF WAR AND THE BORDER FRONTIER

1. Moderates preferred to pass "scarecrow" policies that funded military bills to frighten England into making concessions. See Jasper Trautsch, "Origins of the War of 1812," *Journal of Military History* 77, no. 1 (2013): 285–288; Bradford Perkins, *Prologue to War: England and the United States, 1805–1812* (Berkeley: University of California Press, 1961), 348.
2. Troy Bickham, *The Weight of Vengeance: The United States, the British Empire, and the War of 1812* (Oxford: Oxford University Press, 2012), 214.

3. Perkins, *Prologue to War*, 30; Bickham, *Weight of Vengeance*, 25.
4. Trautsch, "Origins of the War of 1812," 278–279.
5. Adam Nicolson, *Seize the Fire: Heroism, Duty, and the Battle of Trafalgar* (New York: Harper Collins, 2005), 20; Scott Thomas Jackson, "Impressment and Anglo-American Discord, 1787–1818" (PhD diss., University of Michigan, 1976), 17, 28; Alexander Brunsman, *The Evil Necessity: British Naval Impressment in the Eighteenth-Century Atlantic World* (Charlottesville: University of Virginia Press, 2013), 59, 246.
6. Jackson, "Impressment and Anglo-American Discord," 28.
7. Jackson, 3–4; Bickham, *Weight of Vengeance*, 59–61; Brunsman, *Evil Necessity*, 48.
8. Bickham, *Weight of Vengeance*, 62; Jackson, "Impressment and Anglo-American Discord," 10–11.
9. Order from Vice Admiral G. C. Berkeley, June 1, 1807, in *American History Told by Contemporaries*, ed. Albert Hart (New York: The Macmillan Company, 1898), 3:395; Jackson, "Impressment and Anglo-American Discord," 270.
10. Perkins, *Prologue to War*, 1–2, 5–6; Bickham, *Weight of Vengeance*, 66–68.
11. *Staffordshire Advertiser*, January, 13, 1810.
12. James Richardson, *James Madison: A Compilation of the Messages and Papers of the Presidents*, Vol. 1, Part 4 (Washington, DC: Government Printing Office, 1896), 81; Jeremy Black, *The War of 1812 in the Age of Napoleon* (Norman: University of Oklahoma Press, 2009), 36; Madison to Jefferson, May 25, 1812, in *The Writings of James Madison, Comprising his Public Papers and His Private Correspondence, Including Numerous Letters and Documents Now For the First Time Printed*, ed. Gaillard Hunt (New York: G. P. Putnam's Sons, 1908), 8:190–191.
13. Joseph Bouchette, *The British Dominions in North America* (London: Longman, Rees, Orme, Brown and Green, 1832), 1:108.
14. Edwin Guillet, *Pioneer Travel in Upper Canada* (Toronto: University of Toronto Press, 1933), 155–162; Glenn Steppler, "Logistical Considerations in the Canadian War of 1812" (PhD diss., McGill University, 1974), 134–137; John Grodzinksi, "The Vigilant Superintendence of the Whole District: The War of 1812 on the Upper St Lawrence" (PhD diss., Royal Military College of Canada, 2002), 58.
15. Oliver Holmes, "The Turnpike Era," *History of the State of New York* 5 (1934): 259–261.
16. Guillet, *Pioneer Travel in Upper Canada*, 155–162; Holmes, "The Turnpike Era," 262–263; Steppler, "Logistical Considerations in the Canadian War of 1812," appendix 19, 292; traveler quote cited in Guillet, *Pioneer Travel in Upper Canada*, 155.
17. Holmes, "The Turnpike Era," 262–263.
18. Grodzinksi, "Vigilant Superintendence of the Whole District," 11; Steppler, "Logistical Considerations in the Canadian War of 1812," 130, 134, 239; traveler quote cited in Guillet, *Pioneer Travel in Upper Canada*, 155; Guillet, 181.
19. Nelson Vance Russell, "Transportation and Naval Defense in the Old Northwest

during the British Regime, 1760–96," in *University of Michigan Historical Essays*, ed. A. E. R. Boak (Ann Arbor: University of Michigan Press, 1937), 114–115; "The Diary of John Macdonell," in *Five Fur Traders*, ed. Charles Gates (Minneapolis: University of Minnesota Press, 1933), 82; Brereton Greenhous, "A Note on Western Logistics in the War of 1812," *Military Affairs* 34, no. 2 (1970): 42–43; "Northwestern Country," in *NWR*, 3:106.

20. William Hull, *Memoirs of the Campaign of the Northwestern Army* (Boston: True & Greene, 1824), 8; Martin Kaatz, "The Black Swamp: A Study in Historical Geography," *Annals of the Association of American Geographers* 45, no. 1 (1995): 1; Samuel Brown, *Views of the Campaigns of the North-Western Army* (Troy, NY: Printed by F. Adancourt, 1814), 2; Samuel Williams, *Two Western Campaigns in the War of 1812–1813* (Cincinnati: R. Clarke, 1870), 18–20.
21. Greenhous, "A Note on Western Logistics in the War of 1812," 43; Jeffrey Kimball, "Strategy on the Northern Frontier: 1814" (PhD diss., Louisiana State University and Agricultural and Mechanical College, 1969), 45.
22. Water navigation was the preferred method of travel along the route, but sometimes low water levels forced transporters to use turnpikes that ran along the Mohawk River, but carts or wagons could not carry as many supplies as a boat. Also, the Mohawk and Schenectady turnpike ran from Utica to Schenectady and on to Albany, and the Seneca turnpike ran west from Utica; see DeWitt Clinton, *The Life and Writings of DeWitt Clinton* (New York: Baker and Scribner, 1849), 40, 55, 77.
23. Robert Malcomson, *Lords of the Lake* (Quebec: Robin Brass Studio, 1998), 45–46; Chauncey to Hamilton, September 26, 1812, in *NW*, 1:314–317; Anderson to Hamilton, October 8, 1812, in *NW*, 1:322–323.
24. Steppler, "Logistical Considerations in the Canadian War of 1812," 130; Robinson to Prevost, August 27, 1814, in *DHCNF 1814*, 1:182.
25. Prevost to Brock, July 27, 1812, in *DRIC 1812*, 97; J. P. Riley, *A Matter of Honour: The Life, Campaigns and Generalship of Isaac Brock* (Montreal: Robin Brass Studio, 2011), 77.
26. Steppler, "Logistical Considerations in the Canadian War of 1812," 112, 238; *Rutland County Herald*, May 25, 1810; Joseph Bouchette, *A Topographical Description of the Province of Lower Canada* (London: W. Faden, 1815), 157–158; Hugh Gray, *Letters from Canada Written during a Residence There, in the Years 1806, 1807, 1808* (London: Printed for Longman, Hurst, Rees, and Orme, 1809), 69–70, 148.
27. Grodzinksi, "Vigilant Superintendence of the Whole District," 12–16; Bouchette, *A Topographical Description of the Province of Lower Canada*, 136–137; L. H. Tasker, "The United Empire Loyalist Settlement at Long Point, Lake Erie," *Ontario Historical Society Papers and Records* 2 (1900): 31.
28. Russell, "Transportation and Naval Defense in the Old Northwest," 116–124.
29. Mark Lardas, *Great Lakes Warships, 1812–1815* (Oxford: Osprey, 2012), 12.

30. Lardas, *Great Lakes Warships*, 6–7.
31. Eugene Ware, *Pennsylvania Lighthouses on Lake Erie* (Charleston, SC: The History Press, 2016), 12; Bouchette, *A Topographical Description of the Province of Lower Canada*, 38; Nelson Vance Russell, "Transportation and Naval Defense in the Old Northwest during the British Regime 1760–96," in Boak, ed., *University of Michigan Historical Essays*, 131–132; K. Crisman and W. Rybka, *Coffins of the Brave: Lake Shipwrecks of the War of 1812* (College Station: Texas A&M University Press, 2014), 10; Oliver Spencer, *Narrative of Oliver M. Spencer*, 2nd ed. (London: John Mason, 1842), 253–254; *Buffalo Gazette*, November 11, 1812; "View of the Lakes," *Connecticut Gazette*, May 31, 1813.
32. C. Winton-Clare, "A Shipbuilder's War," in *The Defended Border: Upper Canada and the War of 1812*, ed. Morris Zaslow (Toronto: Macmillan Company, 1964), 166.
33. The Provincial Marine Department was divided into two divisions, with one at Kingston (1789), which was responsible for Lake Ontario, and a second western division (1796) at Amherstburg, which retained responsibility for Lakes Erie and Huron. See W. A. B. Douglas, "The Anatomy of Naval Incompetence: The Provincial Marine in Defence of Upper Canada before 1813," *Ontario History* 22 (1979): 9–10; John Grodzinski, *Defender of Canada: Sir George Prevost and the War of 1812* (Norman: University of Oklahoma Press), 62; C. P. Stacey, "Another Look at the Battle of Lake Erie," *Canadian Historical Review* 39, no. 1 (1958): 43; David Curtis Skaggs and Gerard T. Altoff, *A Signal Victory: The Lake Erie Campaign, 1812–1813* (Annapolis, MD: Naval Institute Press, 1997), 111–112.
34. Gray to Prevost, March 12, 1813, in *DHCNF 1813*, 1:107–108; Skaggs and Altoff, *A Signal Victory*, 61, 65; Riley, *A Matter of Honour*, 99; E. A. Cruikshank, "The Contest for the Command of Lake Ontario in 1812 and 1813," *Transactions of the Royal Society of Canada*, series 3, vol. 10 (September 1916): 161.
35. Lardas, *Great Lakes Warships*, 7–10; Alec Gilpin, *The War of 1812 in the Old Northwest* (East Lansing: Michigan State University Press, 2012), 67.
36. Greenhous, "A Note on Western Logistics in the War of 1812," 43.
37. Steppler, "Logistical Considerations in the Canadian War of 1812," 65–66, 236, 240–241, appendix 11, 278; Tasker, "The United Empire Loyalist Settlement at Long Point," 56.
38. Steppler, "Logistical Considerations in the Canadian War of 1812," 240–241; Jon Latimer, "Smuggling and Contraband in the War of 1812," *War of 1812 Magazine* 8 (February 2008). Accessed on July 15, 2018. https://www.napoleon-series.org/military-info/Warof1812/2008/Issue8/c_pirates.html.
39. Procter wrote to Noah Freer, the military secretary for the governor-in-chief of Canada; see Procter to Freer, September 6, 1813, in *SBD*, 2:269–270.
40. John Abbot, *The History of Fort St. Joseph* (Toronto: Dundurn Group, 2000), 45, 55.
41. C. Edward Skeen, *Citizen Soldiers in the War of 1812* (Lexington: University Press

of Kentucky, 1999), 18, 21; Robert Quimby, *The U.S. Army in the War of 1812: An Operational and Command Study* (East Lansing: Michigan State University Press, 1997), 1:7–8.

42. Skeen, *Citizen Soldiers in the War of 1812*, 12; Smyth to Eustis, June 5, 1812, in *ASP*, 1:319.
43. Edward Coffman, *The Old Army: A Portrait of the American Army in Peacetime, 1784–1898* (New York: Oxford University Press, 1986), 8, 10, 12.
44. Jean-Pierre Beugoms, "The Logistics of the United States Army 1812–1821" (PhD diss., Temple University, 2018), 14–15, 17.
45. US Statute at Large, II, 12th Congress, Session 1, chap. 47, 696–699; Carl Skeen, "John Armstrong and the Role of the Secretary in the War in the War of 1812" (PhD diss., Ohio State University, 1966), 46–48; Beugoms, "The Logistics of the United States Army," 21–22.
46. Skeen, "John Armstrong and the Role of the Secretary," 46–48; Beugoms, "The Logistics of the United States Army," 14–15, 27.
47. Gregory Urwin, *The United States Infantry: An Illustrated History, 1775–1918* (New York: Sterling, 1988), 37; Strong to Eustis, August 5, 1812, in *ASP*, 1:1:323.
48. Kevin Linch, *Britain and Wellington's Army: Recruitment, Society, and Tradition, 1807–1815* (New York: Palgrave Macmillan, 2011), 16–20; J. A. Houlding, *Fit for Service: The Training of the British Army, 1715–1795* (New York: Oxford University Press, 1981), 5–6, 10–13; Chris McNab, *Armies of the Napoleonic Wars: An Illustrated History* (New York: Osprey, 2009), 102, 106.
49. Richard Glover, *Peninsular Preparation: The Reform of the British Army, 1795–1809* (Cambridge: Cambridge University Press, 1963), 121.
50. Rory Muir, *Tactics and the Experience of Battle in the Age of Napoleon* (New Haven, CT: Yale University Press, 1998), 68–104.
51. Muir, *Tactics and the Experience of Battle in the Age of Napoleon*, 22–23; Matthew Spring, *With Zeal and Bayonets: The British Army on Campaign in North America, 1775–1783* (Norman: University of Oklahoma Press, 2008), 99–102.
52. John Richardson, *A Canadian Campaign: Operations of the Right Division of the Army of Upper Canada, during the American War of 1812* (Simcoe, ON: Davus, 2011), 20.
53. Spring, *With Zeal and Bayonets*, 252–262; Muir, *Tactics and the Experience of Battle in the Age of Napoleon*, 51–67; C. W. Robinson, "The Expedition to Plattsburg, upon Lake Champlain Canada, 1814," *Royal United Services Institution Journal* 61, no. 443 (1916): 508.
54. Dennis Carter-Edwards, "The War of 1812 along the Detroit Frontier: A Canadian Perspective," *Michigan Historical Review* 13, no. 2 (1987): 26; Gilpin, *The War of 1812 in the Old Northwest*, 67; Grodzinksi, "Vigilant Superintendence of the Whole District," 52–54.
55. Grodzinksi, "Vigilant Superintendence of the Whole District," 52–55; Michelle Guitard, *The Militia of the Battle of the Châteauguay: A Social History* (Ottawa,

ON: National Historic Parks and Sites Branch, Parks Canada, Environment, 1983), 11–12; Robinson to Prevost, July 30, 1812, in *DRIC 1812*, 111.

56. Grodzinski, *Defender of Canada*, 52–53; Steppler, "Logistical Considerations in the Canadian War of 1812," 4–6, 30–31, 115–116; Robinson to Prevost, July 30, 1812, in *DRIC 1812*, 111; Prevost to Brock, July 27, 1812, in *DRIC 1812*, 97.
57. J. C. A. Stagg, *Mr. Madison's War: Politics, Diplomacy, and Warfare in the Early American Republic, 1783–1830* (Princeton, NJ: Princeton University Press, 1983), 47; Henry Clay, *The Papers of Henry Clay: The Rising Statesman, 1797–1814*, ed. James Hopkins and Mary Hargreaves (Lexington: University of Kentucky Press, 1959), 1:842.
58. Donald Hickey, *The War of* 1812: *A Forgotten Conflict* (Chicago: University of Illinois Press, 1995), 80; C. Edward Skeen, *Citizen Soldiers in the War of 1812*, 78; *NWR*, 2:288.
59. *Carthage* (Tennessee) *Gazette*, July 11, 1812.

CHAPTER 2. CONFLICT IN THE OLD NORTHWEST

1. Gillum Ferguson, *Illinois in the War of 1812* (Urbana: University of Illinois Press, 2012), 2–4; William M. Darlington, *Christopher Gist's Journals* (Pittsburgh, PA: J. R. Weldin & Co., 1893), 31–32; Mr. Williams to his wife, August 3, 1812, in Samuel Williams, *Two Western Campaigns in the War of 1812–1813* (Cincinnati: R. Clarke, 1870), 21.
2. Darlington, *Christopher Gist's Journals*, 43.
3. Isaac Lippincott, "The Early Salt Trade of the Ohio Valley," *Journal of Political Economy* 20, no. 10 (1912): 1029–1033.
4. Malcolm Rohrbough, *Trans-Appalachian Frontier: People, Societies, and Institutions, 1775–1850* (Bloomington: Indiana University Press, 2008), 103–104; William Bergmann, "A Commercial View of This Unfortunate War: Economic Roots of an American National State in the Ohio Valley, 1775–1795," *Early American Studies* 6, no. 1 (2008): 144.
5. Ferguson, *Illinois in the War of 1812*, 2–4; Bergmann, "Commerce and Arms," 488; Matthew Ward, "The British Army and Epidemic Disease among the Ohio Indians," in *The Sixty Years' War for the Great Lakes, 1754–1814*, ed. David Skaggs and Larry Nelson (East Lansing: Michigan State University Press, 2001), 73.
6. Rohrbough, *Trans-Appalachian Frontier*, 104–105.
7. Frank Ross, "The Fur Trade of the Ohio Valley," *Indiana Magazine of History* 34, no. 4 (1938): 418–419; Ann Keating, *Rising Up from Indian Country: The Battle of Fort Dearborn and the Birth of Chicago* (Chicago: University of Chicago Press, 2012), 23–24
8. Ross, "The Fur Trade of the Ohio Valley," 420–424.
9. Ross, 426–430.

10. *The Debates and Proceedings of the British House of Commons from 1765 to 1768* (London: Printed for J. Almon, 1772), 181.
11. Ross, "The Fur Trade of the Ohio Valley," 431–434.
12. W. Wallace Carson, "Transportation and Traffic on the Ohio and the Mississippi before the Steamboat," *The Mississippi Valley Historical Review* 7, no. 1 (1920): 29–30.
13. George Stanley, "The Indians in the War of 1812," *The Canadian Historical Review* 31, no. 2 (1950): 147; John Bowes, *Land Too Good for Indians: Northern Indian Removal* (Norman: University of Oklahoma Press, 2016), 22–23.
14. Maria Campbell, *Revolutionary Services and Civil Life of General William Hull* (Philadelphia: G. S. Appleton, 1848), 309; Bowes, *Land Too Good for Indians*, 117; Sandy Antal, *Wampum Denied: Procter's War of 1812* (Montreal: McGill-Queen's University Press, 2011), 44, 72, 261.
15. Ferguson, *Illinois in the War of 1812*, 20; David Edmunds, "The Illinois River Potawatomi in the War of 1812," *Journal of the Illinois State Historical Society* 62, no. 4 (1969): 344; Bergmann, "A Commercial View of This Unfortunate War," 148; Bowes, *Land Too Good for Indians*, 24.
16. David Curtis Skaggs, *William Henry Harrison and the Conquest of the Ohio Country: Frontier Fighting in the War of 1812* (Baltimore: Johns Hopkins University Press, 2014), 11; "Invoice for Michilimackinac 10 September 1814," *Michigan Pioneer and Historical Society* 15 (Lansing, MI: Wynkoop, Hallenbeck, Crawford Co., 1909), 648–649.
17. Dwight Smith, "A North American Neutral Indian Zone: Persistence of a British Idea," *Northwest Ohio Quarterly* 61, no. 2–4 (1989): 46–50.
18. Smith, "A North American Neutral Indian Zone," 52–54.
19. Smith, 52–54; Reginald Horsman, "The British Indian Department and the Resistance to General Anthony Wayne, 1793–1795," *Mississippi Valley Historical Review* 49, no. 2 (1962): 272.
20. Allan Millett, "Caesar and the Conquest of the Northwest Territory: The Wayne Campaign, 1792–1795," *Timeline* 14 (May/June 1997): 2–21; Bergmann, "A Commercial View of This Unfortunate War," 159.
21. Millett, "Caesar and the Conquest of the Northwest Territory," 2–21.
22. Julius Pratt, "Fur Trade Strategy and the American Left Flank in the War of 1812," *American Historical Review* 40, no. 2 (1935): 247–250.
23. Brian Dunnigan, "The British Army at Mackinac 1812–1815," *Reports in Mackinac History and Archeology* 7 (1980): 5–6.
24. Ferguson, *Illinois in the War of 1812*, 24; Edmunds, "The Illinois River Potawatomi in the War of 1812," 347; David Skaggs, *William Henry Harrison*, 11; Keating, *Rising Up from Indian Country*, 64–65.
25. Glenn Tucker, *Tecumseh: Vision of Glory* (New York: Cosimo Classics, 2005), 26, 71.

26. David Edmunds, "Forgotten Allies: The Loyal Shawnees and the War of 1812," in *The Sixty Years' War for the Great Lakes, 1754–1814*, ed. David Curtis Skaggs and Larry Nelson (East Lansing: Michigan State University Press, 2001): 338–340; Keating, *Rising Up from Indian Country*, 86.
27. John Sugden, *Tecumseh's Last Stand* (Norman: University of Oklahoma Press, 1985), 49, 115; Anonymous, "The Capitulation," in *War on the Detroit: The Chronicles of Thomas Verchères de Boucherville and The Capitulation*, ed. Milo Quaife (Chicago: The Lakeside Press, 1940), xx, 253.
28. Robert Allen, *His Majesty's Indian Allies* (Toronto: Dundurn Press, 1992), 121–122; Robert Allen, "His Majesty's Indian Allies: Native Peoples, the British Crown and the War of 1812," *Michigan Historical Review* 14, no. 2 (1988): 6–7, 9–10.
29. Brock to Prevost, December 2, 1811, in *LCMGIB*, 125.
30. Prevost to Brock, December 24, 1811, in *LCMGIB*, 133–135.
31. Glegg to Baynes, November 11, 1812, in *DRIC 1812*, 228; Toussaint Pothier, "Memorandum on Loyalty of Inhabitants of Michilimackinac Country," in *DRIC 1812* 15; Elliott to Claus, July 15, 1812, in *DRIC 1812*, 63.

CHAPTER 3. OPENING MOVES

1. Maria Campbell, *Revolutionary Services and Civil Life of General William Hull* (Philadelphia: G. S. Appleton, 1848), 2–24.
2. Campbell, *Revolutionary Services*, 93–97.
3. Campbell, 306, 308–309.
4. Alec Gilpin, *The War of 1812 in the Old Northwest* (East Lansing: Michigan State University Press, 1958), 40–41.
5. J. P. Riley, *A Matter of Honour: The Life, Campaigns and Generalship of Isaac Brock* (Montreal: Robin Brass Studio, 2011), 55–56; *LCMGIB*, 12–15.
6. Riley, *A Matter of Honour*, 83–86; Wesley Turner, *British Generals in the War of 1812: High Command in the Canadas* (Montreal: McGill-Queen's University Press, 1999), 58–67.
7. Riley, *A Matter of Honour*, 99–100, 104.
8. Riley, 131, 151–153.
9. Dennis Carter-Edwards, "The War of 1812 along the Detroit Frontier: A Canadian Perspective," *Michigan Historical Review* 13, no. 2 (1987): 29; Riley, *A Matter of Honour*, 159–160; Prevost to Brock, July 10, 1812, in *LCMGIB*, 200–201; Brock to Baynes, February 12, 1812, in *LCMGIB*, 147–149.
10. Bathurst to Prevost, August 10, 1812, in LAC, CO 43/23/68; Prevost to Bathurst, July 30, 1812, in *DHCNF 1812*, 110.
11. Prevost to Brock, April 30, 1812, in *LCMGIB*, 149.
12. Carter-Edwards, "The War of 1812 along the Detroit Frontier," 26–27; John Mahon, "British Command Decisions in the Northern Campaigns of the War of 1812," *The Canadian Historical Review* 46, no. 3 (1965): 220.

13. John Grodzinski, *Defender of Canada: Sir George Prevost and the War of 1812* (Norman: University of Oklahoma Press, 2013), 73–74.
14. William Hull, *Memoirs of the Campaign of the North Western Army of the United States, A.D. 1812* (Boston: True & Greene, 1824), 34; quote from William Hatch, *A Chapter of the History of the War of 1812 in the Northwest: Embracing the Surrender of the Northwestern Army and Fort, at Detroit, August 16, 1812* (Cincinnati: Miami Printing and Publishing Company, 1872), 19 (original emphasis); Anthony Yanik, *The Fall and Recapture of Detroit in the War of 1812: In Defense of William Hull* (Detroit: Wayne State University Press, 2011), 44–45.
15. Anonymous, "The Capitulation," in Thomas Verchères de Boucherville, *War on the Detroit: The Chronicles of Thomas Verchères de Boucherville and The Capitulation by an Ohio Volunteer*, ed. Milo Quaife (Chicago: The Lakeside Press, 1940), 207–209; Yanik, *The Fall and Recapture of Detroit*, 44–46.
16. "Expedition of Captain Henry Brush with Supplies for General Hull," in Samuel Williams, *Two Western Campaigns in the War of 1812–1813* (Cincinnati: R. Clarke, 1870), 34; Anonymous, "The Capitulation," 209.
17. Yanik, *The Fall and Recapture of Detroit*, 135.
18. Campbell, *Revolutionary Services*, 444.
19. Eustis to Hull, June 18, 1812, in *DRIC 1812*, 35; Yanik, *The Fall and Recapture of Detroit*, 48.
20. William Beall, "Journal of William K. Beall, July–August 1812," *American Historical Review* 17, no. 4 (1912): 788; de Boucherville, *War on the Detroit*, 78.
21. Gilpin, *The War of 1812*, 24; Yanik, *The Fall and Recapture of Detroit*, 53.
22. Hull to Meigs, July 11, 1812, in Williams, *Two Western Campaigns*, 12.
23. R. David Edmunds, "Forgotten Allies: The Loyal Shawnees and the War of 1812," in *The Sixty Years' War for the Great Lakes*, ed. David Curtis Skaggs and Larry Nelson (East Lansing: Michigan State University Press, 2001), 342–434.
24. Dixon to Bruyeres, July 8, 1812, in *DRIC 1812*, 48–49.
25. St. George to Brock, July 15, 1812, in *DRIC 1812*, 47.
26. Alan Taylor, *The Civil War of 1812: American Citizens, British Subjects, Irish Rebels, & Indian Allies* (New York: Alfred A. Knopf, 2010), 152; Talbot to Brock, July 27, 1812, in *DRIC 1812*, 93–94; Brock to Prevost, July 28, 1812, in *DRIC 1812*, 99; Dixon to Bruyeres July 8, 1812, in *DRIC 1812*, 49.
27. Yanik, *The Fall and Recapture of Detroit*, 55.
28. Hull, *Memoirs of the Campaign*, 46.
29. St. George to Brock, July 15, 1812, in *DRIC 1812*, 61; Robert Lucas, *The Robert Lucas Journal of the War of 1812 during the Campaign under General William Hull*, ed. John Parish (Iowa City: State Historical Society of Iowa, 1906), 30; Prevost to Bathurst, August 26, 1812, in *DRIC 1812*, 182; Carl Benn, *The Iroquois in the War of 1812* (Toronto: University of Toronto Press, 1998), 44–45; John Norton, *The Journal of Major John Norton*, ed. Carl Klinck and James Talman (Toronto: Champlain Society, 1970), 297; Robert Allen, *His Majesty's Indian Allies: Brit-*

ish Indian Policy in the Defence of Canada, 1774–1815 (Toronto: Dundurn Press, 1992), 136; Sandy Antal, *Wampum Denied: Procter's War of 1812* (Montreal: McGill-Queen's University Press, 2011), 44.

30. Lucas, *The Robert Lucas Journal*, 30–34; William Bealle, "Journal of William K Bealle, July-August 1812," *The American Historical Review*, vol. 17, no. 4 (1912): 802.
31. de Boucherville, *War on the Detroit*, 239; William Hull, *William Hull, Report of the Trial of Brig. General William Hull, Commanding the North-Western Army of the United States: by a court martial held at Albany on Monday, 3d January, 1814 and Succeeding Days*, ed. Lieutenant Colonel Forbes (New York: Eastburn, Kirk, and Co., 1814), 22, 55–56, 78; Hull to Eustis, August 4, 1812, in William Hull, *Report of the Trial*, appendix 2, 11.
32. Brock to Prevost, July 20, 1812, in *LCMGIB*, 193.
33. Hull, *Memoirs of the Campaign*, 162–163.
34. Beall, "Journal of William K. Beall," 805.
35. Barry Gough, *Fighting Sail on Lake Huron and Georgian Bay: The War of 1812 and Its Aftermath* (Annapolis, MD: Naval Institute Press, 2002), 20–21.
36. Francis Jennings, *The History and Culture of Iroquois Diplomacy: An Interdisciplinary Guide to the Treaties of the Six Nations and Their League* (Syracuse, NY: Syracuse University Press, 1985), 73–76; Robert Malcomson, *A Very Brilliant Affair: The Battle of Queenston Heights*, 1812 (Toronto: Robin Brass Studio, 2003), 50–51.
37. Benn, *The Iroquois in the War of 1812*, 48; Gough, *Fighting Sail on Lake Huron*, 25–26; Brian Dunnigan, "The British Army at Mackinac 1812–1815," *Reports in Mackinac History and Archeology* 7 (1980): 11–12.
38. Hull, *Memoirs of the Campaign*, 58–60; Hull to Eustis, August 4, 1812, in Hull, *Report of the Trial*, appendix 2, 11; Myers to Prevost, August 17, 1812, in *DRIC 1812*, 185.
39. David Lomax, *A History of the Services of the 41st (The Welch) Regiment* (Devonport: Printed by Hiorns & Miller, 1899), 24, 30, 47.
40. Yanik, *The Fall and Recapture of Detroit*, 52, 66–67; Prevost to Bathurst, August 24, 1812, in *DRIC 1812*, 62.
41. Hull, *Memoirs of the Campaign*, 63, 70; Cass to Eustis, September 10, 1812, in Hull, *Report of the Trial*, appendix 2, 25; Hull to Wells August 11, 1812, in *New York Gazette Office*, Sunday Evening August 23, 1812; de Boucherville, *War on the Detroit*, 277.
42. Brock to Liverpool, August 29, 1812, in *DRIC 1812*, 192.
43. Shadrach Byfield, *A Narrative of a Light Company Soldier's Service in the Forty-First Regiment of Foot (1807–1914)*(New York: Reprinted by W. Abbatt, 1910), 352.
44. Cass to Eustis, September 10, 1812, in Hull, *Report of the Trial*, appendix 2, 26; Hull, *Memoirs of the Campaign*, 95–96; William Hatch, *A Chapter of the History*

of the War of 1812 in the Northwest: Embracing the Surrender of the Northwestern Army and Fort, at Detroit, August 16, 1812 (Cincinnati: Miami Printing and Publishing Company, 1872), 40; Talcott Wing, *History of Monroe Country Michigan* (New York: Munsell & Company, 1890), 1:91; Yanik, *The Fall and Recapture of Detroit*, 84.

45. Robert Quimby, *The U.S. Army in the War of 1812: An Operational and Command Study* (East Lansing: Michigan State University Press, 1997), 1:44; Hatch, *A Chapter of the History of the War of 1812*, 42.
46. John Richardson, *Richardson's War of 1812* (Toronto: Historical Publishing Co., 1902), 51.
47. Richardson, *Richardson's War of 1812*, 53, 55; Jon Guttman, "War of 1812: Detroit Showdown," *Military History Quarterly Magazine* 25, no. 1 (2012): 69.
48. Richardson, *Richardson's War of 1812*, 55; Sandy Antal, *Wampum Denied: Procter's War of 1812* (Montreal: McGill-Queen's University Press, 2011), 95; *Missouri Gazette and Public Advertiser*, September 19, 1812.
49. Ferguson, *Illinois in the War of 1812*, 61–62; David Curtis Skaggs, *William Henry Harrison and the Conquest of the Ohio Country: Frontier Fighting in the War of 1812* (Baltimore: Johns Hopkins University Press, 2014), 104.
50. Ferguson, *Illinois in the War of 1812*, 63–65.
51. Ferguson, 67–69; Heald to Hull, October 23, 1812, in John Brannan, *Official Letters of the Military and Naval Officers of the United States During the War with Great Britain* (Washington City: Printed by Way & Gideon, 1823), 84–85.
52. Hull, *Report of the Trial*, appendix, 99–100.
53. Hull's read testimony, in *Report of the Trial*, appendix, 46, 51.
54. Brock to Prevost, August 16, 1812, in *LCMGIB*, 247; Cass to Eustis, September 10, 1812, in Hull, *Report of the Trial*, appendix 2, 26.
55. Richardson, *Richardson's War of 1812*, 58–59; Byfield, *A Narrative of a Light Company*, 353; Lomax, *A History of the Services of the 41st*, 59; Lucas, *Robert Lucas Journal*, 69; Charles Askin, "Journal of the Detroit Campaign," in *John Askin Papers* (Detroit: Detroit Library Commission, 1931), 2:719–720; Benson Lossing, *The Pictorial Field Book of the War of 1812*, (New York, Harper & Brothers, 1868), 291.
56. Edmunds, "Forgotten Allies," 342–343; James Reynolds, *Journal of an American Prisoner at Fort Malden and Quebec in the War of 1812*, ed. G. M. Fairchild (Quebec: Priv. print. by F. Carrel, Limited, 1909), 18–19; *Nashville Whig*, September 2, 1812.
57. Cass to Eustis, September 10, 1812, in Hull, *Report of the Trial*, appendix 2, 28.
58. *Niles Weekly Register*, May 7, 1814. For analysis of the trial, see Yanik, *The Fall and Recapture of Detroit*, 106–127. Yanik notes that "the trial was devoid of any hard evidence to support the verdict and such an extreme sentence."
59. *Times of London*, October 21, 1812. Historian Donald Hickey lays the blame for the surrender on Hull for his "lack of nerve"; see Donald Hickey, *Don't Give Up*

the Ship! Myths of the War of 1812 (Urbana: University of Illinois Press, 2006), 54–56.

CHAPTER 4. THE BATTLE OF QUEENSTON

1. Rensselaer to Tompkins, August 19, 1812, in Solomon Van Rensselaer, *A Narrative of the Affair of Queenstown: In the War of 1812* (Boston: Crocker & Brewster, 1836), appendix, 28, and Dearborn to Rensselaer, August 3, 1812, appendix, 22.
2. It is possible that the section of road from Burlington to the Grand River Village was the only stretch that could not handle heavy ordnance. Cannon probably could have been floated down the Grand River from this point, depending on the time of year; see Glenn Steppler, "Logistical Considerations in the Canadian War of 1812" (PhD diss., McGill University, 1974), 133; E. A. Cruikshank, "A Sketch of the Public Life and Services of Robert Nichol," *Ontario Historical Society Papers and Records* 19 (1922): 30; "Upper Canada," *Daily National Intelligencer*, January 26, 1813.
3. Daniel Barnard, *A Discourse on the Life, Services, and Character of Stephen Van Rensselaer* (Albany, NY: Printed by Hoffman & White, 1839), 27–58; Robert Malcomson, *A Very Brilliant Affair: The Battle of Queenston Heights* (Toronto: Robin Brass Studio, 2003), 62–63.
4. *Assault and Battery: Report of the Trials of the Causes of Elisha Jenkins vs. Solomon Van Rensselaer* (Albany, NY: Croswell & Frary, 1808), 6; Catharina Bonney, *A Legacy of Historical Gleanings* (Albany, NY: J. Munsell, 1875), 1:159–183.
5. Bonney, *A Legacy of Historical Gleanings*, 1:228.
6. Lovett to Alexander, August 16, 1812, in Bonney, *A Legacy of Historical Gleanings*, 1:209; Lovett to Alexander, August 23, 1812, in HCHC, John Lovett Papers; Lovett to Van Vechten, August 28, 1812, in Bonney, *A Legacy of Historical Gleanings*, 1:221.
7. Solomon to Van Vechten, September 5, 1812, in Bonney, *A Legacy of Historical Gleanings*, 1:227; Solomon to Arriet, August 31, 1812, in HCHC; Arriet to Solomon, September 6, 1812, in HCHC, Arriet Van Rensselaer Papers, 1:228.
8. Prevost to Brock August 12, 1812, in *LCMGIB*, 236.
9. Van Rensselaer to Dearborn, September 1, 1812, in Van Rensselaer, *A Narrative of the Affair*, appendix, 37; Bonney, *A Legacy of Historical Gleanings*, 1:216; Edward Skeen, *Citizen Soldiers in the War of 1812* (Lexington: University Press of Kentucky, 1998), 14.
10. Lovett to Joseph, September 2, 1812, in HCHC, John Lovett Papers (original emphasis).
11. Herbert Gardiner, *Nothing but Names: An Inquiry into the Origin of the Names of the Counties and Townships of Ontario* (Toronto: G. N. Morang and Company, 1899), 9–11; John Macdonell, *Sketches Illustrating the Early Settlement and History of Glengarry in Canada* (Montreal: W. Foster, Brown & Co., 1893), 6–8; Wesley Turner, *British Generals in the War of 1812: High Command in the Cana-*

das (Montreal: McGill-Queen's University Press, 1999), 80; Dearborn to Rensselaer, August 25, 1812, in Van Rensselaer, *A Narrative of the Affair*, appendix, 36.

12. Van Rensselaer, *A Narrative of the Affair*, 21n.
13. Prevost to Brock, September 14, 1812, in *LCMGIB*, 291–292; Prevost to Brock, September 25, 1812, in *LCMGIB*, 303.
14. Ernest Cruikshank, *Queenston Heights* (Welland: Printed by W.T. Sawle & Co., 1890), 23–24; John Symons, *The Battle of Queenston Heights* (Toronto: Thompson & Co., Printers, 1859), 10.
15. Stephen Van Rensselaer to Dearborn, October 8, 1812, in Van Rensselaer, *A Narrative of the Affair*, appendix, 8; Theodore Crackel, "The Battle of Queenston Heights, 13 October 1812," in *America's First Battles*, ed. Charles Heller and William Stofft (Lawrence: University Press of Kansas, 1986), 43.
16. Stephen Van Rensselaer to Dearborn, September 5, 1812, in Van Rensselaer, *A Narrative of the Affair*, appendix, 43, and Stephen Van Rensselaer to Tompkins September 15, 1812, appendix, 50. Stephen Van Rensselaer to Dearborn, September 17, 1812, in Bonney, *A Legacy of Historical Gleanings*, 1:234.
17. Malcomson, *A Very Brilliant Affair*, 110; Winfield Scott, *Memoirs of Lieut.-General Winfield Scott*, ed. Timothy Johnson (Knoxville: University of Tennessee Press, 2015), 55n; Smyth to Stephen Van Rensselaer, September 29, 1812, in Bonney, *A Legacy of Historical Gleanings*, 1:239.
18. Malcomson, *A Very Brilliant Affair*, 110–111; Van Rensselaer to Smyth, September 30, 1812, in Bonney, *A Legacy of Historical Gleanings*, 1:240.
19. Elliott to Hamilton, October 9, 1812, in *Abridgement of the Debates of Congress, from 1789–1856*, ed. Thomas Hart Benton (New York: D. Appleton and Company, 1857), 4:571–572; Benson Lossing, *Pictorial Field Book of the War of 1812* (New York: Harper & Brothers, 1868), 386; Hall to Stephen Van Rensselaer, October 10, 1812, in Bonney, *A Legacy of Historical Gleanings*, 1:246.
20. Malcomson, *A Very Brilliant Affair*, 117–120. Van Rensselaer to Dearborn, October 14, 1812, in Van Rensselaer, *A Narrative of the Affair*, appendix, 63, and numerous letters from Van Rensselaer to Smyth, appendix, 68–73.
21. Van Rensselaer, *A Narrative of the Affair*, 21–22; Malcomson, *A Very Brilliant Affair*, 119, 128.
22. Solomon to Arriet, October 10, 1812, in Bonney, *A Legacy of Historical Gleanings*, 1:247–248.
23. Malcomson, *A Very Brilliant Affair*, 120, 127–128; Van Rensselaer, *A Narrative of the Affair*, 21–22.
24. Malcomson, *A Very Brilliant Affair*, 123–124; Brock to Prevost, October 12, 1812, in *LCMGIB*, 328; Robert Quimby, *The U.S. Army in the War of 1812: An Operational and Command Study* (East Lansing: Michigan State University Press, 1997), 1:68.
25. Smyth to Van Rensselaer, October 12, 1812, in *DHCNF 1812*, 4:68; Scott, *Memoirs*, 57; Statement of Lieutenant Colonel Thompson Mead, in *DHCNF 1812*, 4:91.

26. *DHCNF 1812*, 4:93; Van Rensselaer, *A Narrative of the Affair*, 24; Scott, *Memoirs*, 57.
27. Van Rensselaer, *A Narrative of the Affair*, 24; Philip Van Rensselaer to Solomon, October 13, 1812, in Bonney, *A Legacy of Historical Gleanings*, 1:248.
28. Van Rensselaer, *A Narrative of the Affair*, 13; Lovett to Alexander, October 14, 1812, in Bonney, *A Legacy of Historical Gleanings*, 1:266; John Robinson "Account of the Battle of Queenston Heights, October 13, 1812," in LAC, F44, John Beverly Robinson Papers.
29. Bonney, *A Legacy of Historical Gleanings*, 1:254.
30. Chrystie to Cushing, February 22, 1813, in John Armstrong, *Notices of the War of 1812* (New York: Wiley & Putnam, 1840), 1:210–211; Scott, *Memoirs*, 63.
31. Wool to Stone, September 13, 1838, in *Bulletin of the New York Public Library* 9, no. 1 (New York: 1906), 120; *LCMGIB*, 329–330; Lovett to Alexander, October 14, 1812, in Bonney, *A Legacy of Historical Gleanings*, 1:266.
32. York militiaman to his father, October 14, 1812, in LAC, MG 13/W044/245.
33. Wool to Stone, September 13, 1838, in *Bulletin of the New York Public Library*, 120; Malcomson, *A Very Brilliant Affair*, 141–142; Chrystie to Cushing, February 22, 1813, in Armstrong, *Notices of the War*, appendix, 1:211–212; Lovett to Alexander, October 14, 1812, in Bonney, *A Legacy of Historical Gleanings*, 1:266.
34. Cruikshank, *Queenston Heights*, 29; Chrystie to Cushing, February 22, 1813, in Armstrong, *Notices of the War*, appendix, 1:214; Scott, *Memoirs*, 57. Lovett to Alexander, November 2, 1812, in Bonney, *A Legacy of Historical Gleanings*, 1:275, and Lovett to Alexander, October 14, 1812, 1:268. Journal of James Mullany, cited in Malcomson, *A Very Brilliant Affair*, 150; Chrystie to Cushing, February 22, 1813, in Armstrong, *Notices of the War of 1812*, appendix, 1:214; Robinson "Account of the Battle of Queenston Heights."
35. W. H. Merritt, *Journal of Events Principally on the Detroit and Niagara Frontiers During the War of 1812* (St. Catherine's C.W.: Historical Society B.N.A., 1863), 15; Malcomson, *A Very Brilliant Affair*, 144; Evans to [?], October 15, 1812, in *DHCNF 1812*, 4:111, 113; Sheaffe to Prevost, October 18, 1812, in "Documents Relating to the War of 1812: The Letter Book of Gen. Sir Roger Hale Sheaffe," in *Buffalo Historical Society Publications*, ed. Frank Severance, vol. 17 (Buffalo: Buffalo Historical Society, 1913), 275–277.
36. Malcomson, *A Very Brilliant Affair*, 145–147; "Letter from One of the York Militia Present at the Battle of Queenston," October 14, 1812, in Matilda Ridout Edgar, *Ten Years of Upper Canada in Peace and War, 1805–1815* (Toronto: W. Briggs, 1890), 150–152; McLean to McNab, July 22, 1860, in *Bulletin of the Niagara Historical Society* 23 (Niagara: Pickwell Bros.), n.p., http://nhsm.ca/media/NiagaraHistoricalSocietyNo.23.pdf.
37. J. P. Riley, *A Matter of Honour: The Life, Campaigns and Generalship of Isaac Brock* (Montreal: Robin Brass Studio, 2011), 285–286; Van Rensselaer, *A Narrative of the Affair*, 25–26; Wool to Stone, September 13, 1838, in *Bulletin of the New*

York Public Library, 120; Cruikshank, *Queenston Heights*, 32; Evans to [?], October 15, 1812, in *DHCNF 1812*, 4:113, and narrative of Jarvis, 4:116; Merritt, *Journal of Events*, 16; McLean to McNab, July 22, 1860, *Bulletin of the Niagara Historical Society* 23; Robinson "Account of the Battle of Queenston Heights"; Lossing, *Pictorial Field Book of the War*, 397. For a comprehensive discussion of how the Americans reached the top of the heights, see Guy St-Denis, "In Search of the Fisherman's Path: Rethinking the American Assault on Queenston Heights," *Canadian Military History* 27, no. 1 (2018): 1–12.

38. Robinson "Account of the Battle of Queenston Heights"; Wool to Solomon Van Rensselaer, October 23, 1812, in Van Rensselaer, *A Narrative of the Affair*, 14–15; Cruikshank, *Queenston Heights*, 33.
39. Cruikshank, *Queenston Heights*, 33; McLean Letter, October 15, 1812, in *DHCNF 1812*, 4:114, and Evans to [?], October 15, 1812, 4:113.
40. Quimby, *The U.S. Army in the War of 1812*, 1:71.
41. Wool to Solomon Van Rensselaer, October 23, 1812, in Van Rensselaer, *A Narrative of the Affair*, 14–15; Van Rensselaer to Dearborn, October 14, 1812, in Van Rensselaer, *A Narrative of the Affair*, appendix, 66; Malcomson, *A Very Brilliant Affair*, 156; Scott, *Memoirs*, 60.
42. Turner, *British Generals*, 84–88; Riley, *A Matter of Honour*, 83–85.
43. John Norton, *The Journal of Major John Norton*, ed. Carl Klinck and James Talman (Toronto: Champlain Society, 1970), 305.
44. Carl Benn, *The Iroquois in the War of 1812* (Toronto: University of Toronto Press, 1998), 93–94, 97; Statement of Thompson Mead, November 18, 1812, in *DHCNF 1812*, 4:92; Norton, *The Journal of Major John Norton*, 306–307; Wilson to a Friend, November 8, 1812, "A Rifleman at Queenston," in *Publications of the Buffalo Historical Society* 9 (Buffalo, 1906), 374; Isaac Roach," Journal of Major Isaac Roach," *Pennsylvania Magazine of History and Biography* 17, no. 2 (Historical Society of Pennsylvania, 1893), 138.
45. Cruikshank, *Queenston Heights*, 37–38.
46. Sheaffe to Prevost, October 18, 1812, in *The Letter Book of Gen. Sir Roger Hale Sheaffe*, n.p.; James Crooks, "Recollections of the War of 1812," in *Niagara Historical Society* 28 (Niagara, NY: Pickwell Bros., 1916), 28–41; Malcomson, *A Very Brilliant Affair*, 182–183, 186; Merritt, *Journal of Events*, 17; William Woodruff to Thorburn, July 29, 1840, in *DHCNF 1812*, 4:77; Cruikshank, *Queenston Heights*, 38; Turner, *British Generals in the War of 1812*, 90.
47. Cruikshank, *Queenston Heights*, 38, 40; Crooks, "Recollections of the War of 1812," 28–41; Robinson, "Account of the Battle of Queenston Heights"; Lovett to Alexander, October 14, 1812, in Bonney, *A Legacy of Historical Gleanings*, 1:267; Scott, *Memoirs*, 60–61; Extract of a Letter from Fort George, October 14, 1812, in LAC, MG13/ W044/245.
48. Scott, *Memoirs*, 60–61; Benn, *The Iroquois in the War of 1812*, 95.
49. Crooks, "Recollections of the War of 1812," 28–41.

50. Prevost to Bathurst, April 21, 1813, in TNA, CO 42/150/ 143–146.
51. Rideout to his brother at York, October 21, 1812, in *DHCNF 1812*, 4:147.
52. Riley, *A Matter of Honour*, 302–304.
53. Jefferson to Madison, November 6, 1812, in LOC, Thomas Jefferson Papers, Series 1, General Correspondence; Malcomson, *A Very Brilliant Affair*, 126; Crackel, "The Battle of Queenston Heights," 49.
54. Dearborn to Smyth, October 21, 1812, in NARA, RG94; Smyth's Proclamation, in *DHCNF 1812*, 4:194.
55. Smyth to Secretary of War Eustis, October 20, 1812, in *DHCNF 1812*, 4:141, Smyth's Proclamation, *DHCNF 1812*, 4:194, Smyth to the Commander at Fort Erie, November 28, 1812, 4:246, and *New York Evening Post*, December 13, 1812, 4:281–282.
56. Eustis to Dearborn, December 18, 1812, in NARA, RG94/254.

CHAPTER 5. HARRISON ENTERS THE WAR

1. Robert Gunderson, "William Henry Harrison: Apprentice in Arms," *Northwest Ohio Quarterly* 65, no. 1 (1993): 4.
2. Gunderson, "William Henry Harrison," 14.
3. David Skaggs, *William Henry Harrison and the Conquest of the Ohio Country: Frontier Fighting in the War of 1812* (Baltimore: Johns Hopkins University Press, 2014), 32–35, 41.
4. Thomas Case, "The Battle of Fallen Timbers," *Northwest Ohio Quarterly* 35 (1963): 54–68; Isaac Jackson, *A Sketch of the Life and Public Services of William Henry Harrison: Commander in Chief of the North-western Army, during the War of 1812* (New York: Office of the New York Express, 1839), 5–6; William B. Northcutt Journal, 1797–1866, Kentucky Historical Society, Special Collections, SC 159; *Nashville Whig*, September 2, 1812.
5. Lewis Collins, *Historical Sketches of Kentucky, Embracing its History, Antiquities, and Natural Curiosities, Geographical, Statistical, and Geological Descriptions* (Maysville, KY: L. Collins, 1850), 168; Anderson Quisenberry, *Kentucky in the War of 1812* (Frankfort: Kentucky State Historical Society, 1915), 47–48; Northcutt, "Journal," Kentucky Historical Society.
6. *Western Spy*, as reported in *Western Citizen*, September 12, 1812, in G. Glenn Clift, *Remember the Raisin! Kentucky and Kentuckians in the Battles and Massacre at Frenchtown, Michigan Territory, in the War of 1812* (Frankfort: Kentucky Historical Society, 1961), 23–24; Elias Darnell, *A Journal Containing an Accurate and Interesting Account of the Hardships, Sufferings, Battles, Defeat, and Captivity of Those Heroic Kentucky Volunteers and Regulars, Commanded by General Winchester, in the Years 1812–13* (Philadelphia: Lippincott, Grambo, and Co., 1854), 11.
7. Harrison to Secretary of War Eustis, September 27, 1812, in *MLWHH*, 2:156–157, and Harrison to Secretary of War Eustis, October 13, 1812, 2:177.

8. Darnell, *A Journal*, 12; Northcutt, "Journal," Kentucky Historical Society.
9. "Letter from a Volunteer in the Bourbon Troop," September 13, 1812, published in *Western Citizen*, September 26, 1812, and referenced in Clift, *Remember the Raisin!*, 28.
10. Thomas Smith to W. W. Worsley, September 17, 1812 in Clift, *Remember the Raisin!*, 29; Northcutt, "Journal," Kentucky Historical Society.
11. Robert McAfee, *History of the Late War in the Western Country* (Bowling Green, OH: Historical Publications Company, 1816), 203.
12. Northcutt, "Journal," Kentucky Historical Society.
13. Winchester, General Orders, October 1, 1812, in "Papers and Orderly Book of Brigadier General James Winchester," in Michigan Pioneer and Historical Society, *Historical Collections* (Lansing, MI: Wynkoop, Hallenbeck, Crawford Co. 1902), 31:258; McAfee, *History of the Late War*, 202–203.
14. Harrison to Secretary of War Monroe, December 12, 1812, in *MLWHH*, 2:240; McAfee, *History of the Late War*, 202–204; Carl Skeen, "John Armstrong and the Role of the Secretary in the War in the War of 1812" (PhD diss., Ohio State University, 1966), 46–47; account of the quartermaster's journey taken from Jeffrey Kimball, "Strategy on the Northern Frontier: 1814" (PhD diss., Louisiana State University and Agricultural and Mechanical College, 1969), 45–47.
15. Darnell, *Journal*, 41–42; Clift, *Remember the Raisin!*, 39–40; McAfee, *History of the Late War*, 205; Northcutt, "Journal," Kentucky Historical Society.
16. Colonel John Allen to Judge William Logan, October 2, 1812, in Clift, *Remember the Raisin!*, 34.
17. Harrison to Eustis, December 12, 1812, in *MLWHH*, 2:240–242.
18. Eustis resigned on December 3, 1812, and Monroe took over from that point until February 5, 1813, after which Armstrong took over; then Monroe permanently replaced Armstrong on August 27, 1814.
19. Monroe to Harrison, January 17, 1813, in WHHP, reel 7, 232–233 (original emphasis); Monroe to Harrison, January 21, 1813, in WHHP, reel 7, 274.
20. Darnell, *Journal*, 43; Perkins to Harrison, January 6, 1813, in WWHP, reel 7, 159; Harrison to Piatt, January 7, 1813, in WWHP, reel 7, 161.
21. *Harper's New Monthly Magazine* 27 (New York: Harper & Brothers, 1868), 156; Harrison to Shelby, January 24, 1813, in John Richardson, *Richardson's War of 1812* (Toronto: Historical Publishing Co., 1902), 146; Harrison to Meigs, January 24, 1814, in WHHP, reel 7, 309–311; Winchester to Harrison, January 17, 1813, in *MLWHH*, 2:314.
22. Lewis to Winchester, January 20, 1813, in *NWR*, 4:49; Harrison to Eustis, December 12, 1812, in *MLWHH*, 2:243.
23. *Commonwealth*, June 9, 1871, in Clift, *Remember the Raisin!*, 54; Kentucky Yeoman Extra, "The Democratic Candidate for Governor and Lieutenant Governor of Kentucky," in Clift, 55.
24. Darnell, *Journal*, 48–50; William Atherton, *Narrative of the Suffering and De-*

feat of the Northwestern Army under General Winchester (Frankfort, KY: A.G. Hodges, 1842), 38–39; E. Whittlesey to his wife, January 25, 1813, in *Western Reserve Historical Society* 92, part 2 (November 1913): 100.

25. Harrison to Winchester, January 20, 1813, in Charles Todd, *Sketches of the Civil and Military Services of William Henry Harrison* (Cincinnati: J. A. & U. P. James, 1847), 56; Harrison to Winchester, January 21, 1813, in WHHP, reel 7, 293.
26. "Memorandum of Statements made by General Winchester and Major Madison to the Secretary of War, on return from their captivity in John Armstrong," in *Notices of the War of 1812* (New York: Wiley & Putnam, 1840), 1:199; McAfee, *History of the Late War*, 228; Clift, *Remember the Raisin!*, 58, 60; Harrison to Winchester, January 21, 1813, in WHHP, reel 7, 293; Roger Rosentreter, "Remember the River Raisin," *Michigan History Magazine*, no. 5 (November/December 1998), 43; Atherton, *Narrative of the Suffering*, 41; Quisenberry, *Kentucky in the War of 1812*, 39.
27. Atherton, *Narrative of the Suffering*, 42.
28. William Coffin, *1812: The War, and Its Moral: A Canadian Chronicle* (Montreal: Printed by John Lovell, 1864), 203; Richardson, *Richardson's War of 1812*, 134.
29. Atherton, *Narrative of the Suffering*, 42–43; Shadrach Byfield, *A Narrative of a Light Company Soldier's Service in the Forty-First Regiment of Foot, 1807–1914* (New York: W. Abbatt, 1910), 13.
30. Richardson, *Richardson's War of 1812*, 135; Byfield, *Narrative*, 13.
31. Richardson, *Richardson's War of 1812*, 136–137.
32. McClanahan to Harrison, January 26, 1813, in *MLWHH*, 2:340; Laurent Dorucher letter, Monroe County Library, *War of 1812 Digital Collection*, https://library.biblioboard.com/viewer/a1a7bcd4-c507-40c7-82e2-a028348cd6da; Robert Quimby, *The U.S. Army in the War of 1812: An Operational and Command Study* (East Lansing: Michigan State University Press, 1997), 1:136.
33. McClanahan to Harrison, January 26, 1813, in *MLWHH*, 2:340; McAfee, *History of the Late War*, 233; James Price to his wife, January 16, 1813, in Clift, *Remember the Raisin!*, 160–161; Clift, 65.
34. Atherton, *Narrative of the Suffering*, 47–49; McAfee, *History of the Late War*, 233–234; Richardson, *Richardson's War of 1812*, 135.
35. "Statements of Prisoners of War on their Return to Pittsburgh," in *NWR*, 4:10–13.
36. Quisenberry, *Kentucky in the War of 1812*, 41.
37. Armstrong, *Notices*, 1:74–75, 77; Clift, *Remember the Raisin!*, 70; Atherton, *Narrative of the Suffering*, 52–54.
38. Richardson, *Richardson's War of 1812*, 132, 140.
39. Darnell, *Journal*, 58–59; McAfee, *History of the Late War*, 244; Testimony of John Todd, May 2, 1813, published in *NWR*, 5:140–141.
40. Testimony of John Todd, May 2, 1813, published in the *NWR*, 5:140–141.
41. Laurent Dorucher letter, Monroe County Library, *War of 1812 Digital Collection*;

numerous depositions of eyewitness recorded in *ASP*, 1:367–371; Benson Lossing, *Pictorial Field Book of the War of 1812* (New York: Harper & Brothers, 1868), 357–359.

42. Testimony of John Todd, May 2, 1813, published in the *NWR*, 5:140–141.
43. In WHHP: Harrison to Shelby, January 25, 1813, reel 7, 330; Harrison to Monroe, January 26, 1813, reel 7, 335–336; Harrison to Meigs, reel 7, 357 Harrison to Morrison, January 29, 1813, reel 7, 362.
44. Procter to Sheaffe, January 25, 1813, in *SBD*, 2:7–9; Prevost to Procter, February 9, 1813, in *DHCNF 1813*, 1:63; Quimby, *The U.S. Army in the War of 1812*, 1:137; Dr. Robert Richardson to Askin, February 7, 1813, in *John Askin Papers*, 2:750, Detroit Public Library; Bathurst to Prevost, August 1812, LAC, C042, 147, 168.
45. Winchester to Monroe, January 13, 1813, in *MLWHH*, 2:328; McAfee, *History of the Late War*, 238. In *NWR*: testimony of Alexis Labadie, February 3, 1813, 4:93; Baker to Winchester, February 25, 1813, 4:93; testimony of John Todd, May 2, 1813, 5:140–141; testimony of Joseph Robert, February 14, 1813, 4:92. Report of Ensign Isaac Baker to Winchester, February 26, 1813, in *ASP*, 1:370.
46. Robert Quimby, *The U.S. Army in the War of* 1812, 1:137; Tony Horwitz, "Remember the Raisin," *Smithsonian* 43, no. 3 (2012): 28–35; Harrison to Meigs, January 24, 1814, in WHHP, reel 7, 309–311; Harrison to Monroe, January 24, 1813, in WHHP, reel 8, 313–316; editorial in *NWR*, 4:98.
47. William Orlando Butler, "The Field of Raisin," in William Coggeshall, *The Poets and Poetry of the West* (Columbus : Follett, Foster, 1860), 172.
48. "Journal of Lieutenant Eleazer Wood," in George Cullum, *Campaigns of the War of 1812–15 against Great Britain* (New York: James Miller, 1879), 371–372.
49. Cullum, *Campaigns of the War of 1812–15*, 108; Glenn Bradley, "Fort Meigs in the War of 1812," *Bulletin of Historical Society of Northwestern Ohio* 2 (1930): 6.
50. "Minutes of the Principal Occurrences Which Have Taken Place During the Siege of Fort Meigs," in *Niles Weekly Register*, June 12, 1813, 242–244.
51. Henry Compton, "The Siege of Fort Meigs," *Ohio Archeological and Historical Quarterly* 10 (1902), 325–326; "Joseph Underwood Narrative," cited in Horace Knapp, *History of the Maumee Valley* (Toledo, OH: Blade Publishing House, 1872), 161n; Bradley, "Fort Meigs in the War of 1812," 6.
52. "Account from Eleazer Wood," in McAfee, *History of the Late War*, 285; Bradley, "Fort Meigs in the War of 1812," 6.
53. Bradley, "Fort Meigs in the War of 1812," 7.
54. "Journal of Lieutenant Eleazer Wood," in Cullum, *Campaigns of the War of 1812–15*, 395–397; Earl Saliers, "The Siege of Fort Meigs," *Ohio State Archeological and Historical Society* 18 (1909): 532; "Joseph Underwood Narrative," cited in Knapp, *History of the Maumee Valley*,168–170n; "Official Report from Captain Leslie Combs to General Green Clay, May 6, 1815," in Leslie Combs, *Col. Wm. Dudley's Defeat Opposite Fort Meigs, May 5th, 1813* (Cincinnati: Spiller & Gates, 1869), 6–8.
55. "Official Report from Captain Leslie Combs to General Green Clay, May 6, 1815,"

in Combs, *Col. Wm. Dudley's Defeat*, 9–11; "Joseph Underwood Narrative," cited in Knapp, *History of the Maumee Valley*, 170–171n; Cullum, *Campaigns of 1812–15*, 113; "Journal of Lieutenant Eleazer Wood," in Cullum, *Campaigns of the War of 1812–15*, 397; "For shame to desist . . . " quote in McAfee, *History of the Late War*, 294.

56. McAfee, *History of the Late War*, 295; Harrison's reply to Procter, in H. L. Hosmer, *Early History of the Maumee County* (Toledo, OH: Hosmer & Harris, 1858), 45; Procter to Prevost, May 14, 1813, in *SBD*, 2:35; Procter to Prevost, August 9, 1813, in *SBD*, 2:44; Byfield, *Narrative*, 16.
57. Procter to Vincent, June 15, 1813, in *DHCNF 1813*, 2:85; Procter to Prevost, August 22, 1813, in *SBD*, 2:48, and Prevost to Procter, July 11, 1813, 2:251; Bruce Bowlus, "A Signal Victory: The Battle for Fort Stephenson," *Northwest Ohio Quarterly* 63 (1991): 45; Procter to Prevost, August 9, 1813, in *SBD*, 2:45.
58. Bowlus, "A Signal Victory," 45–46.
59. Holmes to Croghan, July 27, 1813, in WHHP, reel 8, 633; Bowlus, "A Signal Victory," 47–48; Croghan to Harrison, July 30, 1813, in McAfee, *History of the Late War*, 323.
60. Shipp quote in Lossing, *Pictorial Field Book*, 501; "Address of Charles Fairbanks," in Lucy Keeler, *93d Anniversary of the Battle of Fort Stephenson* (Columbus: Ohio State Archeological and Historical Society, 1907), 28; McAfee, *History of the Late War*, 350–351.
61. Bowlus, "A Signal Victory," 49; McAfee, *History of the Late War*, 351; Croghan to Harrison, August 5, 1813, in *MLWHH*, 2:515.
62. Lossing, *Pictorial Field Book*, 503; Richardson, *Richardson's War of 1812*, 179–180; "Account of the Battle of Fort Stephenson," in *Kentucky Gazette*, August 17, 1813; Croghan to Harrison, August 5, 1813, in *MLWHH*, 2:515.
63. McAfee, *History of the Late War*, 351–352; Richardson, *Richardson's War of 1812*, 180; Procter to Prevost, August 9, 1813, in *SBD*, 2:45–46; "Account of the Battle of Fort Stephenson," *Kentucky Gazette*, August 17, 1813; Croghan to Harrison, August 5, 1813, in *MLWHH*, 2:515; Byfield, *Narrative*, 18.
64. Byfield, *Narrative*, 18; Richardson, *Richardson's War of 1812*, 180; "Account of the Battle of Fort Stephenson," in *Kentucky Gazette*, August 17, 1813; Harrison to Perry, August 4, 1813, in OHPP, Series 1, Correspondence and Documents.
65. Byfield, *Narrative*, 19.
66. Harrison to Secretary of War Armstrong, August 4, 1813, in *MLWHH*, 2:512.

CHAPTER 6. AMERICA SEIZES THE NIAGARA FRONTIER

1. *Buffalo Gazette*, September 29, 1812.
2. Glenn Steppler, "Logistical Considerations in the Canadian War of 1812" (PhD diss., McGill University, 1974), 130; Prevost to Bathurst, August 14, 1814, in *Report on the Canadian Archives*, ed. Douglas Brymner (Ottawa: S. E. Dawson, 1897), 36.

3. Jeff Seiken, "To Obtain Command of the Lakes: The United States and the Contest for Lakes Erie and Ontario, 1812–1815," in *The Sixty Years' War for the Great Lakes, 1754–1814*, ed. David Skaggs and Larry Nelson (East Lansing: Michigan State University Press, 2001), 356.
4. Hamilton to Chauncey, August 31, 1812, in *NW*, 1:297; Woolsey to Chauncey, September 7, 1812, NARA, RG45/C/1812; Chauncey to Hamilton, October 8, 1812, in *NW*, 1:336–337.
5. David Curtis Skaggs, *Oliver Hazard Perry: Honor, Courage, and Patriotism in the Early U.S. Navy* (Annapolis, MD: Naval Institute Press, 2006), 54; Chauncey to Hamilton, October 8, 1812, in *NW*, 1:336–337.
6. Elliot to Dobbin, October 2, 1812, in *NW*, 1:321; Skaggs, *Oliver Hazard Perry*, 56–57; Robert Malcomson, *Lords of the Lake: The Naval War on Lake Ontario, 1812–1814* (Annapolis, MD: Naval Institute Press, 1998), 74; Gerry Altoff, *Oliver Hazard Perry and the Battle of Lake Erie* (Put-in-Bay, OH: Perry Group, 1990), 4–9; Hamilton to Dobbins, September 15, 1812, in *NW*, 1:310.
7. Anderson to Hamilton, October 8, 1812, in *NW*, 1:323; C. P. Stacey, "Naval Power on the Great Lakes, 1812–1814," in *After Tippecanoe: Some Aspects of the War of 1812*, ed. Philip Mason (East Lansing: Michigan State University Press, 2012), 51.
8. Rapids toward the end of the river often forced transporters to traverse the final miles to Oswego overland. Seiken, "To Obtain Command of the Lakes," 358; Malcomson, *Lords of the Lake*, 45–46; Anderson to Hamilton, October 8, 1812, in *NW*, 1:323; *ASP*, class 10, vol. 1, miscellaneous (1834), 250; Stacey, "Naval Power on the Great Lakes," 51.
9. Chauncey to Hamilton, November 26, 1812, in *NW*, 1:353; Wood to Stevens, February 3, 1813, in *The Town of York 1793–1815*, ed. Edith Firth (Toronto: University of Toronto Press, 1962), 289–290.
10. E. A. Cruikshank, "The Contest for the Command of Lake Ontario in 1812 and 1813," *Transactions of the Royal Society of Canada*, series 3, vol. 10 (September 1916): 167, 171; Malcomson, *Lords of the Lake*, 66–70; *Lancaster Intelligencer and Journal*, September 18, 1812.
11. Armstrong to Dearborn, February 24, 1813, in *ASP*, 1:440; Armstrong to Dearborn, April 19, 1813, in *ASP*, 1:442; Armstrong to Dearborn, April 8, 1813, in NARA, RG94, 2.1, Correspondence.
12. Steppler, "Logistical Considerations in the Canadian War of 1812," 10–11.
13. Multiple letters from Dearborn to Armstrong, dated March 3, 9, 14, 16, 1813, in *ASP*, 1:441–442; Chauncey to Jones, March 18, 1813, in *NW*, 1:1813, 431.
14. Armstrong to Dearborn, April 19, 1813, in *ASP*, 1:442; Armstrong to Dearborn, March 29, 1813, in *ASP*, 1:442.
15. Bruyeres to Sheaffe, February 19, 1813, in *DHCNF 1813*, 5:219, and Prevost to Sheaffe, March 27, 1813, 5:34.
16. MacDonell to Harvey, February 25, 1813, in *SBD*, 2:20–24.

17. Robert Malcomson, *Capital in Flames: The American Attack on York, 1813* (Annapolis, MD: Naval Institute Press, 2008), 166, 202; Pike to his father, n.d., in *Niles Weekly Register*, 4:304.
18. The term "squadron" and "fleet" are used interchangeably in this book. Chauncey to Jones, April 24, 1813, in *NW*, 2:448.
19. Malcomson, *Capital in Flames*, 173; Bruyeres to Sheaffe, February 19, 1813, in *DHCNF 1813*, 1:219; Charles Humphries, "The Capture of York," *Ontario History* 51 (1959): 3.
20. Malcomson, *Lords of the Lake*, 115; Bathurst to Sheaffe, June 8, 1813, in *DHCNF 1813*, 2:58.
21. Myers to Baynes, May 20, 1813, in *DHCNF 1813*, 1:238; Wesley Turner, *British Generals in the War of 1812: High Command in the Canadas* (Montreal: McGill-Queen's University Press, 1999), 93, 98.
22. Robert Malcomson, *Capital in Flames*, 163; Ridout to Sheaffe, March 19, 1813, in LAC, RG8 688c.
23. Brigade Order, Sackets Harbor, April 25, 1813, in *DHCNF 1813*, 1:162–163; W. E. Hollon "Zebulon Montgomery Pike and the York Campaign," *New York History* 30, no. 3 (1949): 267.
24. James Cooper, *Ned Myers* (New York: AMS Press, 2009), 1:51.
25. Cooper, *Ned Myers*, 1:51–52.
26. "An Account of the Capture of York," in *DHCNF 1813*, 1:175–176, and Sheaffe to Prevost, May 5, 1813, 1:187.
27. Humphries, "The Capture of York," 5; Richard Cannon, *Historical Record of the Eighth, or the King's Regiment of Foot* (London: Parker, Furnivall, and Parker, 1844), 77–79.
28. "Account of Events at York," May 8, 1813, in *DHCNF 1813*, 1:193.
29. "Journal of Colonel Cromwell Pearce," in *War of 1812 in Person: Fifteen Accounts by United States Army Regulars, Volunteers and Militiamen*, ed. John Fredricksen (Jefferson, NC: McFarland & Co., 2010), 75; Malcomson, *Capital in Flames*, 194–196.
30. Malcomson, *Capital in Flames*, 197–198; Dearborn to Armstrong, April 28, 1813, in *ASP*, 1:443.
31. Fraser to Pike, May 1813, in *DHCNF 1813*, 1:179–182.
32. Dearborn to Armstrong, April 28, 1813, in *ASP*, 1:443–444.
33. Dr. Trowbridge to John Trowbridge, May 1814, in Francis Trowbridge, *The Trowbridge Genealogy: History of the Trowbridge Family in America* (New Haven, CT: Tuttle, Morehouse & Taylor Company, 1908), 537; P. Finan, "From Journal of a Voyage to Quebec in the Year 1825," in *DHCNF 1813*, 1:208, and "Extract of a Letter from Kingston," 1:192.
34. Colonel William Allan Manuscript, May 8, 1813, in *DHCNF 1813*, 1:192–202, and "The War," in *DHCNF 1813*, 1:212–213; Finan, *From Journal of a Voyage to Quebec*, 209.

35. John Fredericksen, "A Poor but Honest Sodger: Colonel Cromwell Pearce," *Pennsylvania History* 52 (July 1985): 139; Dr. Trowbridge to John Trowbridge, May 1814, in Trowbridge, *The Trowbridge Genealogy*, 537; Malcomson, *Capital in Flames*, 217–218; Ely Playter's Diary, April 27, 1813, AO, F556; "The War," in *DHCNF 1813*, 1:213.
36. "An Account of the Capture of York," in *DHCNF 1813*, 1:175–177; John Beikie to John Macdonell, May 5, 1813, in AO, F548.
37. Malcomson, *Capital in Flames*, 228–229; Fredericksen, "A Poor but Honest Sodger," 137.
38. Fredericksen, "A Poor but Honest Sodger," 139; Strachan to Brown, April 4/June 4, 1813, AO, F983, Strachan Fonds; Malcomson, *Capital in Flames*, 18–19.
39. Ely Playter Diary, April 29, 1813, in AO, F556.
40. Cooper, *Ned Myers*, 1:122–225; Colonel William Allan Manuscript, May 8, 1813, in *DHCNF 1813*, 1:201.
41. Dearborn to Secretary of War Armstrong, May 3, 1813, in *DHCNF 1813*, part 1, 186; Memorandum by Thomas Ridout, in *DHCNF 1813*, part 1, 223–224. For a balanced discussion of who might have started the York fires, see Humphries, "The Capture of York," 13–15.
42. Colonel William Allan Manuscript, May 8, 1813, in *DHCNF 1813*, 1:192–202.
43. Sheaffe to Bathurst, May 13, 1813, in *DHCNF 1813*, 1:227; Charles Ingersoll, *Historical Sketch of the Second War between the United States of America* (Philadelphia: Lea and Blanchard, 1849), 1:273; Dearborn to Armstrong, May 3, 1813, in *ASP*, 1:443–444; General Ripley's statement, August 15, 1815, in *NWR*, 9:161; Malcolmson, *Capital in Flames*, 245; Chauncey to Jones, May 7, 1813, in *NW*, 1:453.
44. *From Journal of a Voyage to Quebec in the Year 1825, with Recollections of Canada during the late America War*, in *DHCNF 1813*, 1:210, and *Quebec Mercury*, Tuesday, May, 25, 1813, in 1:211.
45. Bruyeres to Prevost, February 13, 1813, in *DHCNF 1813*, 1:218; E. A. Cruikshank, *The Battle of Fort George* (Welland, ON: Tribune Print, 1904), 21; Prevost to Bathurst, May 26, 1813, in *DHCNF 1813*, 1:242.
46. Dearborn to Armstrong, May 18, 1813, in *DHCNF 1813*, 1: 229.
47. Vincent to Prevost, May 19, 1813, in *DHCNF 1813*, 1:235–237.
48. Harvey to Baynes, May 25, 1813, in *SBD*, 2:102.
49. Chauncey to Jones, May 28, 1813, in *DHCNF 1813*, 1:255; Cruikshank, *The Battle of Fort George*, 27–28.
50. William Worth, "First Campaign of an A.D.C.," *Military and Naval Magazine of the United States* 2 (September 1833 to February 1834): 11–12; Brigade Order, May 26, 1813, in *DHCNF 1813*, 1:241–242.
51. John Fredricksen, "Memoirs of Captain Ephraim Shaler," *New England Quarterly* 57 (September 1984): 411–420; Worth, "First Campaign of an A.D.C.," 13.
52. Worth, "First Campaign of an A.D.C.," 16; John Fredricksen, "Chronicle of

Valor: The Journal of a Pennsylvania Officer in the War of 1812," *Western Pennsylvania Historical Magazine* 67 (July 1984): 262.

53. Fredricksen, "Chronicle of Valor," 262.
54. Captain John Walworth to his father, May 29, 1813, in LAC, MG24/F16; Worth, "First Campaign of an A.D.C.," 18–19; Fowler to Baynes, May 29, 1813, in *DHCNF 1813*, 1:257–258.
55. Boyd quote referenced in Cruikshank, *The Battle of Fort George*, 29; Fredricksen, "Chronicle of Valor," 264; Fowler to Baynes, May 29, 1813, in *DHCNF 1813*, 1:257–258.
56. Fredricksen, "Chronicle of Valor," 263–264.
57. Captain John Walworth to his father, May 29, 1813, in LAC, MG24/F16; Vincent to Prevost, May 28, 1813, in *DHCNF 1813*, 1:250–251.
58. Winfield Scott, *Memoirs of Lieut.-General Winfield Scott*, ed. Timothy Johnson (Knoxville: University of Tennessee Press, 2015), 90–91; Worth, "First Campaign of an A.D.C.," 78–79; John Boyd quote referenced in Cruikshank, *The Battle of Fort George*, 29; Fredricksen, "Chronicle of Valor," 265; Lewis to Dearborn, May 27, 1813 in *ASP*, 1:445.
59. "Agreement Governing Joint Operations," in *NW*, 2:434–435, and Jones to Chauncey, April 8, 1813, 2:434.
60. John Grodzinski, *Defender of Canada: Sir George Prevost and the War of 1812* (Norman: University of Oklahoma Press, 2013), 125.

CHAPTER 7. BRITAIN STRIKES ON LAKE ONTARIO

1. Yeo to Croker, May 26, 1813, in *NW*, 2:469; Yeo to Croker, July 16, 1813, in *DHCNF 1813*, 2:246; Robert Malcomson, *Lords of the Lake: The Naval War on Lake Ontario, 1812–1814* (Annapolis, MD: Naval Institute Press, 1998), 335; C. P. Stacey, "The Ships of the British Squadron on Lake Ontario," *Canadian Historical Review* 34, no. 4 (1953): 317–323.
2. Prevost to Bathurst, June 1, 1813, in *DHCNF 1813*, 1:292.
3. Chauncey to W. Chauncey, May 20, 1813, in *NW*, 2:467; Brown to Tompkins, June 1, 1813, in *DHCNF 1813*, 1:283–287.
4. Brown to Tompkins, June 1, 1813, in *DHCNF 1813*, 1:285; John Morris, *Sword of the Border: Major General Jacob Jennings Brown, 1775–1828* (Kent, OH: Kent State University Press, 2000), 40–43; Dearborn to Armstrong, May 13, 1813, in *ASP*, 1:444.
5. *Four Years on the Lakes of Canada in 1813, 1814, 1815 and 1816 by a Naval Officer Under Command of the Late Sir James Lucas Yeo*, LAC, MG24-F18; Morris, *Sword of the Border*, 42; Patrick Wilder, *Battle of Sackett's Harbour* (Baltimore: Nautical & Aviation Pub. Co. of America, 1994), 77–78; "Viger to his wife, June 12, 1813," in *Watertown Daily Times*, May 28 to June 4, 1963.
6. "Viger to his wife, June 12, 1813"; *Four Years on the Lakes of Canada*, LAC, MG24-F18.

7. Wilder, *Battle of Sackett's Harbour*, 82, 85, 88; Brown to Tompkins, June 1, 1813, in *DHCNF 1813*, 1:283–287.
8. Brown to Tompkins, June 1, 1813, in *DHCNF 1813*, 1:286.
9. Wilder, *Battle of Sackett's Harbour*, 91–92; John Le Couteur, *Merry Hearts Make Light Days: The War of 1812 Journal of Lieutenant John Le Couteur*, ed. Donald Graves (Montreal: Robin Brass Studio, 2012), 116; Brenton to Freer, May 30, 1813, in *DHCNF 1813*, 1:281.
10. Brown to Tompkins, June 1, 1813, in *DHCNF 1813*, 1:286.
11. "Viger to his wife, June 12, 1813."
12. Wilder, *Battle of Sackett's Harbour*, 96; Brenton to Freer, May 30, 1813, in *DHCNF 1813*, 1:282; "Viger to his wife, June 12, 1813."
13. Le Couteur, *Merry Hearts Make Light Days*, 116; Brenton to Freer, May 30, 1813, in *DHCNF 1813*, 1:281.
14. Brown to Tompkins, June 1, 1813, in *DHCNF 1813*, 286; Morris, *Sword of the Border*, 53.
15. Morris, *Sword of the Border*, 47; Brown to Tompkins, June 1, 1813, in *DHCNF 1813*, 1:286; Wilder, *Battle of Sackett's Harbour*, 103. For a comprehensive summary of Drury's court-martial, see Morris, *Sword of the Border*, 50–52.
16. In *DHCNF 1813*: Brenton to Freer, May 30, 1813, 1:279–282; Yeo to Croker, May 31, 1813, 1:289; Baynes to Prevost, May 30, 1813, 1:276–278. Le Couteur, *Merry Hearts Make Light Days*, 116.
17. Le Couteur, *Merry Hearts Make Light Days*, 116.
18. *Four Years on the Lakes of Canada*, LAC, MG24-F18, 9; Graves, *Merry Hearts Make Light Days*, 116.
19. Yeo to Croker, May 31, 1813, in *DHCNF 1813*, 1:289–290; *Four Years on the Lakes*, LAC, MG24-F18, 10.
20. James Elliott, *Strange Fatality: The Battle of Stoney Creek, 1813* (Montreal: Robin Brass Studio, 2009), 107, 120; John Fredricksen, "Memoirs of Captain Ephraim Shaler," *New England Quarterly* 57 (September 1984): 411–420.
21. Fredricksen, "Memoirs of Captain Ephraim Shaler," 411–420; G. F. G Stanley, *Battle in the Dark: Stoney Creek, 6 June 1813* (Toronto: Balmuir Publishing, 1991), 13; Elliott, *Strange Fatality*, 107–110; George Talbot, "General John Chandler on Monmouth Maine with Extracts from His Autobiography," *Collections of the Maine Historical Society* 9 (1887): 190–191; Johnson to Dearborn, June 7, 1813, in Talbot, "General John Chandler on Monmouth Maine with Extracts from his Autobiography," *Collections of the Maine Historical Society* 9 (1887): 196–197.
22. Vincent to Prevost, June 6, 1813, in *DHCNF 1813*, 2:8, and Harvey to Baynes, June 6, 1813, 2:7. Ruth McKenzie, *James Fitzgibbon: Defender of Upper Canada, 1805* (Toronto: Dundurn Press, 1983), 29; C. S. Jones, *The Battle of Stoney Creek* (Brantford, 1889), 11.
23. Fitzgibbon to Somerville, June 7, 1813, in *DHCNF 1813*, 1:13, and Harvey to Baynes,

June 6, 1813, 2:7. Stanley, *Battle in the Dark*, 16–17; Mabel Thompson, "Billy Green: The Scout," *Ontario History* 44 (1952): 175–176; Hazel Corman, "An Account of the Battle of Stoney Creek," in *Papers & Records of the Wentworth Historical Society* 7 (Hamilton, ON: The Griffin & Richmond Co., 1916), 29–30.

24. Thompson, "Billy Green: The Scout," 176–177; *Niles Weekly Register*, June 19, 1813; John Norton, *Journal of John Norton*, ed. Carl Klinck and James Talman (Toronto: Champlain Society, 1970), 328; Fredricksen, "Memoirs of Captain Ephraim Shaler," 411–420.
25. Fredricksen, "Memoirs of Captain Ephraim Shaler," 127.
26. "Reports of the Battles at Stoney Creek," *The Washingtonian* 3, no. 156 (1813), 2; Johnson to Dearborn, June 7, 1813, in Talbot, "General John Chandler on Monmouth Maine," 197; Fitzgibbon to Somerville, June 7, 1813, in *DHCNF 1813*, 2:13; Stanley, *Battle in the Dark*, 17; Thompson, "Billy Green: The Scout," 177; William Merritt, *A Desire of Serving and Defending My Country* (Toronto: Iser Publications, 2001), 6; Harvey to Baynes, June 6, 1813, in *DHCNF 1813*, 2:7; Emerson Biggar, "Battle of Stoney Creek," in *The Hamilton Spectator*, June 5, 1889, 6; Fredricksen, "Memoirs of Captain Ephraim Shaler," 411–420.
27. Plenderleath to Vincent, July 23, 1813, in *SBD*, 2:158; Elliott, *Strange Fatality*, 136–137.
28. Talbot, "General John Chandler on Monmouth Maine with Extracts from his Autobiography," 192–193; Burns to Ingersoll, July 1, 1813, in John Fredricksen, "Colonel James Burns and the War of 1812," *South Carolina Historical Magazine* 90 (1989): 299–312; "Extract of a Letter from an Officer in the Army of the United States," in *Niles Weekly Messenger*, June 22, 1813, 2; *Richmond Enquirer*, June 2, 1813; Fitzgibbon to Somerville, June 7, 1813, in *DHCNF 1813*, 1:14; Chandler to Dearborn, June 18, 1813, in *ASP*, 1:448.
29. James Fitzgibbon, "From a Memorandum of the Services of Lt. Colonel Charles Plenderleath, C. B., Sent to his Widow after his Death, on Jan. 1, 1854," in *DHCNF 1813*, 2:16; Harvey to Baynes, June 6, 1813, in *DHCNF 1813*, 2:7; Elliott, *Strange Fatality*, 154–156, 202; Fitzgibbon to Somerville, June 7, 1813, in *DHCNF 1813*, 2:2,14; Thompson, "Billy Green: The Scout," 177.
30. Burns to Ingersoll, July 1, 1813, in Fredricksen, "Colonel James Burns and the War of 1812," 299–312; Dearborn to Secretary of War Armstrong, June 6, 1813, in *DHCNF 1813*, 2:6.
31. Vincent to Prevost, May 19, 1813, in *DHCNF 1813*, 2:236; Stanley, *Battle in the Dark*, 25.
32. F. H. Keefer, *Beaverdams* (Thorold, Canada: Thorold Post Printers, 1914), 5–6; *Memoir of Mrs. Secord*, in *SBD*, 2:164–165; *Fitzgibbon's Certificate*, in *SBD*, 2:165–166; Peggy Leavey, *Laura Secord: Heroine of the War of 1812* (Toronto: Dundurn, 2012), 11. For an analysis of Secord's trek, see Donald Hickey, *Don't Give Up the Ship! Myths of the War of 1812* (Urbana: University of Illinois Press, 2006), 196–197.

33. "Account of Major Chapin," *Niles Weekly Register*, August 7, 1813; Bishop to Vincent, June 24, 1813, in *DHCNF 1813*, 2:112; Stanley, *Battle in the Dark*, 26.
34. Fitzgibbon to Dearborn, June 25, 1813, in *SBD*, 2:162.
35. *Montreal Gazette*, July 6, 1813, in *DHCNF 1813*, 2:116; Fitzgibbon to Major De Haren, June 24, 1813, in *SBD*, 2:159–160; "Account of Beaverdams," *Niagara Historical Society & Museum, Scrap Book*, ed. Janet Carnochan (Niagara-on-the-Lake, ON: Niagara Historical Society Museum, 1913), n.p.; "Account of Major Chapin," *Niles Weekly Register*, August 7, 1813.
36. Ernest Cruikshank, *Drummond's Winter Campaign, 1813* (Welland, ON: Lundy's Lane Historical Society, 1900), 15; McClure to Armstrong, December 10, 1813, in *ASP*, 1:486.
37. Armstrong to McClure, October 4, 1813, in *ASP*, 1:486.
38. Murray to Drummond, December 19, 1813, in *DHCNF 1812–1814*, 9:11–12, and General Order, December 19, 1813, 9:14–15; Shadrach Byfield, *A Narrative of a Light Company Soldier's Service in the Forty-First Regiment of Foot, 1807–1914* (New York: reprinted, W. Abbatt, 1910), 25–26; "Campaign of 1814 in Upper Canada," in LAC, 24/F23.
39. Cruikshank, *Drummond's Winter Campaign*, 19–20.
40. Glenn Steppler, "Logistical Considerations in the Canadian War of 1812" (PhD diss., McGill University, 1974), 133; E. A. Cruikshank, "A Sketch of the Public Life and Services of Robert Nichol," *Ontario Historical Society Papers and Records* 19 (1922): 30.
41. Wesley Turner, *British High Generals: High Command in the Canadas* (Montreal: McGill-Queen's University Press, 1999), 102–104; Rottenburg to Prevost, July 7, 1813, in *DHCNF 1813*, 2:200.
42. Steppler, "Logistical Considerations," 133.

CHAPTER 8. AMERICA RETAKES THE NORTHWEST

1. Chauncey to Jones, January 1, 1813, in *NW*, 2:406–407.
2. *ASP*, class 10, vol. 1, miscellaneous (1834), 735; C. P. Stacey, "Naval Power on the Great Lakes, 1812–1814," in *After Tippecanoe: Some Aspects of the War of 1812*, ed. Philip Mason (East Lansing: Michigan State University Press, 2012), 51; C. P. Stacey, "Another Look at the Battle of Lake Erie," *Canadian Historical Review* 39, no. 1 (1958): 46–47.
3. Jones to Chauncey, January 27, 1813, in *NW*, 2:419; Jeff Seiken, "To Obtain Command of the Lakes: The United States and the Contest for Lakes Erie and Ontario, 1812–1815," in *The Sixty Years' War for the Great Lakes, 1754–1814*, ed. David Skaggs and Larry Nelson (East Lansing: Michigan State University Press, 2001), 358–359.
4. Barclay could also not retrieve the cannon even if they made it to Long Point because he already had abandoned the depot. David Curtis Skaggs and Gerard Altoff, *A Signal Victory: The Lake Erie Campaign, 1812–1813* (Annapolis, MD: Naval

Institute Press, 1997), 61–68; Barclay to Yeo, August 5, 1813, in *NW*, 2:547; Barclay to Prevost, June 29, 1813, in *SBD*, 2:248–259; "Narrative of the Proceedings during the Command of Captain Barclay of His Majesty's Squadron on Lake Erie," in *SBD*, 2:298–318; E. A. Cruikshank, "A Sketch of the Public Life and Services of Robert Nichol," *Ontario Historical Society Papers and Records* 19 (1922): 30.

5. Barclay to Vincent, June 17, 1813, in *DHCNF 1813*, 2:89, and Freer to Procter, August 25, 1813, 3:62. In *SBD*: "Narrative of the Proceedings," 2:311–312; Prevost to Procter, September 6, 1813,2: 270–271; Prevost to Bathurst, August 25, 1813, 2:289–290.
6. Prevost to Procter, June 20, 1813, in *DHCNF 1813*, 2:101; Barclay to Prevost, July 16, 1813, in *SBD*, 2:257–259; Rottenburg to Procter, July 1, 1813, in *DHCNF 1813*, 2:172, and "Notes by Captain W. H. Merritt," 2:174.
7. Shelby to Harrison, March 20, 1813, WWHP, reel 8, 734.
8. Stacey, "Naval Power on the Great Lakes," 51–52; *Pittsburgh Gazette*, January 24, 1812; Stacey, "Another Look at the Battle of Lake Erie," 46–47; Perry to Chauncey, April 10, 1813, in *NW*, 2:440.
9. Perry to Chauncey, June 12, 1813, in NARA, RG45; Skaggs and Altoff, *A Signal Victory*, 71.
10. Perry to Chauncey July 23, 1813, in Lossing, *Pictorial Field Book of the War of 1812*, 513; Perry to his father, August 9, 1813, in OHPP, Series 1, Correspondence; Skaggs and Altoff, *A Signal Victory*, 77, in *NW*: Jones to Chauncey, July 3, 1813, 2:509–512; Perry to Chauncey, July 27, 1813, 2:529-530; Chauncey to Perry, July 30, 1813, 2:530.
11. Skaggs and Altoff, *A Signal Victory*, 84.
12. "Narrative of the Proceedings," in *SBD*, 2:300; Skaggs and Altoff, *A Signal Victory*, 85; Gerard Altoff, *Deep Water Sailors, Shallow Water Soldiers: Manning the United States Fleet on Lake Erie, 1813* (Put-in-Bay, OH: Perry Group, 1993), 23–24; Perry to Harrison, August 5, 1813, in WWHP, reel 9, 725.
13. Altoff, *Deep Water Sailors*, 23–24; David Curtis Skaggs, "Creating Small Unit Cohesion: Oliver Hazard Perry at the Battle of Lake Erie." *Armed Forces and Society* 23, no. 4 (1997): 636, 645–647.
14. Skaggs, "Creating Small Unit Cohesion," 648–651.
15. Perry to his father, August 9, 1813, in OHPP, Series 1, Correspondence; Skaggs and Altoff, *A Signal Victory*, 90–93, 103; Harrison to Perry, August 4, 1813, in OHPP, Series 1, Correspondence; David Curtis Skaggs, *William Henry Harrison and the Conquest of the Ohio Country: Frontier Fighting in the War of 1812* (Baltimore: Johns Hopkins University Press, 2014), 214–215; Harrison to Perry, September 4, 1813, in WHHP, reel 8, 123; Perry to Harrison, September 5, 1813, in WHHP, reel 7, 137.
16. Michael Palmer, "A Failure of Command, Control, and Communications: Oliver Hazard Perry and the Battle of Lake Erie," *Journal of Erie Studies* 17 (Fall 1988): 12–13.

17. Glenn Steppler, "Logistical Considerations in the Canadian War of 1812" (PhD diss., McGill University, 1974), 49, 52.
18. Procter to Freer, September 6, 1813, in *SBD*, 2:269–270, and Barclay to Yeo, September 1, 1813, 2:268.
19. "Narrative of the Proceedings," in *SBD*, 2:304; Yeo to Prevost, September 14, 1813, in TNA, CO 42/151/150; Yeo to Warren, October 10, 1813, in *DHCNF 1813*, 3:219; Harrison to Perry, September 4, 1813, in OHPP, Series 1, Correspondence; Ernest Cruikshank, "The Contest for the Command of Lake Erie," in *The Defended Border: Upper Canada and the War of 1812*, ed. Morris Zaslow (Toronto: Macmillan Company of Canada, 1964), 96.
20. "Narrative of the Proceedings," in *SBD*, 2:311, 313, 317; Chad Fraser, *Lake Erie Stories: Struggle and Survival on a Freshwater Ocean* (Toronto: Dundurn Press, 2008), 61; *Caledonian Mercury*, December 5, 1814.
21. Skaggs and Altoff, *A Signal Victory*, 108–110; Palmer, "A Failure of Command, Control, and Communications," 14; "Narrative of the Proceedings," in *SBD*, 2:317.
22. Usher Parsons, *Battle of Lake Erie, A Discourse, Delivered Before the Rhode-Island Historical Society, on the Evening of Monday, February 16, 1852* (Providence, RI: B. T. Albro, 1854), 8–9; Palmer, "A Failure of Command, Control, and Communications," 14; Richard Cox, "Account of the Battle of Lake Erie by Samuel Hambleton," *U.S. Naval Institute Proceedings* 104 (February 1978): 71; Skaggs and Altoff, *A Signal Victory*, 125, 127; David Bunnell, *The Travels and Adventures of David C. Bunnell* (Palmyra, NY: J. H. Bartles, 1831), 110–111.
23. Parsons, *Battle of Lake Erie*, 8–9; Palmer, "A Failure of Command, Control, and Communications," 16–18; Skaggs and Altoff, *A Signal Victory*, 127–129.
24. Skaggs and Altoff, *A Signal Victory*, 129; Palmer, "A Failure of Command, Control, and Communications," 17–18; "Narrative of the Proceedings," *SBD*, 2:298–318; C. S. Forester, *The Age of Fighting Sail* (Garden City, NY: Doubleday, 1956), 183.
25. Perry to Jones, September 13, 1813, in *NW*, 2:557–559; Skaggs and Altoff, *A Signal Victory*, 134, 137–138.
26. Parsons, *Battle of Lake Erie*, 11–13; Skaggs and Altoff, *A Signal Victory*, 132.
27. Frank Allaben, "The Log Book of the Lawrence," *Journal of American History* 8 (January–March 1914): 120; Cox, "Account of the Battle of Lake Erie by Samuel Hambleton," 71, 73; W. W. Dobbins, *History of the Battle of Lake Erie, (September 10, 1813) and Reminiscences of the Flagship* Lawrence (Erie, PA: Ashby & Vincent, 1876), 81; "William V. Taylor's Account of The Battle of Lake Erie," in John Fredriksen, "A Grand Moment for our Beloved Commander," *Journal of Erie Studies* 17 (1988): 119.
28. Dobbins, *History of the Battle of Lake Erie*, 83. Perry to Jones, September 13, 1813, in *NW*, 2:557–559, and Perry to Jones, September 13, 1813, 2:558.
29. Barclay to Yeo, September 12, 1813, in *NW*, 2:555–557; Dobbins, *History of the*

Battle of Lake Erie, 84; Inglis to Barclay, September 10, 1813, in *SBD*, 2:278; Perry to Harrison, September 10, 1813, in *NW*, 2:553.

30. Parsons, *Battle of Lake Erie*, 13–14, 20; "William Taylor's Account of the Battle of Lake Erie," in Fredriksen, "A Grand Moment for Our Beloved Commander," 116; Parsons, *Battle of Lake Erie*, 20; Laura Sanford, *History of Erie County, Pennsylvania* (Erie, PA, 1894), 1:311.
31. Palmer, "A Failure of Command, Control, and Communications," 20.
32. Casselman, *Richardson's War of 1812*, 204; "Tecumseh's Speech," in Casselman, *Richardson's War of 1812*, 205; Procter to Rottenburg, October 23, 1813, in *SBD*, 2:323; Harrison to Meigs, October 11, 1812, in *MLWHH*, 2:576; Prevost to Procter, September 23, 1813, in *SBD*, 2:284; Prevost to Bathurst, September 22, 1813, in *DHCNF 1813*, 3:161; Skaggs, *Harrison*, 193.
33. Skaggs, *Harrison*, 198–200; Harrison to Armstrong, September 27, 1813, in *ASP*, 1:455.
34. A. R. Millet, "Caesar and the Conquest of the Northwest Territory," *Timeline* 14 (May-June 1997): 19; Bennet Young, "Battle of the Thames in Which the Kentuckians Defeated the British, French, and Indians, October 5, 1813," *Filson Club Publications* 18 (1903): 53.
35. Harrison to Armstrong, October 9, 1813, in WHHP, reel 9, 323; Harrison to Armstrong, September 27, 1813, in *ASP*, 1:455; Harrison to Perry, September 4, 1813, in OHPP, Series 1, Correspondence; Young, "Battle of the Thames," 45–46.
36. Harrison to Armstrong, October 9, 1813, in WHHP, reel 9, 323–325.
37. Charles James, *A Collection of the Charges, Opinions, and Sentences of General Courts* (London: T. Egerton, 1820), 683; Procter to Rottenburg, October 23, 1813, in *SBD*, 2:325; Young, "Battle of the Thames," 58–60.
38. The sentence for General Procter's court-martial, in James, *A Collection of the Charges, Opinions, and Sentences of General Courts*, 683.
39. William Coffin, *1812: The War, and Its Moral* (Montreal: John Lovell, 1864), 227–228; John Sugden, *Tecumseh's Last Stand* (Norman: University of Oklahoma Press, 1985), 113–114; Norton, *Journal*, 130; Casselman, *Richardson's War of 1812*, 212.
40. Harrison to Armstrong, October 9, 1813, in WHHP, reel 9, 323–333.
41. Young, "The Battle of the Thames," 76, 80; Sugden, *Tecumseh's Last Stand*, 125.
42. Young, "The Battle of the Thames," 78; Procter to Rottenburg, October 23, 1813, in *SBD*, 2:326; Casselman, *Richardson's War of 1812*, 209; Extract of a Letter from Colonel George Trotter, October 6, 1813, in the *Kentucky Gazette*, October 26, 1813; Byfield, *Narrative*, 21. The sentence for General Procter's court-martial, in James, *A Collection of the Charges, Opinions, and Sentences of General Courts*, 685–687.
43. "Charles Wickliffe to the editor of the *Bardstown Gazette*, November 25, 1859," in Charles A. Wickliffe Papers, Kentucky Historical Society; Harrison to Meigs, October 11, 1812, in *MLWHH*, 2:575–576; Captain James Sympson diary, in An-

derson Quisenberry, *Kentucky in the War of 1812* (Frankfort: Kentucky State Historical Society, 1915), 104–105; Harrison to Armstrong, October 9, 1813, in WHHP, reel 9, 323–333.

44. Young, *The Battle of the Thames*, 87–88; Sandy Antal, *Wampum Denied: Procter's War of 1812* (Montreal: McGill-Queen's University Press, 2011), 346; James Knaggs, "Account of the Battle of the Thames," in *History of Monroe County Michigan*, ed. Talcott Wing (New York: Munsell & Co., 1890), 70–71. Sugden examines various reports regarding Tecumseh's death and the location of his body after the battle in Sugden, *Tecumseh Last Stand*, 139–140.
45. Harrison to Armstrong, October 9, 1813, in WHHP, reel 9, 323–333; James Hammack, *Kentucky and the Second American Revolution: The War of 1812* (Lexington: University Press of Kentucky, 1976), 85; *Kentucky Gazette*, October 26, 1813; Harrison to Armstrong, October 9, 1813 in *WHHP*, reel 9, 434–436.
46. Harrison to Armstrong, October 16, 1813, in *ASP*, 1:455.
47. Bullock to Baynes, October 21, 1813, in "Historical Collections," *Michigan Pioneer and Historical Society* 15 (Lansing, MI: Wynkoop, Hallenbeck, Crawford Co., 1909), 421, and Bullock to Freer, October 23, 1813, 423, and Bullock to Freer, December 30, 1813, 465–466. Brian Dunnigan, *The British Army at Mackinack 1812–1815* (Lansing, MI: Mackinac Island State Park Commission, 1980), 16–17.

CHAPTER 9. THE MONTREAL CAMPAIGN

1. Armstrong to Eustis, January 2, 1812, in John Armstrong, *Notices of the War* (New York: Wiley & Putnam, 1840), 1:234.
2. Carl Skeen "John Armstrong and the Role of the Secretary in the War in the War of 1812" (PhD diss., Ohio State University, 1966), 44–51.
3. David Curtis Skaggs, *William Henry Harrison and the Conquest of the Ohio Country: Frontier Fighting in the War of 1812* (Baltimore: Johns Hopkins University Press, 2014), 94–95.
4. Armstrong to Dearborn, February 24, 1813, in *DHCNF 1813*, 1:72–73; Armstrong to Wilkinson, August 8, 1813, in *DHCNF 1813*, 2:323.
5. J. C. A. Stagg, *The War of 1812: Conflict for a Continent* (New York: Cambridge University Press, 2012), 98–99. Hampton to Armstrong, August 23, 1813, in *DHCNF 1813*, 3:54, and Armstrong to Wilkinson, August 9, 1813, 2:329. Donald Graves, *Field of Glory: The Battle of Crysler's Farm, 1813* (Toronto: Robin Brass Studio, 1999), 31–32.
6. In *DHCNF 1813*: Wilkinson to Hampton, August 16, 1813, 3:29; Hampton to Armstrong, August 23, 1813, 3:54; Wilkinson to Armstrong, August 26, 1813, 3:75.
7. "Minutes of a Council of War, Held at Sackett's Harbour, August 26, 1813," in James Wilkinson, *Memoir of My Own Times* (Philadelphia: Abraham Small, 1816), 3:497–498.
8. Hugh Gray, *Letters from Canada Written during a Residence There, in the Years 1806, 1807, 1808* (London: Printed for Longman, Hurst, Rees, and Orme, 1809),

69, 144–146; John Grodzinski, *Defender of Canada: Sir George Prevost and the War of 1812* (Norman: University of Oklahoma Press), 65; John Grodzinksi, "The Vigilant Superintendence of the Whole District, The War of 1812 on the Upper St Lawrence" (PhD diss., Royal Military College of Canada, 2002), 10–11, 233–234.

9. In *DHCNF 1813*: "From the Journal of the Secretary of War," October 5, 1813, 3:197; Wilkinson to Armstrong, August 24, 1813, 56; Armstrong to Wilkinson, September 20, 1813, 3:153.
10. In *DHCNF 1813*: Chauncey to Secretary of Navy William Jones, September 13, 1813, 3:123–124; Yeo to Prevost, September 14, 1813, 3:126.
11. Robert Malcomson, *Lords of the Lake: The Naval War on Lake Ontario, 1812–1814* (Annapolis, MD: Naval Institute Press, 1998), 203–207. In *DHCNF 1813*: Yeo to Warren, September 29, 1813, 3:175–176; "Extract of a Letter from York," September 29, 1813, 3:177; Chauncey to the Secretary of the Navy William Jones, October 1, 1813, 3:180–182.
12. Armstrong to Wilkinson, October 19, 1813, in *DHCNF 1813*, 4:81–82, and Wilkinson to Armstrong, October 19, 1813, 84. Armstrong, *Notices of the War*, 2:209.
13. Chauncey to Jones, October 30, 1813, in *NW*, 2:594–595.
14. Armstrong to Hampton, October 16, 1813, in *ASP*, 1:461; Donald Graves, *Field of Glory: The Battle of Crysler's Farm, 1813* (Toronto: Robin Brass Studio, 1999), 70, 83, 90; Prevost to Bathurst, October 8, 1813, in *DHCNF 1813*, 3:205–208; William Lighthall, *An Account of Châteauguay* (Montreal: W. Drysdale & Co., 1889), 13.
15. Patrick Wohler, *Charles de Salaberry: Soldier of the Empire, Defender of Quebec* (Toronto: Dundurn Press, 1984).
16. Graves, *Field of Glory*, 83; William Gray, *Soldiers of the King: The Upper Canadian Militia, 1812–1815* (Erin, ON: Boston Mills Press, 1995), 32; Michelle Guitard, *The Militia of the Battle of the Châteauguay: A Social History* (Ottawa: National Historic Parks and Sites Branch, Parks Canada, 1983), 12. Michael O'Sullivan, "Account of the Battle of the Châteauguay," in *SBD*, 2:402–403, and Salaberry to Baynes, November 1, 1813, 2:397–398. Lighthall, *Account of Châteauguay*, 14.
17. Robert Sellar, *The U.S. Campaign of 1813 to Capture Montreal* (Huntingdon, QB: Gleaner Office, 1914), 5–9; Lighthall, *Account of Châteauguay*, 17; "Colonel Purdy's Report to Major General Wilkinson, of the Action at Châteauguay, & Transmitted by the General to the Secretary of War," in *ASP*, 1:479–480; Hampton to Armstrong, November 1, 1813, in *ASP*, 1:461; "Report from General Wade Hampton in Armstrong," in Armstrong, *Notices of the War*, 2:193; Neef to Bell, December 20, 1813, War of 1812 Papers, William L. Clements Library, University of Michigan.
18. Neef to Bell, December 20, 1813, War of 1812 Papers; "Colonel Purdy's Report to Major General Wilkinson, of the Action at Châteauguay, & Transmitted by the General to the Secretary of War," in *ASP*, 1:479–480; Sellar, *U.S. Campaign of 1813*, 9.

19. Lighthall, *Account of Châteauguay*, 18–19; Michael O'Sullivan, "Account of the Battle of the Châteauguay," in *SBD*, 2:405–406; "Journal of Brigadier General George Izard," in *War of 1812 in Person: Fifteen Accounts by United States Army Regulars, Volunteers and Militiamen*, ed. John Fredriksen (Jefferson, NC: McFarland & Co., 2010), 226; Victor Suthren, "The Battle of Châteauguay," *Canadian Historic Sites*, 11:129–130, http://parkscanadahistory.com/series/chs/11/chs11-3j.htm.
20. Suthren, "The Battle of Châteauguay," 130; Lighthall, *Account of Châteauguay*, 20–21; Salaberry to de Watteville, October 26, 1813 in *SBD*, 2:386.
21. "Colonel Purdy's Report to Major General Wilkinson, of the Action at Châteauguay, & Transmitted by the General to the Secretary of War," in *ASP*, 1:479; Salaberry to his father, October 29, 1813, in *SBD*, 2:391.
22. Baynes, General Order, in *SBD*, 2:390; Salaberry to Baynes, November 1, 1813, in *SBD*, 2:398; Salaberry to de Watteville, October 26, 1813, in *SBD*, 2:387.
23. Sellar, *U.S. Campaign of 1813*, 12–13; Graves, *Field of Glory*, 111–112; Wool quoted in Benson Lossing, *Pictorial Field Book of the War of 1812* (New York: Harper & Brothers, 1868), 648.
24. Graves, *Field of Glory*, 77–78.
25. "General Wilkinson to the Secretary of War," November 3, 1813 in Wilkinson, *Memoir of My Own Times*, Vol. 3, 557–558; Graves, *Field of Glory*, 77–78.
26. Grodzinksi, "The Vigilant Superintendence of the Whole District," 167; Ridout to his father, November 9, 1813, in Matilda Edgar, *Ten Years in Upper Canada in Peace and War, 1805–1815* (Toronto: W. Briggs, 1890), 252.
27. Sellar, *U.S. Campaign of 1813*, 16; Richard Feltoe, *The Flames of War: The Fight for Upper Canada, July–December 1813* (Toronto: Dundurn Press, 2013), 94–95.
28. Ronald Way, *The Day of Crysler's Farm, November 11, 1813* (Morrisburg, ON: Ontario-St. Lawrence Development Commission, 1961), 14–15.
29. Graves, *Field of Glory*, 189–190; Way, *The Day of Crysler's Farm*, 17; Sellar, *U.S. Campaign of 1813*, 18–19.
30. "Testimony of Elizear Ripley," in Wilkinson, *Memoir of My Own Times*, 3:142; Boyd to Wilkinson, November 12, 1813, in *DHCNF 1813*, 4:171.
31. Harvey Letter in Edgar, *Ten Years in Upper Canada in Peace and War*, 252; *Campaign of 1814 in Upper Canada*, LAC, MG/F23.
32. Graves, *Field of Glory*, 215; Boyd to Wilkinson, November 12, 1813, in *DHCNF 1813*, 4:171; "Account of Dr. Amasa Trowbridge," in Franklin Hough, *History of St. Lawrence and Franklin Counties, New York* (Albany, NY: Little & Co., 1853), 647.
33. John Fredricksen, "A Poor but Honest Sodger," *Pennsylvania History* 52 (1985): 145; "Account of Dr. Amasa Trowbridge," 647–648.
34. Harvey Letter, in Edgar, *Ten Years in Upper Canada in Peace and War*, 253, and Ridout to his father, November 20, 1813, 255; "From a memorandum of the services of Lt. Col. Charles Plenderleath," in *DHCNF 1813*, 4:166; Graves, *Field of*

Glory, 222–224; Edward Coss, *All for the King's Shilling: the British Soldier under Wellington, 1808–1814* (Norman: University of Oklahoma Press, 2010), 208; "Account of Dr. Amasa Trowbridge," 648. Plenderleath was awarded a gold medal for his courage on this day; see "From a Memorandum of the Services of Lt. Col. Charles Plenderleath," in *DHCNF 1813*, 4:166.

35. "Testimony of John Boyd," in Wilkinson, *Memoir of My Own Times*, 3, 91, and "Testimony of BG Swartout," 3:49. Mordecai Myers, *Reminiscences, 1780 to 1814, Including Incidents in the War of 1812–14* (Washington, DC: The Crane Co., 1900), 42; Boyd to Wilkinson, November 12, 1813, in *DHCNF 1813*, 4:171; Way, *The Day of Crysler's Farm*, 26–27.
36. Boyd to Wilkinson, November 12, 1813, in *DHCNF 1813*, 4:171.
37. Hampton to Armstrong, November 8, 1813, in *ASP*, 1:462, and Armstrong to Hampton, November 12, 1813, 1:463.
38. David Gates, *The Napoleonic Wars, 1803–1815* (London: Arnold, 1997), 221, 232, 244–251; Rory Muir, *Britain and the Defeat of Napoleon, 1807–1815* (New Haven, CT: Yale University Press, 1996), 229.
39. Castlereagh to Liverpool, August 28, 1814, in Robert Castlereagh, *Memoirs and Correspondence of Viscount Castlereagh, Second Marquess of Londonderry* (London: H. Colburn, 1850–53), 2:101–102; Jeremy Black, *The War of 1812 in the Age of Napoleon* (Norman: University of Oklahoma Press, 2009), 149–150; *Times of London*, October 19, 1814.
40. Wellington to Bathurst, February 22, 1814, in John Gurwood, *The Dispatches of Field Marshal The Duke of Wellington* (London: William Clowes and Sons, 1837–1839), 11:525-526; Wellington to Liverpool, November 9, 1814, in Wellington, *Supplementary Despatches and Memoranda*, 9:424–426; *Times of London*, December 24, 1814.
41. John Grodzinski, *Defender of Canada: Sir George Prevost and the War of 1812* (Norman: University of Oklahoma Press, 2013), 161–163; Donald Graves, "The Redcoats Are Coming! British Troops Movements in North American in 1814," *Journal of the War of 1812* 6, no. 3 (2001): 12–13; Bathurst to Prevost, June 3, 1814, in TNA, CO 43/23/150–155. Britain dispatched twelve units of Wellington's veterans to the Canadas, one to the maritime provinces, and eight campaigned on American territory; see Graves, "The Redcoats Are Coming,"12–13.

CHAPTER 10. SEEDS OF A DISCIPLINED AMERICAN ARMY

1. Armstrong to Brown, February 28, 1814, in John Armstrong, *Notices of the War* (New York: Wiley & Putnam, 1840), 2:213–214.
2. Armstrong to Brown, February 28, 1814, in Armstrong, *Notices of the War*, 2:213–214; Jeffrey Kimball, "Strategy on the Northern Frontier: 1814" (PhD diss., Louisiana State University and Agricultural and Mechanical College, 1969), 111–116.
3. Armstrong to Madison, April 31, 1814, in Armstrong, *Notices of the War*, 2:216–

217; Robert Malcomson, *Lords of the Lake: The Naval War on Lake Ontario, 1812–1814* (Annapolis, MD: Naval Institute Press, 1998) 285.

4. Armstrong to Madison, April 31, 1814, in Armstrong, *Notices of the War*, 2:216–217.
5. Donald Graves, *Where Right and Glory Lead: The Battle of Lundy's Lane, 1814* (Toronto: Robin Brass, 1997), 20–23. Armstrong to Madison, April 31, 1814, in Armstrong, *Notices of the War*, 2:216–217, and "Head of Plan of Campaign Within District No 9," 2:218.
6. Jon Latimer, *Niagara 1814: The Final Invasion* (New York: Osprey, 2009), 14.
7. Robert Malcomson, *Lords of the Lake* (Annapolis, MD: Naval Institute Press, 1998), 253–254; Chauncey to Jones, May 23, 1814, in *NW*, 3:494, in Chauncey to Jones, April 18, 1814, 434–435.
8. Croker to Yeo, January 29, 1814, in *NW*, 3:388; Drummond to Prevost, May 7, 1814, in TNA, CO 42/156/299–303; Yeo to Drummond, June 3, and Drummond to Yeo, June 6, 1814, in *SBD*, 3:75–78.
9. Shipwrights put the *Mohawk* into the water on June 11, but many of Chauncey's blacksmiths became sick and couldn't finish the vessel, which delayed it being fully operational until July 24 or 25. See Chauncey to Jones, August 10, 1814, in *NW*, 3:585–586; Brown to Chauncey, April 18, 1814, in *NW*, 3:444; Chauncey to Brown, June 25, 1814, in *NW*, 3:527; Malcomson, *Lords of the Lake*, 285.
10. Harvey to Riall, March 23, 1814, in *DHCNF 1814*, 1:3–6, and Drummond to Yeo, June 6, 1814, 1:19.
11. Brown to Chauncey, June 21, 1814, in *NW*, 3:526, and Chauncey to Brown, June 25, 1814, 3:527.
12. Graves, *Where Right and Glory Lead*, 77–78; Jacob Brown, "Memoranda of Occurrences and Some Important Facts Attending the Campaign on the Niagara," in Charles K. Gardner Papers, New York State Library.
13. Winfield Scott, *Memoirs of Lieutenant General Winfield Scott*, ed. Timothy Johnson (Knoxville: University of Tennessee Press, 2015), 1:125; Brown to Secretary of War Armstrong, July 7, 1814, in *DHCNF 1814*, 1:138; Robert Quimby, *The U.S. Army in the War of 1812: An Operational and Command Study* (East Lansing: Michigan State University Press, 1997), 2:524.
14. William Merritt, *A Desire of Serving and Defending My Country: The War of 1812 Journals of William Hamilton Merritt*, ed. Stuart Sutherland (Toronto: Iser Publications, 2001), 40; Harvey to Riall, March 23, 1814, in *DHCNF 1814*, 1:4.
15. Scott, *Memoirs*, 1:120–121; Lester Smith "A Drummer Boy in the War of 1812: The *Memoirs of Jarvis* Frary Hanks," *Niagara Frontier* 7 (Summer 1960): 55.
16. Porter to Stone, May 26, 1849, in *DHCNF 1814*, 2:364; John Norton, *The Journal of Major John Norton*, ed. Carl F. Klinck and James J. Talman (Toronto: Champlain Society, 1970), 350; "Memoranda of Occurrences and Some Important Facts Attending the Campaign on the Niagara," in Charles K. Gardner Papers, New York State Library.

17. Scott, *Memoirs*, 1:127–128.
18. Scott, 1:127–128.
19. Riall to Drummond, July 6, 1814, in *DHCNF 1814*, 1:31–32; Graves, *Where Right and Glory Lead*, 85–86; Scott to Adjutant General, July 15, 1814, in *DHCNF 1814*, 1:46; Scott, *Memoirs*, 1:129.
20. Scott to Adjutant General Gardner, July 15, 1814, in *DHCNF 1814*, 1:46; Scott, *Memoirs*, 1:129; Smith, "A Drummer Boy," 56.
21. *NWR*, 6:306; Scott, *Memoirs*, 1:131; Edward Mansfield, *Life of General Winfield Scott, Commander-in-Chief of the United States Army* (New York, A. S. Barnes & Co, 1852), 42; "Extract from a Letter Written by an Officer in the United States," July 7, 1814, in *DHCNF 1814*, 1:49.
22. Brown to Secretary of War Armstrong, August 7, 1814, in *DHCNF 1814*, 1:97–101; Graves, *Where Right and Glory Lead*, 87–88; *George Howard Letter Book*, Connecticut Historical Society Library Manuscripts, 110.
23. Merritt, *Journals*, 41; Scott, *Memoirs*, 1:131; "The Narrative of Alexander McMullen," in *DHCNF 1814*, 2:373; Benson Lossing, *Pictorial Field Book of the War of 1812* (New York, Harper & Brothers, 1868), 811; Quimby, *The U.S. Army*, 2:526.
24. *George Howard Letter Book*, Connecticut Historical Society Library Manuscripts, 111; Riall to Drummond, July 6, 1814, in *DHCNF 1814*, 1:32; Merritt, *Journals*, 41; Brown to Secretary of War Armstrong, July 6, 1814, in *DHCNF 1814*, 1:38.
25. Graves, *Where Right and Glory Lead*, 97.
26. Eleazer Ripley, *Facts Relative to the Campaign of the Niagara of 1814* (Boston: Patriot Office, 1815), 7–8; Scott, *Memoirs*, 1:136; Robert Malcomson, *Lords of the Lake: The Naval War on Lake Ontario, 1812–1814* (Annapolis, MD: Naval Institute Press, 1998), 287–288; Chauncey to Brown, June 25, 1814, in *NW*, 3:527.
27. Norton, *Journal*, 355–356.
28. Drummond to Prevost, July 27, 1814, in *DHCNF 1814*, 1:87–92; Ernest Cruikshank, *Battle of Lundy's Lane* (Welland, ON: Printed at the Tribune office, 1893), 26.
29. Cruikshank, *Battle of Lundy's Lane*, 26; Brown to Secretary of War Armstrong, August 7, 1814, in *DHCNF 1814*, 1:97–101; Scott, *Memoirs*, 1:138; David Bates, "An Original Narrative of the Niagara Campaign of 1814," ed. John Horton in *Niagara Frontier* 11, no. 1 (1964): 13.
30. Bates, "A Original Narrative," 13.
31. Drummond to Prevost, July 27, 1814, in *DHCNF 1814*, 1:87–92; Graves, *Where Right and Glory Lead*, 119–121; Cruikshank, *Battle of Lundy's Lane*, 29; Merritt, *Journals*, 43.
32. Cruikshank, *Battle of Lundy's Lane*, 30; Scott, *Memoirs*, 1:141.
33. Leavenworth, January 15, 1815, in Ripley, *Facts*, 20–21; Brady to Vincent, July 28, 1814, in John Linn, *Annals of Buffalo Valley, Pennsylvania, 1755–1855* (Lewisburg, PA: Mary Belle Lontz, 2003), 419–420; Graves, *Where Right and Glory Lead*, 127, 131; Smith, "A Drummer Boy," 57.

34. Merritt, *Journals*, 43; *Horton, "An Original Narrative,"* 21; Graves, *Where Right and Glory Lead*, 139–140.
35. Testimony of McDonald, in Ripley, *Facts*, 111–112; Graves, *Where Right and Glory Lead*, 136–137.
36. Graves, *Where Right and Glory Lead*, 141; Cruikshank, *Battle of Lundy's Lane*, 31.
37. Miller to—, July 28, 1814, in *DHCNF 1814*, 1:105–106; Bates, "A Original Narrative," 15–16.
38. Miller to—, July 28, 1814, in *DHCNF 1814*, 1:105–106.
39. Scott, *Memoirs*, 1:143–144; Leavenworth, January 15, 1815, in Ripley, *Facts*, 23.
40. Testimony of McDonald in Ripley, *Facts*, 13; Miller to—, July 28, 1814, in *DHCNF 1814*, 1:105–106; Drummond to Prevost, July 27, 1814, in *DHCNF 1814*, 1:87–92; Norton, *Journal*, 358.
41. Graves, *Where Right and Glory Lead*, 178–179; Scott, *Memoirs*, 1:142; Testimony of McDonald, in Ripley, *Facts*, 15.
42. Horton, "An Original Narrative," 21.
43. Ripley ordered his men to wait until they saw muzzle flashes before they fired. Testimony of McDonald, in Ripley, *Facts*, 14; "Extract of a letter from Dr. E. L. Allen, of the 21st regiment, to his brother," in *Niles Weekly Register*, 6:413; Graves, *Where Right and Glory Lead*, 181.
44. Drummond to Prevost, July 27, 1814, in *DHCNF 1814*, 1:87–92; Testimony of McDonald, in Ripley, *Facts*, 15–16; John Morris, *Sword of the Border: Major General Jacob Jennings Brown, 1775–1828* (Kent, OH: Kent State University Press 2000), 138–139; Bates, "An Original Narrative," 21; Graves, *Where Right and Glory Lead*, 184; McDonald to Ripley, March 20, 1815, in Ripley, *Facts*, 29; Quimby, *The U.S. Army*, 2:542; Porter to Tompkins, July 29, 1814, in *DHCNF 1814*, 1:101.
45. Dr. Bull to—, in *DHCNF 1814*, 1:104.
46. Norton, *Journal*, 359; Quimby, *The U.S. Army*, 2:543; Morris, *Sword of the Border*, 138–139.
47. Ripley, *Facts*, 39–40; Brown to Ripley, July 27, 1814, in Lossing, *Pictorial Field Book*, 829.
48. Quimby, *The U.S. Army*, 2:546–547; Louis Babcock, *The Siege of Fort Erie: An Episode of the War of 1812* (Buffalo, P. Paul Book Co., 1899), 26.
49. Quimby, *The U.S. Army*, 2:550–551; Babcock, *The Siege*, 38–39.
50. MacMahon to Mr. William Jarvis, August 22, 1814, in *DHCNF 1814*, 1:166–168, and J. Le Couteur to H. Le Couteur, 1:168–169. Lossing, *Pictorial Field Book*, 833–835; Smith, "A Drummer Boy," 59; Bates, "An Original Narrative," 27–29; "Campaign of 1814 in Upper Canada," in LAC, M24/F23.
51. Drummond to Prevost, August 21, 1814, in *DHCNF 1814*, 1:184–185; Babcock, *The Siege*, 26n.
52. Babcock, *The Siege*, 55–58; Lossing, *Pictorial Field Book*, 837–840; Smith, "A Drummer Boy," 60; "Campaign of 1814 in Upper Canada," in LAC, M24/F23.

53. G. K. Mills, "The Nottawasaga River Route," *Ontario Historical Society Papers and Records* 8 (1907): 43.
54. Brian Dunnigan, "The British Army at Mackinac 1812–1815," *Reports in Mackinac History and Archeology* 7 (1980): 21–22; Croghan to Armstrong, August 9, 1814, in Roger Andrews, *Old Fort Mackinac on the Hill of History* (Menominee, MI: Herald-Leader Press), 137.
55. Dunnigan, *The British Army at Mackinac*, 22; Sinclair to Jones, August 9, 1814, in Andrews, *Old Fort Mackinac*, 143.
56. Andrews, *Old Fort Mackinac*, 135.
57. Croghan to Armstrong, August 9, 1814, in Andrews, *Old Fort Mackinac*, 139; John Elting, *Amateurs, to Arms! A Military History of the War of 1812* (Chapel Hill, NC: Algonquin Books of Chapel Hill, 1991), 278–279; McDouall to Prevost, August 14, 1814, in *SBD*, 3:273–277.
58. Ernest Cruikshank, "The Story of the Schooner Nancy," in *The Defended Border, Upper Canada and the War of 1812*, ed. Morris Zaslow (Toronto: Macmillan, 1964), 150–152; Sinclair to Jones, August 9, 1814, in Andrews, *Old Fort Mackinac*, 144.
59. Cruikshank, "The Story of the Schooner Nancy," 150–152; Bulger to McDouall, September 7, 1814, in *SBD*, 3:279–281; McDouall to Drummond, September 9, 1814, in *SBD*, 3:277–279.
60. Brown to Chauncey, September 4, 1814, in *NWR*, 7:121; Morris, *Sword of the Border*, 140–141, 159.
61. Historian Donald Hickey points out that the uniforms were already grey before 1814 because of a shortage of blue cloth, so they adopted that color for financial reasons after the war. Later the uniform's color was recognized to honor the Battle of Chippawa; see Hickey, *Don't Give Up the Ship: Myths of the War of 1812* (Urbana: University of Illinois Press, 2006), 73.

CHAPTER 11. PREVOST INVADES NEW YORK

1. David Skaggs, *Thomas Macdonough: Master of Command in the Early U.S. Navy* (Annapolis, MD: Naval Institute Press, 2003), 44.
2. Bathurst to Prevost, June 3, 1814, in TNA, CO 43/23/150–155; C. S. Forester, "Victory on Lake Champlain," *American Heritage Magazine* 15, no. 1 (1963): 3; Jeffrey Kimball, "Strategy on the Northern Frontier: 1814" (PhD diss., Louisiana State University and Agricultural and Mechanical College, 1969), 43.
3. Bathurst to Prevost, July 11, 1814, in TNA Co43/23/157–159; Bathurst to Prevost, August 22, 1814, in TNA, Co43/23/163.
4. John Schroeder, *The Battle of Lake Champlain: A Brilliant and Extraordinary Victory* (Norman: University of Oklahoma Press, 2015), 49–50; Donald Alcock, "The Best Defence Is . . . Smuggling? Vermonters during the War of 1812," *Canadian Review of American Studies* 25, no. 1 (1995): 73; Schroeder, *Battle of Lake Champlain*, 41; Forester, "Victory on Lake Champlain," 7–8.

5. Bathurst to Prevost, August 22, 1814, in TNA, CO 43/23/163.
6. Forester, "Victory on Lake Champlain," 3; Donald Graves, *And All Their Glory Past: Fort Erie, Plattsburgh and the Final Battles in the North, 1814* (Montreal: Robin Brass Studio, 2013), 148–149.
7. David Fitz-Enz, *The Final Invasion: Plattsburgh, The War of 1812's Most Decisive Battle* (Lincoln: University of Nebraska Press, 2009), 57–58, 94.
8. Macdonough to Jones, November 23, 1813, in NARA, RG45; Allan Everest, *The War of 1812 in the Champlain Valley* (Syracuse, NY: Syracuse University Press, 1981), 147–148; "Vergennes," *Vermont Historical Magazine*, ed. Abby Hemenway (Burlington, VT: Published by Ms. A. M. Hemenway, 1867), 1:106; Walter Crockett, *Vermont the Green Mountain State* (New York: The Century History Company, 1921–23), 3:87; Jones to Macdonough, July 5, 1814, in *NW*, 3:539; Kimball, "Strategy on the Northern Frontier," 43; Jones to Macdonough, December 7, 1813, in NARA, RG45; "Advertisement," *Middlebury Mercury*, February 17, 1808.
9. Forester, "Victory," 8; Macdonough to Jones, August 16, 1814, and Izard to Macdonough, August 17, 1814, in *NW*, 3:540–541.
10. In *NW*: Macdonough to Wilkinson, April 9, 1814, 3:426; Macdonough to Jones, May 14, 1814, 3:480–481; Macdonough to Jones, April 30, 1814, 3:430–431.
11. Macdonough to Wilkinson, April 9, 1814, in *NW*, 3:426, and Macdonough to Jones, June 19, 1814, 3:507; Keith Herkalo, *The Battles at Plattsburgh: September 11, 1814* (Charleston, SC: History Press, 2012), 57; "Extraordinary Expedition," *Columbian Patriot*, May 18, 1814.
12. Jones to Macdonough, July 5, 1814, in *NW*, 3:539.
13. Donald Graves, "The Redcoats Are Coming! British Troops Movements in North American in 1814," *Journal of the War of 1812* 6, no. 3 (2001): 13; Schroeder, *Battle of Lake Champlain*, 54.
14. John Grodzinski, *Defender of Canada: Sir George Prevost and the War of 1812* (Norman: University of Oklahoma Press, 2013), 161–163; Donald Graves, "The Redcoats Are Coming!," 17; Graves, *And All Their Glory Past*, 147.
15. Macomb to Armstrong, September 12, 1814, in Alexander Macomb Letters, Benjamin F. Feinberg Library, Plattsburgh State University College; Robert Quimby, *The U.S. Army in the War of 1812: An Operational and Command Study* (East Lansing: Michigan State University Press, 1997), 2:607; Izard to Armstrong, August 11, 1814, in George Izard, *Official Correspondence with the Department of War* (Philadelphia: Published by Thomas Dobson, 1816), 65.
16. Freligh to his brother, January 11, 1814, in Freligh Family Papers, Benjamin F. Feinberg Library, Plattsburgh State University College; Quimby, *The U.S. Army*, 2:608–609; Macomb to Armstrong, September 15, 1814, and Macomb to Armstrong, August 31, 1814, in Alexander Macomb Letters.
17. Schroeder, *Battle of Lake Champlain*, 60; Graves, "The Redcoats Are Coming!," 12–18.
18. Fitz-Enz, *The Final Invasion*, 58, 94; Schroeder, *Battle of Lake Champlain*, 57.

19. Skaggs, *Thomas Macdonough*, 110; Fitz-Enz, *The Final Invasion*, 58, 94–97.
20. Herkalo, *Battles at Plattsburgh*, 57, 81; Macomb, General Orders, September 5, 1814, in *Niles Weekly Register*, 7:68; Macomb to Armstrong, September 15, 1814, in Alexander Macomb Letters; Allan Everest, *The War of 1812 in the Champlain* Valley (Syracuse, NY: Syracuse University Press, 1981), 172.
21. Wool to Roberts, January 6, 1859, in John Ellis Wool Papers, Benjamin F. Feinberg Library, Plattsburgh State University College; Herkalo, *Battles at Plattsburgh*, 57; Amos Barber quote referenced in Herkalo, *Battles at Plattsburgh*, 86; Everest, *The War of 1812 in the Champlain Valley*, 173; Quimby, *The U.S. Army*, 2:611; Macomb to Armstrong, September 8, 1814, in Alexander Macomb Letters; Keith Herkalo, ed. *The Journal of Henry Ketchum Averill, Sr.* (Plattsburgh, NY: Battle of Plattsburgh Association, 2001), 7.
22. Macomb to Armstrong, September 15, 1814, in Alexander Macomb Letters; Pring to Yeo, September 12, 1814, in *NW*, 3:609–612, and Prevost to Downie, September 9, 1814, 3:598.
23. Numerous letters, Downie to Prevost, Prevost to Downie, September 7 to September 10, 1814, in *SBD*, 3:379–383.
24. Macomb to Armstrong, September 15, 1814, in Alexander Macomb Letters; Quimby, *The U.S. Army*, 2:611–612; numerous letters, Downie to Prevost, Prevost to Downie, September 7 to September 10, 1814, in *SBD*, 3:379–383.
25. "Testimony of Henry Cox Court Martial of Captain Pring," in *SBD*, 3:421; "Testimony of Robert Anderson Brydon Court Martial of Captain Pring," in *SBD*, 3:412; Pring to Yeo, September 12, 1814, in *NW*, 3:611; "Testimony of Henry Cox Court Martial of Captain Pring, in *SBD*, 3:421.
26. Testimony of Robert Anderson Brydon Court Martial of Captain Pring, in *SBD*, 3:414; Testimony of Captain Pring, Court Martial of Captain Pring, in *SBD*, 3:442; Testimony of Lieutenant James Robertson, Court Martial of Captain Pring, in *SBD*, 3:440.
27. Herkalo, *Battles at Plattsburgh*, 101–105; C. W. Robinson, "The Expedition to Plattsburg, upon Lake Champlain Canada, 1814," *Royal United Services Institution Journal* 61, no. 443 (1916): 510.
28. Skaggs, *Thomas Macdonough*, 126.
29. Testimony of Robert Anderson Brydon Court Martial of Captain Pring, in *SBD*, 3:413, 416–417, 419; Pring to Yeo, September 12, 1814, in *NW*, 3:610; James Cooper, *History of the Navy of the United States of America* (London: R. Bentley, 1839), 2:504.
30. Cooper, *Naval History*, 2:217n; Benson Lossing, *Pictorial Field Book of the War of 1812* (New York: Harper & Brothers, 1868), 867.
31. Macdonough to Jones, September 13, 1814, in *NW*, 3:614–615.
32. Robertson to Yeo, September 12, 1814, in *NW*, 3:612–613; Herkalo, *Battles at Plattsburgh*, 113–114; Judge Hubbel quote referenced in Herkalo, *Battles at Plattsburgh*, 114; Lee to his brother, December 14, 1814, in Lossing, *Picto-*

rial Field Book, cite 2, 871; Macdonough to Jones, September 13, 1814, in *NW*, 3:614–615; Testimony of Henry Cox Court Martial of Captain Pring, in *SBD*, 3:422; Testimony of Robert Anderson Brydon Court Martial of Captain Pring, in *SBD*, 3:418.

33. Lossing, *Pictorial Field Book*, 872–873; Macdonough to Jones, September 11, 1814, in *NW*, 3:607, and Pring to Yeo, September 12, 1814, 3:612.

34. Herkalo, *Battles at Plattsburgh*, 115–116; David Fitz-Enz, *Plattsburgh: The War of 1812's Most Decisive Battle*, ed. John Elting (Lincoln: University of Nebraska Press, 2009), 167; Wool to Lossing, May 10, 1860, in the John Ellis Wool Papers, Benjamin F. Feinberg Library, Plattsburgh State University College; Robinson to Merry, September 22, 1814, in LAC, MG 24/F21; Robinson, "The Expedition to Plattsburg," 511.

35. *Times of London*, October 24, 1814; Robinson to Merry, September 22, 1814, in LAC, MG 24/F21.

36. Schroeder, *Battle of Lake Champlain*, 87–88; Grodzinski, *Defender of Canada*, 188–190; Robinson to Merry, September 22, 1814, in LAC, MG 24/F21.

37. *Times of London*, October 24, 1814; Liverpool to Castlereagh, October 21, 1814, in Arthur Richard Wellesley, Duke of Wellington, *Supplementary Despatches and Memoranda of Field Marshal Arthur Duke of Wellington* (London: J. Murray, 1862), 9:367; Robinson, "The Expedition to Plattsburg," 518–519.

38. Grodzinski, *Defender of Canada*, 237, 241; Grodzinski, "Sir George Prevost: Defender of Canada in the War of 1812," *The War of 1812 Magazine* 18 (June 2012), 2–3; *Cobbett's Weekly Political Register*, November 5, 1814.

39. Prevost to Drummond, September 16, 1814, in *NW*, 3:616–617; Testimony of Lieutenant William Drew Court Martial of Captain Pring, in *SBD*, 3:458, and Testimony of Lieutenant William Drew in Court Martial of Captain Pring, 3:408; Grodzinksi, *Defender of Canada*, 214.

40. J. C. A. Stagg, *The War of 1812: Conflict for a Continent* (Cambridge: Cambridge University Press, 2012), 145–146; Wellington to Liverpool, November 9, 1814, in Wellington, *Supplementary Despatches and Memoranda*, 9:424–426; Liverpool to Canning, December 28, 1814, in Charles Yonge, *The Life and Administration of Robert Banks, Second Earl of Liverpool, K. G., Late First Lord of the Treasury* (London: Macmillan and Co., 1868), 2:74–77; *Cobbett's Weekly Political Register*, November 5, 1814.

41. Bickham, *Weight of Vengeance*, 227–228, 252–253; Liverpool to Canning, December 28, 1814, in Yonge, *Life and Administration of Robert Banks*, 2:75.

42. Liverpool to Castlereagh, November 18, 1814, in Yonge, *Life and Administration of Robert Banks*, 2:73, and Liverpool to Canning, December 28, 1814, 2:74–77; Frank Updyke, *Diplomacy of the War of 1812* (Baltimore: Johns Hopkins, 1915), 347–350, 355.

43. Liverpool to Canning, December 28, 1814, in Yonge, *Life and Administration of Robert Banks*, 2:75.

44. Wellington to Liverpool, November 9, 1814, in Wellington, *Supplementary Despatches*, 9:425–426.

EPILOGUE

1. These vessels, if completed, would be larger than all but one ship that participated in the Battle of Trafalgar in 1805.
2. Robert Malcomson, *Lords of the Lake: The Naval War on Lake Ontario, 1812–1814* (Annapolis, MD: Naval Institute Press, 1998), 321.
3. Malcomson, *Lords of the Lake*, 321–322.

BIBLIOGRAPHY

SPECIAL COLLECTIONS/MANUSCRIPTS

Archives of Ontario(AO)
- Crysler Family Fonds
- David Kinnear Fonds
- Duncan Clark Fonds
- Ely Playter Fonds
- John Beverley Robinson Papers
- Joseph Willcocks Papers
- Military History Collection (F 895)
- Ridout Family Correspondence

Connecticut Historical Society Library Manuscripts
- George Howard Letter Book

Duke University, Rubenstein Rare Book & Manuscript Library

Filson Historical Society

Historic Cherry Hill Manuscript Collections (HCHC)

Jacques Viger Papers
- *Watertown Daily Times*, May 28 to June 4, 1963

Kentucky Historical Society
- Charles A. Wickliffe Papers

Library and Archives Canada (LAC)
- Manuscript Group 11
  - Colonial Office 42 (CO42) Original Correspondence Canada 1811–1815
- Manuscript Group 13
  - War Office 25 Registers various
  - War Office 44 Ordnance Office: In-Letters
  - War Office 57, Commissariat Department: In-Letters
  - War Office 71, Transcript of Court Martial of Major General Henry Proctor
- Manuscript Group 19
  - Duncan Clark Papers
  - William Claus Papers
- Manuscript Group 23
  - Edward Winslow Papers
  - John Graves Simcoe Papers
  - Murray Papers
  - Samuel Jarvis Letter
  - Sewell Papers
- Manuscript Group 24
  - Charles K Gardner Papers

- Correspondence of Colonel Hercules Scott, 103rd foot, 1814
- Salaberry Correspondence
- Drummond Letterbook
- Four years on the lakes, Lt David Wingfield, RN
- General Francis de Rottenburg Papers
- Great Britain, Lakes Papers
- Gustavus Nicholls Papers
- John Macdonnell Papers
- Merritt Papers
- Prevost Family Papers
- Ryland Letterbook
- Sir Isaac Brock Papers
- William Robinson, Letter on Plattsburgh

Manuscript Group 30
- Ernest Cruikshank Papers

Library of Congress (LOC)
- Andrew Jackson Papers
- Battle of New Orleans Descriptive Account
- Daniel Carroll Papers
- Daniel Tompkins Papers
- Dolley Madison Papers
- Jacob Brown Papers
- James Madison Papers
- James Wilkinson Papers
- John Ellis Wool Papers
- Samuel Smith Papers
- Sir Alexander Forrester Inglis Cochrane Correspondence
- Sir George Cockburn Papers
- United States Army Division of the North Orderly Book, 1814–1815
- William Henry Harrison Papers

National Archives of the United Kingdom
- Admiralty Records (AMD Series)
- Colonial Official Correspondence (CO 42)
- War Office (WO)

National Archive of the United States
- Correspondence of the Office of the Secretary of the Navy, Record Group 80
- General Records of the Department of Justice, Record Group 60
- Naval Records Collection of the Office of Naval Records and Library, Record Group 45
- Office of the Secretary of War, Record Group 107
- Records of the Adjutant General's Office, Record Group 94

Records of the Office of the Secretary of War, Record Group 107
War of 1812 Pension Record
New York State Library, Manuscripts and Special Collections
Charles K. Gardner Papers
Plattsburgh State University College, Benjamin F. Feinberg Library
Alexander Macomb Letters
Freligh Family Papers
John Ellis Wool Papers
State University of New York, Feinberg Library, Special Collections
University of Georgia, Hargrett Rare Book and Manuscript Library
William and Catherine Nicholson Few Papers
University of Michigan, William Clements Library, Special Collections
Jacob Brown Papers
Oliver Hazard Perry Papers
War of 1812 Papers
Western Reserve Historical Society, Cleveland Ohio

BOOKS/ PUBLISHED MANUSCRIPTS

Abbot, John. *The History of Fort St. Joseph*. Toronto: Dundurn Group, 2000.

Adams, John. *Writings of John Quincy Adams*. Vol. 5. New York: Macmillan Co., 1915.

Allen, Robert. *His Majesty's Indian Allies: British Indian policy in the Defence of Canada, 1774–1815*. Toronto: Dundurn Press, 1992.

Altoff, Gerard. *Deep Water Sailors, Shallow Water Soldiers*. Put-in-Bay, OH: The Perry Group, 1993.

———. *Oliver Hazard Perry and the Battle of Lake Erie*. Put-in-Bay, OH: The Perry Group, 1990.

American State Papers (ASP). Class 5. Military Affairs. Washington, DC: Gales and Seaton, 1832.

Andrews, Roger. *Old Fort Mackinac on the Hill of History*. Menominee, MI: Herald-Leader Press, 1938.

Antal, Sandy. *A Wampum Denied: Procter's War of 1812*. Montreal: McGill-Queen's University Press, 2011.

Armstrong, John. *Notices of the War of 1812*. 2 vols. New York: G. Dearborn, 1836–1840.

Assault and Battery: Report of the Trials of the Causes of Elisha Jenkins vs. Solomon Van Rensselaer. Albany, NY: Croswell & Frary, 1808.

Atherton, William. *Narrative of the Suffering and Defeat of the Northwestern Army under General Winchester*. Frankfort, KY: A. G. Hodges, 1842.

Averill, Henry. *The Journal of Henry Ketchum Averill*. Plattsburgh, NY: Battle of Plattsburgh Association, 2001.

Babcock, Louis. *The Siege of Fort Erie: An Episode of the War of 1812*. Buffalo: P. Paul Book Co., 1899.

———. *The War of 1812 on the Niagara Frontier*. Buffalo: Buffalo Historical Society, 1927.

Barnard, Daniel. *A Discourse on the Life, Services, and Character of Stephen Van Rensselaer*. Albany, NY: Hoffman & White, 1839.

Benn, Carl. *The Iroquois in the War of 1812*. Toronto: University of Toronto Press, 1998.

Benton, Thomas. *Abridgement of the Debates of Congress from 1789 to 1856*. 16 vols. New York: D. Appleton & Company, 1860.

Bickham, Troy. *The Weight of Vengeance: The United States, the British Empire and the War of 1812*. Oxford: Oxford University Press, 2012.

Black, Jeremy. *The War of 1812 in the Age of Napoleon*. Norman: University of Oklahoma Press, 2009.

Boak, A. E. R., ed. *University of Michigan Historical Essays*. Ann Arbor: University of Michigan Press, 1937.

Bonney, Catharina. *A Legacy of Historical Gleanings*. 2 vols. Albany, NY: J. Munsell, 1875.

Borneman, Walter. *The War That Forged a Nation*. New York: Harper, 2004.

Bouchette, Joseph. *The British Dominions in North America*. Vol. 1. London: Longman, Rees, Orme, Brown and Green, 1832.

———. *A Topographical Description of the Province of Lower Canada*. London: W. Faden, 1815.

Bowes, John. *Land Too Good for Indians: Northern Indian Removal*. Norman: University of Oklahoma Press, 2016.

Brannan, John. *Official Military Letters of the Military and Naval Officers of the United States during the War with Great Britain*. Washington City: Way & Gideon, 1823.

Brumwell, Stephen. *Redcoats: The British Soldier and War in the Americas*. Cambridge: Cambridge University Press, 2006.

Brunsman, Denver. *The Evil Necessity: British Naval Impressment in the Eighteenth-Century Atlantic World*. Charlottesville: University of Virginia Press, 2013.

Brymner, Douglas, ed. *Report on the Canadian Archives*. Ottawa: S. E. Dawson, 1897.

Bunnell, David. *The Travels and Adventures of David C. Bunnell*. Palmyra, NY: J. H. Bartles, 1831.

Byfield, Shadrach. *A Narrative of a Light Company Soldier's Service in the Forty-First Regiment of Foot*. New York: Reprinted, W. Abbatt, 1910.

Calloway, Colin. *The Shawnees and the War for America*. New York: Viking, 2007.

Campbell, Maria. *Revolutionary Services and Civil Life of General William Hull*. New York: D. Appleton & Co., 1848.

Canney, Donald. *Sailing Warships of the US Navy*. Annapolis, MD: Naval Institute Press, 2001.

Cannon, Richard. *Historical Record of the Eighth, or the King's Regiment of Foot*. London: Parker, 1844.

Carnochan, Janet, ed. *Niagara Historical Society & Museum, Scrap Book*. Niagara-on-the-Lake, ON: Niagara Historical Society Museum, 1913.

Carstens, Patrick. *Searching for the Forgotten War: 1812*. Philadelphia: Xlibris Corporation, 2011.

Castlereagh, Robert. *Memoirs and Correspondence of Viscount Castlereagh, Second Marquess of Londonderry*. Vol 2. London: H. Colburn, 1848.

Christie, Robert. *Memoirs of the Administration of the Colonial Government of Lower Canada By Sir James Henry Craig and Sir George Prevost from the Year 1807 Until the Year 1815*. Quebec: Robert Christie, 1818.

Clift, G. Glenn. *Remember the Raisin: Kentucky and Kentuckians in the Battles and Massacre at Frenchtown, Michigan Territory, in the War of 1812*. Frankfort: Kentucky Historical Society, 1961.

Clowes, W. Laird. *The Royal Navy: A History from the Earliest Times to the Present*. Vol. 6. London: S. Low, Marston and Company, 1897–1903.

Coffin, William. *1812: The War and Its Moral: A Canadian Chronicle*. Montreal: Printed by John Lovell, 1864.

Coffman, Edward. *The Old Army: A Portrait of the American Army in Peacetime, 1784–1898*. New York: Oxford University Press, 1986.

Collins, Gail. *William Henry Harrison*. New York: Henry Holt and Company, 2012.

Collins, Lewis. *Historical Sketches of Kentucky: Embracing Its History, Antiquities, and Natural Curiosities, Geographical, Statistical, and Geological Descriptions*. Cincinnati: J. A. & U. P. James, 1850.

Combs, Leslie. *Colonel William Dudley's Defeat, Opposite Fort Meigs*. Cincinnati: Spiller & Gates, 1869.

Cooper, James. *Ned Myers; or a Life before the Mast*. Annapolis, MD: Naval Institute Press, 1989.

Cooper, James Fenimore. *History of the Navy of the United States of America*. New York: G. P. Putnam & Co., 1853.

Cooper, John. *Rough Notes of Seven Campaigns, 1809–1815*. Staplehurst: Spellmount, 1996.

Coss, Edward. *All for the King's Shilling: The British Soldier Under Wellington, 1808–1814*. Norman: University of Oklahoma Press, 2010.

Crisman, K., and W. Rybka. *Coffins of the Brave: Lake Shipwrecks of the War of 1812*. College Station: Texas A&M University Press, 2014.

Crockett, Walter. *Vermont the Green Mountain State*. Vol. 3. New York: The Century History Company, Inc., 1921–1923.

Cruikshank, Ernest. *The Battle of Fort George*. Welland, ON: Tribune Print, 1904.

———. *The Battle of Lundy's Lane, 25th July,1814*. Welland, ON: Tribune Print, 1893.

———, ed. *Documentary History of the Campaign upon the Niagara Frontier 1812–1814*. 9 vols. Welland, ON: Lundy's Lane Historical Society, 1896–1908.

———, ed. *Documents Relating to the Invasion of Canada and the Surrender of Detroit, 1812*. Ottawa, ON: Government Printing Bureau, 1912.

———, ed. *Documents Relating to the Invasion of the Niagara Peninsula by the United States Army, Commanded by General Jacob Brown, in July and August 1814*. Niagara-on-the-Lake, ON: Niagara Historical Society, 1920.

———. *Drummond's Winter Campaign, 1813*. Welland, ON: Lundy's Lane Historical Society, 1900.

———. *Queenston Heights: A Thrilling Narrative of the Famous Battle Where General Brock Died Defending His Country*. Welland, ON: Printed by W. T. Sawle & Co., 1890.

Cullum, George. *Campaigns of the War of 1812–15*. New York: J. Miller, 1879.

Cumberland, Barlow. *The Navies on Lake Ontario in the War of 1812*. Toronto: William Briggs, 1907.

Darnell, Elias. *A Journal, Containing an Accurate and Interesting Account of the Hardships,* Sufferings, Battles, Defeat and Captivity of Those Heroic Kentucky Volunteers and *Regulars, Commanded by General Winchester, in the years 1812–13*. Philadelphia: Grigg & Elliott, 1834.

Daughan, Charles. 1812: *The Navy's War*. New York: Basic Books, 2011.

Dobbins, William. *History of the Battle of Lake Erie (September 10, 1813) and Reminiscences of the Flagships* Lawrence *and* Niagara. Erie, PA: Ashby Printing Company, 1913.

Drake, Benjamin. *Life of Tecumseh, and Of His Brother the Prophet; With a Historical Sketch of the Shawanoe Indians*. Cincinnati: E. Morgan & Co., 1841.

Drake, Francis. *Dictionary of American Biography*. Boston: J. R. Osgood and Company, 1872.

Dudley, William. *The Naval War of 1812: A Documentary History*. 3 vols. Washington, DC: Naval Historical Center, 1985.

Dunnigan, Brian. *The British Army at Mackinack, 1812—1815*. Lansing, MI: Mackinac Island State Park Commission, 1980.

Eayrs, Hugh. *Sir Isaac Brock*. Toronto: Macmillan Company of Canada, 1918.

Edgar, Matilda. *Ten Years in Upper Canada in Peace and War, 1805–1815*. Toronto: W. Briggs, 1890.

Edmunds, Russell. *Shawnee Prophet*. Lincoln: University of Nebraska Press, 1983.

Elliott, James. *Strange Fatality: The Battle of Stoney Creek, 1813*. Toronto: Robin Brass, 2009.

Elting, John. *Amateurs, to Arms! A Military History of the War of 1812*. Chapel Hill, NC: Algonquin Books of Chapel Hill, 1991.

Esarey, Logan. *Messages and Letters of William Henry Harrison*. 2 vols. New York: Arno Press, 1922.

Everest, Allan. *The War of 1812 in the Champlain Valley*. Syracuse, NY: Syracuse University Press, 1981.

Fay, Heman. *Collection of the Official Accounts*. New York: Printed by E. Conrad, 1817.

Feltoe, Richard. *The Call to Arms: The 1812 Invasions of Upper Canada*. Toronto: Dundurn, 2012.

———. *The Flames of War: The Fight for Upper Canada, July–December 1813*. Toronto: Dundurn Press, 2013.

Ferguson, Gillum. *Illinois in the War of 1812*. Urbana: University of Illinois Press, 2012.

Fitz-Enz, David. *The Final Invasion: Plattsburgh, The War of 1812's Most Decisive Battle*. Lincoln: University of Nebraska Press, 2009.

Forester, C. S. *The Age of the Fighting Sail*. Garden City, NY: Doubleday, 1956.

Fraser, Chad. *Lake Erie Stories: Struggle and Survival on a Freshwater Ocean*. Toronto: Dundurn Press, 2008.

Fredriksen, John. *War of 1812 in Person: Fifteen Accounts by United States Army Regulars, Volunteers and Militiamen*. Jefferson, NC: McFarland & Co., 2010.

Fremont-Barnes, Gregory. *The Napoleonic Wars: The Peninsula War, 1807–1814*. Oxford: Osprey Publishing, 2002.

Gardiner, Herbert. *Nothing but Names: An Inquiry into the Origin of the Names of the Counties and Townships of Ontario*. Toronto: G. N. Morang and Company, 1899.

Gates, David. *The British Light Infantry Arm: Its Creation, Training, and Operational Role*. London: Batsford, 1987.

———. *Napoleonic Wars, 1803–1815*. London: Arnold, 1997.

Gilje, Paul. *Free Trade and Sailors' Rights in the War of 1812*. New York: Cambridge University Press, 2013.

Gilpin, Alec. *The War of 1812 in the Old Northwest*. East Lansing: Michigan State University Press, 1958.

Glover, Richard. *Britain at Bay: Defence against Bonaparte, 1803–14*. London: Allen & Unwin, 1973.

———. *Peninsular Preparation: The Reform of the British Army, 1795–1809*. Cambridge: Cambridge University Press, 1963.

Gough, Barry. *Fighting Sail on Lake Huron and Georgian Bay: The War of 1812 and Its Aftermath*. Annapolis, MD: Naval Institute Press, 2002.

Graves, Donald. *And All Their Glory Past: Fort Erie, Plattsburgh and the Final Battles in the North, 1814*. Montreal: Robin Brass Studio, 2013.

———. *Field of Glory: The Battle of Crysler's Farm, 1813*. Toronto: Robin Brass, 1999.

———. *Merry Hearts Make Light Days: The War of 1812 Journal of Lieutenant John Le Couteur, 104th Foot*. Ottawa, ON: Carleton University Press, 1993.

———. *Where Right and Glory Lead! The Battle of Lundy's Lane, 1814*. Toronto: Robin Brass, 1997.

Gray, W. M. *Soldiers of the King: The Upper Canadian Militia, 1812–1815*. Erin, ON: Boston Mills Press, 1995.

Grodzinski John. *Defender of Canada: Sir George Prevost and the War of 1812*. Norman: University of Oklahoma Press, 2013.

Guillet, Edwin. *Pioneer Travel in Upper Canada*. Toronto: University of Toronto Press, 1933.

Guitard, Michelle. *The Militia of the Battle of the Châteauguay*. Ottawa, ON: National Historic Parks and Sites Branch, Parks Canada, Environment, 1983.

Hammack, James. *Kentucky and the Second American Revolution: The War of 1812*. Lexington: University Press of Kentucky, 1976.

Hart, Albert. *American History Told by Contemporaries*. New York: The Macmillan Company, 1897.

Hastings, Hugh ed., *Public Papers of Daniel D. Tompkins*. 3 vols. Albany, NY: J. B. Lyon, 1902.

Hatch, William. *A Chapter of the History of the War of 1812 in the Northwest: Embracing the Surrender of the Northwestern Army and Fort, at Detroit, August 16, 1812*. Cincinnati: Miami Printing and Publishing Company, 1872.

Hecht, Robert. *Continents in Collision: The Impact of Europe on the North American Indian Societies*. Lanham, MD: University Press of America, 1980.

Heidler, David. *Encyclopedia of the War of 1812*. 3 vols. Santa Barbara, CA: ABC-CLIO, 1997.

———. *The War of 1812*. Westport, CT: Greenwood Press, 2002.

Heller, Charles, and William Stofft, eds. *America's First Battles, 1776–1965*. Lawrence: University Press of Kansas, 1986.

Helm, Linai. *The Fort Dearborn Massacre*. Chicago: Rand McNally & Company, 1814.

Herkalo, Keith. *The Battles at Plattsburgh: September 11, 1814*. Charleston, SC: History Press, 2012.

Hickey, Donald. *Don't Give Up the Ship! Myths of the War of 1812*. Urbana: University of Illinois Press, 2006.

———. *The War of 1812: A Forgotten Conflict*. Urbana: University of Illinois Press, 1989.

Hickey, Donald, and Connie Clark, eds. *The Routledge Handbook of the War of 1812*. New York: Routledge, 2016.

Hitsman, J. Mackay. *Incredible War of 1812: A Military History*. Toronto: University of Toronto Press, 1965.

Holmes, Richard. *Redcoat: The British Soldier in the Age of Horse and Musket*. London: Harper Collins, 2001.

Hosmer, H. L. *Early History of the Maumee County*. Toledo, OH: Hosmer & Harris, 1858.

Hough, Franklin. *A History of St. Lawrence and Franklin Counties, New York: From The Earliest Period to the Present Time*. Albany, NY: Little & Co., 1853.

Houlding, J. A. *Fit for Service: The Training of the British Army, 1715–1795*. New York: Oxford University Press, 1981.

Howe, Henry. *Historical Collections of the Great West*. Cincinnati: H. Howe, 1855.

Hulbert, Archer. *The Ohio River: A Course of Empire*. New York: G. P. Putnam's Sons, 1906.

Hull, William. *Memoirs of the Campaign of the North Western Army of the United States, A.D.1812*. Boston: True & Greene, 1824.

———. *Report of the Trial of Brig. General William Hull, Commanding the North-Western Army of the United States*. New York: Eastburn, Kirk, and Co., 1814.

Hunt, Gaillard, ed. *The Writings of James Madison, Comprising His Public Papers and His Private Correspondence, Including Numerous Letters and Documents Now for the First Time Printed*. Vol. 8. New York: G. P. Putnam's Sons, 1908.

Ingersoll, Charles. *Historical Sketch of the Second War between the United States of America*. 3 vols. Philadelphia: Lea and Blanchard, 1845.

Izard, Ralph. *Official Correspondence with the Department of War, Relative to the Military Operations of the American Army under the Command of Major General Izard, on the Northern Frontier of the United States in the Years 1814 and 1815*. Philadelphia: Thomas Dobson, 1816.

Jackson, Isaac. *A Sketch of the Life and Public Services of William Henry Harrison: Commander in Chief of the North-western Army, during the War of 1812*. New York: Office of the New York Express, 1839.

James, Charles. *A Collection of the Charges, Opinions, and Sentences of General Courts Martial*. London: T. Egerton, 1820.

James, William. *Naval Occurrences of the War of 1812: A Full and Correct Account of the Naval War between Great Britain and the United States of America, 1812–1815*. 2 vols. London: Printed for T. Egerton, 1817.

Jennings, Francis. *The History and Culture of Iroquois Diplomacy*. Syracuse, NY: Syracuse University Press, 1985.

Jones, C. S. *The Battle of Stoney Creek*. Brantford, ON, 1889.

Keating, Ann. *Rising Up from Indian Country: The Battle of Fort Dearborn and the Birth of Chicago*. Chicago: University of Chicago Press, 2012.

Keefer, Frank. *Beaverdams*. Thorold, ON: Thorold Post Printers, 191

Keeler, Lucy. *93d Anniversary of the Battle of Fort Stephenson*. Columbus: Ohio State Archaeological and Historical Society, 1907.

Knapp, Horace. *History of the Maumee Valley, Commencing With Its Occupation By The French in 1680*. Toledo, OH: Blade Publishing House, 1872.

Langguth, A. J. *Union 1812: The Americans Who Fought the Second War of Independence*. New York: Simon & Schuster, 2006.

Lardas, Mark. *Great Lakes Warships, 1812–1815*. Long Island City, NY: Osprey, 2012.

Latimer, Jon. *1812: War with America*. Boston: Harvard University Press, 2010.

———. *Niagara 1814: The Final Invasion*. New York: Osprey, 2009.

Leavey, Peggy. *Laura Secord: Heroine of the War of 1812*. Toronto: Dundurn, 2012.

Lighthall, William. *An Account of the Battle of Châteauguay*. Montreal: W. Drysdale & Co., 1889.

Linch, Kevin. *Britain and Wellington's Army: Recruitment, Society and Tradition, 1807–15*. New York: Palgrave Macmillan, 2011.

Lomax, David. *A History of the Services of the 41st: From Its Formation in 1719 to 1895*. Devonport: Printed by Hiorns & Miller, 1899.

Lossing, Benson. *The Pictorial Field-Book of the War of 1812*. New York: Harper & Brothers, 1868.

Lucas, Robert. *The Robert Lucas Journal of the War of 1812 during the Campaign Under General William Hull*. Iowa City: State Historical Society of Iowa, 1906.

Macdonell, John. *Sketches Illustrating the Early Settlement and History of Glengarry in Canada*. Montreal: W. Foster, Brown & Co., 1893.

Madison, James. *The Writings of James Madison, Comprising his Public Papers and his Private Correspondence, Including Numerous Letters and Documents Now for the First Time Printed*. Vol. 8. New York: G. P. Putnam's Sons, 1900–1910.

Mahan, Alfred. *Sea Power in Its Relations to the War of 1812*. 2 vols. New York: Greenwood Press, 1905.

Mahon, John. *The War of 1812*. New York: Da Capo Press, 1972.

Malcomson, Robert. *Capital in Flames: The American Attack on York, 1813*. Annapolis, MD: Naval Institute Press, 2008.

———. *Lords of the Lake: The Naval War on Lake Ontario, 1812–1814*. Annapolis, MD: Naval Institute Press, 1998.

———. *A Very Brilliant Affair: The Battle of Queenston Heights, 1812*. Annapolis, MD: Naval Institute Press, 2003.

Mansfield, Edward. *Life of General Winfield Scott*. New York: A. S. Barnes & Co., 1846.

Mason, Philip, ed. *After Tippecanoe: Some Aspects of the War of 1812*. East Lansing: Michigan State University Press, 2012.

Markham, Edwin. *The Real America in Romance: Valor and Victory*. Vol. 10. Chicago: W. H. Wise & Company, 1909.

McAfee, Robert. *History of the Late War in the Western County*. Bowling Green, OH: Historical Publications Company, 1919.

McKenzie, Ruth. *James Fitzgibbon: Defender of Upper Canada, 1805*. Toronto: Dundurn Press, 1983.

McNab, Chris. *Armies of the Napoleonic Wars*. New York: Osprey, 2009.

Merritt, William. *A Desire of Serving and Defending My Country*. Toronto: Iser Publications, 2001.

———. *Journal of Events Principally on the Detroit and Niagara Frontiers, during the War of 1812*. St. Catharines, ON: Historical Society, BNA, 1863.

Morris, John. *Sword of the Border: Major General Jacob Jennings Brown, 1775–1828*. Kent, OH: Kent State University Press, 2000.

Muir, Rory. *Britain and the Defeat of Napoleon, 1807–1815*. New Haven, CT: Yale University Press, 1996.

Nicolson, Adam. *Seize the Fire: Heroism, Duty, and the Battle of Trafalgar*. New York: HarperCollins, 2005.

Norton, John. *The Journal of Major John Norton, 1816*. Toronto: Champlain Society, 1970.

Parsons, Usher. *Battle of Lake Erie. A Discourse, Delivered Before The Rhode-Island Historical Society*. Providence, RI: B. T. Albro, 1853.

Perkins, Bradford. *Prologue to War: England and the United States, 1805–1812.* Berkeley: University of California Press, 1961.
Pirtle, Alfred. *The Battle of Tippecanoe, Read before the Filson Club.* Louisville, KY: J. P. Morton and Company, 1900.
Quaife, Milo. *The John Askin Papers.* Detroit: Detroit Library Commission, 1928.
———. *War on the Detroit: The Chronicles of Thomas Verchères de Boucherville and The Capitulation, by an Ohio Volunteer.* Chicago: The Lakeside Press, 1940.
Quimby, Robert. *The U.S. Army in the War of 1812: An Operational and Command Study.* 2 vols. East Lansing: Michigan State University Press, 1997.
Quisenberry, Anderson. *Kentucky in the War of 1812.* Baltimore: Genealogical Pub. Co., 1969.
Reynolds, James. *Journal of an American Prisoner at Fort Malden and Quebec in the War of 1812.* Quebec: Print. by F. Carrel, Limited, 1909.
———, ed. *A Compilation of Messages and Papers of the Presidents: 1789–1897.* Vol. 1. Washington, DC: U.S. Gov. Printing Office, 1896.
Richardson, John. *A Canadian Campaign: Operations of the Right Division of the Army of Upper Canada, during the American War of 1812.* Edited by David Beasley. Simcoe, ON: Davus Publishing, 2011.
———. *Richardson's War of 1812.* Toronto: Historical Publishing Co., 1902.
Riley, J. P. *A Matter of Honour: The Life, Campaigns and Generalship of Isaac Brock.* Montreal: Robin Brass, 2011.
Rohrbough, Malcolm. *Trans-Appalachian Frontier: People, Societies, and Institutions, 1775–1850.* Bloomington: Indiana University Press, 2008.
Roosevelt, Theodore. *The Naval War of 1812.* Vol. 1. New York: G. P. Putnam's Sons, 1889.
Royle, Trevor. *The Argyll and Sutherland Highlanders: A Concise History.* Edinburgh: Mainstream, 2008.
Sanford, Laura. *History of Erie County Pennsylvania.* Vol. 1. Philadelphia: J. B. Lippincott & Co., 1862.
Schroeder, John. *The Battle of Lake Champlain: A Brilliant and Extraordinary Victory.* Norman: University of Oklahoma Press, 2015.
Scott, James. *Recollections of a Naval Life.* Vol. 3. London: R. Bentley, 1834.
Scott, Winfield. *Memoirs of Lieut.-General Scott, LL.D.* New York: Sheldon & Company, 1864.
Sellar, Robert. *The U.S. Campaign of 1813 to Capture Montreal: Crysler, the Decisive Battle of the War of 1812.* Huntingdon, QB: Gleaner Print, 1913.
Severance, Frank H. *Documents relating to the War of 1812: The Letter-Book of Gen. Sir Roger Hale Sheaffe.* Vol 17. Buffalo: Buffalo Historical Society, 1913.
Shorto, Russell. *Tecumseh and the Dream of an American Indian Nation.* Englewood Cliffs, NJ: Silver Burdett, 1989.
Skaggs, David Curtis. *Oliver Hazard Perry: Honor, Courage, and Patriotism in the Early U.S. Navy.* Annapolis, MD: Naval Institute Press, 2006.

———. *Thomas Macdonough: Master of Command in the Early U.S. Navy*. Annapolis, MD: Naval Institute Press, 2003.

———. *William Henry Harrison and the Conquest of the Ohio Country: Frontier Fighting in the War of 1812*. Baltimore: Johns Hopkins University Press, 2014.

Skaggs, David Curtis, and Gerard Altoff. *A Signal Victory: The Lake Erie Campaign, 1812–1813*. Annapolis, MD: Naval Institute Press, 1997.

Skaggs, David Skaggs, and Larry Nelson, eds. *The Sixty Years' War for the Great Lakes, 1754–1814*. East Lansing: Michigan State University Press, 2001.

Skeen, Carl. *Citizen Soldiers in the War of 1812*. Lexington: University Press of Kentucky, 1999.

Skelton, William. *An American Profession of Arms: The Army Officer Corps, 1784–1861*. Lawrence: University Press of Kansas, 1992.

Smyth, Benjamin. *History of the XX Regiment*. Manchester: The Examiner Printing Works, 1889.

Snider, C. H. J. *In The Wake of The Eighteen-Twelvers: Fights & Flights of Frigates & Fore-'n'-Afters in the War of 1812–1815 on the Great Lakes*. London: Cornmarket, 1969.

Spencer, Oliver. *Narrative of Oliver M. Spencer*. London: John Mason, 1842.

Spring, Matthew. *With Zeal and with Bayonets Only: The British Army on Campaign in North America, 1775–1783*. Norman: University of Oklahoma Press, 2008.

Stagg, J. C. A. *Mr. Madison's War: Politics, Diplomacy, and Warfare in the Early American Republic, 1783–1830*. Princeton, NJ: Princeton University Press, 1983.

———. *The War of 1812: Conflict for a Continent*. Cambridge: Cambridge University Press, 2012.

Stanley, George. *Battle in the Dark, Stoney Creek, June 6, 1813*. Toronto: Balmuir, 1991.

Sugden, John. *Tecumseh's Last Stand*. Norman: University of Oklahoma Press, 1985.

Symons, John. *The Battle of Queenston Heights Being a Narrative of the Opening of the War of 1812*. Toronto: Thompson & Co., 1859.

Taylor, Alan. *Civil War of 1812: American Citizens, British Subjects, Irish Rebels, & Indian Allies*. New York: Alfred A. Knopf, 2010.

Tebbel, John. *American Indian Wars*. New York: Harper, 1960.

Therry, R. *The Speeches of the Right Honourable George Canning with a Memoir of His Life*. Vol. 3. London: James Ridgway & Sons, 1836.

Todd, Charles. *Sketches of the Civil and Military Services of William Henry Harrison*. Cincinnati: Published by U. P. James, 1840

Trowbridge, Francis. *The Trowbridge Genealogy: History of the Trowbridge Family in America*. New Haven, CT: Tuttle, Morehouse & Taylor Company, 1908.

Tucker, Glenn. *Tecumseh; Vision of Glory*. Indianapolis, IN: Bobbs-Merrill, 1956.

Tucker, Spencer, ed. *The Encyclopedia of the War of 1812*. 3 vols. Santa Barbara, CA: ABC-CLIO, 2012.

Tupper, Ferdinand. *Family Records; Containing Memoirs of Major-General Sir Isaac Brock*. Guernsey: S. Barbet, 1835.

———. *The Life and Correspondence of Major-General Sir Isaac Brock*. London: Simpkin, 1845.

Turner, Wesley. *British Generals in the War of 1812: High Command in the Canadas*. Montreal: McGill-Queen's University Press, 1999.

———. *The War of 1812: The War That Both Sides Won*. Toronto: Dundurn Press, 1990.

Updyke, Frank. *The Diplomacy of the War of 1812*. Baltimore: Johns Hopkins, 1915.

Urwin, Gregory. *The United States Infantry: An Illustrated History, 1775–1918*. New York: Blandford Press, 1988.

Van Rensselaer, Solomon. *A Narrative of the Affair of Queenstown: In the War of 1812*. Boston: Crocker & Brewster, 1836.

Walker, Adam. *A Journal of Two Campaigns of the Fourth Regiment of U.S. Infantry: In The Michigan and Indiana Territories, under the Command of Col. John P. Boyd, and Lt. Col. James Miller, during the Years 1811 & 12*. Keene, NH: Printed at the Sentinel Press, by the Author, 1816.

Ware, Eugene. *Pennsylvania Lighthouses on Lake Erie*. Charleston, SC: The History Press, 2016.

Way, Ronald. *The Day of Crysler's Farm November 11, 1813*. Morrisburg, ON: Ontario-St. Lawrence Development Commission, 1961.

Wellesley, Arthur Richard, Duke of Wellington. *Supplementary Despatches and Memoranda of Field Marshal Arthur, Duke of Wellington*. London: J. Murray, 1858–1872.

Wilder, Patrick. *Battle of Sackett's Harbour: 1813*. Baltimore: Nautical & Aviation Pub. Co. of America, 1994.

Wilkinson, James. *Memoirs of General Wilkinson*. 3 vols. Philadelphia: Abraham Small, 1816.

Williams, Samuel. *Two Western Campaigns in the War of 1812–13*. Cincinnati: R. Clarke, 1870.

Winchester, James. *Historical Details Having Relation to the Campaign of the North-Western Army*. Lexington: Worsely & Smith, 1818.

Wing, Talcott. *History of Monroe County Michigan*. Vol. 1. New York: Munsell & Company, 1890.

Wohler, Patrick. *Charles de Salaberry: Soldier of the Empire, Defender of Quebec*. Toronto: Dundurn Press, 1984.

Wood, William, ed. *Select British Documents of the Canadian War of 1812*. 3 vols. Toronto: The Champlain Society, 1920–28.

Yanik, Anthony. *The Fall and Recapture of Detroit: In Defense of William Hull*. Detroit: Wayne State University Press, 2011.

Yonge, Charles. *The Life and Administration of Robert Banks, Second Earl of Liverpool, K. G., Late First Lord of the Treasury*. Vol. 2. London: Macmillan and Co., 1868.

Young, Bennett. *The Battle of the Thames, In Which Kentuckians Defeated the British, French, and Indians, October 5, 1813*. Louisville, KY: J. P. Morton and Company, 1903.

Zaslow, Morris, ed. *The Defended Border: Upper Canada and the War of 1812*. Toronto: Macmillan Company, 1964.

ARTICLES/BOOK CHAPTERS

Alcock, Donald. "The Best Defence Is . . . Smuggling? Vermonters during the War of 1812." *Canadian Review of American Studies* 25, no. 1 (1995): 73–92.

Allaben, Frank, ed. "The Log Book of the Lawrence." *Journal of American History* 8 (January–March 1914): 117–121.

Allen, Robert. "His Majesty's Indian Allies: Native Peoples, the British Crown and the War of 1812." *Michigan Historical Review* 14, no. 2 (1988): 1–24.

Barrett, Robert "Naval Recollections of the Late American War, No. 2." *United Service Journal and Naval and Military Magazine* 1 (April 1841): 455–467.

Beall, William. "Journal of William K. Beall, July-August, 1812." *American Historical Review* 17, no. 4 (July 1912): 783–808.

Bergmann, William. "A Commercial View of this Unfortunate War: Economic Roots of an American National State in the Ohio Valley, 1775–1795." *Early American Studies* 6, no. 1 (2008): 137–164.

Biggar, E. B. "The Story of the Battle of Stony Creek." *Hamilton Spectator*, June 6, 1873.

Black, Jeremy. "A British View of the Naval War of 1812." *Naval History* 22, no. 4 (2008): 16–25.

Bowlus, Bruce. "A Signal Victory: The Battle for Fort Stephenson." *Northwest Ohio Quarterly* 63, no. 3/4 (1991): 43–57.

Bradley, Glenn. "Fort Meigs in the War of 1812." *Historical Society of Northwestern Ohio Quarterly Bulletin* 2, no. 1 (1930): 1–10.

Carson, Wallace. "Transportation and Traffic on the Ohio and the Mississippi before the Steamboat." *Mississippi Valley Historical Review* 7, no. 1 (1920): 26–38.

Carter-Edwards, Dennis, "The War of 1812 along the Detroit Frontier: A Canadian Perspective." *Michigan Historical Review* 13, no. 2 (1987): 25–50.

Case, Thomas. "The Battle of Fallen Timbers." *Northwest Ohio Quarterly* 35 (1963): 54–68.

Checkland, S. G. "American versus West Indian Traders in Liverpool, 1793–1815." *Journal of Economic History* 18, no. 2 (1958): 141–160.

Compton, Henry. "The Siege of Fort Meigs." *Ohio Archeological and Historical Quarterly* 10 (1902): 315–330.

Corman, Hazel. "An Account of the Battle of Stoney Creek." *Wentworth Historical Society* 7 (1916): 26–34.

Cox, Richard. "An Eyewitness Account of the Battle of Lake Erie by Samuel Hambleton." *U.S. Naval Institute Proceedings* 104 (February 1978): 72–73.

Crook, James. "Recollections of the War of 1812." *Niagara Historical Society Publication* 28 (1916): 28–41.

Cruikshank, E. A. "The Contest for the Command of Lake Ontario in 1812 and 1813." *Transactions of the Royal Society of Canada* 10, no 3 (1916): 161–223.

———. "A Sketch of the Public Life and Services of Robert Nichol." *Ontario Historical Society Papers and Records* 19 (1922): 6–81.

Douglas, W. A. B. "The Anatomy of Naval Incompetence: The Provincial Marine in Defence of Upper Canada before 1813." *Ontario History* 22 (1979): 3–26.

Douglass, David. "An Original Narrative of the Niagara Campaign of 1814." *Niagara Frontier* 11 (1964): 1–36.

Eckert, Edward. "William Jones: Mr. Madison's Secretary of the Navy." *Pennsylvania Magazine of History and Biography* 96, no. 2 (1972): 167–182.

Edmunds, David. "The Illinois River Potawatomi in the War of 1812." *Journal of the Illinois State Historical Society* 62, no. 4 (1969): 341–362.

"First Campaign of an A.D.C." *Military and Naval Magazine of the United States* 2 (September 1833–February 1834): 10, 73, 200, 278.

Forester, C. S. "Victory on Lake Champlain." *American Heritage Magazine* 15, no. 1 (1963): 4–11, 88–90.

Fredriksen, John, ed. "Chronicle of Valor: The Journal of a Pennsylvania Officer in the War of 1812." *Western Pennsylvania Historical Magazine* 67 (July 1984): 243–284.

———, ed. "A Grand Moment for Our Beloved Commander: Sailing Master William V. Taylor's Account of the Battle of Lake Erie." *Journal of Erie Studies* 17 (1988): 113–122.

———. "The War of 1812 in Northern New York: General George Izard's Journal of the Chateauguay Campaign." *New York History* 76, no. 2 (1995): 173–200.

Golder, F. A. "The Russian Offer of Mediation in the War of 1812." *Political Science Quarterly* 31, no. 3 (1916): 360–391.

Graves, Donald. "The Redcoats Are Coming! British Troops Movements to North America in 1814." *War of 1812 Journal* 6, no. 3 (2001): 12–18.

Greenhous, Brereton. "A Note on Western Logistics in the War of 1812." *Military Affairs* 34, no. 2 (1970): 41–44.

Grodzinksi, John. "The Duke of Wellington, the Peninsular War and the War of 1812, Part II: Reinforcements, Views of the War and Command in North America." *War of 1812 Magazine* 6 (April 2007). https://www.napoleon-series.org/military/Warof1812/2007/Issue6/c_Wellington1.html.

———. "Sir George Prevost: Defender of Canada in the War of 1812." *War of 1812 Magazine* 18 (June 2012): 1–8.

———. "The Vigilant Superintendence of the Whole District: The War of 1812 on the Upper St. Lawrence." Master's Thesis, Royal Military College of Canada, 2002.

Gunderson, Robert. "William Henry Harrison: Apprentice in Arms." *Northwest Ohio Quarterly* 65, no. 1 (1993): 3–29.

Guttman, Jon. "War of 1812: Detroit Showdown." *Military History Quarterly Maga-*

zine 25, no. 1 (2012). https://www.historynet.com/war-of-1812-detroit-showdown.htm.

"Historical Collections." *Michigan Pioneer and Historical Society* 15 (Lansing, MI: Wynkoop, Hallenbeck, Crawford Co., 1909): 421.

Hollon, W. E. "Zebulon Montgomery Pike and the York Campaign." *New York History* 30, no. 3 (1949): 259–275.

Holmes, Oliver. "The Turnpike Era." *History of the State of New York* 5 (1934): 259–261.

Horsman, Reginald. "The British Indian Department and the Resistance to General Anthony Wayne, 1793–1795." *Mississippi Valley Historical Review* 49, no. 2 (1962): 269–290.

Humphries, Charles. "The Capture of York." *Ontario History* 51 (1959): 1–24.

Latimer, Jon. "Smuggling and Contraband in the War of 1812." *War of 1812 Magazine* 8 (February 2008). https://www.napoleon-series.org/military-info/Warof1812/2008/Issue8/c_pirates.html.

Lippincott, Isaac. "The Early Salt Trade of the Ohio Valley." *Journal of Political Economy* 20, no. 10 (1912): 1029–1052.

Mahon, John. "British Command Decisions in the Northern Campaigns of the War of 1812." *Canadian Historical Review* 46, no. 3 (1965): 219–237.

"McLean to McNab, July 22, 1860." *Niagara Historical Society*, no. 23, 1913. http://nhsm.ca/media/NiagaraHistoricalSocietyNo.23.pdf.

Millett, Allan. "Caesar and the Conquest of the Northwest Territory: The Wayne Campaign, 1792–1795." *Timeline* 14 (May/June 1997): 2–21.

Mills, G. K. "The Nottawasaga River Route." *Ontario Historical Society Papers and Records* 8 (1907): 40–48.

Naylor, Isaac. "The Battle of Tippecanoe, as Described by Judge Isaac Naylor, a Participant." *Indiana Magazine of History* 2 (December 1906): 161–169.

Palmer, Michael. "A Failure of Command, Control, and Communications: Oliver Hazard Perry and the Battle of Lake Erie." *Journal of Erie Studies* 17 (Fall 1988): 7–26.

"Papers and Orderly Book of Brigadier General James Winchester." In Michigan Pioneer and Historical Society, *Historical Collections* (Lansing, MI: Wynkoop, Hallenbeck, Crawford Co. 1902): 31:253–313.

Roach, Isaac. "Journal of Major Isaac Roach." *Pennsylvania Magazine of History and Biography* 17, no. 2 (1893): 129–158.

Robinson, C. W. "The Expedition to Plattsburg, upon Lake Champlain Canada, 1814." *Royal United Services Institution Journal* 61, no. 443 (1916): 499–522.

Rosentreter, Roger. "Remember the River Raisin!" *Michigan History Magazine* 5 (November/December 1998): 40–48.

Ross, Frank. "The Fur Trade of the Ohio Valley." *Indiana Magazine of History* 34, no. 4 (1938): 417–443.

Ross, Nicholas. "The Provision of Naval Defense in the Early American Republic: A

Comparison of the U.S. Navy and Privateers, 1789–1815." *Independent Review* 16, no. 3 (2012): 417–433.

Saliers, Earl. "The Siege of Fort Meigs." *Ohio State Archeological and Historical Society* 18 (1909): 520–541.

Seiken, Jeff. "To Obtain Command of the Lakes: The United States and the Contest for Lakes Erie and Ontario, 1812–1815." In *The Sixty Years' War for the Great Lakes, 1754–1814*, edited by David Curtis Skaggs and Larry Nelson, 353–373. East Lansing: Michigan State University Press, 2001.

Skaggs, David Curtis. "Creating Small Unit Cohesion: Oliver Hazard Perry at the Battle of Lake Erie." *Armed Forces and Society* 23, no. 4 (1997): 635–668.

Smith, Dwight. "A North American Neutral Indian Zone: Persistence of a British Idea." *Northwest Ohio Quarterly* 61, no. 2–4 (1989): 46–63.

Smith, Lester, ed. "A Drummerboy in the War of 1812: *The Memoirs of Jarvis Frary Hanks.*" *Niagara Frontier* 7 (Summer 1960): 53–62.

St-Denis, Guy. "In Search of the Fisherman's Path: Rethinking the American Assault on Queenston Heights." *Canadian Military History* 27, no. 1 (2018): 1–12.

Stacey, C. P. "Another Look at the Battle of Lake Erie." *Canadian Historical Review* 39, no. 1 (1958): 41–51.

———. "Naval Power on the Great Lakes, 1812–1814." In *After Tippecanoe: Some Aspects of the War of 1812*, edited by Philip Mason, 49–59. East Lansing: Michigan State University Press, 2012.

Suthren, Victor. "The Battle of Châteauguay." *Canadian Historic Sites* 11 (1974): 95–150.

Talbot, George. "General John Chandler on Monmouth Maine with Extracts from his Autobiography." *Collections of the Maine Historical Society* 9 (1887): 167–206.

Tasker, L. H. "The United Empire Loyalist Settlement at Long Point, Lake Erie." *Ontario Historical Society Papers and Records* 2 (1900): 9–124.

Thompson, Mabel. "Billy Green: The Scout." *Ontario History* 44 (1952): 173–181.

Trautsch, Jasper. "Origins of the War of 1812." *Journal of Military History* 77, no. 1 (2013): 273–293.

"Vergennes." In *Vermont Historical Magazine*, edited by Abby Hemenway, 1:106–108. Burlington, VT: Published by Ms. A. M. Hemenway, 1867.

"Wellington to Longford, May 22, 1815." *Louisiana Historical Quarterly* 9, no. 1 (1926): 8–9.

Wilson, J. "A Rifleman at Queenstown." *Publications of the Buffalo Historical Society* 9 (1906): 373–376.

Winchester, James. "Papers and Orderly Book of Brigadier General James Winchester." *Michigan Historical Collections* 31 (1902): 253–313.

"Wool to Stone, September 13, 1838." *Publications of the Buffalo Historical Society* 9 (1906): 120.

Young, Bennet. "Battle of the Thames in Which the Kentuckians Defeated the British, French, and Indians, October 5, 1813." *Filson Club Publications* 18 (1903):1–272.

DISSERTATIONS/THESES

Beugoms, Jean-Pierre. "The Logistics of the United States Army 1812–182." PhD diss., Temple University, 2018.

Grodzinksi, John. "The Vigilant Superintendence of the Whole District: The War of 1812 on the Upper St Lawrence." PhD diss., Royal Military College of Canada, 2002.

Jackson, Scott. "Impressment and Anglo-American Discord 1787–1818." PhD diss., University of Michigan, 1976.

Kimball, Jeffrey. "Strategy on the Northern Frontier: 1814." PhD diss., Louisiana State University and Agricultural and Mechanical College, 1969.

Skeen, Carl. "John Armstrong and the Role of the Secretary in the War in the War of 1812." PhD diss., Ohio State University, 1966.

Steppler, Glenn. "A Troublesome Duty beyond Measure: Logistical Consideration in the Canadian War of 1812." Master's thesis, McGill University, Montreal, 1974.

SELECT NEWSPAPERS AND MAGAZINES

Albany Register

Balance and State Journal

Buffalo Gazette

Carthage Gazette

Cobbett's Weekly Political Register

Gentleman's Magazine

Hamilton Spectator

Harper's New Monthly Magazine

Kentucky Gazette

Kingston Gazette

Missouri Gazette and Public Advertiser

Montreal Gazette

Nashville Whig

New Jersey Journal

New York Evening Post

New York Gazette Office

Niagara Bee

Niagara Chronicle

Niagara Mail

Niles Weekly Register

Oxford University and City Paper

Public Advertiser

Quebec Gazette

Quebec Mercury

Richmond Enquirer

Rutland County Herald

Staffordshire Advertiser
Times
The Washingtonian

INDEX